The
Bumper Bundle Book
Of Modelling

NLP Modelling Made Simple

Fran Burgess

KILMONIVAIG PUBLISHING
www.nlpand.co.uk

First published by:

Kilmonivaig Publishing, 22 Painterwood, Billington, Clitheroe, Lancashire, BB7 9JD, UK

www.nlpand.co.uk : admin@nlpand.co.uk

© Fran Burgess 2014

The right of Fran Burgess to be identified as the author of this work has been asserted by her in accordance with the Copyright Designs and Patents Act 1988.

All rights reserved. Except as permitted under current legislation, no part of this work may be photocopied, stored in a retrieval system, published, performed in public, adapted, broadcast, transmitted, recorded or reproduced in any form or by any means, without the prior permission of the copyright owner.

Enquiries should be addressed to Kilmonivaig Publishing.

British Library of Cataloguing-in-Publication Data

A catalogue entry for this book is available from the British Library.

Print   ISBN 978-0-9928361-0-8

ePub   ISBN 978-0-9928361-1-5

Printed and bound by Lightning Source Chapter House, Pitfield Kiln Farm, Milton Keynes, MK11 3LW

Contents

The Introduction

The Foreword

A User's Guide to Connecting to the Spirit of NLP: Modeling

The *Bumper Bundle Book of Modeling* is certainly aptly named, and it is more than an assembled collection of knowledge related to the mastery and artistry of modeling.

It is a modeling project done with love, curiosity and the desire to make a contribution. Fran spent fifteen years as a modeller herself in order to bring this book to the community, so she knows about the relationship of the *Hero's Journey* and a big modeling project.

Modeling is the spirit of NLP; its life force so to speak. It is through the ongoing desire to re-create structures of the success factors in human experience that brings freshness to the field of Neuro Linguistic Programming. This book is a kind of 'unified field' of knowledge that pertains to modeling. It brings together the various strategies used by the successful modellers in the field; it defines the patterns that connect all the different strategies.

I believe that this book can bring us back to the roots of the NLP of Alfred Korzybski and the presupposition that 'the map is not the territory'. Not just because Fran has respectfully brought so many different maps of modeling together, but she has successfully shown how they fit into a mosaic of thinking, feeling and doing that is captured in the activity of modeling. Bringing together these different mental maps demonstrates how holding multi-perspectives is at the core of wisdom, genius, humor and effective symbolic thinking. This was what Korzybski was pointing us toward – *another way of thinking*. Sadly in the NLP community, people often forget this particular presupposition and form fixed schools of thought, defining some to be orthodox and some heretical, depending on one's particular fixed point. So at least in the form of this beautiful book, wholeness is brought through the acknowledgement of both diversity and connectedness.

NLP is now in its third description or generation. The developments over the 35 plus years have yielded many useful tools, processes and technology. The applications vary from leadership, education, creativity, health, law and more. Organizations have come and gone, materials have been updated and some material has fallen out of favor. Many, many books have been written applying NLP to one or another area of life. There have been many who desired only the technology of NLP and those who continue to express their knowledge through Gandhi's words: *'being the change they want to see in the world.'* In between their two points are the amazing strategies of the modelers in NLP and the natural modelers of the world.

There are certain books in any field, I suppose, that give a deeper understanding, or they give a fuller vision or description, or perhaps a more accessible form of knowledge. I feel that this is one of those special books in the field NLP. However, this book does all of the above. This is the book for anyone who loves NLP and loves the activity of modeling.

This book is a reflection of Fran's passion and gift for modeling and a guide forward toward the roots of NLP and multiple descriptions. Here's to Fran, and others who continue to support the building of bridges between the diverse ideas inside and outside of NLP.

Thank you Fran, for this extraordinary offering. It is joy to walk the NLP Modeling path with you.

Judith Delozier
Santa Cruz, January 2014

The Preframe

Origins

In 1998, in a hotel on Primrose Hill, London, at his workshop on Patterns, John Grinder declared:

> If we do not produce more modellers and models, NLP will become a footnote in history of the late 20th and early 21st century.

That was my Call to Action, and fifteen years later this book is the result. On that day, I decided that learning about modelling, growing modellers and learning how to teach modelling, would be my contribution to the field of NLP. This would be my payback for the fantastic changes NLP had enabled in my life.

From that day, my husband Derek Jackson and I invited the world's best modellers to The Northern School of NLP, so that not only could they teach our students but us as well. Robert Dilts, David Gordon, Judith Delozier, Steve Gilligan, John McWhirter, Shelle Rose Charvet, James Lawley and Penny Tompkins all stalk the pages of this book, their energies, wisdom and spirit contributing to the experiences I have had and the conclusions I have come to. Starting back then, with next to no knowledge, skills or understanding, I was a willing apprentice.

I was very fortunate to have had lots of learners to test my learning, and those who travelled onwards onto NLP Trainer's training could plot the stages of my thinking. Progressive Master Practitioners benefited from my increased coherence, as well as my improved methods of teaching the mysteries of modelling. But most of all, the fantastic group of learners who became part of our Explorer's Club did much to help me bring my thoughts together into a series of simple frameworks.

There were some great breakthrough moments. Without being fully aware of my background churn of confusion, my modeller's system was continuously filtering for patterns relating to my quest. Newspaper articles, talks on the radio, events in training, and chance conversations could turn an everyday event into a moment of epiphany. So obvious the insight, there would be a moment when I would suspect everyone knew this, and what had taken me so long?

Just as I was initially overwhelmed by the enormity and naivety of the task I had set myself, I also reluctantly accept that the NLP world at large seems to have a limited appetite for the concept and rigours of modelling; being more content to work with the techniques and apply the known skills. Though the optimist within me suspects that there are many adherents out there, operating below the radar, who don't consider what they do to be modelling. I do believe ultimately, that when the appeal of standalone skills and techniques wane, the art of modelling will always remain a relevant attribute and will always provide an essential contribution.

I smile wryly when I think that my life's work – well the last fifteen years of it – has been devoted to something so apparently esoteric that possibly a fraction of those within our global NLP community may be interested to find out what I have come up with! But this could be the very justification for the pursuit. Make the modelling process easier, accessible and relevant, and many more people will naturally be able to become identified with it, and involved. Show how all the NLP skills and knowledge can dance together to unfold powerful information, and NLP will rise in credibility and prominence.

I fully believe that this book can raise the level of a practitioner's NLP tradecraft to a level of practice where he or she will have the confidence to decide the many differences they want to make. As my knowledge became integrated, I realised that what I am offering here is a comprehensive coverage not just of an advanced NLP syllabus, but a joined up way of thinking about NLP. Hopefully I have made NLP and modelling both interchangeable, as well as simple and obvious.

The Process

What you won't find here is a well-documented investigation of materials already published – not least because there is not very much published on NLP modelling. Whilst several of the modellers featured have written up their own modelling methodologies, they tend to focus on how to deliver these methodologies, rather than focus at a meta level on the process of modelling itself.

What you will find here are the conclusions arising from the overview I have gained. The bulk of the material is gleaned through personal exposure to key players, and from direct experience of their workshops, reference to their handouts, my notes, and videoed performance. I have also had occasion to consult their writings and YouTube materials. I am also extremely grateful for the conversations I've had over email with many of my mentors, who have been able to correct my thinking, offer suggestions and above all give support. The integration and meta level of understanding have come through testing my understanding on myself, with our learners and my clients; and through the continuous thinking, referring, comparing, generalising, tussling, and occasional despairing and recovery from overwhelm.

Possibly because this is not an academic pursuit, the content is easier to read – but that might be my non-academic bias coming out! Given that NLP is a practical endeavour, I am comfortable that I have taken a practical approach. That's not to say that I have shied away from accommodating the technology, or the theory – far from it. I believe it is essential that all professional NLP practitioners should have at their fingertips a complete grasp of the technical language, constructions and principles that govern our modality. How else can we hope for creativity, inspiration, and pioneering applications? And how else will we be able to clearly teach subsequent generations?

I also believe that this practice needs to be well grounded in the thinking that holds its own in the world of academia and medicine. This way we can keep standards high and resist the advances of dilution and dumbing down of training and thinking, to ensure the longevity and authority of our modality.

I also hope I have presented my understandings in a style that you'll find readable and stimulating, sufficiently light of touch to keep you motivated, but with enough gravitas to make the reading rewarding.

For consistency, I have referred to exemplar and modeller. Depending on context, exemplar could mean customer, student, learner as well as holder of the desired behaviour. Similarly, modeller could refer to the practitioner, therapist, trainer, coach, teacher or consultant. And where appropriate I have adopted a he/she approach, without being too cumbersome.

I have been challenged for my occasional departure into modal operators of certainty and necessity, and a smattering of universal quantifiers, which are counter to the map not being the territory. I hold my hands up. My defence is that this is my book and my take. Of course it comes from within my map. It has taken me long enough to believe that I have a right to my opinion – though rest assured I am prepared to hold it lightly. So I offer it to you freely, and you can savour it or reject it, as you will. I would relish feedback and good argument to amend and mature my thinking.

I am pleased with the range of original ideas that I am contributing to the field of modelling. Within these pages you will find new frameworks, models, methodologies, and interventions all of which I hope serve to simplify the whole field of modelling and expand awareness and thinking, and take the field that bit further forward. A full listing of these models and frameworks is found in the Appendix.

It is not a decorative filly of a book – not like the fabulous *NLP Cookbook*. It is a working carthorse – a textbook with diagrams. It is long enough, without taking up more space with lots of indulgent pictures and cartoons or other such distractions that you can find elsewhere. If you need a visual distraction, look round the room, out the window, or at the face of a future client or customer who is bowled over by your elegant skills and competence.

I've received significant feedback saying that the hard book format is much easier to follow. Because I drill down into so much detail, and operate within a range of all frameworks, readers have needed the option of easy referral backwards and forwards throughout the book. Electronic versions didn't provide this facility, although they do have the great benefit of operating a search function – and of course are much easier to carry.

The bibliography is not extensive. My strength is not in research but in making sense of my experiences. In the section on modelling methodologies, for example, I have been happy to explore to some degree the modeller's own published materials, but on the whole I have drawn from my first-hand experiences. There was no point going into great detail – that is the role of the respective developer. Instead, I want to serve as a signpost giving direction to further specialist training and development. I'm the Red Bus tour guide, and you can choose when to get off and where to explore further.

The Overall Framework

This is a textbook for all trained practitioners, a source of learning as well as a source of reference. I hope that the invaluable band of Master Trainers, who are training the next generation of NLP

Trainers, find what I have to offer useful. I like to think you will find many gems here, and much that will confirm and provide resolution to your own experiences.

Part 1 – The Nature of a Modeller

In this chapter I explore the nature, mindset, attributes, and characteristics of what makes a modeller. I draw up a composite description of the Identity of an NLP Modeller. Starting with John Grinder's description, from *Whispering in the Wind* 2001, of himself and Richard Bandler, I then cover a wide range of explorers and learners, followed by a model of the collective attributes of modelling experts.

Knowing what is required of a modeller, I offer a developmental model giving you an overview of how a NLP modeller can grow and mature from being beginner in the earliest days of their training to an expert, who has instant access to their technologies and expertise. Then there is a brief description of how these modellers could be operating in business, education, therapy and coaching, before inviting you to consider your own Call to Action and your own direction for your modelling endeavours.

Part 2 – The Principles of Modelling

No study is complete without consideration being given to the underpinning thinking which drives any endeavour. So for the field of modelling it is important to understand the philosophy behind our actions. Without this we are unable to make congruent decisions and might be tempted to stray into less rigorous areas of application. We are certainly unable to justify our performance in the wider field of academia. From first principles I spell out the thinking to explain why we as NLPers do what we do, and how we do it and what it delivers as a result. Here I offer in layman's terms, a light overview of Post-Modernism, Constructivism, and our underpinning rationale.

Then I touch on the emergent field of Neuroscience, which has been the missing link for many. We are gaining more and more evidence on how the brain works, how it influences personality, and how it responds to particular inputs. I have only selected accounts of published material that serve to explain the neurological mechanics behind our brilliance.

Finally I cover the range of great minds within cybernetics, therapy and philosophy that were operating in the mid '70s, who collectively established a relational field of influence, significantly infecting the direction of Bandler and Grinder's exploration. Out of this collection of thinkers emerged our NLP Presuppositions, the beliefs on which our whole approach is based.

Part 3 – The Methodologies of Modelling

We now approach the powerhouse of modelling – the formal approaches designed to reveal inner structure. This is the first of two chapters looking at depth into HOW we go about finding out about HOW someone does what they do. In my travels I have found that How? is the question least asked, though the one we modellers need to be asking all the time. We have been weaned on Why? and What? but it seems that few have an instinctive muscle that asks How?

First of all I consider the nature of a Modelling Methodology and its requirements. Then I bring you a unique framework that integrates *thirteen* methodologies classified under one roof. Instead of focussing on the usual differences between them, I've shown how they are all connected and so give a coherence and legitimacy to each. Then I provide a developed description for each – all thirteen of them.

This compilation is a first! Previously you would have had to go directly to the work and writings of the respective developer. And most practitioners know of only one or two methodologies. So here is your chance not only to sample thirteen but also gain an understanding of how each works, how you can use them, and how they contribute overall to the field.

Part 4 – The Skills of Modelling

Continuing the focus on the HOW behind NLP, it is now the turn of modelling skills. The methodologies would be nothing without an advanced set of skills. Much of what is taught in Practitioner and Master Practitioner doesn't equip a practitioner to become a skilled modeller, which is why many understandably find modelling difficult. The hidden skills of modelling are not generally recognised or understood. Many of the modellers themselves are naturally talented and possibly underestimate their instinctive skills of systemic thinking, pattern detecting and classifying.

One of my outcomes was to fill in the gaps and enable learners to acquire conscious competence in these areas. Many of the skills required coding and a means of accessing them. So the sixteen skills I include, required either throughout the modelling process or at certain stages, hopefully give you a shortcut to acquiring them.

The sister publication *The Bumper Bundle Companion Workbook* offers you nearly one hundred exercises to flex and strengthen your modelling muscle.

Part 5 – The Results of Modelling

Change can happen the moment a modeller begins to model. However interventions can have many different guises. This chapter looks at the range of interventions, in addition to apply a modelling methodology, that the modeller can choose from, with plenty of practical and tested examples of modelling working across the areas of business, training, therapy and coaching. Only some of these interventions will result in the production of a model.

For many however, the end point *is* the production of a model, which often explains why modellers drop by the wayside, or don't appreciate that they are modelling. I provide a classification of models that are present, and then focus on the area of constructed models. This is a neglected area in most teaching of modelling and answers the question 'what do you do with all the data you've got?' I am delighted to offer you some very practical pointers to model construction so that the process becomes really easy.

Finally I offer a detailed account of the Inside Out Process which I have devised which is a process that ultimately provides a technique designed around a model which has been constructed from the exemplar's own data – all in about 45 minutes.

Part 6 – The Formal Acquisition Process

The end is in sight! At last we arrive at the point where the whole modelling endeavour is formalised into final acquisition by a third party. Formal acquisition is the point where others who were not part of the modelling process to date, now experience its benefits in the form of a structured intervention. This is the realm of technique productions.

This Part starts off with the model for Technique Construction and the components required – so simple that anyone can now turn a model into a magical experience. Whilst not seeking to turn you into trainers, I take you through the wide range of Delivery Methods available so you have a choice about the sort of experience you create. Then I include full coverage of our unique Neurological and Linguistic Frames that are the building blocks of NLP. Selecting from submodalities, perceptual positions, metaphors etc., and then Meta Model patterns, reframing, and sensory predicates for example, provide your technique with NLP's special engineering.

Once the design is established, the final stage in the whole process is the writing up – the production of written instructions. All that work encapsulated on an standard-size sheet of paper!

Appendices

Here you will find the whole process wrapped up in a case study, taking you explicitly through the modelling experience, gathering information, coding, model construction, technique design and production of written instructions.

This is then followed by a short Bibliography and details of *The Bumper Bundle's Companion Workbook* that provides you with loads of exercises to test your understanding of the material contained within these covers.

Outcomes

Having read the framework of this book, some elements may appeal to you more than others. It is all a question of your preferred chunk size, sorting traits, thinking style, current need-to-knows and future requirements; plus a benchmark for what you already know ; and a ready source of reference.

So know that, whilst there is a connection running through the six Parts, there is no rational requirement to read from beginning to end. You can select specific topics as required, or top up your awareness through dipping in and out. I do hope that the book has a life beyond the first few weeks of your purchase. I do hope it becomes a well-thumbed companion on your own modelling journey.

Specifically I wish that this book:

- Re-awakens the spirit of modelling within you
- Demystifies what is in fact a process natural to all of us
- Serves to recommit and rededicate you to the first principles of NLP
- Renews your admiration and fascination for the tradecraft that NLP brings to the world
- Develops your place within the congruence and authority of our modality
- Provides a different and simplified view on the whole modelling process, from beginning to end
- Gives you new ideas and stretches your awareness of what can be possible in the pursuit of hidden structure
- Generates confidence in your abilities to consciously pursue a modelling approach
- Gives new direction and inspiration for your development, and new areas of application
- Refreshes your enthusiasm to play, explore, test out, expand, discover, and learn.

The 7 + 1 Myths of Modelling

There are unchallenged myths surrounding the process of NLP Modelling, sound bites that get trotted out without the speaker having any real understanding of the whole process. These myths are handed down possibly from trainers who don't know enough to question them. As a result, this folklore limits the huge potential of modelling, prejudices a needful market, and prolongs the embryonic understanding of the early developers.

In the fascinating learning journey responding to Grinder's call, I worked towards filling in the gaps and factoring in my own instinctive practices and I have been delighted to discover that modelling is so much more than I was originally led to believe. The more experience and exposure I gained, the more I understood just how misleading the modelling myths actually are.

I don't know if you have reached the stage in your NLP development where you appreciate just how flexible NLP can be, and how creative you can become as a result. You will certainly have experienced some of the magic of its potential. You may already know that in the right hands, NLP provides a gift to understanding, and a doorway into enlightened communication and behaviour. All because of the process of modelling – finding the structure responsible for behaviour. As you will see, the potential to make a difference is absolutely enormous – possibly infinite.

The following table outlines the range of routes a modeller can take through the modelling process. It covers the wide number of options so much so that the permutations are literally endless. As we go through it, I will offer you up-to-date thinking instead of the myths that you may be running.

And here's a big thought. Whilst the time may come when the fairly recent constructs of NLP Practitioner and NLP Master Practitioner certifications become obsolete, the concept of NLP modelling will endure and remain constant under whichever promoted label or banner. There will always be a market for NLP modellers. The concept of NLP can't die out. It is too useful.

The Modelling Route Map

This is the last piece of the jigsaw that emerged for me, and as I see it, this framework encompasses the territory of modelling. I know that is an ambitious statement, so you will have to judge it for yourselves. The summarised explanations that accompany it will hopefully answer many of the questions you may realise you've been holding, and hold the doors open for the rest of the book.

Application Area	End User	Focus of Enquiry	Source(s) of Information	Intervention	Modelling Outcome
Personal Development Therapy / Coaching Consultancy / Training Others	Third Party Self Exemplar Host Organisation	Structure of Desired Behaviour (DB) Structure of Unwanted Behaviour (UB) Relationships between exemplar / DB / UB	Self Exemplar Exemplars Literature and other media Systems	Product and Process Models Modelling Methodologies Neurological Modelling Linguistic Modelling Combination of above	Exploration / Identification of Structure Remodelling of Structure Model Construction Formal Acquisition

The Modelling Route Map – Burgess 2013

Application Area

Modellers can be operating in as many vocational and personal areas as there are people. Wherever there is a desire to understand, communicate that understanding and possibly disseminate that understanding, there is a place for an NLP modeller to excel.

For the professional purposes of this book, in addition to personal development, I have considered only four major areas of application – Therapy, Coaching, Business Consultancy and Training. These are the four most common vocational areas of those undertaking NLP training and development. However, the creative and imaginative practitioner can come from any walk of life and apply their modelling skills wherever they are operating, for example in the area of parenting, professional caring, marketing and any area requiring communication and understanding.

In the book we spend time exploring the modelling mindset that can operate across the board, from explorers to detectives to sports people, with a particularly interesting handle of what the world would be like if consultants, teachers, trainers, therapists and coaches operated as modellers. And throughout I offer many practical examples and suggestions of how the process of modelling, methodologies and models can be use in these areas.

End User

Myth 1: The purpose of modelling is to produce a model to be installed into a third party.

The ultimate end user sets the direction of the enquiry, which adds to the options available to the modeller.

- *Third party:* traditionally the requirement of a modeller was to meet identified needs of a third y, or to find a third party who could benefit from what the modeller had discovered. This therefore discounted all the fantastic modelling activity that took place in therapy and coaching, as well as any personal consumption by modellers themselves.

- *Self:* the modeller may be modelling for his or her own personal learning or development. Often this might be informal exploration, in the name of problem solving. Or we may be motivated through self-interest to use our NLP understanding to gain insight to 'sort' something within our own lives.

- *Exemplar:* the modeller may be working with an exemplar, in this instance a client, to help that individual make sense of his or her own current model of the world. This is the one-to-one working of a therapist or coach, where the client is both the source of the information and the consumer of the knowledge gained.

- *Host organisation:* the modeller may be commercially contracted by a host organisation to explore specific activities within that organisation and then possibly use the knowledge gained to change behaviour in identified areas of the business.

It is worth noting that more than one type of end user can benefit. It is down to the imagination of the modeller, or the subsequent developer to see the potential in the information and models that are produced.

Focus of Enquiry

Myth 2: Modelling is about seeking out excellence.

The mythology in NLP is that modelling is all about exploring 'excellence', which is usually interpreted as behaviour desired by others.   This myth has been the source of much of the malignment of modelling.   It has led to sloppy declarations of 'overnight' success, 'easy quick results' and 'achievement with little effort'. It is responsible for workshop and book titles of '7 Secrets of X', '5 Steps to Y,' which can be useful, and less usefully 'How to Chat Up Women Successfully' or 'How To Make Your First £Million'.

This thinking not only limits the scope of the modeller's activities, it narrows the area where the skills of modelling can usefully be deployed. Happily today's modeller has more options than this to choose from.

- *Desired behaviour:* focussing on desired behaviour can lead to the production of models suitable for a waiting market. 'I'll have some of what she's eating.' But it doesn't have to be the heady heights of 'excellence'.   In fact excellence may come with an unacceptable price. It could be merely 'good enough' or the desirability of the behaviour could rest merely in the eye of the beholder – the modeller.

A consultant may be asked to model key sales personnel or identified leaders within a particular environment, to find out what characteristics, or beliefs or values they have in common, or what particular responses they have to specific situations. Once identified this can be disseminated to others in the same roles in various ways.

It may not be the behaviour that is desired. It may be the strategy for how that behaviour is generated that is the key, because of its potential to be transferred to another context. So say working with the Gordon/Dawes Array, the individual selects something that he or she accepts they do well; the structure that emerges can be applied to a less satisfactory aspect that is not working well for them.

- *Unwanted behaviour:* just as usefully the modeller can concentrate on the structure of a consistent unwanted behaviour and either seek to restructure this or reframe this successful structure by applying it where it could be more useful.

With restructuring, the consultant may be called in to discover how a particular problem keeps occurring and to find out what causes it and how it might be avoided. The coach may seek to find out what is happening to the singer who freezes in front of the large audience, or can't speak to strangers. In therapy it might be sufficient for the individual to realise just how they get the results they do, without intensive analysis and recrimination.

As a reframe, the unwanted behaviour can generate something desirable in a different context. For example, an individual may feel bad about not paying attention to housework, dusting and vacuuming. This could be interpreted as an example of being able to withstand the 'ought's and should's' of others. Taking this aptitude and applying it to being bullied, or making an alternative career choice, could strengthen resolve and generate confidence.

- *Relationships holding the behaviour:* in true Bateson fashion, in may be necessary to explore the system holding the behaviours. This system is made up of the exemplar, the desired and the unwanted behaviour, plus any external injunctions. Vital information may come from discovering how the exemplar is viewing, holding and/or hearing the desired behaviour in the future, or the unwanted behaviour in the past. There is information to be found in exploring the dynamics between the desired and unwanted behaviours, and taking the system as a whole. Issues of secondary gain, ecology, submodalities, modal operators may make themselves known.

Sources of Information

Myth 3: At least three live exemplars are required to provide sufficient information.

Traditionally the modeller identifies three exemplars to model, each being particularly good at doing the identified skill or behaviour. Why three? Because it takes three occurrences to confirm a pattern. The modeller spends time with each exemplar and then goes off with the gathered information to devise a model.

Not so – sources of information can be multifarious leaving the modeller once more at flexible choice.

- *Self:* it might be that the modeller is exploring his or her own system and acts as the exemplar. This narrow field of enquiry may be sufficient because the idiosyncratic information gleaned is sufficient for purpose. Obviously this can fall foul of the belief that the exemplar rarely knows what he or she does, as key elements lie outside of conscious awareness. But if the tested results deliver the intended outcome then this isn't a problem. If they don't then an additional dissociated perspective may be required.

- *Exemplar:* the modeller may seek to emulate how a particular individual achieves the results he or she does, certainly in the manner that they do. So the exemplar is required to identify a range of occasions when this behaviour is delivered in the desired manner, and the modeller through possible observation and interview gathers the evidence and explores the common patterns found across them.

- *Exemplars:* it might be that the modeller is after a generalised description of an identified behaviour and therefore consults three or more exemplars that demonstrate the same ability. Again through possible observation and interview the modeller can discover patterns common to all or to the majority. The modeller may include himself or herself in this mix.

- *Literature and other media:* in the absence of sufficient or suitable exemplars, or to underpin or supplement understanding, the modeller may go to written or recorded sources of information, removed from the living experience. Care needs to be taken to differentiate between direct reportage from the exemplar, and commentary about the exemplar – the difference between autobiography and biography. Again the testing of the resulting model will adjudicate here.

- *Systems:* the modeller may not seek to model a specific individual or group of people. Instead the modeller may focus on the system that is holding the behaviour, good or bad, factoring in common inputs, influences, problems, successes, and consequences. This is often the case for consultants within an organisation.

Interventions

Myth 4: Modelling an exemplar can impair the exemplar's future performance.

This brings up another of the myths surrounding modelling – the fear that modelling can make the exemplar self-conscious, disrupt the natural patterns of their excellence and then arrest future performance. Enough to put any budding modeller off! However experience has demonstrated the reverse is in fact the case. Enhanced self-knowledge can generate further improvements in performance, and in self-esteem.

Myth 5: Some methodologies are 'better', 'the right ones', 'more sophisticated' than others.

I have deliberately chosen the word 'Intervention' mindful of Bateson's mantra: 'When you view a system you change it.' The process of modelling is an intervention in its own right. Change will inevitably take place.

- *Product and process models:* for many new practitioners applying a technique based on a particular model is the primary means of modelling out what is happening on the inside with an exemplar or explorer. Neurological Level Alignment is a great example of this. Unfortunately in some quarters the use of techniques is discredited as being unsophisticated and robotic, especially if the modeller's choice of techniques is limited.

- *Modelling methodologies:* over the past forty years we are very fortunate to have at our disposal a wide range of modelling methodologies to choose from. I've included thirteen different approaches in the book. Unfortunately there is a tendency for vested interest to emerge, with some developers promoting their own methodology's validity over those of others. This unhelpful myth can result in budding modellers having only one or two approaches available, and running a prejudice against other equally useful ones, restricting their personal flexibility as a result.

- *Neurological modelling:* here we have the gifts of NLP's building blocks, held within no formal procedures and available to be freely selected and worked with. The modeller can choose to model out structures revealed through sensory representation systems, multiple perspectives, time frames, submodalities, parts, metaphor, and mentors.

- *Linguistic modelling:* we are equally uniquely blessed with our rich choice of available language frameworks. The richness of the Meta and Milton Models, the impact of frames and reframing, and the subtleties of predicates can directly target specific areas of internal processing.

The modeller has the additional option of picking and mixing their approaches, provided the information gathered is compatible across exemplars and contexts. I offer lots of examples of how these can be used in direct response to the individual's needs and feedback.

Modelling Outcomes

Myth 6: The production of a model is required as part of the modelling process.

Myth 7: The modeller is required to replicate the excellent behaviour in others.

Because of these particular requirements, many modellers' motivation falls by the wayside, or excellent modellers don't realise that they are in fact modelling, just because they haven't produced a standalone model or designed a new technique.

If these requirements were the case, we would be brimming over with new models, new techniques and cloned experts – and we're not. Few of the modelling approaches actually specifically demand these requirements or even teach us how to do them. So we find that the reality does not match the reported theory. Happily the reality is much more useful.

Before going into the range of possible outcomes, let's knock on the head the notion of replication. *It is impossible to replicate behaviour in another.* Taking aside the requirement of like-for-like physiology and like-for-like bank of pre-existing skills, this is because the acquirer has his or her own neurology and has to process all information through it. The best a modeller can achieve – should that be desired – is a *close approximation* of the exemplar's behaviour, processed through the character and nature of the acquirer's essence: my Fran-ness in my case. Actually close approximation is not always required: something *like* the behaviour may be sufficient, or a movement *towards* the behaviour is enough. Should close replication be required then significant adjustments to the acquirer's system have to be made to accommodate the new demands, and the behaviour needs to be broken down into pretty small pieces – all doable but laborious.

- *Exploration/identification of structure:* it may be sufficient for the exemplar – or the modeller – just to absorb the insight and understanding 'merely' through informally acquiring new information that had been tucked away in the nether regions of the exemplar's system. The acquisition of the knowledge and awareness allows for incubation within the system, which in turn can self-regulate and alter behaviour autonomously. No third party is involved.

- *Remodelling of structure:* based on fundamental Constructivist principles, once a structure is identified it can be added to, modified or restructured, with the aim of altering subsequent behaviour desirably. This is the key feature of NLP therapy and coaching and the process most often stops with the exemplar.

- *Model construction:* out of all the data, patterns emerge which can be reduced down and refined into a discrete digitised description, the elements of which when taken together encapsulate the modelled ability. Stepping into the model, second positioning it, can provide insight into the subtleties lying within the behaviour. Up until now, little has been written on the nature of models and their construction.

- *Formal acquisition:* the icing on the cake of the whole modelling process is the design and delivery of a technique that acts as the carrier of the model's dynamics and intrinsic wisdom. Here the original intentions of modelling come into play, as a technique can be offered to anyone who would gain from its effects, in any context or culture.

The Final Myth

Myth 8: Modelling is difficult.

Not true. To my mind modelling has only been allowed to become difficult because so many pieces were ill defined and uncoded, making coherent teaching impossible. Trainers were operating out of either unconscious incompetence or unconscious competence, hoping their noses didn't grow in the process.

I hope you'll find that I have conveyed just how simple modelling is, through laying out the system that holds it, and providing context for all the elements that are involved within it. NLP is really a simple modality, once you become aware of the purpose of its components and the relationship between them.

I fondly hope that what you will find in this book is a whole bunch of information, ideas, practical explanations and examples, congruent and simple, which will accelerate your learning, broaden your understanding and sharpen your motivation.

Finally

I hope you are now raring to go. I promise you, there is so much more to come! You will not be disappointed. Use the Index and the Table of Contents to direct your attention if your want to pick your way through the vast amount of information available here. This is a resource to dip into again and again, as well as read through. Should I ever meet you and you present me with a copy of this book, I want it to be well thumbed with notes in the margins and question marks, asterisks and exclamation marks!

The potential that modelling presents is endless and the benefits, both to others and yourself, are there for the taking. I can think of no better way to launch this inspirational journey than these words of Robert Dilts:

> I've seen what the right tools can do in terms of bringing real healing; not just pushing the shadow off somewhere else but real transformation. So I think if we all do that, then we have a possibility for incredible growth – to bring health, to bring creativity, to bring more of these great gifts of being the human being.

> Basic things like health, love, joy, those are the drivers. We can create that. I believe that life is about abundance – actually abundance is the natural seed. The earth is always capable of producing abundance but with some sort of human tending, you can increase that. An interaction with proper tools and you can just magnify the abundance.

> That's potential. Use that potential.

> From an interview conducted by Fran Burgess at The Northern School of NLP, 2006

The Introduction

Part 1
The Nature of a Modeller

Introduction

For many people within the NLP field, modelling is some esoteric activity practised by the few and irrelevant to most. It is seen as something separate within NLP, compartmentalised as an optional specialism. Or it is seen as a particular narrow activity for NLP geeks, who are given the role of devising new models and producing new materials, for the rest of us to use.

For the non-creative, or the easily satisfied, devising new models seems to be unnecessary. We have enough available skills and techniques already. And if they don't work, then we can cobble on practices learnt elsewhere.

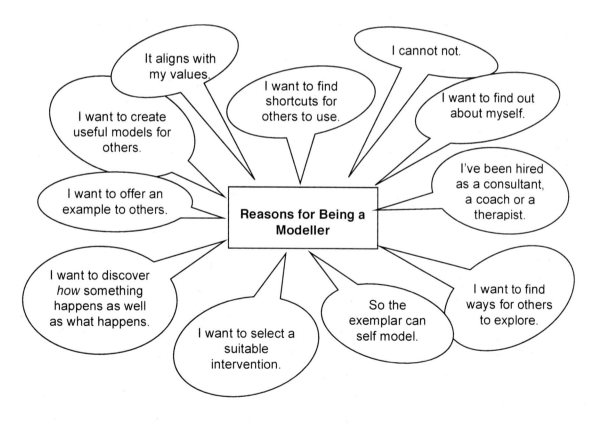

Reasons for Being a Modeller – Burgess : 2005

Modelling has somehow become detached from the body of NLP, and as attendances at NLP Conference workshops on modelling demonstrate, modelling is of interest to a distinct minority. Whereas the 'truth of it' is quite the opposite! Modelling lies at the heart of NLP. It is the pulse of NLP. It is its lifeblood.

- All the models used within NLP have been identified through the process of modelling. Submodalities, perceptual positions, effects of time, effects of metaphors and parts, the nature of neurological levels and meta programmes all became known through the detection and isolation of their patterns at work within our subjective experience.

- All the linguistic patterns were identified and refined through the modelling process.

- All the techniques – the basic repertoire and those that have been developed subsequently – resulted from these exploratory processes, and were tested through modelling.

- All the skills within our repertoire – outcome setting, rapport, sensory acuity and flexibility, and pattern detection and systemic thinking, were originally identified as essential requirements for excellence through the process of modelling.

- All the modelling methodologies have resulted from the process of modelling. All methods of teaching and acquiring these methodologies have come through modelling.

- All effective interventions are sourced through the process of modelling the exemplar; finding out the structure of the current system, determining the desired situation, and mapping the intervention against the structure of a known process – or creating something totally unique for that individual.

- Arguably, if we are NLP practitioners worthy of our name, we cannot not be modelling. We may just not know it, or acknowledge it, or know that what we are doing passes for modelling. If we are making sense of the structure that lies beneath behaviour, we are modelling.

So often the process of modelling has become confused with the end product of modelling – a model. The two are very distinct. The process of modelling may never reach the fully coded stage of a portable model. It may be sufficient for the source of the information, the exemplar, to learn what their inner structure is. Or the process may stop with the modeller, once the structure is known. It all depends on the modeller's outcome.

Our Origins

Neurolinguistic Programming might never have made the light of day if it hadn't been down to the particular characteristics and attributes of our founders. If Bandler and Grinder had been different types of people, they may have been content to merely become acolytes of the experts Perls, Satir, Bateson and Erickson. With this scenario, they would have become highly skilled and proficient in delivering the body of skills performed by these experts. Or they may through happenstance have landed on another way of doing things and carried on practicing that, without any concern for *how* they were getting the results they were getting. It would have been enough just to know that what they did worked, and get on with it.

But they didn't. They didn't take either of these approaches. They instinctively sought to find out

HOW the experts achieved their results, and HOW they themselves could achieve them, and HOW other people could also achieve them. They didn't have a ready-made label to describe their approach. They didn't even have any ready-made tools to assist their approach. They went into the pursuit blind, enthusiastically and with the optimism born out of arrogance and fearlessness. They found themselves involved in a process of discovery, one that only later they would name as Modelling.

In *Whispering in the Wind*, Part 1 Chapter 4, Grinder describes the characteristics that he possessed which enabled him to do the pioneering work he did. He starts off by listing the characteristics he and Bandler shared (p121-2):

> Arrogant, curious, unimpressed by authority or tradition; strong personal boundaries where each has responsibility for their own experience; willingness to try nearly anything rather than be bored or boring; utterly lacking in self-doubt – egotistical; playful, full capability as players in the Acting As If game; and full behavioural appreciation of difference between form (structure) and content.

He then goes on to provide further specific detail regarding himself (p123-136). I offer the outline here, and strongly suggest you read further to gain his full description of what he means by each of these:

* A hypnotic fascination with competency and excellence

* A clean behavioural distinction between form and substance, process and content

* A positive affinity for what others call risk-taking

* A recognition of the value of formalisation and explicit representations

* A positive response to ambiguity and vagueness

* A sharpened alertness for unusual events.

If our founders had been any different, then I for one would not be here exploring the art and science of modelling. It is also unlikely that I would have made the extraordinary personal and commercial gains that came my way in the last twenty-five years. And I doubt if I would have been able to make the significant impact on my own learners and clients through my resulting skills and understanding. My life would have taken a very different turn, or perish the thought, would have continued in the unfulfilling direction it was previously taking.

I suspect this would be true for many others that NLP has touched. We are all where we are today *because* of the unique natures of both Bandler and Grinder, creating their heady magic on the fringes of behavioural science. However, without the steadying influence of the developers that followed them, most significantly Robert Dilts, we would not be finding ourselves within the mainstream of personal development forty years on. We are truly indebted to the work and energies of these fine minds.

The Modeller's Identity

It was a natural progression to model the fabulous modellers that came to The Northern School of NLP. But not to limit my consideration on 'just' these NLP experts, but to extend and test my understanding with those in other fields of operations who pursue the same class of activity, namely exploration.

As babies we come into a world full of mysteries. Our instinct as we grow in these early years is to make sense of this confusing unscripted world: navigate between safety and danger; discover pleasure and avoid pain; set up our signposts; and accommodate familiarity and difference. We learn to survive.

Some of us continue in this vein naturally and uninterrupted, constantly exploring, finding new meanings, and updating existing learning. These people may go on to make a living out of their fascination with structure and model-making, as engineers, diagnosticians, artists. For this group, discovering that NLP is all about modelling and structure would be music to the ears. Happily many have found their way to NLP and delight in what it has to offer.

Others among us may find, as we grow older that the intensity and frequency of our explorations becomes less wide-ranging and we become satisfied that the range of models we have gathered are sufficient for our needs and aspirations. Our model-making abilities lie dormant, or are occasionally activated. Should this outcome not be challenged, and alternatives presented, then our world risks becoming narrower and less stimulating. We adopt conformity and compliance, and let go the belief that the world is a fascinating place and our take on it is something totally unique and worth cherishing. Harry Chapin's incredibly poignant song '*Flowers are Red*' records this distressing process. I urge you to find it and listen to it.

Happily this condition is not terminal!

Interestingly I found that the majority of participants on NLP practitioner courses are within the 35-50 age range, when often people are looking for something more, and are no longer fully satisfied with 'good enough'. As an NLP practitioner, I suspect your early experience of NLP learning reintroduced you to your primal states of wonder and curiosity, reawakened your sense of adventure and reactivated your desire to learn – specifically about going beyond the obvious and discovering how behaviours and responses were activated.

But for how long? For all too many Master Practitioners, the last time they were conscious of modelling was for certification. And many other learners may have dropped by the wayside because the whole process seemed too complicated and confusing. They were unlikely to have sustained the connection between structure and behaviour, and how NLP skills were designed to discover it.

The question I grappled with was how to stop this haemorrhage of motivation and energy, and channel it purposefully. So modelling out the process of modelling itself was the next logical step.

NLP has attracted some fantastic natural modellers, who have demonstrated to us the power and influence models and modelling can have. It makes sense to find out who they are and what makes them do what they do. But we can go beyond that world of NLP and expand our studies to take in many other types of modellers – explorers, those whose efforts exceed the ordinary, whose work demands the ability to dig below the surface.

Just take a moment to consider all the jobs around that require the ability to clear away lots of detail to get to the nub of the issue, or whose job is to track a truth, create a structure, resolve confusion and clarify understanding.

Here's a few to be getting on with: archaeologists, painters, detectives, film directors, pathologists, research scientists, architects, anthropologists, therapists, IT help desk personnel, explorers, choreographers, engineers, gossip columnists, judges, business consultants, car mechanics, trackers, and coaches. Modellers are all around us.

Living Through Modelling

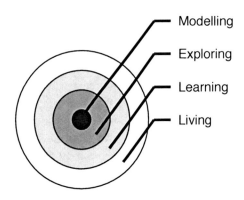

Modelling as a Life Skill – Burgess: 2005

Let me unashamedly expose my bias. Without it, this book would never have been written. To my mind, modelling is a direct pathway to living a purposeful life. I come to this complex equivalence through the following argument.

Learning

To continue living in an active and dynamic fashion, we need to keep on learning. This doesn't mean endless diplomas and degrees – more being curious about the world, challenging assumptions, exposing ourselves to new experiences, and being open to changing our perceptions and conclusions, so that we can enhance the contribution we are able to make to the world.

At The Northern School of NLP, our NLP Practitioner training was built round the need to reactivate our adult learners, restore their faith in their abilities to learn, and to reignite the pleasure and safety found in discovering. Early on we would focus on our learners becoming comfortable with Not-Knowing, identifying personal patterns which supported or hindered learning, and begin to shift the limiting beliefs around looking foolish, getting it wrong, or being judged badly, to the realisation that mistakes, not knowing and questions are essential for learning. Since learning and vulnerability go hand in hand, we can find ways to be safely unsafe and comfortably uncomfortable.

Being an active Learner is essential if we are to have an active life.

The *Learner Readiness Questionnaire*, which I developed in 2002, highlights the following categories of learner, as revealed through their beliefs.

- *Self-sufficient learner:* these are excellent learners. They enjoy learning and gain tremendously from it. They are up for learning whatever life presents. They are realistic and set their goals accordingly. They have high levels of motivation and their past successes fuel their future endeavours. Others would be well served to learn their secrets of success.

- *Operational learner:* these are effective learners, and generally can overcome most obstacles they meet. However, there are some beliefs they hold which prevent them from realising all of their learning potential – and prevent them fully enjoying the learning process. These beliefs will cause occasions of low motivation, which might make them think of giving up – or certainly aiming for less.

- *Vulnerable learner:* these are cautious and possibly anxious learners. Learning for them has had its ups and downs, and varying successes. They rely on the learning conditions being right for them, otherwise their chances of success are limited. They would gain tremendously from developing a wider range of learning skills and becoming more self-assertive.

- *Dependent learner:* these are not instinctive learners, and their experiences of learning have probably not been very rewarding for them. However, they know they can learn. Look at what they learnt between the ages of 0-5. They need to re-discover those skills of learning and so realise that 'you are a swan!' after all. Doing a pre-study learning-to-learn course would help them enormously.

You may identify people who come under the various categories. Much of this outcome rests with the range of beliefs they hold about themselves, their expectations regarding learning, the nature of learning, their level of learning competence, and the levels of support they seek. Shifting these beliefs and introducing alternative ways of thinking can radically shift performance and self-efficacy – a truly worthwhile outcome.

Our *Learning Readiness Questionnaire* – www.nlpand.co.uk, not only identifies the level of learning inclination, but also provides in-depth supportive ways to consider alternative thinking.

Exploring

There are two major ways to approach learning – learning from the experiences of others, or learning from your own experience.

Learning from others means you will gain ready-made conclusions, be free of the arduous task of generating your own conclusions, and arguably fast track yourself to knowledge. You can tap into the finer minds of others, and accrue the wisdom produced over the centuries. Stand on the shoulders of genius. As such, you will learn nothing new – new to you perhaps but not to the world. Your learning will not be original. However such externally referenced learning is not to be discounted, since it can catalyse new thinking, and inspire you to plough your own furrow.

Alternatively you may be compelled to learn from your own experiences, trusting your own discoveries, testing them and moulding them into the manner of yourself. This is the longer route, but much more stimulating and profoundly personal – particularly for those who are strongly internally referenced. You may find that you have reinvented a wheel, but it will be *your* wheel with your own particular stamp on it. And if you do, then you share your genius alongside others. If however you come up with something totally original, well what a contribution you have made! And now you are in the position to inspire others.

Exploration is the major route to discovery for those of us who are experiential learners: pursuing uncharted waters; plotting our way through unknown territory; exposing ourselves to the unfamiliar and sometimes the uncomfortable; and in the process strengthening our own resourcefulness and making a contribution for others.

Actual explorers are a particular type of learner, and I believe they exemplify in a physical dimension all the activities that we as modellers strive to deliver in the mental domain. Explorers manifest learning through discovery, from first-hand experience and from living with their own conclusions.

Explorers come in all shapes and forms. Some are traditional travellers finding fulfilment by literally entering unknown territories. Others are explorers within their own field of work, carving out new processes, discovering hidden elements, combining old and new thinking and going outside current parameters. They are the mavericks and the rule breakers, or those that recognise happy happenstance and develop it further.

I find such people so stimulating, and not a little awesome. They have so much to teach us, yet they don't see themselves as being particularly special. For many, they couldn't not be like this. Life would be unbearable if they couldn't let their mind and talents roam unfettered. It is in their blood and written in their DNA.

As exemplars they can reveal once more the basic patterns that drive discovery. As NLPers, whilst we know that 'the map is not the territory', the challenge for us is consciously and consistently to put ourselves out to discover what actually does lie outside our map. Our own map can only be enhanced if we deliberately set the intention to explore and learn from the maps of others, or from territory hitherto unexplored. We will grow when we are happy to let go the safety of our familiar world – be it the world of physical or emotional or mental or spiritual comfort. Some of us are braver in some of the worlds over others.

Modelling

Learning through Exploring is the hallmark of an NLPer. We come from a place where the map is not the territory, and our own map is not relevant in the process of making sense of another's. Our approach to training – at least for those who provide thorough training experiences – encourages testing and trying out of the material within the training programme. Our approach regarding an exemplar or a situation is one we have when addressing those Magic Eye 3D pictures. At first glance the image looks like a geometric design, or an ordinary scene, and then when we look at it with a totally different focus – voila! – a completely unexpected new image emerges. As modellers, we work on the belief that there is always a picture behind the picture, always a hidden structure lurking behind the presented behaviour and our job is to find it. This is modelling.

Therefore as modellers, we are Explorers and Learners and fully engaged with Living. To become better modellers, it serves us to become better Learners and Explorers. Here's your chance to explore the world of Learners, Explorers and finally modellers themselves.

Explorers

The Hero's Journey

Before we look at particular explorers, it is worth being familiar with Joseph Campbell's book *The Hero of a Thousand Faces* (1949). Campbell modelled out the great journeys told in the tales of mythology across cultures and religions. There he cites that often the Hero, for it usually was a young boy of insignificant origin – a shepherd or fisher boy – experiences a Call whilst he is going about his everyday life. The Call often comes in the form of a bird, or animal, or in a dream.

Initially he refuses the Call when he is first aware of it, disbelieving it, or be unwilling to undertake the upheaval to his life that following the Call might make. However, the Call persists and eventually the Hero submits to its insistence and agrees to follow: at which point his Guardian appears.

His Guardian offers him protection, words of wisdom and gives him a talisman to help him on his journey – a sword, cloak, or a ring.

The Hero then goes forward and has many adventures, meeting many assailants and sources of support and shelter. He develops great skills and achieves feats way beyond any imagining. After some time, his adventures bring him to a moment of epiphany, and he receives profound insight into the purpose of his travels – an overwhelming universal truth. Strengthened, he continues, seeing the truth of this wisdom at every turn of the road.

After this point, he receives another Call – A Call to Return, demanding he returns to the land from whence he came. And he refuses this Call. He wants to travel further, and learn more from the wonders of the world. He has begun to relish this life of adventure and exploring. But the Call to Return persists, and he is compelled to return to the land of his birth. He accepts that the whole purpose of the adventure is to bring back the wisdom he has gained.

Physical Explorers and Travellers

- *Benedict Allen:* Benedict Allen is my hero. His first planned expedition at the age of 23 took him travelling across perhaps the most remote forest on earth, which lies between the mouths of the Orinoco and the Amazon. From there on he has lived with remote peoples in Papua New Guinea, crossed the Namib desert with camels, and taken a dog team across Siberia in one of the coldest winters on record. He has been shot at, stolen from and abandoned, crippled by malaria, stranded and left near to death at least six times, yet he cannot not explore.

  I first came across his existence one Sunday morning. As you know, once you set the filters new information comes your way in the strangest of places. I was reading one of *The Sunday Times*

Magazine features: *The Best of Times, Worst of Times* (a feature sadly now discontinued) and Benedict Allen's opening paragraph just jumped out at me.

> For me, exploration is not about conquering natural obstacles or planting flags, or going where nobody has gone before. It's about making yourself vulnerable, opening yourself up to whatever's there, and letting a place leave its mark on you.

For him the purpose of an explorer is to disconnect from home and test or immerse himself with what is unfamiliar to him. This requires not taking along objects from his known world (in Allen's case GPS, sponsorship logos), but instead breaking the link so that he adjusts the world he is now in. He learns the technology of the local peoples, usually simple, locally sourced, based on long-serving skills and handed down knowledge. How else is he going to learn what it is really like to be in this alien and seemingly hostile environment? From his website, www.benedictallen.com, he says

> These remote communities only look after me because I'm harmless. They adopt me, like you might a child. It's also a sound philosophy to be ready to learn from scratch, just like an infant.

His description of the arduous nature of exploration totally mirrors the experiences of a modeller, who may tussle in the chaos of confusion for quite some time before the emerging patterns begin to provide clarity.

> The best thing being an Explorer is that special moment when you realise that you have overcome your obstacles and you stagger out of the forest, knowing that dream you had two years ago has been achieved. It is a wonderful thing when you realise that your struggle has been vindicated.

He addresses the tenacity required, when giving up might seem such a desirable outcome.

> An Explorer has a steely resolve, clear vision of where he's going, adapts to changing circumstances, uses the resources within and around him, and pushes himself to the limit.

Resonant with The Hero's Journey, Allen sees it as essential to bring back useful information that has to be meaningful.

> My job is to go to unknown, little known or misunderstood parts of the planet and describe and challenge our ideas about them. The difference between you and say, someone travelling as a tourist, traveller, or adventurer, is that you set out with the specific objective of systematically tackling that frontier of knowledge and – here's an equally important bit – you then report back your findings. You can't claim to be an explorer unless you bring back some new insight.

To find out more about this fascinating man, go to his website: http://www.benedictallen.com.

- *Michael Palin:* Michael Palin is the Monty Python man and inveterate traveller, producer of eight memorable travel programmes and lots of books, and a recent past-President of the Royal Geographical Society. At one point it was reported that he was about to hang up his walking boots. The following extract is from his response printed in The Times, Saturday April 30 2005.

> The truth is that I could no more stop travelling than I could stop drawing breath. Travel tests me physically and mentally. It sharpens my reactions, my appetites and my judgment. It's in the blood.

> In a world some seek to smear with bigotry and prejudice, travel has given me valuable

reassurance. In all the journeys I've made, I've rarely been greeted with the fist of anger or the wagging finger of accusation. From what I've seen the instinct to befriend and assist is much stronger than the urge to do harm.

It is not an easy option. The essence of travel is letting go of habit and prejudice and relishing the unfamiliar. Food you've never eaten before, a language you've never spoken before, religion that mystifies, customs that confuse, politics that perplex, all question everyday assumptions about how you live your life.

But the more unusual and exotic you want your experience to be, the tougher it is on the system. Certainly, crossing the Sahara and travelling the length of the Himalaya tested myself and my team to the limits and I feel the need for some thinking time before deciding on another journey.

But there are many different ways to cut the cake, from a single one-off programme to a series that doesn't necessarily involve a huge journey. One of the most rewarding episodes we shot was one of the slowest. It was way back on Around the World in Eighty Days and followed our progress from Dubai to Bombay at a steady four miles an hour on a dhow, with neither radio or radar, crewed by Gujarati fishermen.

As a result of the confined space and the length of time spent together, extraordinary friendships grew up between people from two different worlds. For a short magical few days everyone was equal. All our material and technical superiority meant nothing. The Indians knew how to sail the boat and we didn't. And that was all that mattered.

Whatever shape or form my future plans assume, I could never conceive of a life that didn't offer the possibilities of such encounters happening again.

And that's a travelling life.

© 2005 Michael Palin

There is so much here that is reflects the pursuit of modelling. I just love it when I find a good resource!

Athletes

- *Tanya Streeter – Free Diver:* Tanya Streeter became the first person to free dive to depths of 400ft. In doing so she established another first – setting a world record for women that bettered the men's world record. Free diving is a death defying activity, requiring athletes to survive on one breath for over 3½ minutes and withstand the enormous pressure on their bodies. You may well wonder why she does it, to which she says in a radio interview:

  Our human limit is way more than where we think it is. We need to redefine our limits. Whilst there are limits, they simply are nowhere near where we think they are.

  From a radio interview

- *Shaun Baker – Kayaker:* Shaun Baker is a record-breaking kayaker who took to paddling down waterfalls – an extension he said of the white-water rivers he used to seek out. Always going for a challenge and ignoring advice on when to carry the boat, he would seek out those waters previously unvisited. He has the notion of man challenging and finding atonement with nature.

  When you know water, the noise and the power, it's your friend. And a waterfall is just a vertical river. Making the first descent is the main thing for me. If it is a world record, that's a bonus. I always analyse each fall logically and if I think I won't come out with my life intact then I won't run it. It's the scariest feeling ... you only get the merest glimpse of what is about to happen as you start to fall.

This extract is taken from a Toyota Members' magazine article written by Ben Webb, Autumn 1998.

- *Chris Yates – Angler:* Chris Yates, an international angler and writer of many books on the subject of fishing, describes his early morning arrival at his chosen river.

    I see the river and stop. That's a magical moment – the river sort of says something to me in a way that's almost indescribable. You want to know what state the water is in, which is easy to see. But this other thing, which comes through after, is mysterious, and it's the key to how I'll fish that day.

When describing a recent crossroads in his life, he described it like this:

    It's like you've reached a fork in the stream, and you think it looks good one way, but it doesn't look at all fishy. And yet I might find something a bit unusual, where it's shadowy and murky, and that's where I've gone – I've gone up this little side-stream, which is a backwater in life, and I don't know where it's going to lead but I like it, and it's completely unknown to me, where I am at the moment.

A Life In The Day 2006 interview by Seb Morton-Clark

© Reproduced with permission from Times Newspapers Ltd 2006

Creative Artists

- *Ida Bagus Anom – Carver:* Ida Bagus Anom is a famed Master Balinese Mask maker and dancer himself. He produces beautiful masks, working with the contours of the wood and creating illusions that are instantly impactful. Some of the dance masks are then painted with over 40 layers of paint creating the characters of the dance. As soon as you put them on, you become transformed, almost possessed by the mask's character.

    He described his process to me: 'I receive pieces of wood and wait ... and wait, until the wood tells me what mask I need to make. I am a servant of the wood.'

- *Emma Sergeant – Painter:* the artist describes her approach to the empty canvas.

    When I look at my canvas, I feel there is a drawing or painting already there. If I have to disturb the rhythms or impose what I want, it is going to go dead on me. But if I go along with what I am seeing and feeling on the canvas, then I find it instructs me. Then I have to discover it and nurture it to life.

Source unknown

- *Unknown choreographer:* an interview on the radio caught my ear. Unfortunately I didn't catch the name of the guest speaker. She was talking about the creative process of dance and the interviewer asked if she went in knowing the dance she was going to make. 'Oh no! I have the music, but until I meet the dancers and we work with the music, only then I will know what might be possible.'

- *Unknown sculptor:* on the Census survey a Sculptor entered 'Sculpting Stone Lions' under occupation. When then asked what does this specifically involves, he wrote: 'Chipping away at anything that is not Lion.'

Investigation Specialists

- *Ed Uthman – Forensic Pathologist:* MD, Diplomate, American Board of Pathology provides the following answer to the question 'what personality characteristics are required in a good forensic pathologist?' Apart from having a thick skin and a strong stomach he says:

  > A talent for and interest in science – involving an appreciation of structure and spatial relationships. Good communication skills – liaising and convincing a wide range of people. The mind of a detective – having some insight into the heart and mind of a criminal.

  > http://web2.airmail.net/uthman/forensic_career.html

- *Detective:* here are some of the characteristics required of a good detective

  > As an excellent detective you must have a thirst for adventure and must like solving puzzles. Solving puzzles requires patience – lots of it. You will be able to combine creative thinking with logic and analysis and the ability to know when to use either. You avoid being gullible. You value detail even in its minutes form, being prepared to look beyond those clues found in plain sight, whilst at the same time looking beyond the situation or case. You are tenacious and never give up. Most importantly, you have a desire for truth and justice as your main goal.

  > http://www.theprivatedetective.com

- *Crime scene investigation:* Here is a description of Crime Scene Investigation Skills taken from the eHow website written by Robert Vaux.

  > Crime scene investigation skills involve the ability to notice small details, to make intuitive leaps and to ferret out important pieces of evidence from an ocean of incidental details. A successful crime scene investigator will be able to deduce what happened at the scene with a fair amount of accuracy and provide solid evidence that is admissible in court. A poor one will overlook important details, bury solid facts behind inconsequential trivialities and even destroy important evidence through mishandling.

  > A good investigator has the ability to notice things – to take in the totality of a given room or space and identify as many pertinent details as possible. This includes obvious crime scene elements like bloodstain patterns or the marks used on an open safe as well as more subtle elements like an off-kilter picture in the house of a compulsive neat freak or a brand of cigarette in the ashtray that no one in the household smokes. A good memory can serve the investigator well too, allowing him to conjure up details of the crime scene after the fact at a point when they may be useful.

  > http://www.ehow.com

NLP Modellers

I have been privileged to spend time with some of the best modellers within our field – Robert Dilts, Steve Gilligan, David Gordon, Judith Delozier, John McWhirter, Shelle Rose Charvet, James Lawley and Penny Tompkins. Unsurprisingly they share many similar characteristics and traits, which I realised I also share to a greater or lesser extent.

These can be grouped into three areas: Being – their qualities and personal makeup; Thinking – their approach to information; Doing – their expression of their nature and thinking.

It's important to point out that not all our modellers displayed all these characteristics, and certainly some were more dominant than others. And since we all have these resources already within our system, all of us have the potential to develop each of them further.

As you read through the listings, just notice how much of that characteristic is already a part of you, or is around but could do with flexing. Take time to isolate occasions where you demonstrated the trait in your own inimitable way, and notice how you felt. If it gave you a buzz, then this is a great way for you to know how to come into your own more often. If your response to the trait was less fulsome, then you could seek to reframe it, or challenge the limiting belief restraining it.

The listings also provide an excellent means of diagnosing what you could develop further, or even 'borrow' from elsewhere. It stands to reason, the stronger these traits, the more consistent and effective you will be as a modeller.

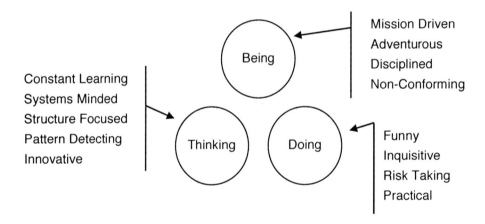

The Characteristics of an NLP Modeller – Burgess 2012

Being

1   **Mission driven:** modellers cannot not model, whether it's because modelling itself is an activity at mission, or that the modeller can serve their mission through modelling.

Gordon's mission is 'to participate fully, and help others to participate fully, in life's variety of experiences.' And therefore he is focused on understanding more and more about how we construct our experiences, delighting in the differences and the opportunity to engage fully in the perception of others.

Dilts puts it: 'It (modelling) is not about having the information. It's not just about, "I am going to try and figure out what someone else does". It is my path, my own path of growth.'

Sometimes the modeller can feel in awe of the project they have decided to undertake, unequal to its demands and challenges. That's usually a good sign that this is something worthy of committing your life to.

McWhirter came early to NLP, way back in the 1980s, when he co-trained with Bandler in the States. Over the years he became more and more dissatisfied by what he considered to be the messiness and incompleteness of many of the models within NLP. So initially he set about remodelling it – a pretty big task in itself – that has led to a lifetime's pursuit designing Developmental Behavioural Modelling (DBM).

For myself my Purpose is to Connect with Spirit, which is what happens when I enter another's model of the world, and which is why training and therapy work are so satisfying. Even putting this book together is meeting this need, and I knew I couldn't move on with what is to come next until I had completed this work and was in a position to share it with others.

> **When have you felt compelled to pursue a particular path? When have you been touched and gratified by your actions? When have you sensed a deep felt sense of satisfaction, connection and even completion? Have you a sense of your own Purpose?**

2 **Adventurous:** I would ask our modellers what sorts of books they read when they were little, as a way of finding out the golden thread that has been running throughout the years.

Dilts identified from a young age with pioneers, those who had to seek and track animals. He would read things about Daniel Boone the frontiersman, and the Jack London books, which are about going to Alaska and then surviving in the wilderness.

The fictional stateside girl detective Nancy Drew attracted Delozier and Tompkins as children. Nancy was famous for solving mysteries and behaving more as a tomboy than a little girl in dresses. Personally I was an Enid Blyton Famous Five devotee, with George being my favourite. I was also a Second Lieutenant in my brother's gang.

Delozier's study of anthropology and comparative religions took her willingly into many different cultures within North and Central America as well as Bali, and of course all the other countries she has travelled to subsequently.

After quitting the rat race of business, in a year off Lawley joined an expedition to look for undiscovered Mayan temples in the jungle of Belize.

Lawley and Tompkins set sail on totally uncharted waters, namely the mapping of David Grove's work, with no cooperation from him. They had no way of knowing what the results might be, and if this would be a good investment of their time. They also forfeited earning time to pursue what became a passion. They little realised that they were at the start of creating a totally new modelling methodology, attracting learners from around the world.

> **What has drawn you away from the beaten track? When has exploring been compulsive? When have you been inspired 'to boldly go where no man/person has gone before'?**

3   **Disciplined:** tenacity is present within most of our modellers. Even if they don't seem to be making any breakthroughs, they don't give up and seek another diversion. Whatever they are working on may be put aside to be picked up at a later stage, when the missing pieces have made themselves known.

Tompkins has a lovely story of how she finally persuaded a very adamant David Grove to allow her and Lawley to sponsor some of his workshops, so that they could not only spread the word, but also carry on with their modelling endeavours. He had already refused to be involved in the modelling process. He was very reluctant, but she was not going to take, '*No*' for an answer. She asked him what it would take for him to agree, and he said, 'Seeing her request in writing.' So she snuck into his room just before he was planning to leave the country and left a written request in his suitcase that he would immediately see when opening it. It worked.

Rigour accompanies Tenacity. This attribute stands out for all our modellers. They will work and rework a model until it meets all the tests and stands up in chosen contexts. They don't rest on their laurels after the first draft. Their model stays with them and is being constantly applied to discover what works and what doesn't where and when. They seek to find different uses for it, specialist modifications, and spin offs, with an eye on whatever will be the next one.

McWhirter is the most notable. He has been working on modelling out the territory of human experience for nearly 20 years, and only by 2012 was he ready to commit pen to paper and write up his work. He couldn't/wouldn't do so until he was satisfied that he was ready to say what there was to say. This rigour has come from thoroughly testing, refining, retesting his many, many models, until he achieved and tested an awesome framework of overwhelming cohesion, accommodating over 553 models at the last count.

The same is true for Lawley and Tompkins. Whilst they published their book *Metaphors in Mind* in 2000, they have constantly revisited it, adding, modifying and continuing to expand their understanding of its processes. Their website is outstanding for the many papers they have written on the symbolic modelling approach. http://www.cleanlanguage.co.uk.

Gordon and Dawes continue to add and refine their thinking regarding their Experiential Array. Again you will find these insightful essays on their website http://www.expandyourworld.net

I know it has taken me a long time to consolidate my learning regarding modelling, working away at the frameworks and models that have emerged along the way. Unless the model holds up and is consistently robust, the job is not done. There is no satisfaction in producing sloppy models.

> **When have you been a stickler for getting something 'right'? When was 'good enough' not good enough? When have you persevered, despite wanting to give up?**

4   **Non-conforming:** modellers are rarely satisfied with what is already there. They are constantly seeking new, or more elegant, ways to do things. They tend to have a maverick streak running through them, and don't accept the status quo just because it's there. They are independent thinkers and, rather like Benedict Allen the Explorer and Shaun Baker the Kayaker, tend to live slightly apart from the mainstream of thought.

Modellers are likely to be mismatchers – nearly compelled to explore against the flow. The small roads 'unsuitable for long vehicles' attract; as do the doors and stairways in stately homes and castles marked 'No Entry'.

When have you been reluctant to follow the established rules? When have you been dissatisfied by the given norms? When have you known that your thinking was as good as anyone else's?

Thinking

5   **Constant learning:** modellers are on a personal quest. They seem to be constantly in the Operation part of their personal TOTE (Test, Operate, Test, Exit) often not being able to Exit because they know they don't know enough. This doesn't require them to have brilliant academic track records, merely to have an insatiable desire for more.

Our dining table and kitchen has witnessed some absolutely fabulous, invigorating, demanding conversations, which tested thinking and theories, provoked feedback, suggested new ideas, and catalysed new thinking. These have been some fantastically fertile times.

As learners, Dilts, McWhirter and Lawley are avid readers, especially around past and present thinking concerning human experience. They particularly keep abreast of technology and seek ways in which it could enhance their work.

Delozier is a natural befriender of people from different cultures. She would know more about the immediate happenings in our village after two days than I did from living here. She strikes up connections with everyone she meets, in the hotel, the shop, the venue, and obviously the participants in the workshop.

When asked about his call to model something, Dilts says:

> Best I can describe it is somehow a feeling of inexplicable expansion in my own being, being more of the person than I was before and suddenly there was a whole new territory to be in. I mean it is not about understanding it; it is about growing into that. It is a feeling of identity expansion and when the identity expands then for me that means that there are new areas to model because modelling is always about, in a sense, only modelling yourself.

Personally I can remember clearly those apocalyptic insights and the blur for a few days afterwards. But in the months, even years, proceeding from those moments of lucidity, I know I have been storing up experiences, turning them over in my mind, undervaluing some elements and putting too great an importance on others. The gestation period was over when wham! – new connections were made.

When did you find learning absorbing and fascinating? When did your desire to know more, and find out more, dictate your actions? When did you marvel at the connections you were making and the insight you were gaining?

6   **Systems minded:** our modellers all demonstrated the ability to drill down into detail whilst always scanning the bigger picture and wider context.

Gordon cut his teeth on the books of Robert Lawson, and still likes to read them today. Lawson was notable for writing from the perspective of the main character's companion animal, taking the reader to a very different field of vision and experience.

From an early stage in his modelling development, McWhirter embraced Gregory Bateson's thinking that everything is part of a system; hence his company name Sensory Systems. The challenge for him was to widen and widen the system until he ran out of newness. He is still working on it.

Tompkins is a natural system thinker. As a director of a company manufacturing oil field equipment, she had an unerring ability to formulate policy that took in all the variables operating both inside and outside the work environment. For example, she factored in the needs of wives when determining a payment process.

> **When did you find yourself working out the lay of the land, to familiarise yourself and seek direction? When was it important to discover what was causing something, or explore the effects that particular actions would have? When has one change resulted in a very different outcome?**

7 **Structure focused:** modellers resist being seduced by the trappings and noise of content. They unerringly seek to sniff out the structure that lies behind such presentations.

Lawley as a child had a natural desire to find out what lay behind the outside shell. He would be found merrily dismantling the radiogram – an old fashioned wireless to those who don't know – to find out how it worked. I don't know if he succeeded in putting it back together again.

Many modellers have a background in science, which is based on establishing structure and bringing order to the natural world. Having said that, historians and Linguists for example have to have a fine appreciation of logical form as well.

Science was my route in. The Periodic Table of Chemistry, the Linnaeus Plant and Animal Classifications cleanly and clearly encapsulated the logic that linked the vastly differing chemical elements, and flora and fauna. I realise it was here that I connected with the calm certainty and connecting logic that a rigorously thought-out framework can give. This discipline set up the instinctive drive to test a theory by applying it to different contexts and to different scales.

> **When did you find yourself digging behind the obvious to discover what was hidden? When has understanding been possible once you discovered what lay behind the phenomena you were studying? When have you been able to restore order to an apparently chaotic situation?**

8 **Pattern detecting:** the reason for thinking systemically and widening the space for our attention is so that we can increase our opportunities to spot patterns.

NLP was conceived and born at UC Santa Cruz as a result of the vision and imagination of Dean McHenry. He supported the idea of cross-disciplinary study groups, where linguists met with physicists, mathematicians met with anthropologists. He argued that it was likely that the same patterns would emerge across disciplines and a response applied to one area may be useful in another.

Dilts is a natural pattern detector:

> I had always been interested in observation, and kind of interested in science, not in the sense of the mathematical aspect of science, but observing the world for patterns. When I was younger I was always very interested in animals and would watch birds or other creatures and see their pattern and behaviour, learning about what it does, what it is, what is the pattern of this animal's activity

Delozier's background was in Anthropology and Religious Studies and her interests would take her to explore mythologies and rituals common to many diverse cultures. She also thought the physical somatic responses involved in dancing could be transferred to learning in other areas.

When have you noticed similarities between apparently very different situations? When were you aware of repetitive behaviours – your own behaviours or others? When have you noticed the similarities in structure between something large and something very small?

9 **Innovative:** modellers are natural creators. They want to discover something that has possibly not been mapped before, certainly to provide something that serves a need. By definition they are innovative, producing a product or process out of the details they have been immersed in.

However, it is likely that the final output is not the primary motivation to model. The motivation is the itch to fill the gap, to make sense of the differences that perhaps only they are detecting.

One of Gordon's stories involves his school science project. He jettisoned his original plan to use a prescribed science kit because the planarians died on him. Pressed for time, he then noticed that his sister's goldfish acted differently when the light went on and off in her room. This led him to set up a whole experiment to discover the effects that different coloured lights would have on these goldfish. Much to his surprise his project came first, beating the class swot. He learnt: 'Imitation bad. Original thinking good.'

And I like to think that in my own way I have made a contribution to the understanding of the process of modelling itself, through the models and methodologies I have created, as well as the means to train and develop such understanding.

When have you created something that is uniquely yours? When have you found yourself modifying an object or a process? When have you introduced a new idea, strategy, a product, to address a given situation?

Doing

10 **Funny:** all our modellers without exception are funny – at least the ones we have invited to our home and the School. We have had some fabulous times together. They love telling stories, sharing jokes, keeping up with the banter. They all have a lightness of spirit that belies the discipline of their minds.

Such wit and humour probably comes from their innate understanding of structure, patterns and how to create pattern disrupts. The quirks and fallibilities of the human condition are a delight for them.

When did you see the funny side of a situation? When have you enjoyed the wit and nonsense of another person? When have you appreciated unpredictable occurrences?

11 **Inquisitive:** inquisitiveness covers curiosity, fascination, wonder; tail pointed, ears pricked, eyes on stalks and ears on antennae. Our modellers demonstrate that in spades. Gordon cannot not explore things: your glove compartment, the items on your mantelpiece. McWhirter is perpetually scanning the world around him registering what doesn't seem to fit.

For Dilts, 'fascination is about being alive' is a fundamental truth for him. A ten-minute walk with him becomes a fascinating thirty-minute exploration into a previously familiar yet apparently unknown world.

Tompkins, when she first experienced David Grove at work, 'felt pulled to find out more'. Here was a man achieving results in a way she had never experienced before, and she persuaded Lawley that this was what they needed to focus upon.

My own curiosity is thankfully reined in by his model of a modelling state, identified by Leif Smith, the founder of the Explorers' Foundation, (explored further in Part 4 – The Skills of Modelling). I risked sacrificing sensitivity because of the ferocity of my curiosity.

> **When have you found yourself being really nosy? When have you been exasperated because you couldn't explore a particular area? When have you been compelled to discover more and delve more deeply, dissatisfied with what you have so far?**

12 **Risk taking:** as explorers, modellers live outside their maps. They go out into the world, already predisposed not to know. They happily rely on their skills and mindset, since previous learning and generalisations are not relevant and can even get in the way.

Some might see this as risky, but to a modeller it is the natural way to be. Modellers work in the moment, in the unknown, responding to the constructs as these are currently operating, so it is essential that they discard the protective resources valued by less intrepid explorers. Their certainty that they will discover something essential and useful is all the resource they need.

> **When have you taken yourself beyond your comfort zone? When has the need to know been stronger than your need to stay safe? When has conforming not been an option?**

13 **Practical:** Gordon defines a model as a useful description and stresses the word 'useful', requiring it to serve a purpose for an end user.

Dilts stresses that modelling is not about gathering knowledge but about creating something that can be used. He always works with the end user in mind. I love his line, which for me simplified the whole purpose of modelling: 'The reason you model is that something which could take you a year but maybe if you have the right tool it only takes you a week. So it would be nice to create the tool to make things happen more quickly.'

Modelling is essentially a practical pursuit, not some aesthetic pastime. At its source is the desire to provide something that will be of clear benefit to one or to many, and something that is a significant contribution to the wellbeing of others.

> **When did you sort out a mess? When have you got on with doing something whilst others were still talking about it? When have you found a use for theories you've been given?**

Summary

You will have recognised many of these characteristics within yourself, some more strongly current than others. You may not have considered yourself in the same league as the given 'names', but it is really worth reappraising the natural abilities that you do bring. You have ready-made built-in capacity to be a modeller. All that might be missing at the moment are some of the underpinning knowledge and maybe some of the specific skills, which you need to raise your game and give you confidence in your abilities.

All of the content of this book will add to your knowledge base, in I hope an easy-to-understand format. And in Part 4 – The Skills of Modelling, you are given well-developed descriptions of the skills you'll need. So all is possible and within your reach.

The Development Path of Modellers

We all have the attributes that enable us to become active modellers. And the development of any expertise results from the integration of a group of attributes, which combine to determine the quality of our performance.

For a long time, I had been looking for an explanation for the small percentage of practitioners within the NLP community who seem to be actively pursuing a modelling habit. Were they akin to geeky postgraduate students who sought to immerse themselves in 'the ivory tower' of academia or study, whilst the undergraduates went off into the 'real' world and used their learning to practical purpose – or pursued a totally different direction?

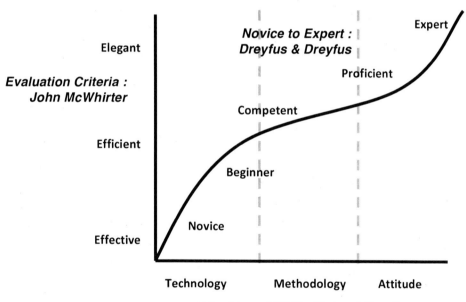

NLP Competence Development Model – Burgess 2006

My heart would have sunk if that were true, because it would mean that modelling was a totally esoteric pursuit – and an academic one at that. Certainly I would never have put myself within that category. Nor would I want to be party to anything that would create barriers, real or imagined, to encouraging *every* practitioner to embrace the pursuit of modelling.

Then I came across the Dreyfus and Dreyfus model – *Novice to Expert: A Five-Stage Model of the Mental Activities Involved in Directed Skill Acquisition.* Washington, DC: Storming Media (1980). This got me thinking. Here was a totally different description of the route to excellence, which didn't rest with 'being better at theory', or 'being really clever'.

Taking this model, I then mapped it with Bandler's description of Neurolinguistic Programming and added to them John McWhirter's Evaluation Model.

The Three Models

Dreyfus and Dreyfus 1984

Dreyfus and Dreyfus plot the progression of competence in a clearly defined manner, based on the level of evolution around five factors, namely:

- Level of knowledge

- Standard of work

- Degree of independence

- Management of complexity

- Perception of context.

This model made such sense to me and served to explain the range of behaviours within our NLP community. There are those who merrily apply the limited techniques to every problem, or infuriate with mindless Meta Model questions. And there are those who demonstrate lovely NLP skills of rapport, sensory acuity and information gathering in their own line of work. And there are those who naturally channel these skills into the whole process of divining underpinning structure. It is just a question of where they are in their development, their awareness of what is next and their motivation to progress further.

Bandler

I added Bandler's alleged description of NLP: that NLP is first and foremost an *Attitude*, of curiosity, a sense of adventure and a desire to learn; followed by a series of skills developed to gather information and replicate behaviour – *Methodology*; which result in a trail of techniques – *Technology*.

It is really worth bearing these distinctions in mind when saying what NLP is. So often saying that it is a set of tools seems sufficient for some, whilst others make reference to communication and relationship skills. You don't hear too many describing NLP as a process for understanding what makes people tick and do what they do. As a result, with these very distinct maps operating, with equal fervour, it is little wonder that we as a community have difficulty in operating from common ground.

That aside, the model of Attitude, Methodology and Technology seems to map across the Dreyfus and Dreyfus distinctions and lend itself to becoming the horizontal axis, with the focus on Technology describing the domain of the novice and beginner, Methodology the area of activity for the competent and emerging proficient, with complete attention on Attitude generating those who are fully proficient and expert.

McWhirter

And then I added McWhirter's simple model of Evaluation Criteria to provide the vertical axis:

- *Effective:* the task is completed somewhat clumsily and at some cost in terms of time and effort to those involved.

- *Efficient:* the task is completed with minimum fuss and disruption.

- *Elegant:* the task is completed smoothly and almost unperceptively, with the fewest stages involved.

As with all of McWhirter's models, this can be regarded as a fractal, so that further distinctions can be made in the field say of Technology, where the practitioner can be effectively effective, efficiently effective or elegantly effective.

NLP Development

As a consequence the finished model, the *NLP Competence Development Model,* seems to make sense of the wide-ranging expressions of NLP in practice, and how practitioners can develop and grow their expertise.

Technology

My suggestion is that newcomers to NLP and recently certificated practitioners focus on NLP's Technology, and when asked what NLP is, will describe it in terms of what it can do. At this stage, they may perform *effectively* according to the instructions in the manual, or mirror their trainer's demonstration. Anything out of the ordinary would floor them and they are likely to abandon the process. If they are successful, they are unlikely to know how that happened and wouldn't be able to self-correct. Since we have all been there, we can remember those times when our skills were clunky and our timing laboured.

NLP *Novices* have a limited grasp of the complexity and potential of the field of NLP. They may suspect that there is rich potential awaiting, but they find it hard to see the wood for the trees. All the pieces they have been offered are much of the time still words on pages, and only some of the processes stand out. Yet inspired and with enthusiasm, they continue with their learning, at which point *Beginners* join Practice Groups and seek to learn more from others, or spend lots of money on books. They will sign up for further training, knowing that there is something here they want to pursue. It is often said that at the end of a Master Practitioner the individual understands that now at last, he or she is a 'proper' Practitioner.

Alarmingly, working from unconscious incompetence, some may set themselves up professionally, marketing phobia cessation or conflict resolution, with no regulation to prevent this.

Methodology

The increasingly *Competent* practitioner logs active practice hours either applying their growing understanding in work situations, or practising with friends and families. Through trial and error, responding to what is happening in the moment, they begin to develop an integrated understanding of how all the various components fit together. They may have woven their knowledge into their existing practice as a trainer, or a coach. They are increasingly comfortable with their growing mastery of their skills. Their sensory acuity and calibration abilities are becoming more second nature. Their use of language and precise questioning is becoming more accurate. Their management of relationships is proving to be more consistent.

They take on more complex problems, and if working professionally as a therapist or coach are likely to be under Supervision. Their focus is to continually improve their skills base and deepen their understanding of the processes involved. They have a deepened identity as an NLP professional and seek to serve both NLP and their clients and customers in a credible and reliable manner. They are growing to trust the 'truth' behind the NLP Presuppositions. These practitioners have become increasingly more *efficient* in terms of time and energy expended. They certainly begin to present greater value for money!

Attitude

Proficient practitioners have their skills in the muscle, their linguistic ability has fluency and they have a fully integrated understanding of the potential of all the elements within their repertoire. Possibly they have begun teaching and supervising the work of others. They are becoming totally immersed in the philosophy and mindset of NLP, with a complete commitment to the efficacy of the process. They are not fazed by the complexity of a problem since they know that it is all part of a system and the answer lies in the underlying structure. They are growing in *elegance*.

Expert practitioners have developed their own authoritative voice, with a deep understanding of the integrated niceties of determining the nature of subjective experience. Working from deep within the principles of Constructivism, they apply their skills effortlessly, almost instinctively, being open to new learning and distinctions. They draw on their learned intuitions, working on that fertile interface between the conscious and unconscious mind. They bring innovation into what they can achieve, develop their own style and find themselves making a contribution to the body of knowledge. They can reduce the seemingly complex system of NLP into a simple framework. With a vision of what may be possible they have pioneered their own area of practice, developed new approaches and extended the boundaries of overall understanding and application. Their *elegance* makes NLP look so easy.

Development and Progression

Of course, not everyone moves onwards and upwards. Many are satisfied with the level they reach. Some may not be aware of how much more they could improve, or not have the time, money, energy or motivation to commit to what it might require. Their priorities lie elsewhere.

However, as Dilts would have it the results of modelling mean that what may have taken ten days can now be done in one. So in this book I am offering many short cuts in thinking, concise descriptions and summary frameworks that can take the sweat out of understanding. I profoundly hope that what you are offered within these covers acts as an accelerant to your journey towards being an Expert.

Application Areas

When NLP was just a twinkle in Bandler and Grinder's collective eye, and they were in that magical maverick period of testing, they didn't necessarily know they would discover the potential to change people's lives. Admittedly at the time, their exemplars were therapists, but Bandler and Grinder were more interested in making sense of *how* these experts achieved their results, not necessarily in the therapeutic work itself or results achieved.

As it turned out, it was within the therapeutic world that they initially put their discoveries to work, and so therapy became the first area of application for this fledgling approach. As more people became involved, the emerging skills and understanding of the language patterns were taken into the areas of business and education, until today there is barely a field of endeavour that hasn't been touched by applied NLP and its tools of intervention.

The flexibility of NLP and its technology has led to high levels of expertise in the professional areas of therapy, coaching, consultancy, and training, with a skilled practitioner being able to apply their talents in any one of these areas. Obviously NLP is applied in areas outside of these: from parenting and caring, to marketing and copy writing and beyond.

It is down to the practitioner to determine what role or roles he or she wants to adopt and at what level they want to pitch their area of operation. Much depends on their own sense of purpose and the area in which their talents feel most at home.

However, developed expertise and comfort as a modeller may not be enough. The professional may require accompanying professional accreditation in the vocational areas as well – for example UKCP accreditation as a Psychotherapist. Nationally recognised qualifications and registration with Professional Bodies legitimises practice and holds within it clearly defined Codes of Ethics and Practice.

1   **Consultancy:** when consultants think and act like modellers, then the process of enquiry can be streamlined and precise, causing minimum disruption to work and relationships. When the consultants are really elegant, they can use the target group to model out for themselves what needs to happen say in a stuck situation and how to get there.

These consultants are not distracted by history, politics, alliances, preferences and prejudices. They can be forensic in the process of detecting what ails the organisation, within the larger system of their industry, economics and trends; or target specific areas of activity so these can be honed and refined for greater efficiency. Consultants can be hired specifically to model out the traits and attributes of key workers with the intention of disseminating this learning across the peer group.

When Consultants are from the field of NLP, they have access to an impressively wide range of information gathering methodologies. Once the data is gathered, these consultants can sort it in many different ways; under different logical types – readiness for change, integration of cultures, communication channels, organisational alignment; or at different logical levels – looking at the culture expressed in values and beliefs, diagnosing strengths and weaknesses in hard and soft skills, reviewing protocols, rituals and procedures.

They can either originate models to illustrate effective systems currently operating, or produce models to overcome deficiencies. Or they can select from the wide range of existing models, sourced from management and systems thinking as well as from within NLP itself.

Sadly many consultants shy away from declaring their NLP provenance and disguise the source of their skills and technology, so that NLP as a well-performed practice does not attain the prominence it so deserves.

2   **Training and teaching:** when Trainers and Teachers are also NLP modellers, the learning domain has the potential to sing! Modelling is learning, learning is modelling. And if trainers and teachers see themselves constantly as learners, they will stay alert to the information they're being offered from their participants and pupils. They will trust that the solution is within the group's or

individual's system, emerging from the generative relational field they're able to create.

The trainer or teacher can model out the dynamics operating within the group at any time, and the influences that may be causing disruption to set patterns. They can match detected undercurrents by pacing, timing, positioning and by the selection and delivery of activity. The trainer or teacher can view learners individually or as an element contributing to a field mind, seeing the whole group as a system, diagnosing and addressing the blockages to energy flow. As modellers they can detect possible causes for limitations in learning and enable the learner to self-model to derive solutions.

The fundamental modeller's questions of 'what has to be happening for this to happen?' and 'what has to be true for that to be true?' when applied to a vulnerable learner, takes the trainer beyond evidence of displacement activity, aggressive questioning, reluctance to participate, over achievement, or non attendance, so that they can discern the limitations that are driving the behaviour.

Believing that learners do have all the resources within can support remedial learning activities, through modelling out strengths and pre-existing useful behaviours and developing easy access to internal representations.

On a subject specific level, the trainer or teacher can encourage a modelling mindset through promoting enquiry and discovery, rewarding individual interpretation against the backdrop of many differing perspectives, developing sensitivity to the occurrence of patterns through time, and encouraging the possibility that any conclusion can alter through staying open and receptive.

Possibly most significantly, trainers or teachers operating as modellers can act as an immediate exemplar to their learners, demonstrating congruently the powerful benefits of enquiry, not-knowing, risk-taking, and trusting that the answer will present itself.

3   **Therapy and coaching:** it is within the domain of therapy and then more recently the area of coaching, that NLP and modelling has made its greatest impact. Certainly that is my experience. Within this area of operation the spirit of constructivism comes alive, as all focus and attention home in on revealing the unique structure of an individual's inner model of the world.

When therapists and coaches are operating as modellers, they automatically set their own map aside and operate from a deeply respectful, non-judgmental base of enquiry. Their fascination to genuinely find out what is the glue that is holding the pieces together makes for the most responsive and productive relationships. Key information can be elicited elegantly and efficiently, relationships can be established quickly and support challenge, and clients can feel fully heard and acknowledged.

NLP therapists and coaches are blessed with a fantastic range of interventions to select from: ten and more modelling methodologies, the range of neurological and linguistic frames and the ever increasing list of tried and tested techniques. Plus whatever emerges on the day. We have come a long way from seeing modelling as merely coding strategies.

Having fluent proficiency with Meta Model, two or three modelling methodologies plus some favourite models and techniques under their belt, the therapist or coach can travel a long way. Add to this a deeper and deeper understanding of their tradecraft and increased desire to respond in the moment, and any practitioner will earn a significantly credible professional reputation.

Your Own Pursuit

Your Purpose

Before you can put any of your skills and knowledge into gear, you need to know what you want to do. What you decide will depend on your Life Purpose and the Mission that is currently driving you. Your choice of activity doesn't have to be major ground breaking work, which will end up in publications, public speaking tours, and lots of Google references, though it might. It might be that your modelling activity serves to resolve some personal limitations, or solve some operating issues at work or home. You may find that you are naturally drawn to a particular area of concern, or that you begin to realise that there is a pattern running through your recent projects which when combined suddenly reveals a far wider sphere of consideration.

It does help however to be clear about where you seek to go, so that you don't waste precious time treading water, or worse going backwards. However for many people this is an elusive goal and they find it hard to put into words what their sense of Purpose is.

The following diagram is a homespun description that I feel ties in the ideas of Destiny, Purpose and Mission with Outcomes and actions.

I have taken the often-used metaphor of 'path' to denote our Life's Path that leads us to our predetermined Destiny – if you were to subscribe to the Hawaiian Huna perspective. Here the energy of our often hidden Purpose draws us positively forwards, informing our operating Missions, our decision-making and our actions.

Sniffer dogs sent off to track a particular scent operate a 'feathering' display. They start off sniffing in a wide arc from side to side, until the scent becomes too weak to detect, which tells them to come back to the centre. As they get closer to their goal, the arc they run becomes narrower as the scent becomes stronger, until they reach the final point.

Our Path to Destiny – Burgess 2009

I suggest that we all have a felt sense of when we are on our Path: those moments when we feel truly happy; we feel fulfilled; we believe we are making a useful contribution; we are using our talents well. I often say that in such moments if I was plucked from this world, I would go without a ripple. These moments of lucidity might be few and far between, but they are the moments when we are aligned with who we are here to be. And even if we haven't experienced such alignment, periods of contentment tell us we are living within the desirable margins of our Path. For some this pull is only hinted at. For others it is unwavering.

In Gordon's Meaningful Existence Model, he plots the route to Life Purpose through those moments of our own excellence: those times when we were effortlessly at our best, where we can admit to being proud of ourselves. Taking these together, there will be a theme which connects and unites them in terms of the deep need that they meet within us, and this is likely to be our Purpose – as simple as that.

At different stages in life we may find ourselves applying our energies to different Missions. The young professional may be concerned with making his or her mark in the world. The parent may live to produce happy, confident, loving and effective young adults. The mid-lifer may discover the contribution they want to make to the external world. The pensioner may seek to ready themselves for leaving this life. All these different Missions will be successful if they are aligned to the individual's Purpose and delivered in the manner aligned to it. So when you or I decide upon a project or a plan of action, we need to ask ourselves: 'is this Mission critical?' If not, then back to the drawing board. Because when it is, everything we do directly or indirectly will be in service to this Mission and therefore our Purpose.

It is unlikely that anyone other than the most self-actualised stays on the centre line of bliss. If we are living, we will be exploring, making mistakes, having doubt, and making poor decisions. If we are lucky we will notice and self-correct, bringing ourselves quickly back to the centre of the mainstream. If however we don't register with ourselves just how far we have strayed from our Emotional/Spiritual North, we will find ourselves becoming disconnected from our Purpose. I believe this is where depression starts and is an immediate indicator that something has to be done to return to the centre. Without listening to this and responding, we may suffer serious consequences in terms of our health and wellbeing.

Defining Moments

You may find yourself naturally using your modelling talents as an everyday part of your working life. It may be that you market your modelling skills in your role of consultant or therapist. But the time may come when you realise that you want to use this unique package of skills and knowledge to produce something that will make a significant difference. And this realisation often is triggered by your Call to Action, as Joseph Campbell would call it. It might be a chance comment made by someone, an object, a TV or radio programme, newspaper article, whatever. Often it may arise unexpectedly out of something else that you are involved in and all of a sudden you are facing a different horizon.

I have already told you of my Call to Action to model modelling – the cry of John Grinder for more models and modellers. I had no idea that attending that workshop would radically affect my life and influence my thinking and practice for at least the next 15 years.

Here are some other fascinating examples from others of their Call to Action and how lives changed as a result.

Part 1 – The Nature of a Modeller

- *Helen Glover:* Helen Glover and Heather Stanning won Britain's first gold medal of the 2012 London Olympics in the women's rowing pair. Helen was remarkable in that she was fairly new to the sport. She only started rowing in 2008 when she got through the Sporting Giants' scheme [UK Sport's fast tracking talent-spotting process] where she was basically chosen for 'being tall and sporty'. They tested 4,500 athletes in groups of 200 at a time. She remembers sitting in a room in Bisham Abbey in 2007 and someone saying: 'A gold medallist in 2012 could be sat in this room. Look around you.' I thought, 'Right, I'm going to make that me.' It was quite surreal.

Four years later that promise came true.

- *Lopez Lomong:* Lopez Lomong, a Somali born athlete and a US Olympian. His first real running experience came when he and three other captured boy soldiers escaped from the rebel army and ran for three days into Kenya. He used to run and play football to forget his hunger. One day all the other kids started talking about the Olympics. He didn't know what the Olympics were but he went with them to a richer Kenyan's house to watch it on TV.

This was the day that Michael Johnson received his gold medal and broke down in tears on the podium. At first, Lomong couldn't understand why Johnson was crying having just won the race, but then Lomong realised it was because Johnson was running for something bigger than this – running for his country. Lomong knew then that he wanted to run for that same country, the United States. 'Johnson was my role model from then on.'

Lomong, as part of a US resettlement programme for Sudan's Lost Boys, arrived in the States and through his foster family he trained for track and field. He even met Michael Johnson. In 2008, he qualified for Beijing in the 1500m and carried the US flag at the opening ceremony.

- *Spencer MacCallum:* I'm grateful to Lara Ewing for this story. It was Spencer MacCallum who in 1979 discovered the Mexican artisan potter Juan Quezada. McCallum is an anthropologist and a great supporter of independent communities. He had been walking along a street in Santa Fe and suddenly saw a shop window displaying pieces of native pottery. He said: 'They jumped out at me calling: "Look at me! I am made by someone who knows who he is."'

He was determined to find their source. He knew they must have come from Mexico but had no way of knowing where. Few others in Mexico seemed to know either. Eventually his search led him to Mata Ortiz, a small dried up ghost town in the Mexican state of Chihuahua. It was miles beyond the end of the rail track and near the ancient Paquime ruins.

There he met Juan Quezada, the potter responsible for the pots. As a young man, collecting firewood, Quezada had stumbled upon remarkable undamaged pots, hundreds of years old, made by the Indians of the Paquime culture that had inhabited the region until the 1400s AD.

From that meeting with MacCallum, a fantastic new life for the village, the villagers and Quezeda grew. MacCullum acted as an agent to take news of the pots to a far wider market. Quezeda began teaching his fellow villagers the techniques and skills involved and the nature of his designs. Buyers and art lovers travelled all the way to the village to see the work for themselves. Pots now sell for thousands of dollars and in 1999; Quezada received the prestigious Premio Nacional de Ciencias y Artes award from Mexican president.

Your Call To Action

A Call to Action may be immediate and leave the receiver in no doubt that this is something they need to pursue, or it may not have surfaced above the threshold point. As with Joseph Campbell's Hero, you may have already refused your own particular Call, without realising how persistent it is going to be. It could be that it has already happened and you have reached the stage when you feel ready to embrace wherever your path will take you next. Alternatively you may think you are too busy for such idealistic folly!

Whatever your situation, your interest in modelling and the pursuit of the *real* purpose of NLP is pulling you. Why else would you be reading this? What matters is that through modelling you may be able to deliver your own sense of Purpose and connect yourself with who you are here to be. Through your endeavours you will be able to make a footprint that is significant, worthwhile, and above all useful.

With Dilts's words ringing in our ears: 'That's potential. Use that potential!'

Summary

We are all modellers. We all have the natural ability to learn, discover and make sense of the world. We all are made up of the attributes that expert modellers draw upon. We just may not hold these at a high value or understand just how useful they are. So whether dormant or not, these attributes can be reactivated through further knowledge and focus.

You may have found yourself within the world of NLP, delighting in the techniques and skills you have found here. But when the technique lets you down, or you find a client that doesn't fit the mould, you want to have alternative strategies; otherwise you may be forced to abandon the NLP ship. This might be completely, or you bolster you knowledge with some other modality learnt elsewhere. Your commitment to what NLP can offer is precariously tenuous.

As Drefus and Drefus state, expertise comes when the practitioner has a holistic understanding of their skill area, and an intuitive ability to make decisions borne out of an integrated understanding of the processes involved. This way, through modelling, we have an exciting channel through which to deliver our very personal Missions and achieve our summoning Purpose.

To accelerate our progress towards elegance in our practice, having a solid foundation on the fundamental principles enhances any decision-making on the ground. Clarity regarding these principles, and what they mean in practice, can give us a strong sense of alignment and an obvious commitment to the fundamental place modelling has within any NLP application. Without this we will become guilty of sending out the message that modelling as an optional extra to the NLP syllabus, as opposed to its core.

In Part 2 – The Principles of Modelling, I offer you some verifiable thinking that serves to explain and validate the claims we can make regarding our fabulous modality. From this you can gain language to support any argument, whilst deepening your own regard for NLP and what it can offer.

You may even find you are able to easily answer the question 'so what *is* NLP?'

Part 2
The Principles of Modelling

Introduction

NLP is fixated on the quest to answer the universal question 'how do you do that?' As will become more obvious in Part 3 – The Methodlogies of Modelling, traditionally those of us in NLP are naturally more inclined to pursue *how* we go about discovering how someone responds the way they do, and give scant attention to the underpinning theory which generates this How. This Part 2 – the Principles of Modelling, looks at *why* we explore human experience the particular way that we do.

By definition NLP is a practical pursuit, getting to the heart of the matter, seeking to find pragmatic solutions, and spending little time theorising on the whys and wherefores in between. Its focus is on how things happen, not on what actually happens, and rarely on why things happen. This arguably has been our downfall. Because we have not given time to articulating the Big Whys behind our work, we have not paced the needs of academics and many important gatekeepers specifically within the fields of mental health and education, and given them the logical imperatives that are the foundations of our actions.

And whilst our founder developers lived within the academic world, they were too busy proving how their new approaches could be used, rather than occupying themselves with the rarefied wisdom of established thinking. It could be that such a backward glance might feel restricting, as they sought to plough their own independent furrow. What thinking they did incorporate was the thinking of their time – that of Korzybski, Chomsky and Bateson, but this they applied retrospectively to their firsthand experiences.

As a consequence of this, we have not been handed down some of the weightier philosophy that serves our practice and provides authenticity to our claims. We don't trade in an overarching 'ology' or 'ism' to stand beside other established fields of thinking. We have been encouraged to make a difference, and not to spend time in providing research results for how we made that difference.

All of which has been our undoing in many ways, since as a collective body, we have found it hard to sit at the table of the 'grown ups' and feel we have rightfully earned our place.

The following sections seek to arrest this incongruence and demonstrate without question the roots of our modality and the assertive justification of our claims. Our theoretical base can be illustrated in three major areas.

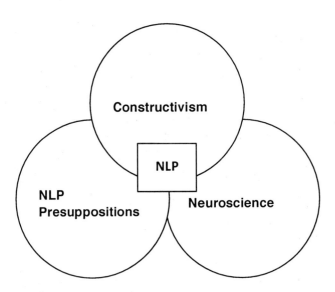

The Theory Underpinning NLP – Burgess 2012

Learning about the philosophy that underpins NLP's approaches can provide a tremendous resource to any theoretical academic argument. Coming from a well thought through philosophical base gains respect and an audience in this world. Holding your own and standing firm can serve to legitimise your position.

Drawing from the empirical world of science can confound the medical detractors. Due to developments in technology, there have been great strides made in the last fifty years to plot and record what happens physiologically within our neurology, when the human system is subjected to different external influences. How we experience change internally can now be plotted and made visible for all to see. It is still early days yet and neuroscience methodology has its detractors. Yet much more can be done to target the connections between the neurolinguistic impact of some of our NLP approaches and their measurable neurological effects on our brain.

Finally we need to consider the major sources of influence that shaped the direction of NLP's development, and guided consciously or otherwise the thinking of the early pioneering developers. NLP did not start with Richard Bandler and John Grinder. It arose out of the relational field of great thinkers operating in the 1960s and 70s in the fields of cybernetics, therapy and philosophy. Having a clear understanding of the sources of the NLP Presuppositions which frame NLP practice is an essential home base for all further application. The NLP Presuppositions act as a filter for all our feedback and determine our decision-making and resultant responses.

Philosophical Base

How often have you found yourself in the untenable position of having to prove the efficacy of NLP without knowing the philosophical basis upon which it is founded? How often have those who come from established 'isms' and 'ologies' undermined your confidence and looked upon your practice as New Age nonsense? Have you ever wished you could trump their smugness with a cogent authoritative description?

NLP comes under the school of thought called Constructivism.

Somehow this really significant piece of information has stayed well under the radar. None of the early developers that I trained with ever mentioned it. Dilts and Delozier do not give any reference to it in their fantastic opus, *The NLP Encyclopaedia* (2000) Only just recently in the *Origins of Neurolinguistic Programming* (2013), does Steve Gilligan very clearly involve the concepts of Constructivism into his explanations.

To my mind, Epistemology is the big answer to the big WHY of NLP. I have James Lawley to thank for my awareness as do the membership of NLPtCA (Neurolinguistic Psychotherapy and Counselling Association). When he spearheaded the affiliation of the UK therapeutic arm of NLP with the Constructivist College within UKCP (United Kingdom Council of Psychotherapy), he established an alliance with other expressions of constructivism within the therapeutic world. Later when he delivered the Northern School of NLP's Psychotherapy Diploma, he embedded all our practice within constructivist concepts.

To enable you to have some fluency around the subject I am offering you a layman's guide. For anything more in depth, Wikipedia awaits with all its extensive bibliographies provided on many of its pages covering the extensive network of topics and thinking. However before that we need to see where Constructivism sits with the wider world of thinking around the study of behaviour.

First of all it is useful to chunk right up to find out where we sit within the world of philosophical thinking. And it may come as a surprise to you to find that NLP does have a place in the philosophical scheme of things. The framework below illustrates where Constructivism and ultimately NLP rests within the broad field of philosophical thought, regarding the nature of human experience. I'm not suggesting that any in-depth knowledge is required here. Just being able to state the context for NLP could be pretty impressive in some circles!

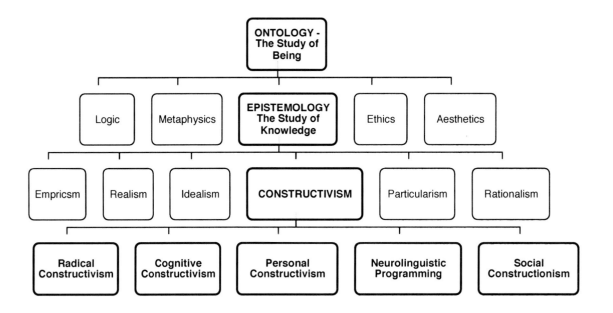

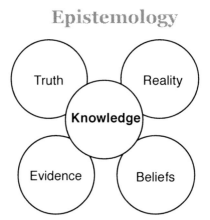

Epistemology

Concepts of Knowledge – Burgess

Epistemology, a term first coined by a Scot James Ferrier 1808-1864, is the theoretical study of Knowledge and Knowing, in answer to the question 'how do we know what we know?' To answer this question, we usefully need to have some understanding of what knowledge is and how it is acquired. And, according to the thinkers, Knowledge is acquired through combining our perception of Truth, Reality, Beliefs and Evidence.

Without going too deeply into the raging philosophical discussions, I hopefully offer you some interesting stuff to think about and relate to your own experience of learning about and applying NLP.

Reality

At last I have found a home for the label Post-Modernism! I have heard others bandy this term around, yet when I asked about it, I have been met with some embarrassed silences.

I am forever grateful to find an article by psychologist Jonathan D. Raskin that quotes the thinking of T L Sexton (1997) in his analysis of the changing nature of knowing. Sexton divided human history into three distinct eras: premodern, modern, and postmodern.

- *Pre-modern era* (sixth century to Middle Ages): during this era knowledge came from the Gods, requiring some religious or spiritual priest or shaman to pass on wisdom to the man in the field.

- *Modern era* (Renaissance to the beginning of 20th Century): by this time the emphasis shifted to the importance of measurement and evidence, and the identification of objective truths and validity. Basically unless science said it was so, it was not so. Anything that science could not explain was either attributed to the vagaries of an unseen God, or fantasy.

- *Post-modern era* (to present time)**:** first coined in 1949, the source of knowledge shifted from imposed external authority to the individual. The awareness that knowledge could only be fully individually constructed, began to explain the many anomalies to prevailing scientific theories. As a result, knowledge for itself becomes less important; *how* it was acquired, identified and categorised becomes the focus. And everyone's perspective and take on reality became as valid as the next person's.

Post-Modernists are therefore sceptical of explanations that claim to be valid for *all* groups, cultures, traditions, or races. Instead of complying with these generalisations, Post-Modernists prefer to focus on the relative truths of each person. Interpretation is everything. Reality is perception.

Post-Modernism relies on experience over theoretical principles, supporting what is personally reported, rather than any universal argument.

Post-Modernism proposes that many, if not all, apparent realities are personal constructs and are therefore subject to change. It claims that there is no absolute truth and that the way people perceive the world is subjective, and emphasises the role of language, power relations and motivations in the formation of ideas and beliefs.

In particular it attacks the use of binary classifications such as male/female, straight/gay, and white/black. The many differing realities, all subjective and dependent on context and experience, provide a spectrum of description between such polarities.

Truth

Truth is slippery, which suggests that there are very few facts to guide us, and our determining indicators are mainly belief based.

Truth requires verification. As we know from Meta Model patterns, much is deleted, distorted and generalised. So when you say 'the jam is on the shelf.' which is true for the speaker, it may be conditional depending on context, source, required evidence and other variables – Which shelf? Which jam? In a jar, or on the surface? Sufficient jam? Jam or marmalade?

Truth requires more than 'gut instinct' or personal satisfaction to make it so. It has to be supported by verifiable facts, which need to be consistent and presented in a coherent manner. If the same results keep occurring then this outcome takes on the status of a fact. But the counter argument here is that there may be some context yet to be discovered where it doesn't work. Bill O'Hanlon's mantra 'X is X except when it isn't' is all part of the Post-Modern thinking of possibilities, as opposed to certainty.

Consensus is not an indication of truth either, especially when it is held in defiance of established facts. Creationism may be regarded as an example of this. The dominant culture may hold sway, yet a cultural truth is unlikely to represent everyone. Nor should the 'truths' handed on through generations, or those standing the test of time, be taken at face value. These 'truths' or more accurately, beliefs, are often very difficult to dislodge, until some new irrefutable evidence is discovered. Just think of the Flat Earth thinking.

Pragmatists would argue that if an idea works, and is sufficiently tested, it must be true. But this unravels say, in the face of the placebo effect gain when the placebo agent gains the same results as the prescribed drug.

The 2012 discovery of the Higgs particle is an interesting illustration of the discovery of truth. Professor Peter Higgs proposed through mathematical calculation in the 1960's, that there had to be something called a Higgs Bosun particle that gives substance to all matter. Finally 50 years later scientists created the context for its occurrence, even though it exists for a tiny fraction of time before breaking up into something else. At last the theory had the evidence to confirm its truth.

Beliefs

Most people accept that for a belief to become knowledge it must, at least, be supported by some evidence.

However knowledge or facts are often confused with theories and beliefs, which means such claims of knowledge often go unchallenged. A table is a table because it performs the functions of a table, and generally conforms to a generic description of a table. It may however be regarded as serviceable, or unattractive or economical, dependent on the perceiver who is creating the opinion and holds beliefs about such things. Post-Modernists hold that beliefs are totally subjective, stored by individuals as core beliefs, or are available for debate and reconsideration. This echos Alice Miller's (1923-2010) line that core beliefs are imprinted between the ages of 0-7 from parents or significant adults and these are the most tenacious. From 7-14 beliefs are formed through modelling of those in the immediate environment – teachers, family friends, etc. And then from 14 onwards, beliefs are adopted through socialisation taking on the thinking of the prevailing group. These are easy to let go of.

Beliefs are negotiable and available for change. This is my belief, shared by many others, supported by evidence arising from the effects of (in my case) NLP based interventions. It is likely that we live far more in a world of unsubstantiated beliefs than verifiable facts.

Evidence

Evidence can tilt the scales, to prove one thing over another, to shift beliefs and strengthen the notion of truth – the burden of proof – and needs to be considered in terms of sufficiency, recency, relevance and currency. Sometimes the truth can be inferred through the combination of facts and contribute to circumstantial evidence.

The quality of this evidence will be determined by how much certainty is needed as opposed to reasonable doubt, which of course is judged by the subjective nature of the assessor. This subjectivity becomes significant depending on what outcome the evidence is serving: is it required to determine justice, assess competence, or simply verify experience? If needs be, finding ways of moderating and verifying these judgments, takes away the over-reliance on one assessor.

Evidence lies at the heart of the limits of human knowing. It is dependent on our ability to access it. In NLP we concentrate on our ability to see, hear, feel, taste and smell, since ours is the study of subjective experience. But this doesn't accommodate those sounds and images outside our range of perception that can be perceived by animals or machines. Nor does NLP acknowledge the possibility of additional sources of evidence, for example perceived energy.

Summary

If you want to read more fully, a taxing port of call would be Jonathan D. Raskin's article *Constructivism in Psychology: Personal Construct Psychology, Radical Constructivism, and Social Constructionism* in American Communication Journal Volume 5, Issue 3, Spring 2002.

However, out of all of this I am persuaded to go with John McWhirter's deceptively simple summary, which no doubt was constructed after long deliberation.

Knowledge: where we have known facts as evidence

Beliefs: where we have some evidence, and are open to counter examples to disprove them

Convictions: where tenacious beliefs are based on limited evidence, held in faith, and are therefore very hard to dislodge through counter example.

Constructivism

I suspect I am offering you more here than you need, for the everyday conversation, to argue NLP's credibility. However the more you know, the more selective you can be with what you introduce to people.

Concepts

Constructivism is one form of Epistemology and is practically interchangeable with Post-Modern thinking. Knowledge is human made and a matter of interpretation of the perceiver. Meaning comes from matching past experience with the present context and not from some external say-so. Language describes our personally held reality, which tends to be formed through relationship and interaction, as opposed to dictates of external 'experts'.

Constructivism becomes distinguished from the other developed theories of Knowing because it focuses on *how* human beings create the internal systems that enable them to make meaning of the world and the experiences they have. First proposed in 1950s by Piaget, Constructivism has only taken hold in the last 30 years, as the understanding of Post-Modern thinking has become established.

The upside of accepting that reality is personally constructed, and therefore our individual responsibility, can be liberating, placing us at cause, in charge of our lives and allowing full expression of our identity and personality. It provides independence for groups and societies, who can take on whatever shape they choose. Most importantly, it creates opportunities for change and choice.

The downside is the distrust that is set up when individuals perceive and label the 'same reality' differently. In fact the removal of empirical truth, that X really is X and not someone's version of Y, can destabilise and call upon far greater demands of personal self-belief. We are also called upon to be accountable for our version, and provide evidence to justify our 'Knowledge' and 'Truths'. Consensus can be hard to achieve.

Taken to its philosophical extreme, reality becomes merely a concept, where there is no such thing as concrete evidence. There is no God which has the power of seeing and understanding that which is unknown and unknowable; no arbiter of reality, adjudicating from the stratosphere, and handing down the tablets in stone. There will never be a place of given certainty.

Such thinking puts enormous demands on self-knowledge, and acceptance of others. It requires individuals to become aware of how they are constructing their reality, where they are finding their evidence and the conclusions and meaning they are making from it. It requires us to approach our fellows with an open non-judgmental mind, in a spirit of enquiry. Maybe we need another chunk of time before such attitudes become the default of human nature. In the meantime we stumble along the best we can!

All constructed meaning represents a point of view. Because of the very lack of observation and measurement, this line of thinking has been poorly represented within the established bodies of medicine and psychology. Its practice eludes valid psychological research. In fact a pure Post-Modern approach would suggest that it is impossible to verify the effects of constructivist practice since everything is in the eye of the perceiver, which includes the scientist.

Interestingly, the current rush to embrace neuroscience could be seen as a way to demonstrate externally the internal workings of an individual's brain. The subjective and objective worlds as they relate to human experience may yet be able to inhabit the same space and illuminate the truths of both.

Constructivist Schools of Thought

Now it may not surprise you to know that there is not one way of applying constructivist thinking, or to think about constructivism. I'm offering the following descriptions so that you can gain some idea of where NLP can sit, should anyone ask you.

Constructivism or Constructionism developed into various ways of thinking and expression, depending on the levels of idealism or realism involved. Realists would have it that objects exist externally to us, whereas idealists argue that everything is dependent on the perception of the mind, and only exists once perceived. The nuances of these arguments are so philosophical, that I will leave it to you to explore further should you choose.

Cognitive Constructivism

Cognitive constructivism is based on the work of Swiss developmental psychologist Jean Piaget. Piaget's theory has two major parts: an 'ages and stages' component that predicts what children can and cannot understand at different ages, and a theory of development that describes how children develop cognitive abilities.

Piaget's theory of cognitive development proposes that humans cannot be 'given' information that they immediately understand and use. Instead, humans must 'construct' their own knowledge. They build their knowledge through experience.

Experiences enable them to create mental models in their heads, from which they navigate the world.

Personal Constructivism

Pioneered by George Kelly, *Personal Construct Theory* proposes that we organise our experiences by developing bipolar dimensions of meaning, which enable us to anticipate and predict how events will turn out. Within these dimensions of meaning, or constructs, we organise our psychological experience, our sense of self, and continually test these constructs to confirm or deny their 'truth'. Should events disprove a construct then we have to revise our construction. Those that don't let go of such faulty constructs, despite the evidence received, are regarded as 'hostile'. The potential for change and the possible combinations and permutations are deemed to be endless.

Kelly emphasises the influence of the external world on an individual's constructs. He argues that events that occur pre-language, form deeply embedded constructs, which he suggests take time to dislodge. He also suggests that when two people share the same profile of constructs their psychological processes will be similar.

Radical Constructivism

Ernst Von Glaserfeld is the originator of this line of thought, which emphasises that we use our understandings that we have created to help us navigate life – regardless of whether or not these understandings match an external reality. The world and people in it are merely models that we ourselves construct.

This theory, advanced from Darwinism and Piaget, suggests that our perception is adaptive, and it has evolved to help us survive. This adaptation is not responding to the needs of the environment, but to the need for a personal sense of equilibrium. Experiences are being constantly reinterpreted based on the constructs we already hold.

The 'real' world is not directly knowable and we only bump into it when our constructs fail us. Behaviour results from the process of cognitively recognising what is happening, taking action associated with these circumstances and expecting that these actions will produce the desired result. Instead of our behaviour being modified by external events, it is influenced by our internalised expectations. If these expectations are misplaced, then we have to revisit our constructs.

This closed systems way of thinking leads us to operate in our own very private self-constructed worlds, where external communication and interaction are merely a result of this inner world. Each of us operates our own private language, since absolute meanings for words are unobtainable.

The Chilean biologist Humberto Maturana is another early Radical Constructivist, even more focussed on the isolation of the individual from the outside world. His focus was on the biology of cognition, what was happening neurologically when thinking and responding. He held the belief that living systems were cognitive systems, whether or not they had a nervous system. He was a precursor of the now blossoming field of neuroscience.

Social Constructionism

Constructivism, with the exception of radical constructivists, generally allows the possibility that people can derive meaning from objects in the environment as well as from social interactions. However, social constructionism denies that deriving meaning directly from objects is possible: meaning is only derived through interaction with others. This is why they prefer to be referred to as Constructionists to avoid any idea that there is a notion of an isolated knower.

Social Constructionists start with the understanding that reality is constructed through human activity and all knowledge is socially and culturally constructed. So reality doesn't exist prior to its social invention. We create meaning through our interaction with others and with the environment. We expand, modify, reject our existing internal constructs, by exchanging views, and accommodating differences in perspectives, as our means of gaining and establishing knowledge. And knowledge is local and fleeting, negotiated between people within a given context and time frame.

Taken to extremes there is no such thing as personality since it is a socially constructed idea, whilst other social constructionists suggest that there are as many realities as there are cultures, contexts and ways of communicating. Personhood becomes a matter of how people are talked about, and the social practices they engage in. Learning is generated from the metacognition that comes with discussion and sharing with others, through what Gilligan would call the Relational Field. Knowledge is only activated and consolidated through social exchange.

Lev Vygotsky strongly influenced the formalisation of the concept of Social Constructionism. He advocated that new learning is accessible in the stretch zone just outside current knowledge. He suggests that our learning is enhanced if we attempt to master new concepts and ideas in the social company of teachers or fellow learners who are more advanced, as opposed to working solely on our own. Whilst still agreeing that our reality is constructed, social constructionists are fully committed to the idea that we are open systems, requiring to interact with our environment and others to sustain our development and learning.

Neurolinguistic Programming

Viewing NLP with these filters, we find much in common. NLP is profoundly the study of subjective experience, perceived through our senses, and therefore rightly placed within the Constructivist field.

We hold that we create our own reality through internal constructs of our internal representations. We assert that these constructions are influenced by the varying sensitivities of our senses, the beliefs we have formed, and the nature of the language expressed. And like the Cognitive Constructivists, we hold that we learn as a result of identifying differences between our constructs and what we actually encounter. These constructs operate at an unconscious level, and are independent of the rational processing of our conscious mind.

We also believe that learning comes outside of our knowing – in Vygotsky's stretch zone, and we recognise that we are influenced by events and people around us. Much of our experiences are context dependent, but not because of the different influence these have to bear, but because of the different meta programmes and traits that we bring to that context. However what separates us significantly from the Social Constructionists is that NLP contends that we are always at cause and that we determine our responses, driven by our known or unknown patterns or programmes.

Summary

Fundamentally the different schools are divided regarding their position on whether or not:

*   We are open or closed systems: Open systems include external objects in the process of making meaning and gaining knowledge, whereas closed systems say that all knowledge is as a result of our internal processing.

*   Knowledge results from cognition or socialisation: is reality and the source of knowledge independent of the knower, or are the knower and known one and the same?

This then places NLP somewhere in the middle of all of them.

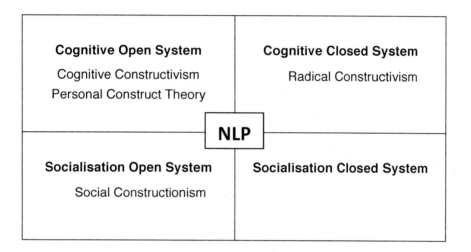

NLP in the World of Constructivism – Burgess 2013

I find it bizarre that we are retrospectively allocating NLP to a particular area of philosophical thinking and practice, running the risk of shoehorning evidence as a means of justifying our credibility.

And in academic quarters it may be regarded as questionable that NLP evolved without any clear philosophical underpinning. Actually this may be NLP's saving grace, since in a totally code congruent manner it evolved as a consequence of the subjective experiences identified by the developers. Going in with a fixed, as opposed to an open, mindset is not the way of the Post-Modern operative.

On that point, as will be illustrated in the next section, NLP was deeply influenced by the ideas of Bateson. Bateson's thinking resonates with so much of the Post-Modern mindset that it was likely that he had instinctively adopted its radical thinking without necessarily being conscious of it or alluding to it. Certainly as far as my limited researches go, he doesn't make reference to Constructivism, whilst he espouses much of the social constructionist approach.

And of course, you need to read this knowing that it is merely a construct and not a truth! This treatise takes the basic NLP presupposition that 'we construct our own reality' as its starting point.

Constructivist Principles

Even though different practices have emerged from the different schools of thought, and the individual expressions of what is or isn't of importance may differ, there is enough commonality to unite us and form a separation from other modalities based on other models of thought.

I had the real privilege to be part of a working group within the Constructivist College of the United Kingdom Council for Psychotherapy (UKCP), with representatives of the various schools and bodies within this College, to come up with a consensus of the operating principles that unite us.

Here they are:

- The central assumption is that people uniquely create their own personal realities, or models of the world. Perception of these realities change through time, and attention can only be usefully placed in the present time.

- This immediacy perspective discounts fundamental pathology, and does not rely on pre-set theories and predetermined approaches. Instead it seeks to be informed by the exemplar and his/her context, without any imposition of any externally construed reality.

- The exemplar's expression of reality acts as the starting point, and the exemplar's desired outcome sets the direction of exploration and determines the evidence of success.

- All behaviour is outcome generated. These outcomes determine where attention is placed and directly influence the information that is deleted.

- Experiences are internally ordered into organised patterns, or systems of structure, the elements of which provide meaningful relationship for that individual.

- Once identified, this structure can be restructured, or elements amplified or reduced, to generate desired and agreed change.

- This internal system of structures generates our sense of self, which is influenced by the nature of social, linguistic and symbolic contexts.

- All experience is experienced through the senses, internally and/or externally. Much of what is being experienced on the inside has the potential to be displayed on the outside through verbal and non-verbal responses.

- We are all part of a system, which allows for this organising activity to be reflected in the operation of a fluid internal & interpersonal communication process. When viewed, the system will undergo change.

- This organisation occurs within an inter-relational context that is contrast-informed & mutually interdependent.

- People can engage in lifelong exploration, elaboration, and differentiation of themselves and the ways by which they organise their living.

It is great to have this broad consensus providing the overall framework for our own NLP Presuppositions – the closest we have to Guiding Principles. These we look at in greater detail later in this chapter.

Neuroscience

Neuroscience focuses on the brain at its functional level. The term covers a wide range of interest and research. For example, as well as surgery, it incorporates the analysis of biological and chemical functions within the brain, the effect of hormones, foods, and events as they influence our internal chemistry. It can readily detect and categorise shifts in emotions and wellbeing.

It has also been applied to the field of NeuroMarketing and NeuroEconomics, which tests and isolates the effects of particular approaches to develop what is referred to as universal neuropatterning. The generalisations learnt through these researches then inform subsequent strategies. In the case of NeuroMarketing, decisions regarding where to place specific products on specific shelves, the nature and designs of packaging and the overall layout of retail areas, all have resulted from studying the neural responses of subjects.

Neuroscience can give us a tangible physical and measurable description of what happens neurologically within an individual when certain events take place. During the last twenty years many technologies have been developed which enable scientists to explore the inner workings of the brain.

In particular, functional and diffusion magnetic resonance imaging (MRI) detects specific neural activity through the increase of blood flow to the particular functional area of the brain. This can be captured through electro imaging, with the subject lying within a cylindrical tube housing a powerful electro magnet that scans activity in the brain. The subject can either watch a screen within the container, or receive verbal instructions, and his or her neural responses are then captured through cross section images. This approach has the advantage of being non invasive, doesn't require the introduction of radioactive substances or dyes to detect activity, and gives good detailed results. Through subsequent computer analysis, patterns can be detected by comparing how the brain itself is responding with how the subject is perceiving, thinking and feeling.

From our interest area, Neuroscience has the potential to give us a scientific explanation for the phenomena we experience whilst undertaking NLP intervention. For some, it is the means of justifying the effects of NLP and providing a credible *scientific* explanation for something we have known for such a long time.

Neuroscience can serve to explain the reasons behind NLP's effectiveness. It is the road inwards to deliver *how* NLP achieves the effects it does.

Our Nervous System

Technology now enables neuroscientists to study the nervous system in all its aspects: how it is structured, how it works, how it develops, how it malfunctions, and how it can be changed.

The most basic component of our nervous system is the neuron. Neurons are cells specialised for communication, and interconnect at synapses, where electrical or electrochemical signals are transmitted from one nerve cell to another. These neurotransmitters can ultimately be responsible for our shifts in mood – serotonin and dopamine for depression or happiness, endorphins for pleasure, and of course adrenalin that provokes the fight, flight, freeze effect under extreme stress.

Once an emotional response has begun, commands are sent to the body and other regions of the brain. The resultant change in the system is global and it is possible for the state of the entire organism to be modified from a response triggered by a relatively small area of the brain.

The nervous system emerges from the assemblage of neurons that are connected to each other. The human brain alone contains around a hundred billion neurons and a hundred trillion synapses. It consists of thousands of distinguishable substructures, connected to each other in synaptic networks whose intricacies have only begun to be unravelled.

In vertebrates, the nervous system can be split into two parts, the central nervous system which takes in the brain and the spinal cord and the peripheral nervous system, which involves the autonomic nervous system and is responsible for our biological functions of breathing, blood flow, cell reproduction, and hormone secretion, and our somatic nervous system, or as Gilligan puts it, our Somatic Mind or 'belly' mind.

> The Somatic is the animal mind shared by all mammals; it is your embodied intelligence, knowing yourself and the world through feeling, action, nonverbal awareness, and emotion. The mammal mind carries a past and a present, but no future awareness. Like your pets and young children, it has the potential for amazing awareness, but no self-awareness; that is, it can't think about itself or represent itself. It is attuned not only to your personal history, but also to ancestral history. It carries instinct, archetypes, and intuitive knowing, all basic elements for transformational change. In terms of trance, it is the first (but not only) 'unconscious mind'.
>
> Steve Gilligan: Three Minds and Three Levels of Consciousness

Our Brain

Through the use of functional Magnetic Resonance Imaging (fMRI), scientists can see which areas of the brain are activated when particular tasks are performed. The subject is placed into the scanning machine and instructions are offered through earpieces or visually on a screen. The resultant neural activity shows up on external monitors.

Therefore to understand more about the precise nature of this detection, it is useful to have some understanding of the brain and what each area does.

The American physician and neuroscientist Paul D. MacLean came up with this 3-part model as far back as 1960s and developed it extensively in his 1990 book *The Triune Brain in Evolution*. He would have it that our brain is made up of three layers:

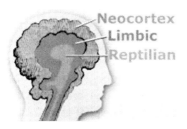

- Reptilian Brain – the innermost core.
- Limbic Brain – the middle layer.
- Neocortex Brain – recognisable convoluted outer layer.

It now appears that the layers are in fact interconnected and are not entirely discrete. Each region continues to evolve and adapt, and they are interconnected by a complex network of bands of nerve fibres, linking not only the left and right hemispheres horizontally, but vertically as well.

Reptilian brain

The reptilian complex, known as the R-complex or 'reptilian brain' was the name given to the basal ganglia, structures derived from the floor of the forebrain during development. It is responsible for the control of instinctive behaviour and motivation.

Neuroscientists once believed that the forebrains of reptiles and birds were dominated by these structures. MacLean proposed that the reptilian complex was responsible for species-typical instinctual behaviours involved in aggression, dominance, territoriality, and ritual displays.

Limbic system

The limbic system is a group of structures that includes the amygdala, the hippocampus, mammillary bodies and cingulate gyrus. These areas are important for controlling the emotional response to a given situation. This system functions precognitively, inducing an immediate and total brain-body response. It has been found that the limbic system can be reconditioned to respond in different ways, and develop adaptive flexibility.

- *Amygdala:* the amygdala activates the instinctive response process. The amygdala is the storehouse for unconscious conditioned emotional patterns and responses, inherent from birth. In times of danger, the cortex – the seat of thinking and reason – is informed while the amygdala takes on responsibility for spontaneous action.

- *Hippocampus:* the hippocampus is important for long-term and explicit memory and learning, developing after the first three years of life, taking on some of the responsibility for considered action, from the instinctive responses of the amygdala.

- *Hypothalamus:* the hypothalamus is composed of several different areas and is located at the base of the brain. The size of a pea, it acts as the body's thermostat and also is responsible for sourcing our emotion, basic responses like hunger and thirst, plus our circadian rhythms that are our sleep cycles. It also controls the pituitary.

- *Thalamus:* the thalamus receives sensory information and relays this information to the cerebral cortex, and vice versa.

- *Brain stem:* the brain stem is a general term for the area of the brain between the thalamus and spinal cord. It influences our breathing, heart rate and blood pressure.

- *Midbrain:* the midbrain is our sensory receptor base, directing our vision, hearing and movement.

Neocortex

- *Cerebral Cortex:* the cortex is the convoluted 2-6mm sheet of tissue that makes up the outer layer of the brain, made up of the right and the left side connected by a thick band of nerve fibres called the corpus callosum. The bumps and grooves of the cortex give the brain its instantly recognisable shape.  The front area is called the frontal lobes, both sides are called the parietal lobes and the back of the cortex is called the occipital lobes. It is responsible for thought, voluntary movement, language, reasoning and perception

  The cortex is the processing powerhouse of the brain, which is made up of a mass of neural connections from all parts of our body, and therefore is the major source of interest to NLP researchers.

  The illustration of the homunculus is a way of representing the distribution of neural space in the cortex for the level of connections to the parts of the body. Our hands have by far the greater number of neural pathways to the cortex than any other part of our body.

- *Cerebellum:* the cerebellum is located behind the brain stem. In some ways, the cerebellum is similar to the cerebral cortex: the cerebellum is divided into hemispheres and has a cortex that surrounds these hemispheres. It is responsible for movement, posture and balance.

Connections with NLP

Here are some examples of how findings from within Neuroscience research go some way to explain the phenomena that we are used to working with in NLP. It is far from an extensive listing since linking the two fields of study only came about in the mid 2000s onwards. This is likely to be an area that will be developed within the next decade. I have provided details under specific NLP phenomena.

Intuitive Modelling

In the early 1990s, a team of neuroscientists at the University of Parma made a surprising discovery. Certain groups of neurons in the brains of macaque monkeys fired not only when a monkey performed an action – grabbing an apple out of a box, for instance – but also when the monkey watched someone else performing that action; and even when the monkey heard someone performing the action in another room.

This firing of neurons through mirroring the actions of others led scientists to believe that these mirror neurons were not concerned with specific movements, but were focussed on the *intentions* of the movements.

By being able to 'replicate' another's neurology through the creation of mirror neurons whilst observing the behaviour or actions of another, we can share that experience. In NLP we call this deep second positioning, or unconscious uptake, which leads us to understand the intentions of other people's actions, without consultation. It is suggested that this process provides the means of attaching meaning to actions, or else encoding such meanings. It is the key to explaining empathy.

Rapport

Dr Uri Hasson, assistant professor of psychology at Princeton University, (Harvard Business Review, *I Can Make Your Brain Look Like Mine.* Dec 2010) conducted a MRI scanning experiment where the brain activity of a woman telling a story was recorded. He then recorded the accounts of people who had listened to the story. What he found was that those who had listened most attentively, and understood the story most accurately, demonstrated brain activity that most closely mirrored that of the speaker whilst telling the story.

This again explains the phenomena of deep second positioning creating profound rapport, when two people just click. Imagining and experiencing what the other is saying naturally leads to the listener resonating with the story through shared physiology and gestures. This requires the listener to let go his or her own map and really connect with the model the other is describing.

State Stability/Instability

The discovery of the Quantum Zeno Effect in the world of Quantum Physics offers up some interesting thinking about state. Here Sudershan and Baidyanath (1977) discovered that by constantly interrupting the natural movement of change, and therefore focussing on a single point in time, the change doesn't occur – the system stabilises.

This thinking can be applied to our brain's response generated by shifting our focus of attention. If we continue to have the same unuseful internal image, or hear the same critical internal dialogue, we will continue to feel grim. Repeating limiting beliefs either visually or auditorily will only deepen the 'truth' of that thought. As we become stuck, our brain establishes specific brain connections, keeping the relevant circuitry open and alive.

Conversely by replacing the unuseful instructions consistently with positive ones, the QZE kicks in and the brain stabilises with the new useful mindset. Rock and Schwartz in *The Neuroscience of Leadership* (2006), argue that attention density shapes identity, with new brain circuitry being developed. Over time shifts in identity arise through deepening individual thought and acts of the mind – a phenomenon that they refer to as self-directed neuroplasticity. New circuits, new chemical links and new structures displace the previous ones that ultimately disappear. We train ourselves to think differently. The effects of pattern disrupts, submodalities changes, visual/kinaesthetic (VK) dissociation all suggest that reconstruction can directly affect state and behaviour.

Resolution of Past Related Emotions

Within NLP, we promote Ericksonian Hypnosis over Traditional Hypnosis, because it is based on permission, utilisation and pacing conscious and unconscious realities. Any resistance is down to the poor skills of the hypnotist, not the nature of the individual.

Kirenskaya, Novototsky-Vlasov, Chistyakov, Zvonikov, written up in *The Relationship Between Hypnotizability, Internal Imagery, and Efficiency of Neurolinguistic Programming* sought to find connections between trance and NLP procedures. Unfortunately the research doesn't identify the trance methodology, or the NLP procedure used. However it does suggest an explanation for the use of trance in state change, visualisations, and many of the walking trances generated by NLP's spatial processes.

Monitored heart rate and skin conduction span were used to verify the reality of inner experience, detected through electrodes placed on the subject's body, plus subjective scoring. Subjects were selected for their varying levels of susceptibility to trance induction, and offered under trance and non-trance conditions to access emotionally neutral, positive or negative memories.

In another experiment they monitored how much the influence of 'hypnotisability' has on the effectiveness of an imagery-based NLP technique.

Results showed that those most susceptible to trance would experience greater emotional intensity and experience more vivid imagery.

This could serve to explain the effectiveness of NLP techniques to access the unconscious mind so readily, since NLP operates in a waking trance state. Through natural use of Ericksonian language and through dissociated focus on internal representations, subjects very quickly let go of the rational control of their conscious mind.

Self-Modelling

Dr Norman Doidge, in his book *The Brain That Changes Itself* (2012), focuses on the neuroplasticity of the brain and its ability to change shape depending on input. For example, he describes how learning can change the number of connections between nerve cells A & B, from 1300 to 2700 connections after several hours of training. New thoughts turn certain genes on and others off in the nerve cell that makes proteins, which then go on to change structure.

So with cognitive and experiential therapies, the brain is given the opportunity to explore and generate new thoughts and connections, often within an integrated system of ideas. Through knocking one set of ideas off its perch through a domino effect, a cascade of new thoughts arise, resulting in a reconstruction of the neural pathways.

This could explain how just the process of forming a well-formed outcome can generate change, without any further action. And certainly holding that outcome firmly deepens the commitment to that change.

Filters

In a BBC Horizon programme, *The Secrets to Personality* (2013), Dr Elaine Fox of the University of Essex talked about a test she had designed that evidences first of all any bias towards optimism or pessimism. Pessimists have more neural activity in the right-hand side frontal lobe. This correlates with higher levels of anxiety and stress.

Using a headdress of electrodes, she then tests reaction times to spotting spots behind one of two faces on the screen. Unbeknown to the subject, the faces have either pleasant happy expressions or unpleasant angry expressions. Pessimists tend towards being in the angry zone already, so their reaction times will be much quicker for these faces – measured in milliseconds.

When the subject is then charged with a thrice-daily exercise of identifying only happy faces out of a changing selection, not only does the pessimist become quicker at identifying them, but also his or her reaction times at identifying the happy faces in the laboratory test improve significantly. And the activity in the frontal cortex becomes more balanced across both spheres. The subject also anecdotally reports feeling more positive and optimistic.

What we filter for can change the construction of our brains at a neurological level.

Space

James Lawley brought to my attention the work of Eric R Kandel *In Search of Memory: The Emergence of a New Science of Mind* (2007). In this book Kandel refers to John O'Keefe at University College London and his discoveries regarding our spatial awareness. Our sense of space is created through the combination of multiple senses and is responsible for our subsequent ability to navigate round our environment rests within the pyramidal cells in the hippocampus. It has been seen that birds that rely on retrieving food from different locations, and London taxi drivers, have an above normally developed hippocampus.

Several points arise that are of interest to the NLPer. The hippocampus is activated both when the subject actually performs an activity related to spatial awareness, and when he or she talks and imagines performing the activity. This can explain the effectiveness of rehearsing desired behaviours through constructed internal and auditory representations, Acting As If and Future Pacing.

The brain represents information about space from a variety of locations and in various configurations depending on the purpose in hand. O'Keefe cites various examples of where the position of the perceiver affects reception, and the significance of how the location and direction of, say, a smell or sound provides orientation. This can provide for us connection between the substantial effects, which associated and dissociated positioning can have on our perception, and the effects of changing spatial submodalities.

You can find out more about Lawley's studies in his article *The Neurobiology of Space*, www.cleanlanguage.co.uk.

Detractors

Having set up my stall by suggesting that the discoveries arising from Neuroscience could provide scientific evidence to explain the effects of specific neurolinguistic input on the brain, and so position NLP's credibility within the research world, I have been made to think again. Lawley presented a far-reaching session on *Neuroscience Myths, Metaphors and Marketing* to the 2012 NLPtCA Conference. Full coverage of the presentation can be found on http://www.slideshare.net/jdlawley/ neurosciencemythsmetaphorsmarketing.

From Lawley's extensive reading round the subject, he highlights the need to be discerning regarding our embrace of neuroscience, and avoid what Raymond Tallis, retired clinical neuroscientist, calls 'Neuromania.'

Technical Problems with fMRI

Whilst hailed as the technology of choice, some suggest fMRI is not fit for purpose.

- The brain is always active and therefore will always be lit up somewhere. It is questionable if the blood flow shifts can be reliably attributed to the sensory input of the experiment. The same cognitive function can show up in different regions of the brain.

- Brain activity and blood flow should not be measured like for like. Millions of neurons have to be activated before blood flow changes can be detected. And neural activity lasts milliseconds, but it takes two to ten seconds to detect blood blow changes.

- The scans are a crude capturing of brain activity since each voxel (cf pixel) isolates a massive 10,000 or more neurons.

- A study could incorporate thousands of scans, each of which may carry 50,000 points of data. This requires massive and very subsequent number crunching. MRI scanning is very expensive.

- Results vary per person, over different scans of the same test and through time.

- Results are not always conclusive given that many false positives are thrown up – results that indicate a condition is present when it isn't, in tests where a single condition is tested for. These often remain uncorrected.

- Given the variability of results, the best results are most likely to be selected to prove the prevailing hypothesis, or emerging theory.

Flaws in fMRI Studies

- Many studies conducted within universities use students as the research group. This group is obviously not representative of the population as a whole. Their age and location presents a cultural, intellectual, life experience bias. They may or may not be motivated by money.

- It has been found that adolescents respond less emotionally to black and white images compared to adults' responses. When the same image is offered in colour, their response increases significantly, more in line with the adults' measurements.

- Activities undertaken within the scanner have to be isolated and simple, compared to the complex everyday actions of humans, which renders the results somewhat simplistic and so need to be taken in context. However, brain scan images are seen to be more credible than the same evidence presented in charts or words.

What They Say

The majority of neuroimaging studies I come across are so flawed, either due to design or statistical errors, they add virtually nothing to my knowledge.

Daniel Bor: Sackler Centre for Consciousness Science, University of Sussex

Mirror neurons have not been demonstrated unequivocally in humans.

Raymond Tallis: Aping Mankind (2011)

As a neuroscientist myself, I have come to know firsthand [the] feeling of dread [when] I speak to the public about the state of our field. The audience [is] curious about brains that malfunction or excel, but even the humdrum lacks explanation. Every day we recall the past, perceive the present, and imagine the future. How do our brains accomplish these feats? It's safe to say that nobody really knows.

Sebastian Seung: Professor of Computational Neuroscience at MIT.

Fifty years of research shows that we don't understand what neural networks are doing.

Michael Harré: Centre for the Mind, University of Sydney

Future Research Possibilities

Currently much of the research activities within the field of NLP centre on the application of NLP techniques and processes to address specific problems, especially those who are accorded DSM V status. Understandably this is an excellent route to gain prominence and credibility with the medical faculty. It reinforces the belief that NLP is a therapy and applicable only as a means of intervention.

This is patently erroneous because NLP is a modelling approach and can address all the vagaries of subjective human experience. To limit it just to the medical psychological world is to do it a disservice.

If research operated at the meta level of modelling and work was done exploring what actually happens neurologically as a consequence of different types of NLP input, then we would be able to demonstrate how universally applicable our modality is. Personally I would love to see research exploring the effects of different types of questions and their delivery, linguistic rapport strategies, multiple perspectives, shifts in temporal predicates. I could go on!

Having said that, given the shortcomings of current technology and know-how, it may be a long time before we will be able to present unequivocally evidence of the connection between neural activity and the neurological and linguistic processes found within NLP.

NLP's Modelling Rationale

Now is the time to discover the key influencers of Bandler and Grinder in the early days, who served to direct their filters and develop the direction of their attention. These thinkers were active in their field, mostly in California, at the time of NLP's inception, and their collective output directly or indirectly contributed to the unique nature and the approach that NLP took. Without this heritage, anything that did emerge would have had a very different shape and feel. We are indebted to these great minds.

NLP's Influencers

Gregory Bateson (1904-1980)

Bateson was a sociologist, philosopher and historian as well as biologist, anthropologist, linguist, psychotherapist and cyberneticist. English by birth and upbringing, he became a naturalised citizen of the United States in his 50s. He met Milton Erikson early in the 1930s as his personal interest in trance developed through his work in Bali.

By the late 50s he found himself in Palo Alto with Donald Jackson, Jay Haley, and Virginia Satir, coming up with the Double Bind Theory – the land of Catch 22 that requires a higher level of thinking to break free of the bind. During this time he developed his thinking round Logical Levels, building upon Bertrand Russell's ideas on Logical Types. As part of the group, he pioneered the practice of systemic Family Therapy. He also happened to be John Grinder's neighbour during the development years of NLP.

Holism

He maintained that the only way we can hope to understand the world around us is by adopting a truly *holistic* attitude towards it and by perceiving the systems that connect, across different fields of study. 'There is at least an impulse still in the human breast to unify and thereby sanitise the total natural world of which we are.'

To view an element outside of its holistic structure invites disaster. Looking at one role in isolation begs the question of how this role fits in the others around it and the context within which it operates. These too have to be known before the role can be understood.

Relationships

In his epistemological search into how things work, and operating within his holistic vision, Bateson soon came to the conclusion that the world is only made of relationships. Every description is relative to the elements involved within it. And these relationships are context dependent. 'Without context, words and actions have no meaning at all.' To illustrate this, he holds up a hand and directs our attention not to the five fingers, but the space between them where the much more significant and critical relationship exists.

> For example, take a molecule of haemoglobin, even if we can know everything about the atoms, structure, interaction, the physics and chemistry, we would still not know that it is its relationship to oxygen that helps the body process energy – life metabolism. And should we find somewhere else in the universe where organisms derive their energy from oxygen, we would find something like haemoglobin but nothing like what we recognise but it would do the same thing. The function of the haemoglobin is not what it is but what it is in relationship to.

Ecology

Bateson had a deep love of Nature and believed that all nature and art generates science. He also held that all systems seek homeostasis, that is that they want to come to rest. Therefore every influence or impact on one part of a system will generate a series of adjustments elsewhere so that balance can be regained. Feedback is essential to enable systemic self-regulation.

Lasting structures are those with the most flexibility. Our ability to remain stable is a measure of our flexibility, since we have to be constantly micro correcting to maintain that homeostasis. If we couldn't, we would fall over. Similarly having flexibility in thinking makes generating new connections possible, which are essential for our continued survival.

Systems

Everything needs to be seen in relation to very other thing. His extraordinarily varied background allowed him to draw across disciplines, seeking analogies that would help explain what he was looking at. He was fascinated to discover the 'patterns that connect', and because he believed they were there he would go looking at them. He saw life as a series of fractals and the large pattern would be found intact in a much smaller scale, if we were to look for it, and vice versa.

This thinking applied through time as well, since learning never stops and there is no such thing as an identical experience – 'You can't step into the same river twice.' (because you and the river will be different at time$_2$). Generalisations have to be constantly revisited. We have to stand back and view them in a different way. Everything can be infinitely examined. Says his daughter Nora:

> Like a Rubik cube, he would twist and revaluate the rules and twist it again so that he wouldn't get stuck in his thinking. He was happy to handle several right answers!

Patterns

Pattern Detection involves looking for redundancies, similarities, themes and variation, which immediately points to something behind the content itself. It is within the structure that new information lies.

Bateson would pose the question 'What pattern connects the crab to the lobster and the orchid to the primrose and all the four of them to me – and me to you?' as a means of testing his listeners. He knew there is no answer since patterns are always changing, but he wanted to strengthen the act of questioning to develop intuitive curiosity so that the patterns-that-connect are given 'wiggle room' to self correct to new information.

Thinking and learning

Bateson's thinking patterns relied heavily on both his intuitive unconscious mind and his cognitive conscious mind. A process of detection would be triggered by a somatic 'hunch' that there was something here to be discovered. This would alert him to search for an analogy that shared the pattern in question. Once he had settled on an analogy, usually through image, he would then rigorously enter the cognitive conscious domain and rigorously apply his thinking to test if that analogy would hold true in this circumstance.

He coined the term 'abduction' where creative thinking would emerge through the illogical mixing of structures and relationships to come up with a deeper truth. This type of thinking was often attributed to the insane! However, he would argue that there would always be a connection if we look for it. However he did not favour 'abduction' over 'deduction'. Rather he saw that advances of scientific thought come from a combination of loose and strict thinking, and this combination is the most precious tool of science.

He pioneered the idea of different levels of thinking, each responsible for making corrective changes and refinements to those below and above it.

The basis for a Logical Level is that the higher level describes the Class of Things, that are occurring on the lower level.

I explore the nature of Logical Levels and Logical Types in greater detail as part of the process of constructing a Model in Part 5.

Difference

The interaction between parts of our mind is triggered by detecting difference. Quality interactions are those that bring the crucial information that is required to regain balance, new understanding, new connections – to use Bateson's phrase, to find 'the difference which makes a difference'. And the quest for establishing new connections comes to an end when there is no longer any 'news of difference'.

Bateson is undoubtedly the most significant contributor and influencer of the development of NLP. He was teaching at Santa Cruz at the same times as Grinder, and several of the students who were part of the crazy Bandler and Grinder development group, were also students of his. Whilst it is often repeated that NLP is based on the work of Perls, Satir and Erickson, it is the thinking of Bateson that gave shape to the final results.

I am very appreciative of his younger daughter Nora Bateson for her fabulously sensitive and deeply informative film, *An Ecology of Mind – a Daughter's Portrait of Gregory Bateson,* released 2012. Well worth a viewing.

Noam Chomsky (b 1928)

Chomsky has been described as the father of modern linguistics and the founder of Transformational Grammar. He argued that, as children from whatever culture are able to acquire language in a relatively short time, there needs to be some universal grammar that is instinctively tapped into.

A demonstration of this lies in the grammatically correct yet nonsensical sentence: 'Colourless green ideas sleep furiously.'

He introduced the terms Deep Structure where our experiences are without language and Surface Structure where we package our inner experience linguistically. As we seek to share a description of these experiences, the process of bringing them to the surface requires linguistic coding. By definition, in the process, the surface account will be a lightweight facsimile of what is actually residing deeply within.

John Grinder, then Professor of Linguistics, was significantly influenced by Chomsky's thinking and used this 'structure' rationale to provide the foundation of the Meta Model creation.

Milton Erickson (1901-1980)

Largely self-taught, dyslexic and colour blind, Milton Erickson became aware of the power of the unconscious mind during his first bout of polio at 17. His mobility led him to study non-verbal behaviours and develop his sensory acuity. Through watching his baby sister learn to walk, and activating 'body memories' he taught himself to walk again.

He gained a psychology degree whilst studying medicine, and went on to practice psychotherapy as a consultant. His polio returned in later life, and he managed to control the pain through self-hypnosis.

He developed a unique approach to trance, induction and hypnotherapy, specifically developing the ideas of permission, utilisation and confusion, which paced and led the patient's reality. He also became famous for his telling of isomorphic stories and setting tasks that mirrored the presenting issues and underlying solutions.

He believed that trance was a normal everyday occurrence and that everybody had the ability to enter an altered state, through confusion and pattern disruption. He taught that the unconscious mind was creative, solution generating, and often positive, and didn't respond to the prescriptive dictates of traditional hypnotherapists. He believed the unconscious mind was 'always listening' and so could be receptive to embedded suggestions received outside of conscious awareness. He developed specific 'artfully vague' linguistic patterns that would support and develop internal processing, through directly addressing the unconscious mind. These became Bandler and Grinder's Milton Model.

Alfred Korzybski (1879 –1950)

Korzybski, a Polish-American philosopher and scientist, an early Constructivist, and founder of General Semantics, argued that human knowledge of the world is limited both by the human nervous system and by the structure of language. He thought that people do not have access to direct knowledge of reality; rather they have access to perceptions and to a set of beliefs which human society has confused with direct knowledge of reality. When people enter into argument about what is real, all they are doing is sparring with their own perception and interpretation of the object of their debate. They are confusing their own models of reality with reality itself (whatever that is).

In 1931 he coined the phrase 'The map is not the territory', although the map may have structure similar or dissimilar to the structure of the territory. Famously quoted as saying: 'The menu is not the meal. If it was you would be eating the menu.'

In General Semantics he explored the physiological effects that can be triggered by language – an early reference to a form of Anchoring.

Carl Rogers (1902-1987)

Working mostly in Chicago and Wisconsin, Rogers was one of the founders of the person-centred approach, which held that the individual, student or exemplar was the determinant of change, not the teacher, therapist or counsellor. This therefore made demands on the professional to find ways of understanding how each individual was operating and responding to the world. He introduced the notion of facilitation that enabled response to emerge without judgment of a person's worth, constraint, or expectation of content. Along with Maslow, he pioneered Humanistic Psychology that was widely adopted in the 60's.

He was highly regarded by his peers and honoured many times over, posthumously nominated for the Nobel Peace Prize.

W Ross Ashby (1903-1972)

A Scot, Ross Ashby moved to the United States in 1960 and worked at the leading edge of cybernetics.

In *An Introduction to Cybernetics* (1956), Ross Ashby formulated his Law of Requisite Variety stating, 'Variety absorbs variety, defines the minimum number of states necessary for a controller to control a system of a given number of states.' Or as our NLP Presupposition goes – 'Those who are most flexible have the most influence.'

Virginia Satir (1916-1988)

An American psychotherapist, Satir is known for her pioneering work in family therapy. 'The family is a microcosm. By knowing how to heal the family, I know how to heal the world.'

Early on in her life she determined that she would become 'a children's detective on parents', because she was aware that there was much more going on under the surface of any presenting problem. She developed the thinking behind Systemic Constellations, a process whereby individuals undertake to act out different members of the family under direction of the exemplar. She had natural linguistic abilities that enabled family members to open up and this contributed to the formulation of the Meta Model devised by Bandler and Grinder.

Paul Watzlawick (1921-2007)

An Austrian by birth, Watzlawick studied philosophy and later analytical psychotherapy at the Carl Jung Institute. He moved to Palo Alto in 1960 working with Bateson, Virginia Satir and Jay Haley, and was a clinical professor in psychiatry and behavioural science at Stanford University.

He contributed to the thinking on Double Binds and developed a specialism in working with Families. He came up with five axioms that determine how people communicated within families, including our NLP Presupposition 'We cannot not communicate.'

NLP Presuppositions

The closest that NLP has come to stating its philosophy is enshrined within the NLP Presuppositions. These are the beliefs and operating principles that underpin the rationale given to all behaviour. They prescribe the mindset required to drive the skills of NLP and inform its technology. All the methodologies that are coming up are dependent on some or all of what is inherently presupposed within these beliefs.

There is not one agreed definitive listing; however those that I have collated encapsulate the major themes. As you will see, these presuppositions are an eclectic mix and their sources under which I have grouped them, directly influenced the thinking of Bandler and Grinder.

You are likely to be familiar with each of these Presuppositions and have fluency already with their explanations. However just by way of recap, I am offering my version of each of them.

Bateson

We are all parts of the system: everything, living and inanimate is connected through relationship. Change one part of the system and changes will occur elsewhere. Even viewing the system itself can change it, through setting up a self-conscious relationship with the perceiver. Therefore we need to think systemically if we are to be able to uncover what is fuelling the system, or interrupting the flow through it.

There is no such thing as failure only feedback: all information is a source of learning. It is neither good nor bad until we put meaning onto it. Of itself it is neutral and has no power to influence one way or another. Therefore 'failure' can be seen to be only the distance between what we had expected to happen and what actually happened – and a great source of learning.

The meaning of our communication is the response that we get: (which may not be the one intended). More than once I have spelt out my vision to a builder or joiner, who has made all the right noises of understanding my desires, and I return to find a path, or a kitchen layout that bears limited resemblance to my internal representation. And I regard myself as a good communicator! If the message is important, it is essential for the receiver to repeat back what they think they heard from you *in their own words.* This way you can respond to any deviation.

Erickson

There is no such thing as a resistant person – only information about your behaviour: we can establish rapport with anyone, even polarity responders, if we have sufficient commitment, flexibility and sensory acuity. Resistance can be overcome by coming alongside and acknowledging concerns instead of seeking to discount or diminish them. Having the flexibility to adapt and use what we are offered is key to the Ericksonian approach.

This presupposition is often accompanied with **What you resist, persists.**

Korzybski

Our reality is what we believe to be true: if a fire safety officer, a tourist board official, the mother of a toddler, and an interior designer all walked into the same room, they would experience four very different rooms and come to four very different conclusions regarding its suitability. It is worth reminding ourselves in the midst of hard-earned certainty that there may be another way of looking at it.

The map is not the territory: I can draw a rough outline of the motorways of England and Wales and some would guess what it was from just the lines. Others would need the towns and motorway road numbers before making the connection. However it is not England and Wales. There can be many different illustrations to describe England and Wales – topography, population distribution, flood plains, rainfall and sunshine figures, house price variation, economic growth indicators etc., can also which provide a valid description of England and Wales, but never, even taken collectively, come close to providing a full description of the territory that is England and Wales.

Maslow and Rogers

We have all the resources we need or can create them: because we are able to make constructions and build models naturally, and we store experience in our deep structure, we can access existing reference experiences and draw on these resources as and when we choose. Even when we haven't had a reference experience ourselves, we can 'act as if' and draw on the resources of another.

Maturana

All our life experiences are encoded in our neurology: we hold experience in deep structure, uncoded in language, and very often leave it lying dormant as a future resource. Through activating neurology either through language, or physiology, we can re-access these experiences at will.

Miller, Galanter and Pribram

All behaviour is outcome driven: every action that we take seeks to serve a purpose, whether we are conscious of it or not. In a short time frame, every question we ask is underpinned by the desired outcome for specific information. Every shift in direction we take seeks to deliver us closer to an intended destination point. However if we pay no heed to setting our outcomes consciously, our behaviours are at the beck and call of long established outcomes set and stored in our unconscious mind and may not have been revised for some time.

This presupposition is often accompanied with: **If you don't know where you're going, you will**

often end up somewhere else.

This trio also came up with the TOTE (Test, Operate, Test, Exit) model, which reflects this presupposition. If we have no predetermined idea of what is our desired situation, our outcome, we will stay in the operational stage forever – even though we may have met the outcome conditions many times in this process. We are stuck!

W Ross Ashby

Those who are most flexible have most influence: a spontaneous two-year-old has the power to turn the population of a train compartment into a body of silent protesters. Free of the rules that constrain behaviour in social situations, the child can respond to events at will – and does so if parental restraint is not applied to some level.

This presupposition is often accompanied with: **If what you're doing isn't working, do something different.**

Virginia Satir

All behaviour is positively intended: this is a powerful belief of forgiveness and acceptance, more easily offered to others than to ourselves. It is the one presupposition that meets with the greatest resistance, so it is worth highlighting that we don't have to like the intention, or even approve of it. It is merely important to know what it is, so that there is a chance that the intention can be met through behaviour that is more acceptable within the circumstances.

This presupposition if often accompanied with: **We do the best we can with the resources available to us.**

Watzlawick

You cannot not communicate: every movement, gesture, shift in breathing, change in skin tone, as well as all the words we select and the manner in which we deliver them, speaks volumes. What is happening on the inside will show up on the outside. Even if you took yourself off to a darkened room and forbade visitors, your absence and manner of leaving will tell its story. It is down to us to become clearer about the messages we are transmitting.

Summary

NLP would not be NLP if it weren't for the principles that underpin it. NLP wouldn't work the way it does if it weren't informed by the wisdom held within its powerful set of collective beliefs. As natural unconscious modellers, Bandler and Grinder had to have been influenced by the thinking of their teachers, the movers and shakers in Palo Alto, and the great therapists the two of them came across. As ever however, their focus was on How and not Why. Remember, Classic Code NLP concentrated mostly on behaviour and skills. An understanding of the mechanics of beliefs came later with Dilts.

Whilst Grinder was an acknowledged student of Bateson and Chomsky, I suspect he and Bandler didn't spend much time coding the sources of their inspirations – they were more preoccupied with generating the practical effects of their spectacular creations. This would explain the complete lack of reference to Constructivism as our starting point, and the general lack of attribution of the NLP Presuppositions. It also explains why NLP has been so consistently dismissed by the body of academia and the world of medicine.

I contend, however, that we have reached the stage in NLP's evolution when all serious practitioners have to include a clear understanding of the principles that hold NLP in its field of operation. We need to be fluent in our arguments and explanations, as well as being adept in the wizardry of its methodologies. If we do not, then we will continue to be picked off by the established and favoured modalities. We will deserve to continue to be dismissed as snake oil charlatans.

Part 3
The Methodologies of Modelling

Introduction

Understandably the process of Modelling is the engine house of NLP. Here in Part 3, we roll up our sleeves and fully engage with the act of modelling itself – discovering how to find the underpinning structure that delivers the identified activity. In the process we will honour the those modellers who have contributed significantly to the understanding of *how* to go about modelling, through their development of modelling methodologies, which each in their own way enable us to come up with a description of internal experience.

We are really fortunate that at the time of writing, we have nearly 50 years of NLP development behind us. Anyone arriving fresh to the field today can immediately access some wonderful developed technology which just didn't exist thirty, twenty, even ten years ago. This is especially true in the field of developed modelling methodologies.

There is a curious tendency within our field, whilst agreeing that the map is not the territory, to suggest that one approach is 'better' than another. Certainly some approaches are promoted more strongly than others and have adherents who are solely committed to its practice. This partisan thinking is a tad incongruent with our philosophy, and can be unusefully divisive.

However it is understandable. If a developer has invested considerable time and thought to formulating, testing and refining a particular approach, there will naturally be a tendency towards bias. For whatever reason the developer has already considered and rejected other approaches and understandably favours their own.

To address this debate, first of all I seek out common ground and determine what constitutes a modelling methodology, and then I bring together and classify thirteen different modelling approaches into one integrated framework, to illustrate the similarities and connected differences between each of them, giving each of them a legitimacy in the wider scheme of things.

Of these thirteen methodologies, some you will already know; some will be new to you, and others you may not have considered to be a methodology. For each one I give you my description of its nature, identify the developer, and cover background, approach, skills, ecology, coding, concerns and applications. These descriptions are merely my descriptions. So if you find my observations are at variance with what you've been taught, or with your own experience, then it is just information, and a sign of difference that can open up even further exploration for you – and for me.

The Modelling Process

A Framework for Modelling and Acquisition

In the Introduction you were offered an overview of the modelling process, in the Modelling Route Map. This Framework for Modelling and Acquisition is another way of looking at the modelling process, viewed on a smaller scale. There are various descriptions of the stages of modelling already published, but the version I have devised illustrates two key points: the differences between modelling and acquisition, and the significance of analogue and digital expression.

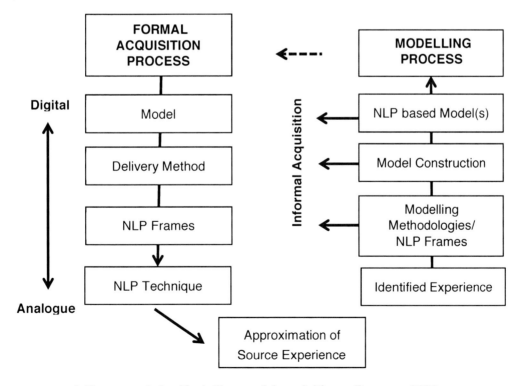

A Framework for Modelling and Acquisition – Burgess 2008

Modelling and Acquisition

The first difference is the relationship between modelling and formal acquisition. Instead of being confusingly lumped together, these need to be seen as two separate operations. Historically, acquisition by a third party (often referred to dubiously as 'installation') was the automatic end point of modelling. There is also an implication that only one model can be constructed and that there is only one technique developed from this model. Whereas I am suggesting that the construction of a model may not be the end point, and many models can emerge from the information gathered and, as will be seen in Part 6 – The Formal Acquisition Process, many techniques can be created using the one model. Every time I remind myself of this, I am bowled over by the infinite potential modelling brings to the world.

Acquisition doesn't just take place with the end user. There will always be informal acquisition by the modeller going on in the process, while testing the significance and sufficiency of the information coming from the exemplar, and then when testing his or her emerging model. And at the same time, there will also be acquisition by the exemplar.

Away from the exemplar, the modeller or another developer creates a technique based on the constructed model to generate a predetermined experience. Here the model can be one devised through NLP modelling or one devised from a totally different area of development. This process is one of formal acquisition, by a third party, and can be delivered as an intervention to generate an approximation of the desired behaviour.

I suspect that, because these processes have not been isolated and fully understood, the pursuit of modelling has not been clearly described, leading to demotivation and a tendency to discount the importance of modelling itself.

Analogue and Digital

The second feature of this framework is the concept of digital and analogue descriptions and the relationship between the two. It is useful to explore the thinking regarding analogue and digital – or my understanding of it at any rate. I was involved in quite a lively web-based forum on the subject and realised that interpretations varied widely, so much so that no definitive answer seemed to emerge.

This therefore makes it doubly important that I offer my own definition of terms, whilst knowing that these could be shot down by other interpretations.

- *Analogue:* behaviour involves movement and so is analogue – dance, music, writing, film. Experience is analogue. Analogue occurs where the individual elements within any behaviour come together to form the final fluid expression.

- *Digital:* when behaviour is broken down into its component parts it becomes a digital expression. These component parts are in and of themselves inert and have no life of their own. They only come into life once more when activated and brought together. So the specific steps or the notation of the choreography is the digital description of the analogue dance; the notes of a score are the digital expression of music; the freeze frames are the digital elements of film; and the words, letters even, are the digital constructs of writing.

  Experience is analogue and the move towards reducing experience down into its key elements is the process of coding, ultimately ending up with a fully digitised model.

Here the end point is a digital description in as few words as possible, which holds within it the essence of the modelled experience. This imminence can then be activated through the judicious selection of NLP wizardry and brought to life so that an approximation of that experience is created.

Stages Involved

The following is a simplified version of the stages involved in the modelling process. The *Modelling Route Map* found in the Introduction, is expanded further in Part 5 – The Results of Modelling.

1 **Identify your end user:** knowing who your customers are and their needs will determine the type of information you go after, how much and what the final results need to look like.

2 **Identify the experience:** identify the ability, the behaviour, or the performance that you want to model, and presumably at least one exemplar who demonstrates a consistent ability to perform this behaviour. You need at least three descriptions occurring in specific contexts so that you can identify common patterns. You now establish your intention to identify the underpinning structure that is generating this behaviour.

3 **Apply your chosen methodology:** if you are working with a range of exemplars, then it is useful to use the same methodology throughout so that you get like-for-like. Where the exemplar doesn't respond to that methodology you need to have a contingency plan.

Here you are using your modelling skills of sensory acuity, rapport, multiple perspectives, holding multiple attention, tracking systems, questioning, second positioning. Many of these skills are covered in Part 4 – The Skills of Modelling.

4 **Reduce and code the information:** once you have gathered sufficient significant information, you go through the process of reducing it down until you are able to produce a simplified version that enables you in the first instance to replicate the behaviour to some level. This vital activity is covered extensively in Part 5 – The Results of Modelling, and involves the skills of pattern detection, systemic thinking, conceptualising, and testing.

5 **Construct your model:** this simplification process can culminate in a fully digitised model, portable and able to be applied to a range of contexts. I have called this an 'NLP Model' since it has been generated using NLP frames. Many other models are out there but they don't have their origins within NLP.

The subsequent formal acquisition process is a reversal of this modelling process, working from the model, determining the vehicle for delivery, selecting the neurological and linguistic frames, so that the end user has a technique that enables him or her to access an experience similar in nature to that of the exemplar(s). Take the model and just add water! Part 6 – The Formal Acquisition Process addresses the process of designing a formal acquisition process.

A good number of potential models have landed on the cutting room floor, not because the data was meaningless, but just because the modeller became stuck at Stage 3 and didn't know where to go next.

Modelling Methodologies

It is at Stage 2 where the Modelling Methodology is applied. This is where you can select from a range of Methodologies, so that you can gather the data that has the potential to be turned into an NLP based Model.

As mentioned earlier, not all modelling results in the construction of a specific model. Very often, especially in the realms of therapy or coaching, it is enough to isolate key information that allows for the exemplar to self-model and restructure the configuration of their internal organisation.

Definition of a Modelling Methodology

After exploring the range of methodologies that I have collated, I have concluded that an approach can be regarded as a modelling methodology if it can:

- Reveal the internal underpinning structure of experience

- Provide the means to do so

- Facilitate self modelling within the exemplar

- Have the potential to be further generalised into a digital coded model.

All the methodologies, with the exception of Grinder's, meet this definition. Grinder's Unconscious Uptake doesn't involve the exemplar and therefore there is no potential for self-modelling.

Modelling Methodology Criteria

Currently the methodologies included are at various stages of their development. The maturity of the methodology can be assessed by the stage it and its developer have reached in its evolution. Whilst relative 'immaturity' of the methodology wouldn't invalidate it, critics could question the claims the developer makes for it.

Part 3 – The Methodologies of Modelling

I have experience in each of the methodologies and received training in most. As a result, in most cases I have been able to evaluate and calibrate the levels of coherence, rigour, and congruence the developer has in relationship with their methodology. Out of this I have identified the following criteria – my personal take on the standards a methodology ideally meets.

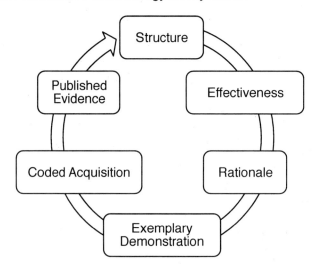

Modelling Methodology Criteria – Burgess 2012

1 **Structure:** fundamentally, all methodologies are required to have the ability to reveal the structure of subjective experience of another. Secondly, they are required to have the potential to transform collected data into a digital coded model, which can be acquired by a third party.

2 **Effectiveness:** it is historically agreed that the output of a modelling process is to enable a third party to acquire the ability of the exemplar, *assuming that the acquirer has the required attributes necessary for that activity.*

The mantra of the early days of NLP was: 'If it is possible to be done by one, it is possible to be done by another.' This required the modeller to find ways of offering the fruits of the modelling process in such a way that an impartial outsider could take on this learning.

Over time, experience has brought awareness that a third party is not the only acquirer and end user of the modelling process.

- The exemplar may be the acquirer, which is the case in therapy or coaching, and which means that there is no need to provide a vehicle for further acquisition by a third party.

- Or the modeller himself or herself may be the acquirer. Again there may be no need to develop a codified model for third party consumption – unless the modeller seeks to generalise his or her discoveries.

3 **Rationale:** developers need to be able to articulate fully the origins of their methodology and basis on which it has developed. They may be able to refer to their own exemplars, or the body of work that stimulated their interest and their subsequent development activities. They need to be able to reference what sets their approach aside from others, to demonstrate that it is a standalone

methodology as opposed to an adjunct to an existing approach.

And they need to be able to account for their development activities, the testing process and modifications that have been undertaken, to establish that this is a credible innovation and not an untested hypothesis. Ideally they can also offer personal experiences of their own consumption and the differences that this has made for themselves.

4   **Exemplary demonstration:** the developer needs to be able to demonstrate their methodology in action. This may be part of their training provision so that they act as exemplars to their learners, and therefore offer the opportunity for unconscious uptake.

They may argue, as does John McWhirter, that providing such a demonstration limits learning. Learners can imprint on that particular demonstration not realising that it was determined by the exemplar at the time. Learners can have lessened reliance on the authority of their own experiences. Learners can become intimidated by 'the expert'.

Whilst the lack of demonstration is code congruent with the modeller entering into a world hitherto unknown, I align with providing the demonstration. Providing several demonstrations allows the patterns within the methodology to emerge, and lets the learners witness the different responses of the trainer. For me, this way avoids the 'one way of doing it' mindset.

5   **Coded acquisition:** trainers who are the original developers often have difficulty delivering their own material since they have blind spots regarding its intricacies. They may overlook something they find naturally easy – pattern detection for example. The exemplar does not know everything they do – hence the need for a modeller's objectivity and awareness of what is operating at an unconscious level.

To be able to train effectively, developers need to be able to deliver the following:

•   They must be operating from meta-cognition. Their understanding needs to be such that they not only know the content, but also understand the integrated relationship between the elements of the content, the context that holds the content, and the application needs of the learner.

   They need to have quantified and coded fully all the processes involved in their methodology, and are able to offer them congruently and confidently in the simplest and most effective way possible. It is not enough to merely know the elements of the methodology – i.e. specifically what to do when. The developers need also to be able to describe and offer an experience of how these elements are delivered.

•   In addition, they need to provide experiences to demonstrate how to manage scenarios when the primary strategies don't work and informed flexibility is called for. This naturally presupposes that the developer also has defined calibration criteria that provide direction and cut-off points for their learners.

•   Different methodologies may require a specific skills set, over and above the recognised NLP repertoire. Where this is the case, then again the developer needs to have fully coded how these skills are constructed, and not only have devised strategies for learners to acquire them, but also opportunities for learners to practise them in observable conditions with coaching and feedback.

These requirements may be difficult to meet if the methodology is still in a state of development and refinement. However when the developer/trainers see the huge value in receiving the intended and unintended feedback from the learners, their methodology and their training input can only gain from further and further fine-tuning.

Often going to the opening night of a show is not the best experience. Waiting till the play has bedded down after a couple of months often provides the more polished experience.

6   **Published evidence:** the developer needs to provide tangible evidence of the effectiveness of their methodology**.**

- Does this methodology indeed deliver the structure that underpins the behaviour?
- Does it highlight the inner workings of the exemplar in a simplified and easy to consume fashion?
- Does it enable altered experience in the acquirer?

Ideally this evidence is presented in the form of a generalised model, which is portable and available to any end user. Evidence may also be offered through favourable feedback by end users.

Furthermore, I would suggest that this evidence is documented in a formal published format, with written up case studies, to underpin its efficacy. At best, the results would be offered as a research project and presented in a formal gathering of peers.

Certainly the current drive to promote research, and publish evidence, would serve to formalise the great work that is currently operating at an informal level. Without it we remain prey to accusations of 'smoke and mirrors'.

Integrated Framework of Methodologies

I can clearly remember one of the many breakthrough moments I've had about the modelling process. It was during an NLP Conference in 2010, and my dear friend Jan Ardui was giving a workshop on modelling on the Saturday. I was due to deliver my workshop on *Conditions for Model Construction* the following day as part of my Cheap and Cheerful Modelling thinking.

Jan had demonstrated a modelling approach he had developed and which seemed to produce good results. The participants definitely seemed to appreciate it. But I was thrown into total confusion. My fundamental hypothesis for Model Conditions was that all models were ideally digital, and at best stripped down to the bare minimum – nominalisations, verbs, or adjectives. Yet here was someone whom I admire tremendously and credit with enormous understanding about modelling, providing as the result of his modelling process, a model that was full of language: analogue structure, sentences, phrases and words.

Being so externally referenced, I felt I had to be wrong. And I had a workshop the next day with my certainty shot to pieces. I remember finally becoming fully awake at about three in the morning, after fitfully sleeping and dreaming of mismatching structure, with the dawning awareness that both were just fine – *it was just a matter of the degree of coding involved.* Phew!

As is the way of breakthroughs, so much else tumbled into place. All the dissention between the various modellers, about 'who had got it right' and 'who was misguided', drained away. From this meta level of awareness I realised that *all* the modelling methodologies could happily co-exist across a spectrum determined by the amount of coding that was expressly involved by each of them.

Everyone is right! I can't tell you how exciting that was, and how affirming if felt to know that we were in fact all coming from the same place and all serving the same aims. Not only that, this inclusive thinking removes divisive barriers and legitimises access to a tremendous range of approaches, giving the modeller options and flexibility.

Classification of Methodologies

Before I could establish a meaningful classification of modelling methodologies, I had to establish the rationale that would differentiate between each of them – without implying that one approach is more sophisticated and 'better' than another. This way I could provide a common language and common understanding. From the thirteen methodologies I've identified – and I fully accept that there are others out there that I have not included – I have grouped them depending on:

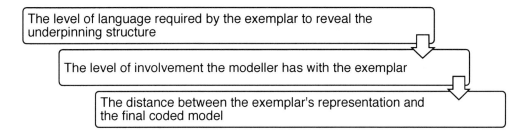

The level of language required by the exemplar to reveal the underpinning structure

The level of involvement the modeller has with the exemplar

The distance between the exemplar's representation and the final coded model

Criteria for Classification of Modelling Methodology – Burgess 2012

This has resulted in identifying four major Classes of Modelling Methodology, each with their own sub-classes.

Note: It's important to know that for some modellers, coding, especially into a digital reduced model, is something not only they don't do, they would never want to do. Some modellers, for example Delozier and Gordon firmly believe that experience is analogue and needs to stay in that format. Lawley and Tompkins use their methodology predominately for therapeutic purposes and rarely apply their approaches to create fully digitised models.

Classes of Modelling Methodologies

For me, Modelling Methodologies fall into four major categories. Each category has links with the one before and after, yet is sufficiently different to merit its own class. Personally I contend that modelling can contain elements from all approaches, and does not need to be a case of either/or.

As you can imagine, the more methodologies you have access to, the greater your choice and flexibility.

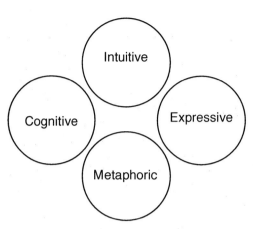

Classes of Modelling Methodologies – Burgess 2012

1 **Intuitive modelling:** the modelling methodologies within this class of modelling require the level of cognition to be at a minimum, and ideally non-existent. To quote Steve Gilligan, here 'the trick is to be in the creative consciousness of the territory without "neuromuscularly locking" into any fixed thought or representation about it.'

Modellers are operating instinctively, intuitively and spontaneously, with no preconceptions, driven only by the dictates of their unconscious mind. Such methodologies require modellers to be in tune with the messages generated from within their unconscious mind and to trust these sufficiently to act upon them.

The exemplar is not directly involved in the modelling process, although may be invited to receive the modellers' conclusions. However the exemplar needs to be present and fully associated into the ability that is being modelled.

I have included the following examples of Intuitive Modelling methodologies:

Unconscious Uptake aka 'The Real NLP Modelling' – *John Grinder and Carmen Bostic St Clair:* taking on the neurology of the exemplar through unconscious uptake.

- *Deep Trance Identification – Steve Gilligan:* taking on the sphere of identity of another.

- *Somatic Modelling – Judith Delozier:* revealing deep structure and the somatic wisdom of the body, through physiology and somatic syntax.

Arguably Somatic Modelling has a place in Expressive Modelling since it is embodied in the kinaesthetic representation system. However due to history and her early involvement in the New Code development of Unconscious Uptake – see *Turtles All The Way Down* (1987) – and because the Expressive Methodologies I have included fit better together, I have kept it here. Certainly Somatic Modelling faces the Expressive Class.

2 **Expressive modelling:** to my mind, Dance, Music, and Art Therapies are based on describing inner structures specifically through the channels of representation systems. Whilst these modelling methodologies have originated outside of the field of NLP, it is surprising that they have

not been incorporated into our practices as modelling approaches in their own right – especially given that we recognise that all our experience is detected through our senses. As you will see in Part 5 – The Results of Modelling, I hold that image, sound, gesture are Natural models in themselves and therefore are capable of being modelling tools and act as neurological frames for technique construction.

Each has a long-established therapeutic process addressing the full range of physical, emotional, mental and spiritual needs. For our purposes as modellers, we can dispense with their respective therapeutic philosophy and its interpretations, and concentrate instead on each process's ability to provide a description of internal structure.

- *Dance/Movement Modelling – various:* using the vehicle of dance and movement to reveal structure.

- *Art Modelling – various:* using images, drawings, painting, sculpting to reveal structure.

- *Music/Sound Modelling – various:* using a range of instruments, including the voice, melodic or otherwise, to reveal structure.

3   **Metaphoric modelling:** the modelling methodologies within this class of modelling access the deep structure patterns through working with symbols and metaphor. They operate on the belief that everyone can access such forms of information, which regularly show up in conversation and gesture.

Operating in mid-structure of experience, this approach allows the exemplar to stay in semi awareness of his or her processes, and provide information from an altered state. In doing so, the modeller and the exemplar are able to access an unedited version of the deep structure, without the imposition of the constraints of rational logic. Modellers need to be aware of what the exemplar is offering linguistically and have sufficient skill to keep the exemplar 'psycho-active' (to quote Lawley/Tompkins), and stay deep within the process.

With these methodologies, the modeller drives the exemplar's attention, leading to further exploration and new information. Depending on outcome, the modeller could work from videoed or written information provided that it is sufficiently rich in the metaphorical references, but can't access further information beyond what's on offer.

Most commonly, the modelling process is completed at the point when the exemplar and modeller part company, although the information will still be 'cooking' within the exemplar's system.

Such approaches are commonly used as therapeutic intervention, first and foremost.

Examples of such methodologies are:

- *Punctuation Modelling – Fran Burgess:* using the form of grammatical punctuation to code deep structure patterns and provide opportunities for repatterning.

- *Sand Play Modelling – various:* an established therapeutic approach which uncovers underpinning structures through the three-dimensional use of sand and a vast selection of objects.

- *Symbolic Modelling – James Lawley and Penny Tompkins:* working with the sub surface structure of metaphor as manifested in words and actions, stimulated by a prescribed range of constructed questions, and delivery intonation.

- *Parts Alignment – Fran Burgess:* working with the cast of parts operating in a given context, to reveal the nature and dynamics between the parts and their appropriateness for the demands of that context.

4   **Cognitive modelling:**   the modelling methodologies within this class of modelling operate cognitively, working with a range of linguistic frames to elicit critical information from the exemplar, and then sort the resultant data using a range of predetermined scoping frameworks.

Cognitive modelling is the methodology most commonly used, principally because most people, both modeller and exemplar, are familiar and comfortable with this, the most conversational approach. Because it operates at surface structure, it lends itself readily to develop product and process models, often for commercial purposes. As a result, there will tend to be a clear third party end user in mind.

The model construction process continues well away from the exemplar, who may be one of many that the modeller has worked with. Moreover the end result may bear little similarity to the specific version offered by any one exemplar.

Again the most desirable scenario is being able to witness the exemplar performing the activity and interviewing them afterwards. Cognitive modellers can work on accounts of such practice from their exemplars, or from third party anecdote and written accounts.

Examples of such methodologies are:

- *Experiential Array – David Gordon and Graham Dawes:* a comprehensive set framework and questions, driven by the operating criterion and supporting beliefs and incorporating strategies, emotions and observed behaviours.

- *Analytical Modelling – Robert Dilts:* eliciting a wide range of information which can then be scoped into familiar frameworks – the most common being Neurological Levels, although the other neurological/linguistic frames of time and perspectives may be used.

- *LAB Profile – Rodger Bailey/Shelle Rose Charvet:* an ingenious means of detecting the meta programme traits an individual is running in particular contexts.

I had intended to include John McWhirter's *Developmental Behavioural Modelling* (DBM), as part of this category since his 500+ models are all reduced down into digital models of few words. His is the ultimate example of Cognitive Modelling. However, I reconsidered this on the basis that DBM is in fact a modality in its own right, and stands alongside NLP and isn't a part of it. Whilst McWhirter started out in NLP being a Master Trainer with Bandler, his work has taken him into a different, though parallel, field of operations.   At the time of writing, he is in the process of writing up his amazing body of work.

The Methodologies Framework

As a means of bringing all the various modelling methodologies together in a cohesive and integrated format, I have devised the following framework. As you will see, it plots the progressive 'evolution' of the range of methodologies and their relationship with each other, relative to the degree of coding.

You can see how the four major classes connect. With Unconscious Uptake there is no coding at all, until the modeller decides to do so. With McWhirter's DBM everything is digital. Whilst Symbolic

Modelling deals with symbols depicted within a metaphoric landscape, the exemplar is providing a linguistic analogue description.

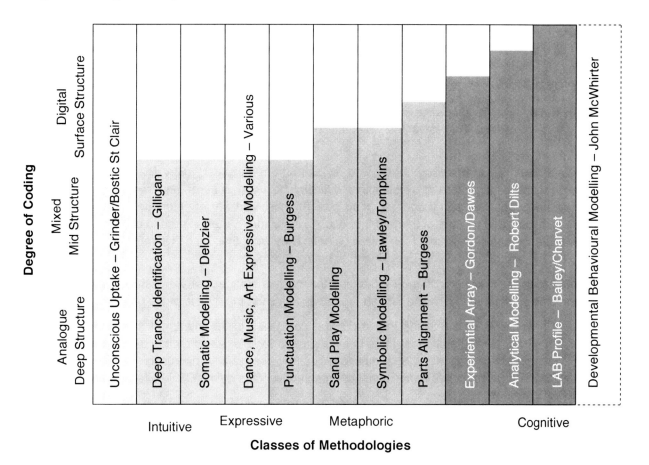

The Methodologies Framework – Burgess 2011

I hope that this view provides a place for the legitimacy for each modelling methodology and the modeller is at liberty to become skilled and selective over the range of them. No one approach is better than another. It is merely a question of what is appropriate for the subject modelled, and the skills of the modeller.

Note: I have conveniently grouped the Expressive Class of Methodologies into one category for the purpose of this framework, given that their origins lie outside of NLP.

Full Coding

Each methodology has the potential to convert the information gleaned into a digital model. It is merely a question of when experience is brought to the surface structure and presented in concise language.

Obviously the cognitive methodologies are just a stone's throw away from producing complete, discrete models. Yet even if the methodology itself doesn't produce fully coded models, these can be developed should the modeller so desire.

The potential harvest of models that modelling can yield is enormous, powerful and of great service to the community at large. I suspect that the narrow path towards coding owes more to ignorance of how to construct a coded model than to any philosophical stance. Happily I have worked to simplify the process as can be seen in the section on model construction in Part 5 – The Results of Modelling.

Coding by a Modeller

A therapist may wish to specialise in a particular behavioural issue. From their modelling activities over a range of clients, they have the potential to reveal commonly held structures that hold the 'problem'.

For example as I was modelling those who suffered from Paruresis (Shy Bladder Syndrome) I identified a consistent pattern of relationship difficulty between sufferer and mother, or nurturing parent, where praise was conditional on good performance, and anxiety stemmed from performing badly. I also identified a range of triggers that caused inhibition. When offered to clients, this created such reassurance and comfort that they weren't alone. They were then able to identify their own trigger that could be another doorway into exploring their inner patterning.

The therapist might discover common strategies for the management of the identified problem and these could be configured to become proven resources to lesson the effects of the problem.

So I learnt a whole list of strategies that a sufferer could use in the interim, if they hadn't already known them – from plotting safe loos (there is even an app for this) to distraction techniques, to urinal etiquette, to resource management, to acquiring a buddy, to self talk, to distraction behaviour. I have to say I was less in favour of this behaviourist approach advocated by the CBT-based support group.

The modeller may seek those who have survived the problem unaided, and so discover patterns that represent the solution to the problem. This was how James Prochaska came up with his six-part model for Change. He and his research team modelled those who had successfully managed to stop addictive behaviour unaided to find out how they did that, subsequently written up in *Changing for Good* (1998).

For this to happen, the therapist needs to be thinking as a modeller, and set out with the intention of holding two very separate outcomes – one fully associated outcome to serve the exemplar towards attaining the exemplar's own outcome, and the other somewhat dissociated outcome is to gain a meta understanding of the condition itself, and the nature of its holder.

Once coded by the modeller, models can be produced. They don't have to be fully digitised – a listing of beliefs may be powerfully effective. The models can then be generalised and offered to new clients.

I suggest that if more therapists adopted this approach, we would be able to present to the world a tremendous body of knowledge and good practice.

Self-Coding

It is usually assumed that the onus lies with the modeller to come up with the coding. Not so. It is arguably much more useful to ask the exemplar to provide the labelling. After all it is their internal structure that is the focus of attention. Whether somatic syntax, a metaphoric landscape, or a gathering of parts, the exemplar can very easily: (a) split the process into its discrete elements, knowing instinctively what is significant and what is incidental: and then (b) label these elements attributing the inherent values of the element, or the action involved, or the dominant description of each.

It is then down to the modeller, who ideally has a deep understanding of the criteria for model construction, to tidy up this description into a meaningful coded model meeting the CASE, coherent, accessible, simple, effective, requirement: see Part 5 – The Results of Modelling.

Methodology Profile

In the next four sections I present my take on each of the methodologies within their respective Intuitive, Expressive, Metaphoric and Cognitive Classes. I will be offering you:

- Biography of the developer(s)
- Background to the methodology
- An overview of the process involved
- Specialised skills required
- Applications
- Ecology Issues
- Coding
- Concerns
- Final thoughts.

As the consumer of this material, you need to be clearly aware of the following:

- I am not offering a definitive description of each of these methodologies.

- What I offer is my take from my own personal experiences. Whilst I have done some reading around the subject of each, my comments and observations come from direct consumption and not from theoretical research.

- I fully recognise that my exposure to the full range of methodologies varies in depth and direct experience, and I am much more familiar with some than others.

- I am also more naturally predisposed to some than others, although I hope I have been even-handed in my approach to each.

- These summaries offered are just that. I wouldn't insult the developers by suggesting that the few pages I provide encapsulate the extent of their years of endeavour.

- I hope to provide the flavour of the methodology to activate your interest and direct your attention to further study. And I hope to provide it in a manner which is easily consumable.

- And then because I know that any subsequent three-day training is just scratching the surface, I urge you to go away and practise, practise and practise, so you begin to really savour the magical connections and engineering inherent within each.

Some of you may question the inclusion of my own methodologies, especially if you are aware of omissions that you think could usefully have been included. You may accuse me of editorial favouritism and you may be right! However, whilst pygmies alongside the other more established approaches, both Punctuation Modelling and Parts Alignment are great processes that produce significant results and I believe have earned their place, meeting most of my self-imposed standards.

Intuitive Methodologies

Intuitive Modelling arguably is the most fundamental approach we can take to learn about another. It is pre-language and is the way we instinctively began to make sense of the world as a child. We may find ourselves unconsciously adopting someone else's mannerisms, their walk, the way they hold their glass, the way they look over the rim of their spectacles. Or we may find ourselves incorporating the tone, accent, syntax and language of someone we admire.

Immersion language learning draws on intuitive modelling as its source of input. Preferably in the country itself, or with native speakers, the learner is intensively exposed to the language, its music and its flow, as well as absorbing the cultural tics and gestures that go with it.

Intuitive modelling seeks to access the deep structure of another, directly, without language, tapping solely into the wisdom on the unconscious mind – that of the modeller, and also of the exemplar. These approaches depend on the degree at which the energies of both parties merge to create a relational field of greater awareness.

It is notable for its lack of verbal communication between modeller and exemplar, and also a seeming passivity on the part of the modeller.

This section seeks to offer you insight into the three of the approaches found within the NLP field of modelling. Specifically you are offered my take on:

- *Unconscious Uptake:*   aka 'The Real NLP Modelling' work headlined by John Grinder and Carmen Bostic St Clair.

- *Deep Trance Identification:* Steve Gilligan, the creator of Self Relations and Generative Self.

- *Somatic Modelling:*   developed and presented by Judith Delozier.

Unconscious Uptake aka 'The Real NLP Modelling'

John Grinder

As you all know John Grinder was the co-founder, with Richard Bandler and Frank Pucelik, of the modality that became known as NLP. You can learn more about Grinder's background and this relationship in Chapter 4 of *Whispering in the Wind* – Grinder and Bostic St Clair (2001). Suffice to say he was an assistant professor at UC Santa Cruz and as a result of his collaborative explorations of the work of Perls, Satir and Erickson, he co-created the process of operating and thinking called Neurolinguistic Programming, which holds a unique place in the field of constructivist endeavour.

Grinder and Judith Delozier, who was also a student at the time in UC Santa Cruz, was involved in the development activities at the time of visiting Milton Erickson. Together they went on to explore the significance of the unconscious mind in subjective experience, strongly influenced by the work of Carlos Castaneda and Don Juan. Delozier as a dancer naturally introduced physiology as the embodiment of the unconscious mind within our extensive neurology. The husband and wife team co-wrote the ground breaking work *Turtles All the Way Down,* published in 1987 and heralding the arrival of 'New Code NLP'.

In 1991 Grinder with his new partner Carmen Bostic St Clair first appeared as co trainers in the UK when they delivered a workshop in London sponsored by Pace Personal Development – PPD, covering the topic of Metaphor. It was one of the most formative workshops I have ever attended, and my first experience of Grinder.

After a seven-year absence Grinder and Bostic St Clair returned to London again sponsored by PPD Learning, this time for a workshop on Patterns. It was here that he uttered his call for more modellers and models – my Call to Action.

At the turn of the century, they then re-emerged into the UK NLP community, becoming a regular fixture with The NLP Academy. They relaunched the concepts of New Code NLP, and established themselves on the modelling moral high ground declaring their approach to be 'The Real NLP Modelling'. In 2001 they co-wrote the rather impenetrable book *Whispering In The Wind*, outlining the evolution of NLP and the thinking behind New Code. Then in 2012 Grinder edited the controversial *Origins*, which was a collection of accounts from those involved in the early days of NLP development.

Intrigued by 'The Real NLP Modelling' labelling, I attended a three-day workshop to find out for myself and to seek recognition for my response to his Call. All I can say is that the weekend disappointed on both counts. I learnt little about Unconscious Uptake and Grinder didn't consider any of my exemplars to be proper modellers.

The Background

In the pre-NLP days there were no modelling methodologies, frameworks or known modelling skills. Bandler in particular was an inspired and unconscious mimic, whilst Grinder was more cerebral. The story goes that they sought to go back to first principles and learn like babies through observing, mimicking, adopting any visible micro-movements, testing, practising. More particularly, like babies, they were able to remove any internal dialogue reprimanding them should they make mistakes, should they fail to understand, or cause upsets. They stayed open and receptive, deeply and enthusiastically curious about the experiences they were being made privy to, and eager to apply what they'd learnt. As an aside, the work done with mirror neurons might explain how this approach succeeds.

Part 3 – The Methodologies of Modelling

Grinder particularly describes their time modelling Erickson this way, whilst Erickson was working with his patients. After spending time in Erickson's company, he and Bandler would rush back to California to practise with anyone within hearing distance with the patterning they were attempting to master.

Interestingly, on my recent visit to Samoa, I learnt that the intricate skills of carving are 'taught' in this manner. There is no official instruction. The apprentice sits with the carver from boyhood and over six or more years the movements and precision are absorbed into the fledgling carver's system. I assume there will be a process of trial and error, but that would be away from the master's awareness.

Grinder contends that the primary motivation of modelling is to find out what the exemplars *do*, not to understand them. Ultimately you would come to understand through living their behaviours; beliefs, values and sense of identity would emerge through the encapsulation of their physiology. He is adamant that the minute we label something, we remove any continued exploration. He tells a story of being captivated by the sight of a hawk swooping down to catch a rabbit. The mood was broken the minute attention was drawn by an external comment about how the bird flew. All of a sudden, the perceiver was taken out of the experience and forced to comment *on* the experience. 'Do not understand what you're doing *until* you can do it.'

Grinder advocates that his 'Real NLP Modelling' is the one and only true method of modelling within NLP. He discounts the validity of any other form of modelling other than Unconscious Uptake, and states that this is the method he and Bandler adopted certainly with Milton Erickson. They may or may not have been consciously aware that they were doing this, and possibly didn't set the intention of adopting a 'Know-Nothing' state. I suspect Erickson had them so deeply in trance that there was no other alternative available.

He contends that this open and receptive state directly leads to uptake of the internal patterning of the other, 'using the ability to filter out anything which is not in front of you'. This emergent awareness then manifests itself as meta-cognition to the point that what had been unconscious incompetence has moved to unconscious competence, ready for the coding phase Stage 4.

As a result of his Metaphors workshop I was inspired to travel to Bali for my Master Practitioner training, working with Judy Delozier. This meant that New Code became well established in my DNA. Bali, the land of trance, was just the place to practise the processes of deep second positioning and unconscious uptake. We had been lent a full gamelan orchestra with their wonderful range of gongs, metal, wood bar instruments, and drums. We were asked to choose our instrument. In the rush I ended up with a tiny insignificant single gong that was lost in amongst the really flashy large bar instruments (like mini-xylophones). We were then asked to second position the player of our instrument in the proper orchestra, to gain insight into the relationship between player and instrument. And finally I became my instrument. Only then did I realise that I was the heartbeat of them all.

The mantra throughout this magnificent training was 'do not try to make known the unknown.'

Buoyed up with my success with the gong, I took my intuitive modelling skills to a cremation. I opted to model the grieving wife. I was dressed in Balinese finery, and to my eyes looked pretty ridiculous, protected only by an umbrella to ward off the intense midday sun. I positioned myself close to the bereaved family without wanting to intrude. Unfortunately I didn't take context into account. For close on two hours rivers of sweat would slough off my modelling state, whilst my exemplar would send curious glances in my direction – along with the rest of the village – from the cool shade of her awning. I gained no insight into the personal effect of a Balinese cremation on the loved ones. I began to suspect there was more to this unconscious uptake than I had realised.

I suspect that Grinder could take exception to being included alongside the others within this chapter, or even this book. He might argue that everything outside his practice falls outside NLP. As he firmly stated in our encounter: 'I invented NLP. I am allowed to call it what I like. Let them call theirs something else.'

Yet curiously, memories and perceptions differ. Pucelik at the 2013 UK NLP Conference talked about the hours they would spend pouring over their recordings of those sessions with Erickson, and Gilligan would talk about having them blasting through the sound system of the house he and Pucelik shared. At their Wednesday evening sessions the students would try out all the tasks they were set by Bandler and Grinder, to find out what worked.

Whatever the story, Unconscious Uptake has its place in the range of modelling methodologies on offer, and forms part of the overall practice of New Code NLP.

Since we don't seem to have access to models produced in the last twenty years, or any case studies, we can't test out the actual outcomes of this process. Both Grinder's and Bostic St Clair's websites are particularly sparse unlike those of his fellow modellers, without papers, blogs, materials, or eBooks, and my own direct enquiries have met with no success.

The Approach

Fundamentally the approach is split into five distinct stages:

1   **Identification of an appropriate model:** or as I prefer to describe the source of the information, the exemplar.

2   **Unconscious uptake of the exemplar's patterning:** this is a key state and central to the process. It involves embracing the full movement involved, refining the steps later only after own physiology can replicate the behaviour. This ability of unconscious uptake is key, and unique to this approach.

3   **Systematic deployment of the patterning:** this phase requires practising results of uptake until you can perform the skill at the same level as the model in approximately the same time frame.

4   **Codify the patterning:** only at this stage do you begin to apply any cognition to the new behaviour emergent within you, integrating your own personal experience with that encountered from within your exemplar.

5   **Testing the model:** now you find out if the coded model works efficiently and effectively. Elegance can come later.

Criteria of Success

Grinder offers very useful criteria of success, which lets the modeller know when they are ready to exit their modelling.

The modeller needs to be able to:

1   **Provide the elements of the pattern:** [model], in sensory specific language, and their required sequencing.

Grinder seems to interchange the words Pattern, Model, Format, and Technique.

2   **Describe the anticipated outcome:** of the pattern [model], again in sensory specific language.

This is where Grinder demands disciplined sensory acuity and calibration, firstly of the effects gained by the exemplar, and secondly the effects gained by the modeller en route to perfecting a description of the pattern. He requires that the modeller is rigorous in achieving a similar standard of performance within the same time period as that of the exemplar.

3   **Know when to select one pattern over another:** in response to the end user's reaction.

Grinder asks:

> Under what specific circumstances/conditions does the genius/exemplar elect to use pattern X as opposed to pattern Y? If the modeller can provide an answer, it is clear the modeller has achieved a meta awareness of the far wider system of operation and is able to work flexibly and with informed creativity as opposed to a linear robotic approach.

I totally agree with this, which is why I support the Gordon/Dawes's requirement of seeking secondary strategies.

The Process

My experiences of Unconscious Uptake have been challenging. I have been very fortunate to be offered the opportunity to learn dances culturally very different to my own. In Bali we had the most beautiful size 8 dancer Cordata Ratih as a teacher. By this time we had been exposed to quite a lot of dancing displays, so for the first and second class I entered into the spirit of things and felt quite good about the Balinese muse that had taken over my body, as my arms and hands and hips seem to be going in the right directions. But by the third self-consciousness hit. I saw this westerner, looking ridiculous in the sarong, stomping through the beauty that Ratih offered. My body seized and I left.

Then in Santa Cruz, I joined the lively class of African Dancing led by Ta Titos Sompa. This time I followed a magnificent, sumptuous, size 16 black woman. As I let my wobbly bits wobble I was right there, until once more I became self-conscious about how ridiculous I looked and departed.

By the time I was at a Tad James Huna training, in Hawaii, and experiencing Hula dancing, I had learnt that I was asking too much of myself to replicate in six hours what these teachers had begun to learn in their mother's womb. All I could ask of myself was to enjoy myself, enter gladly into the 'Know-Nothing' world and go with what happens. Etua, our lovely, enormous and dainty teacher, even asked if I had done this before! If I had had more exposure, with this attitude, I believe I would have learnt so much more.

To understand the process of Unconscious Uptake, you need to understand what Grinder calls the 'Know-Nothing' state. Whilst he concedes that it is impossible to actually know nothing, what we do know needs to be banished from our awareness, and fail to interrupt our openness to absorb the information available from the exemplar.

Grinder first of all requires that we suspend access to our internal maps, and loosen our hold on our own identity. From his descriptions, 'make internal arrangements' and 'subordinate your map', it appears that easy and familiar access to one's unconscious mind is a prerequisite.

1   **Tracker state:** Grinder describes a Tracker State where there is no excess tension. The minute you are aware that you have tensed say facial muscles, shoulders, hands, hips, then you acknowledge the feedback and relax. Internal dialogue is banished or vanquished by overriding it

through creating the metaphor, for example, 'a blanket of snow' to quieten it. And finally eyes remain relaxed with wide peripheral vision, similar to the physiology used in 'seeing' 3D pictures or for speed-reading.

Fundamentally, the conscious mind needs to be sufficiently distracted to allow open connection to the unconscious mind. To develop awareness of this state, he provides various exercises. The Alphabet Game involves the conscious mind being occupied by reading out loud letters of the alphabet whilst performing a set physical movement, leaving the unconscious mind free to zone out and open up.

A similar route to this state can be accessed through rapid ball throwing and catching, as a means of distracting the conscious mind, starting with one and then building up to several balls at one time. Tasks are then added to the process so the conscious mind becomes increasingly loaded. Pretty quickly you let go of the need to catch the ball, and surprise yourself to find that your hand and ball have connected with no conscious bidding. This is very similar to the Zone state favoured by athletes.

Delozier has an exercise where two people sit opposite each other. A is tasked to think of three discrete events and fully associate into them. For each event, B is invited to place his or her hands on A's knees, and after some time come up with a suggestion of the particular scenario. It is surprising the level of accuracy from only a couple of minutes' contact.

There is also the exercise for detecting the Intention to Move, where A holds a £5 note between thumb and forefinger and lets it drop. B is tasked to catch it. The more B is in Tracker State, as opposed to 'trying hard', the greater the success rate.

Given that old habits die hard, and we are culturally wired to avoid failure, and bedevilled with damning internal dialogue, I suspect that significant amounts of time need to be given developing this state to the point that it can be entered into at will and exited, also at will.

2   **Rapport:** rapport is essential for success. Grinder describes this as the relationship between the unconscious mind of the exemplar and that of the modeller. The process starts off from observing consciously and responding in kind until the differences in the energies between both parties reduce and finally merge, resulting in sympathetic movement. For him rapport starts through:

- Breathing, which links to
- Physiology, and so to
- State and therefore
- Behaviour.

He stresses the importance of registering micro muscle movement, which does require high sensory acuity – through peripheral vision, because it belies internal processing. By matching it, you have a gateway into the system of the other.

3   **Playfulness:** echoing how a child experiences the world through a sense of playful exploration, Grinder advocates the importance of a playful spirit. Certainly, Gilligan mentions frequently how much fun and laughter they all experienced in the early days of experimentation and discovery.

Ecology

The possible danger or fear a modeller might have, when entering into the neurology of another, is the likelihood of taking on undesirable elements – for example, in the case of Erickson, his disability. Therefore, arrangements need to be made internally at an unconscious level only to filter those elements that are relevant to the set outcome.

This is relatively easy where the issues are obvious, as in Erickson's case. But it may be that only during the exploration will you discover some really conflicting values, or a mindset, which are totally incompatible with your identity.

To counteract this possible danger, it is useful to establish Life Lines. Although not covered in Grinder's presentation, in Bali with Delozier, we were introduced to the notion of pre-setting strategies for bringing us back fully into self.

These could be required if we had a fixed time allocated to the session and we didn't want to overrun, or if we felt concerned for our own wellbeing, or if there was a threat in our physical environment. Before committing to the endeavour, you are invited to identify a specific signal – the image of a loved one, a particular song, a physical sensation – and arrange with your unconscious mind to alert you should you need to break out of your deep trance state. If there were a time issue, then your time in the state would be pre-set.

Applications

We are *all* able to apply Unconscious Uptake as a means of learning. Some are more susceptible than others. Some people can pick up accents after a short exposure. Others find themselves moving in a particular way after being in the company with someone they admire, or see on TV. There was no conscious desire to emulate, or actively set about practising the accent, gesture or walk. This learning just manifests itself spontaneously, unbidden.

When David Grove eventually agreed to let Lawley and Tompkins model his process, he expressly stated that he didn't want to know what they were doing, nor did he want to be interviewed. So the pair would sit behind him, out of sight, whilst he worked with clients. They would seek unconscious uptake through deep second position and absorbing his 'energies', then comparing experiences and insights afterwards. They combined this approach with the cognitive route of copious notes and transcriptions of taped session after taped session.

Tompkins tells an interesting story. There is a training company whose directors are adherents of Grinder's approach. This is the methodology they champion with their learners. On three occasions, they have invited Lawley and Tompkins to demonstrate the process of Symbolic Modelling, working individually with each of the Master Practitioner participants, often more than once, in a 'goldfish bowl' set up.

The watching students are directed to enter into the Unconscious Uptake state and connect with the inner patterning of Lawley and Tompkins, with the intention of being able to replicate the behaviour of these two excellent modellers. Lawley and Tompkins were not allowed to offer any coding at all, until the very last session.

By day four, overall, the participants did get a sense of the whole process and how it flowed. This experience has led Lawley and Tompkins to introduce more demonstrations and pre-course video study as a result.

However, the participants did not get the exact working of the precise questions, nor the syntax, nor did they identify specific patterns like the PRO Model (see Symbolic Modelling). They were unable to code distinctions that make for quality work, and so would unwittingly go away with a significantly diluted description – *without being aware of their deficiencies.* When the 'correct' coding was offered on the afternoon of the fourth day, it was often too late to shift some of the generalisations that had taken hold.

Coding

Grinder's approach requires there to be two descriptions of the identified behaviour – that of the exemplar and then that of the modeller. It is the modeller's description that is used for subsequent coding, with no further reference to the exemplar. So, hopefully, the modeller has achieved the desired level of performance to meet his or her outcomes. Coding, by which he means conscious labelling, only takes place once these criteria have been met.

He argues that by unpacking what has become the modeller's internal organisation, and through a process of subtraction, the modeller winnows away the chaff of unnecessary detail to reveal the key essentials that generate the behaviour. This process requires rigorous testing and accountable calibration.

Unfortunately, I can't find practical evidence of this process of constructing a model that is congruent and enduring. *In Whispering In The Wind,* Part III, Grinder gives a lot of theoretical consideration to the concept of logical levels, logical types and chunking, amongst other things. However he doesn't seem to provide a specific methodology for selecting the final elements for a pattern/model, nor for its ultimate construction.

Required Conditions

In my opinion, should you choose to adopt Grinder's take on modelling and his teaching of his methodology, some points have to be given serious consideration. Given the possible act of faith involved in handing yourself over to another's neurology, I am suggesting the following conditions are necessary for successful conscious application of the state of unconscious uptake. However, when you move onto Steve Gilligan's work in the next section, because of the approach he takes, you will find that some of these suggestions become irrelevant.

1   **Be strongly motivated to emulate the exemplar:** you are about to let go of who you are and enter into the realms of another's psyche, freely and without fear. You are asking yourself to commit, for a period of time, to disappearing and trusting that all will be well. So the exemplar you choose needs to be an individual that you are willing and eager to visit at a very deep level of intimacy.

2   **Be shielded from any unecological aspects of the exemplar:** whilst you are drawn to particular aspects of your exemplar, there may be undesirable aspects that are independent of the sought behaviour. As there was with Erickson, there may be a disability, or there may be an unsavoury side to the individual whilst he or she is being excellent in a different area. It might be that you have set up lifelines in advance, to bring you out should you feel threatened.

3   **Be in a sufficiently deep trance:** you need to be oblivious of any self-conscious awareness or failure or poor performance, which comes from holding onto your ego identity state. This requires you to enter into a deep trance, self-imposed, which in turn requires you to have significant experience of enabling this. To be effective, you need to be very familiar and conversant with the

conscious/unconscious interface. It is likely that you will have established some powerful anchors that can be guaranteed to trigger this state.

4   **Have full commitment to take on the new sphere of identity:** any incongruence you may have will impede full absorption, and bring you out of your state. Unconscious Uptake is a holistic approach and requires full-bodied acquisition of the behaviour, not selective elements from within. If this happens then you need to revisit issues you may have about ecology, trust your unconscious mind to protect you, and deepen your trance.

Concerns

For me, Grinder's methodology as he presents it raises several issues.

- I totally subscribe to the idea of returning to the 'Know-Nothing' state of a baby, free from judgment within the process of learning. Unfortunately adults are riddled with programmes regarding failure and other injunctions, and unless these limitations are addressed or a means of suppressing their effects is employed, the approach is unlikely to be successful.

- There is some ambiguity concerning his 'Know-Nothing' state. On the one hand he says *'all my acquired generalisations, all previous models, act as a filter that impedes natural uptake.'* (Training Workshop 2005). Yet he says in the video of his mountaineering experience (see YouTube) 'a lot of the fundamental programmes for climbing vertical rocks are there to be subordinated to [the mountaineer exemplar].'

  On the one hand, it is important to act as if you know nothing, and on the other hand you need to integrate your existing learning and knowledge.

- Grinder discounts the inclusion of content in the modelling process, and so dismisses the validity of any other methodology. He refuses to accept that there could be a place for them.

  If, and it is an 'if', the purpose of modelling is to produce a model which can then be acquired by a third party, quickly and effectively, then Grinder's 'first principles' approach is similar to going to a golf professional who has a good reputation for correcting, for example, putting. The golf pro says, 'Yes I could coach you, but go off and spend three months following Tiger Woods, and come back and show me what you've learned to do.' Or, 'Stand there and watch what I do and I am not going to tell you how I'm doing it.' What is the point of the Coach having already coded an excellent strategy?

  Grinder seems to be suggesting that, no matter how many new models within modelling have been coded, the modeller always needs to go back to the drawing board each time.

- This approach may appear to be 'all smoke and mirrors' to the more cognitive learner. Doubters would benefit from the availability of written up evidence, or clear demonstrations illustrating the effectiveness of this approach. It is a shame that this bona fide approach is not better served.

- I am with Grinder on the need to have rigour with our tradecraft. I question, however, the demanding universal requirement of achieving the same standard of performance. To my mind, much is dependent on the needs of the identified end user. The requirement that the modeller achieves the same level of performance in the same time period might explain why few models have been published.

- The approach seems to centre on behavioural replication, which leads to the identification of strategies, and subsequently with the potential to construct product sequential models as opposed to any process or tabular models. The cognitive functions deployed by the exemplar can only be intuited, with the danger of mind-reading being taken as fact.

- My greatest concern is that students and adherents can believe they have obtained the patterning, through this methodology, when they haven't. Obviously they will have something, even something new to them and something useful, but this is not the full working of the exemplar. Grinder talks about the importance of calibration but, where the modeller is determined to delete evidence of difference in performance, the scope for misperceptions running riot is endless.

Finally

Grinder's references mainly relate to the work of intuitively modelling some forty years ago, with nothing to show us since then. Bill O' Hanlon who knew Erickson well, tells of Erickson's comment: 'Bandler and Grinder thought they got my techniques in a nutshell. What they got was the shell.'

I can understand some of Grinder's frustrations. He was a maverick pioneer, loving risk and breaking the rules. He thrived on not knowing, ambiguity and vagueness. With the proliferation of models and prescribed modelling methodologies of today, the need for that pioneering, tracking experience, which he instinctively adopted, has lessened. Arguably from his perspective, modelling has become sanitised – no longer the domain of adventuring explorers. It is now within the realm of tourists. But who is to say that this is something to lament? If new learning to make a difference is the goal, does the method of how we do it really matter?

Deep Trance Identification

Steve Gilligan

Steve Gilligan was an early student of both Gregory Bateson and Grinder, at University of California in 1974. He became part of the evening study groups established by Bandler and Grinder during their early modelling days. These 12-15 students would pioneer exploration of the emerging materials and thinking, working with the Meta Model and exploring personal change.

He then became fascinated with 'the world without maps', discovering learning at an unconscious level. By this time, Bandler and Grinder had been to visit Erickson, on Bateson's suggestion. They came back full of new language patterns and recordings, with a wonderment at a totally different approach, rich in metaphor and stories. The evening study groups became immersed in trance and Gilligan's 'cosmic egg cracked open'. All of this proved to be profoundly meaningful for a 19-year-old, and he set about finding out all he could about trance and hypnosis.

This led him to the work of Russian psychologist Raikov who described 'Deep Trance Identification' where an individual could take on the attributes of another whilst in trance. It naturally followed that he would want to attain such identification with Erickson.

He researched the subject of trance widely, practised and experimented extensively with the language patterns. He even had recordings of Erickson's voice playing throughout the house. A formative year followed, giving rise to the stories of being wheelchair-bound, gathering profound experiences of shifting from personal boundaries of constructed identity, and moving into a generative space.

In 1977 he left the NLP stable to branch out on his own, getting his PhD in Psychology at Stanford University. Whilst he loosened his ties with the Santa Cruz community, he continued his relationship with Erickson until Erickson's death in 1980. In 1987 he wrote *Therapeutic Trances – The Cooperation Principle in Ericksonian Hypnosis* as well as working with Jeff Zeig, Director of The Milton H Erickson Foundation, on co editing *Brief Therapy: Myths, Methods, Metaphors* (1999), and *Therapeutic Conversations* with Reese Price (1980). By this time he was a committed student of martial arts and aikido, and a follower of eastern philosophy. Combining philosophical understanding and meditative practices with his ever deepening relationship with the vastness of the unconscious mind, he pursued his ground breaking work into self relations and generative self, finally writing *The Courage to Love: Principles and Practices of Self-relations Psychotherapy* (1997), a unique approach to therapy not only based on full acceptance and sponsorship of all elements operating within the exemplar's system, but also with high importance placed on the state and attention of the therapist.

After twenty years working independently, he connected up once more with Robert Dilts and together they further developed the notion of sponsorship and field mind, co writing *The Hero's Journey* (2009).

We were delighted to sponsor him five times at The Northern School of NLP and are proud to call him a friend. His worldwide reputation as a teacher is well deserved. He leaves all his students with a feeling of having gained deep personal attention and consistently provides opportunity for profound change. Each year he runs his famous Trance Camps in San Diego which is a mecca for anyone wanting to learn more about the workings of the unconscious mind, and more specifically their own! He is tremendously supportive, and one of the most punctilious email responders, irrespective of where he is in the world.

Much of the following material here has resulted from correspondence with Gilligan, specifically focussing on the activity of modelling, as well as drawing from references in his workshops and handouts on therapeutic trance. He would not say that he is a modeller in the NLP sense, but he has spent his entire professional life seeking to understand the inner patterning of others to support their wellbeing.

Background

Given that reality and identity are personal constructs, it is easy to see how Gilligan regards hypnotic induction as being: 'A set of communications that de-frames or dissolves fixed maps, so allowing new experiences to emerge unhindered by the map bias.'

At the same time, Gilligan embraces the Buddhist concept of 'original mind' that is both 'empty' of form and distinction but luminescent, a pulsating quantum field of subtle light. 'Creative consciousness' can be 'constructed' or 'created' through an observing consciousness.

His early experiences of deep trance identification with Erickson led him to make profound discoveries, which directly contributed to the early development of the Milton Model approach.

- The importance of internal stillness, so that the movements of unconscious awareness can be heard. Erickson, whilst so sharp and witty, and displaying a rapier-like mind, was absolutely quiet on the inside.

- Everybody is already in deep trance. There is no need for any inductions.

- The creative unconscious is already fully active and absorbed.

- Our lives are lived within the rigid boundaries of arbitrary 'identification trances', where we believe the 'truths' tightly held within our maps.

- It is possible to step out of these identification trances, into others, and live from a freer generative space.

He goes on to say:

> It has always been dear to me that trance, when used properly (i.e., relationally and creatively), is a means to deconstruct and reconstruct realities that aren't working. In other words, they are 'experiments in how consciousness creates reality'.

> Given that reality and identity are constructed, it follows that 'the mind', or the two minds – conscious and unconscious – should not be regarded in the singular. Being constructions (though some with hundreds of years in the making), there are always alternate constructions. When Erickson gave primary emphasis to the principle that 'each person's reality is unique,' it is a way of saying that each person is modelling the world in unique ways.

> The interesting challenge for a practitioner of 'map transformation,' then, is the study of how such filters are constructed, deconstructed, and reconstructed ... with special attention of how to apply these understandings to each unique situation.

And in answer to my query as to the role of drugs in the 70s to assist unconscious uptake, he is clear that the only requirement to access the state is 'an experiential willingness to let go of one's conditioned 'self', move into the open space of the creative unconscious, and step into another reality.'

That's all!

The Approach

Generative trance state

Gilligan in his thoroughness has coded how to enter this state. For him 'the trick is to be in the creative consciousness of the territory without "neuromuscularly locking" into any fixed thought or representation about it.'

When I was first introduced to this in 2000, I realised that here was the first clear description of how to gain the modelling state. He offers that this process of Generative Connection allows for the ability to hold multiple attention.

His sensory specific instructions provide us with a step-by-step strategy, and as NLPers we can't ask for more than that.

1   **Centering:** this enables you to open the Somatic Mind. It involves:
    - *Relaxation:* physically, mentally and emotionally, opening to the possibility of becoming even more relaxed
    - *Opening yourself to possibilities:* the energy emerging from your 'belly' mind and expanding out to include the other person and the space in between
    - *Absorption and Detachment:* a sense of being connected with the other whilst being clearly separate.

2 **Setting intention:** this enables you to open the Cognitive Mind. It involves:
  • *Creative Acceptance:* acknowledge what is present and what is not present
  • *Letting Go:* breathing out any unuseful thoughts and states
  • *Acknowledge Intention:* for self and for other person.

3 **Inviting resources:** This enables you to open the Field Mind. It involves:
  • *Dynamic Field:* bringing in awareness of family, friends, ancestors
  • *Unconditional Awareness:* the person you are here to be
  • *Nurturing Energy:* the sense of universal acceptance and support offered to you.

Deep trance identification (DTI)

This process requires existing knowledge and experience of Gilligan's coding of trance: Field of Possibilities, Spirit of Being. It is offered in the second week of Gilligan's Trance Camp, and participants will be well and truly 'cooked' by then.

1 Establish a centred trance state and perform an ecology process with respect to the identified 'identification being' [exemplar].

2 Deepen generative trance and establish a safe place within 'Field of Possibilities'.

3 Let go personal 'sphere of identity' and allow identification spirit of being new 'Sphere of Identity' to guide you.

4 Open your eyes and connect and communicate with others in the room as identification spirit.

5 Return to personal 'Sphere of Identity' and integrate the gifts given from identification being.

6 Future pace and notice continued integration and new responses.

7 Thank spirit, review learnings and simple vows, and reorient.

Applications

All Gilligan's focus is in the field of therapy and personal wellbeing, into which he applies his modelling strategies. The production of models and the devising a formal modelling methodology is of no concern to him.

Yet his profound experiences with deep trance identification with Erickson and his learning gained from working with clients over the years have led him to devise many models centred round how to think about dysfunction (my word) and how to approach an exemplar's identification trance holistically. Three Minds, Sponsorship and Identified Self are some examples.

As a trainer, he has demonstrated the discipline to find a coded route that can enable access, experience, and understanding of the effects he wants created within his students. He has also developed language that approximates the experiences at each stage: Relational Field Mind, Generative Trance, Creative Unconsciousness, and Field of Possibilities.

Any serious therapist would do well to learn from him. He is a constructivist to the core of his being, and his conviction in the strength of spirit resides in everything he thinks and does.

I asked him what his thoughts were about *consciously* adopting Unconscious Uptake as a preferred modelling methodology. His reply:

> When we proceed predominantly with 'conscious modelling', we are constrained by our unconscious adherence to certain values. The value is that this gives us stability and reliability; the down side is that it can be unduly restrictive, relegating us to 'rearranging the chairs on the Titanic.' So when we really want to learn something totally new, that we didn't realise even existed, 'unconscious modelling' is a good starting point.

Interesting differences with Grinder's thinking, namely we need to have a foundation set of skills in place already. It might be that Grinder still relates more to activities and skills, whilst Gilligan may be more oriented towards accessing beliefs and values, which encapsulate identity and require no motor muscular ability.

Ecology

Gilligan's take on the possible danger of absorbing unwanted attributes alongside the desired ones is different from Grinder's. He doesn't live in a world of threat and fear, which he says reflects 'a core identification with an ego identity' – the main obstacle to deeply generative exploration.

> The important thing is to first let go of your constructed identity, realigning with some deeper presence that is not fixed in form. When one is capable of doing this, nothing is really 'sticking' because your identity is not at a content level.

> In generative states, all the patterning is subtle awareness, so it's swishing through the field, not contained or located in any fixed way. Again, this is to me one of the great things that truly generative trance (and its many cousins) mention. A clear parallel would be to ask an artist what the dangers would be if he/she opened deeply to the creative patterns of another artist. I think they would smile …

> Of course, there are concerns; I'm just saying that if they are taken as primary foci, nothing really interesting will happen. Ultimately, you do need to create some reasonably stable social self to house these generative understandings in, but it should be regarded as of secondary importance.

Requiring a 'reasonably stable social self' may be a tall order. If there is any question about the stability of the modeller, then close supervision is required.

Coding

This is not an area of concern for Gilligan in terms of using the identification of other for the production of digitised models. Obviously if the modeller has gained an internal description of the exemplar's patterns, then the modeller has the potential to further refine the experience into a coded description. Certainly the modeller can identify differences from their previous modus operando and code from there.

Concerns

I have not experienced his Deep Trance Identification process – yet – so I'm not in the position to evaluate it. In fact it wasn't until recently that I fully considered his practice to be a modelling methodology. However, I have no doubt that the training and the process is highly ethical, congruent and code congruently delivered. I have always felt totally safe in Gilligan's relational field and look forward to adding to my previous highly positive experiences.

Finally

When Gilligan was learning from Grinder and Bandler, much of the learning was learning without maps – unconscious learning. He shares Grinder's concerns that this unconscious learning element has become lost in the production of models and coded methodologies.

Gilligan sets value in both. He profoundly embraces the generative world of trance – in fact he seems to have taken up residence in this space! Yet his rigour and his desire to share his learning has resulted in him coding very simple, clearly explained procedures which progressively enable his learners to enter the profound altered states productively.

I don't think people within the NLP world have much of an idea of just what an enormous contribution Gilligan has brought to NLP. Much of the approach in NLP II Next Generation is based on his developed thinking of Sponsorship, Relational Field and Centering. And we could do with much more.

He is a quiet leader, rising above the differences held within the global NLP community, probably *because* he took a different route.

Somatic Modelling

Judith Delozier

Judy Delozier is an Oklahoma cowgirl at heart, full of life, funny, irreverent, and what you see is what you get. She is the one person I have met who appears to be totally devoid of ego. She is utterly approachable and makes a point of defusing much of the heady awe that comes her way.

Not for her the © or ® or the ™'s, and her response to copyright is 'Make sure you copy it right!' She has no need for billings, makes no demands to be credited; she has no desire to delve into academic niceties; nor does she choose to champion her valuable contribution to the field of NLP in books or on the internet waves. Her 'apparent' lack of intellectual rigour and her lighthearted delivery attracts comments of 'flakiness' from more erudite quarters – more fool them in my opinion!

Instead she is content to work through quiet collaboration and allow the other to gain top billing. Her grounded and practical personality serves to hold the realms of creative fantasy in check, as she processes all thought through her body to check for its congruence and ecology.

First married to Frank Pucelik, it was the twenty years with John Grinder that led to the development of New Code NLP, written up in *Turtles All the Way Down*. A dancer, Delozier introduced the vital component of physiology into the realms of NLP and the importance of state and personal editing. Her background in cultural anthropology fuels her understanding of multiple perspectives and systems.

She subsequently teamed up with Robert Dilts and Todd Epstein at NLP University, whilst also sharing the vision of Anne Entus and initiating the fantastic NLP trainings in Bali, which Anne continued for about six years. After Epstein's untimely death, she and Dilts continued their summer trainings whilst independently jetting around the world, providing international traininings.

Dilts and Delozier set about the mammoth task of compiling the *NLP Encyclopedia* – the first port of call, I'd say, for any NLP query – and in 2000 this was finally published. Quite an extraordinary feat! We are proud owners of the two hardback volumes personally signed by both. Some would argue that the work is not comprehensive and that only those aligned with NLPU are included. But few could discount the incredible contribution this piece of work makes. Certainly no one else in the field would take on the responsibility of making a similar contribution to our legacy.

With Dilts, Delozier began to formalise some of her thinking and experience of the nature of body as a container of the deep structures of experience – the connection between mind and body, the actual physical neural and linguistic expressions, the integration of the spiritual, mental, emotional and physical systems. Through their work, the understanding of Somatic Syntax and Somatic Modelling emerged, finally finding its way formally into print in *NLP II – The Next Generation* (2010).

I have been blessed with Judy Delozier's sponsorship. I learnt from her in Bali and Santa Cruz, and she certificated me as an NLP Trainer. She was the first to support our first Master Practitioner as a Guest Trainer and, happily, returned on several occasions subsequently. Her brand of simplicity is infectious, and lightened my own potential for earnestness! I am deeply indebted to her for setting my NLP compass. I am so glad my imprinting came from someone who holds integrity lightly and tightly.

Background

Somatic expression first registered on the NLP radar with the introduction of Virginia Satir's four postures – Blamer, Placator, Super Reasonable and Irrelevant – each with their own physiologies and resulting behaviours and verbal patterns. Taking on a specific posture would result in altered behaviour.

Identifying the physiology then connection with such phenomena to language, matching physical sensations caused by emotional disquiet with common phrases – 'gut reaction', 'broken hearted', 'sick to the pit of my stomach', 'flesh creeping', 'frozen inside'.

Eugene Gendlin (1978) described a 'felt sense' – where a problem would have a physical expression totally independent and different in construction to the emotions arising from it. He found that clients who were attuned to this physical expression were more successful at achieving change, than those operating cognitively.

It turns out that we have a variety of secondary brains in our body, through the evidence of high concentrations of neurons and neurotransmitters – around our stomach area, our heart, our feet, our hands. In fact our hands have the greatest number of neural connections to the cortex and take up the greatest surface area there, more than any other part of the body. The area around our stomach is reckoned to be as neurally complex as a cat's brain, operating independently of our brain's activity. This corresponds to Gilligan's thinking about the Somatic Mind.

This all serves to explain what Delozier knew very early on through her experiences of dance and studies of the Alexander Technique. An actor, Frederick Alexander in the 1890s, discovered that he was damaging his voice by the way he was holding his head. He went on to explore the effects of posture on health and wellbeing.

The importance of physiology was acknowledged by Delozier and Grinder in the development of New Code (1987): shifting physiology to change state; personal editing using a desired physiology to drive and displace a state; and discovering internal attention of another through *Walking-in-the-Shoes* process.

Delozier continued to explore the significance of movement and body description as a means of reaching deep structure without the editing by deletions, distortions and generalisations, generated by verbal language. She profoundly subscribes to the New Guinea proverb – 'Knowledge is only rumour until you get it in the muscle.'

> I was teaching a hypnosis certification with Susan Branch around 1992, in upstate New York. I always thought as Alexander did, that the body (or somatic mind) is what people refer to as the unconscious mind. While one of the participants was in a trance I suggested that he allow his body to express each of the states of the SCORE model. It was an amazing unfolding of a timeline with only a physical manifestation.

> I appreciated that the body could problem solve, has memory, and is the 'pattern that connects'; that the body holds the threads of connection, and the web of meanings and can if given space and permission bring movement to life.

It wasn't until 1993 when Delozier began to work formally with the body's ability to reveal the deep structures of patterning through movement alone. Through collaboration with Dilts, they developed the concept of Somatic Syntax that forms the basis of Somatic Modelling. They explored the correlation between the sequence, or syntax, of movement and levels of wellbeing and the effects on resequencing or altering the somatic expression of a problem to generate solution.

> When I mentioned the dancing SCORE to Robert, he was very curious and liked the idea. We talked about taking a state to the edge through the changing of the somatic expression and notice when you have found the edge; go to the space between that movement and the next expression. In other words, go into the unconscious, and let a new awareness emerge.

> The somatic expression was certainly a banner that I carried. Robert and I named the idea, Somatic Syntax during one of the NLPU classes.

Delozier readily recognises there is compatibility in the maps held by herself, Dilts, Gilligan and also Charlie Badenhop, a long established NLP Trainer and Ericksonian Hypnotherapist and Aikido Master, working in Japan. Finally and simply put, she offers:

> The body is a much purer form of communication than the secondary representation of language, since language talks about the experience while it's the body that has the experience. Our body is our primary modelling tool.

Types of Movement

Understandably Delozier is not predisposed to classifying movement. Echoing Isadora Duncan's: 'If I could tell you I wouldn't have to dance it!', she leaves the coding of her practice to others.

In my experience, the exemplar is really keen to oblige and be helpful, especially if they are being asked to perform in a way that is a bit alien to them. Unfortunately, this can lead to them responding consciously and 'making up' movements to please you. You need to be able to distinguish between what's authentic and what is merely sociable compliance.

As a result, I have coded four different types of movement, which can help the modeller navigate through the various non-verbal gestures they are offered, and so encourage the Deep Structure Movement on which Somatic Modelling is based.

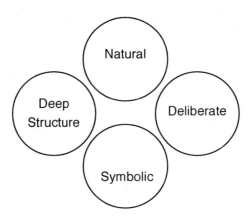

Types of Movement – Burgess 2012

1   **Natural movement:** Serge Kahili King, a specialist in the Polynesian philosophy of Huna, makes the distinction between the conscious and unconscious mind: the conscious mind sets the direction – 'I want to lift this cup.' – and the unconscious mind conducts all the actions required to perform the task, to deliver the desired outcome.

From the minute we wake to the minute we fall sleep, and then onto our nocturnal behaviours, we are a seamless string of analogue movement, most of it without conscious thought, in a fully associated way of being. This is called living. When the movement stops, we've left the room.

The second we place attention onto our natural movement, we run the risk of becoming self-conscious, dissociated and the flow becomes stilted.

2   **Deliberate movement:** this is the term I give to movement that is offered by the exemplar to consciously explain some meaning or give an additional non-verbal description to illustrate what is being said. Someone giving directions uses hand movements to mark out the left and right turns, possible roundabouts and going up or down hills.

It can also be a literal description of an internal representation. For example a woman was being invited to explore a comment about wanting to take the top of her head off and she went through a very calculated enactment of such a process. Her movements were measured and rational as she was acting out her metaphor.

Another occasion where deliberate movement might intrude is during trance. The modeller may be seeking to gain an ideomotor response for a 'Yes' signal, or encouraging arm levitation. You can often spot compliance, when the exemplar feels the need to 'hurry up', and deliberately moves a finger, or raises the arm.

The tell tale sign is usually movement which is too fluid and takes place in real time, as opposed to possibly flickering jerky movement which takes place in its own time. The more in trance the exemplar, the more spontaneous this movement will be, but it takes its own time and makes its own journey, unaided and unscripted.

It is essential that the practitioner is able to detect occurrence of deliberate movement, and not be fooled by it. It is information about the exemplar's intentions and the level of trance being experienced.

3   **Symbolic movement:** we naturally speak with unconscious hand and arm gestures, which indicate internal representations and processing. There may be even unwitting yet significant shifts in posture and gait, as if we are taking on a different persona.

We have all learnt that our unconscious mind can process far more quickly than our lumbering conscious mind, and often our hands will immediately offer a description of an internal experience far more congruently and consistently than our processed words can.

I remember the time when I was at a small workshop with David Grove, where in a 'goldfish bowl' format he was demonstrating his processing which became formalised in Symbolic Modelling. When it came to my first turn, I started to speak and before I had finished the first sentence, his attention went to a 'cutesy little girly' gesture I had unconsciously made, pointing my finger to my cheek. This led me to realise that I had slipped into being a 6-year-old girl; in a very pretty frock, I might add.

These movements are not random or incidental and offer themselves as a way in to deeper exploration. They are a window into internal experiencing and can be useful in and of themselves to be the vehicle for further exploration. Symbolic Modelling uses these physical metaphors to great advantage.

Delozier suggests that these are 'movements trying to get home'.

4   **Deep Structure movement:** to my mind this is the domain of Somatic Modelling. Here all movement seems to be generated from really deeply within, from territory that up until now has not seen the light of day. This movement has not been previously coded and is a totally new formation for the exemplar to behold.

When exemplars give themselves permission to enter into trance and open their channels sufficiently to let the movement grow and manifest itself, this movement is spontaneously conjured. This is when the wisdom of the body speaks, unchecked and unprocessed. This movement is the mouthpiece of the unconscious mind.

Such movement can baffle the exemplar, who has no idea of its origins and no explanation for the shape and form that it takes. Indeed, initially the exemplar can block the manifestation of this information, becoming inhibited by this seeming 'possession' and being self-conscious of what the modeller's response might be. This surprise is the evidence of success.

It is important that the exemplar seeks to put no meaning onto this uncoded language, merely experience its alignment with the invisible truth of the somatic wisdom.

The Approach

So much is down to the modeller's skill of enabling the exemplar to access this hidden action. Delozier has not formally written up the procedures or protocols for facilitating. However she coaches them well in workshops. So, in the absence of existing procedures, I offer the following.

1   **Prepare your state:** you need to be fully congruent about the process to encourage confidence. And you need to be in a relaxed state to set up the light trance required by the exemplar for inner exploration. You yourself need to be centred, open, connected and holding the space of the other.

2   **Offer some explanation:** you describe the various types of movement and indicate that it is the deep structure variety that is desired. This lets the exemplar self correct where possible without

the need for intervention from you.

3   **Provide specific instruction:** the unconscious mind wants to know what information you are specifically looking for, so the frame and scope needs to be offered specifically by the modeller. For example, in Dancing The SCORE, each location is identified and the somatic description for each is called forth. Or in Rossi's Hands the binary parameters are set.

You could ask: 'Let your body describe the mental and emotional process you went through as you prepared for X' which would like as not result in some freeform dance. This would work well for an exemplar very in tune with his or her system. For the average person, such an open instruction would likely be overwhelming. In which case you may ask, 'What were the different states that led up to your decision? Step into each of them and let your body take on the physical expression of this state. Note that the shape you come up with may surprise you.' Once the different 'sculptures' have been established, they then have the potential of being joined up and brought together.

4   **Stand back and observe:** you have no way of knowing how much space the evoked movement will take so your positioning must not in any way compromise the exemplar's ability to move as freely as desired. Also by not crowding the exemplar, you are giving them the space, literally and metaphorically to focus inwardly without distraction. Your energy field is not intruding into theirs. Nor is your will for them to respond chasing away the first stirrings of movement.

From this position you are able to notice patterns of micro movement that you can encourage.

5   **Coach development to fruition:** the exemplar may be satisfied too soon that what they've got is 'It'. This may be because:

•   They are embarrassed, and don't want to become too visible.

•   They have prematurely switched off their channels.

•   Their conscious mind, or inner critic has told them rationally that this is sufficient.

•   They have attempted to provide a contrived deliberate description.

You need to be scanning for signs of incongruence and those micro movements. You may feel there is more energy left in their arms and wonder out loud if they might want them to move higher; you may notice rocking on the ball of the left foot and suggest they might like to step forward; you may notice a general sinking and offer that they might like to bend their knees further, and even further than that; or there is a subtle tilt of the head backwards or forwards, and you encourage them to move it as far as feels right.

By enabling them to take the movement to its possible extremes, you are allowing the exemplar to go beyond their rational limitations and into the realms of surprise and discovery.

6   **Second position the physiology:** take on the movement, accurately yourself, so that you can gain an internal experience of the deep structure of the exemplar. By stepping in you have enlivened it for yourself. This will help you calibrate any shifts in the structure, and detect recurring patterns. You can also gain a sense of the effects of this syntax within your own, neurology and the influence it has on your own ability to perform the given task.

7   **Test the syntax:** amplify or add to the syntax, from within your own system's neurology, to discover if the performance is enhanced. Similarly, reduce or remove elements from the syntax,

until you achieve an optimum expression of the required syntax that generates a consistent experience of the behaviour.

Applications

Business

- One of our students was modelling a line manager who had a reputation for being superb at managing meetings and moving the agenda along, without great posturing or power plays. X had been fortunate to have been given two one hour sessions to interview the manager, not least because the manager herself was intrigued to find out what she did that worked.

  Yet it wasn't until X was able to witness the woman at work, that she detected the 'difference that made the difference', and it was all in the somatic syntax.

  She witnessed the manager sitting at the midpoint side of the table, hands resting motionless on her lap, listening to the contributions of opinion round the table. Once she felt she had heard enough, she took a breath, leant forward and, with her right hand and wrist straight and thumb to the top, about a foot into the table, would make a sweeping movement to the left covering an arc of about 60 degrees. And then she would speak.

  X had us practise the movement. This description facilitates internal calm, dissociated and associated attention, and a moment of decisive punctuation. This short physical description encapsulated all the words that had been written up from the two interviews, simply and succinctly.

- Alternatively, exemplars can be asked to represent, through their physiology, who they are when they address a body of 500 people, or when they comfort the dying, or handle an unruly horse. This somatic expression is unlikely to be the actual physiology the exemplar can be seen holding during the action. Instead it is a description of the inner process that is driving the externally witnessed physiology.

  One student, describing the syntax for tenderness and compassion, could feel the warm glow and bubbling of a lava lamp and moved his cupped hands slowly up and down his centre line.

Therapy

- Somatic Modelling can be used to discover how an individual is experiencing a debilitating emotion or limiting belief, or even physical pain. Generating the somatic syntax of the emotion, belief or pain immediately sponsors it by giving it an opportunity to express itself, as opposed to suppressing it or seeking to destroy it. It also 'names' it, manifesting it and making it known.

- Delozier's trademark application of Somatic Modelling is in the process *Dancing the SCORE*. Here each element of the model is represented through an intuitive physical representation. The technique is designed to develop the Resource element. Yet there can be much to be learned how the exemplar transitions from each element to the next. Where does the movement start? What bit of the body moves first? Powerful metaphors can be evoked: 'I take a deep breath and commit to being different.' 'I turn and put the past behind me.' 'Taking that first step forward and letting go of the immobilisation of that spot made all the difference.'

  Having a somatic representation first and foremost and than consolidating that in language can then become part of the exemplar's self-modelling.

Coaching

- Delozier offers a delightfully simple approach to deal with a particular unwanted pattern. The individual identifies the syntax for the unwanted behaviour. Then just one element of this movement is changed, which then triggers transformation into a very different resourceful somatic pattern. This new pattern is then practised and tested on various situations.

  This can be applied to any pattern that is influencing behaviour. It could be the golfer approaching a bunker shot, an employee entering an appraisal interview, a student settling down to revision. The practised, restructured gesture becomes the anchor to establish the desired filters.

- She further refines this process with the understanding that we will have different somatic syntax for different perceptual positions and through time, for different roles, for different relationships, and for different scenarios, highlighting that somatic modelling can be universally applied, limited only by the imagination of the modeller or therapist.

  This allows us the ability to be really specific regarding our desired responses, and let go of generalisations we have made, which are getting in the way. So a coach could elicit from the exemplar different scenarios where they have felt 'not good enough', yet were able to perform, or were able to perform better than they thought, or were surprised at how well they performed. This could be matched with the present situation. New nuances can be introduced and a firm constructive gesture created.

Associated Applications

Rossi's Hands

Ernest Rossi is a psychologist, chemist, mathematician and co-author with Erickson on Erickson's work. He has been fascinated with the physical working of the brain, in response to therapeutic activity. He has published material on brain plasticity, DNA microarrays, gene expression and many other learned works.

He also has made a specialism based on the Homunculus and the fact that our hands have the greatest number of connections with the cortex. As a great example of therapeutic modelling, rather in the same vein as Visual Squash, he will reduce a problem down to two binary elements. For example, there may be two characters in a dream, or a present self and a desired self, the good me and the bad me, associated me and dissociated me, somatic me and cognitive me, the child me and etc.

Each element is allocated by the individual to one or other of the hands. Placing the hands a foot apart at eye level and focussing at their midpoint, an ideomotor trance develops until both hands make their own spontaneous pathway and then they physically come together at the point of resolution.

Gilligan's Push/Pull

Gilligan has devised a process that follows similar lines, this time addressing a stuck situation matched with the desired one. Rather than allocate them to a hand each, he has the individual identify one movement that sums up the stuck state, and then a separate movement for the desired state. Each are practised separately until they feel right at which point both are run one after the other continuously in a fluid movement. After a period of time a new movement emerges, a combination of both energies and takes hold. This technique is written up in full in *The NLP Cookbook.*

I have taken this process further and the result forms the basis of a fully developed case study of *The Inside Out Process* that I have devised. This is written up at the end of Part 5 – The Results of Modelling.

Coding

Delozier herself has no need to develop the analogue of movement into a coded form. She is not greatly interested in producing digital models.

> NLP is systemic anyway. 'Systemic' means this whole unit of mind. But then when I start to code it, it becomes not so systemic. Right? Because coding is never this whole unit of mind, it is only what consciousness can pull out and say, 'Well, this will represent this, and this will represent that.'

> Coding. That is the paradox. As soon as we code something, is it systemic anymore? At what level do we have to go to in our thinking to maintain the systemic nature of it? For me, there is not any new meaning we discover, rather it is something that we have sort of forgotten and need to recover.

> The question is then, how do we put it back in the body? We look at how the system emerges naturally. We look at how the system punctuates itself naturally. We look at how it goes out of bounds and then re-balances itself naturally. That is holistic, that is systemic. And I think this really is the next challenge for NLP.

An extract from a presentation to The Central London NLP Group, 19 April 1993

However as can be seen in the case study in Part 5 – The Results of Modelling and in the Appendix, it is really easy to generate a model from somatic syntax, one that is highly ecological and honours the exemplar's system. In fact, anyone who has spent months on a modelling project and covered sheets and sheets of paper in their cognitive endeavour might gasp in incredulity at the ease by which a model can be generated through this approach.

Taking up Delozier's concerns about separating the model from the system and the experience, I'm suggesting that there are ways of returning some of the analogue descriptions as part of the acquisition process: see Part 6 – The Formal Acquisition Process.

Ecology

This modelling methodology I believe is very safe for all parties involved.

* The modeller needs to ensure that any replication of the movement is as accurate as possible requiring stringent sensory acuity. Approximations, or worse editing, on the part of the modeller can send a meta message that the exemplar's description is invalid and lead to possible contamination. Certainly such behaviour on the part of the modeller will lessen rapport and reduce credibility.

* Since the modeller sets the focus of attention, this can serve to 'keep the modeller safe', and therefore limit useful exploration. Modellers need to be very aware of their own outcome when they set the focus of attention, to ensure that this is alignment with the exemplar's outcome, or the end user's requirement of the model, as opposed to their own safety. The modeller is seeking to learn and understand. They are at choice with how deeply they associated into the syntax themselves.

* For the exemplar's part, they are working with their own structure, hopefully uncontaminated by the modeller. This may provoke strong emotion and the modeller needs to be ready to hold steadily

such awareness long enough for the information to become available to the exemplar. Should the emotion be too strong, then dissociation and viewing the expression from meta can serve.

Concerns

- The lack of published material on the effects of this modelling methodology has meant that the approach hasn't received the same attention and status as the others in the field.

- Those that favour a more analytical cognitive approach regard somatic modelling as flaky and insubstantial, just because it doesn't come with labels and digitised models.

  Hopefully I have demonstrated that not only is coding possible to generate from somatic syntax, it is infinitely more speedy and possibly more accurate than any cognitive approach could be. It has less structure to travel through.

- It doesn't come with a body of evidence of its effectiveness – either as a modelling methodology to produce models, or to effect change within the therapeutic and coaching fields. This is a bit chicken-and-egg here. Delozier could be well served should one of her many acolytes champion this approach and write up results. I believe it could make for really fascinating reading.

- There may be a misguided belief that somatic modelling only works with those who have a strongly developed kinaesthetic representation system, who are already tuned to calibrating and responding to shifts in internal kinaesthetic submodalities.

- As someone who is predisposed visually, my understanding is that it is less to do with preferred representation system and more to do with developing the permeability of the conscious/ unconscious interface, and the level of receptivity of the perceiver to the messages being received.

- People who are highly cognitive and rational won't respond to this methodology, especially if any non-verbal work is new to them. Inviting them to participate could cause resistance and loss of rapport.

  At the same time, this approach might be what is required to bypass their compulsive cognitions. For such people the modeller needs to establish and test a deep level of rapport so that the exemplar responds to their lead. They will certainly be most surprised by the results and this could be the start of a meaningful conversation they may have with their natural wisdom. What a gift to give!

Finally

Somatic Modelling may remain in the minor league of modelling methodologies, through no fault of its own. I hope this contribution to coding serves to illustrate that this methodology has indeed much to offer the serious practitioner. ('Not too serious!' I hear Delozier cry.) I genuinely believe that it has an enormous contribution to offer the field of modelling, not least because of its rapid access to deep structure, and its undeniable ownership by the exemplar.

However, I doubt that Delozier would thank me for any of this. 'Whatever!' might be her response.

Expressive Methodologies

I had a friend who had terminal lung cancer. She went to the alternative Cancer Treatment Centre in Bristol and was seen by a doctor who gave two days to work in the centre. After she had told her story to him, he invited her to draw it, and he watched her as she did it. Once finished, he then asked if she would like to dance her picture. This was one step too far! Whereupon he came out with the immortal line: 'Would you like me to dance your picture?'

They moved to a large room next door and he danced her picture, stamping away at the point of her mother's illness, curling up at her sadness of her brother's death until the whole picture had been physically expressed and reflected back to her. She said she had never felt so fully heard before. She felt totally affirmed.

These expressive methodologies are based on VAK Models of image, sound and gesture and meet the characteristics of a natural model – see Part 5 – The Results of Modelling.

- *Dance/Movement Modelling:* this approach is akin to Somatic Modelling although used within a wider context.

- *Art Modelling:* this approach divines inner structure visually through external expression in drawing, collages, photographs, painting.

- *Music Modelling:* this approach draws on music and sounds to give expression to inner patterning.

These are methodologies that use the primary representation systems as the vehicle for revealing inner structure. Their place here in the classification is because they connect directly with the unconscious mind, have no requirement for language, have limited requirement for modeller intervention, provide the ability to self model, and can be extrapolated if required to form the basis of a constructed model.

Coming from their own well-developed fields of application, they also come with their own underpinning philosophical perspectives and psychological rationale. However the NLP Modeller can view each approach with a constructivist mind and see representations of that approach as a legitimate description of the subjective experience of the exemplar.

Just because these approaches did not evolve to be modelling methodologies doesn't mean that we should limit our thinking and deprive ourselves of their usefulness. Personally there have been times when I have naturally introduced elements of modelling through art into my therapeutic practice. And I am sure if I was more auditory, I would be encouraging clients to bang drums, radiators, cups and boxes as a means of expressing the way they are structuring their internal organisation.

Dance/Movement Modelling (DMM)

The Background

The first records of dance being used as a form of therapy in the UK date as far back as the 19th century. However Dance/Movement Therapy took hold in the 1940s in the States, pioneered by the choreographer and dancer, Marion Chase. She began to realise the beneficial effects dance had on her students. It is founded on basic principles, namely that:

- Body and mind are inseparable

- Body and mind interact, so that a change in movement will affect total functioning

- Movement reflects personality

- The therapist can influence the process through mirroring the exemplar's movement

- Movement contains a symbolic function and as such can be evidence of unconscious process

- Movement improvisation allows the exemplar to experiment with new ways of being

- Early relationships can be restructured non-verbally through movement

- Mind, body and spirit are united through movement and can generate a sense of wholeness.

Using dance and movement therapeutically has had positive effects on a wide range of disorders and diseases, apart from stress and a lack of balance, extending to working with autism, learning disabilities, visual and hearing impairment, eating disorders, muscular illness, dementia, and depression.

From a modelling perspective, within an identified context of behaviour, or a system of behaviours, the exemplar is free to move as he or she chooses, as the body dictates, possibly connecting with inner rhythms or music, until a 'dance' is identified which depicts the exemplar's internal structure.

As will come through with the other expressive methodologies, there may be sensory synaesthesia, so that movement may incorporate sound, and visual expression may require specific movement.

5 Rhythms

In the 1970s, Gabriel Roth developed the 5 Rhythms practice as a 'soul journey'. Drawing from indigenous traditions, eastern philosophy and the human potential movement, Roth devised a staged process that she maintains connects the energies of the dancer with universal energy accessing unlimited possibilities and potential. Certainly many report feeling invigorated and liberated by the process.

As the name suggests, the whole movement is divided into five stages. Accompanied by drumming, the dancer moves through the expressions of Flow, Staccato, Chaos, Lyrical, and Stillness creating a wave form where chaos is at the point of the wave breaking.

Whilst Roth has coded the process of this liberation into the five stages, the dancer is left to find his or her own expression to the different drum rhythms. They may be offered other stimuli like an image or painting, or their description of a personal experience.

> Remember if you don't do your dance, who will?

> Gabriel Roth

The Approach

Within the therapeutic approach there is a standard Creative Process, following a set procedure: Preparation, Incubation, Illumination and Evaluation. I have taken elements of these and integrated them into this approach:

1 Set up

- The specific area of exploration is clearly stated and understood. The focus may be on desirable or undesirable behaviour, or a system of relationships involving key elements.

- The exemplar needs to feel relaxed and willing to take on this probably unfamiliar means of expression. It may need you to offer some warm-up exercises so that the exemplar gains a real experience of deep structure movement (see the four types of movement in the Somatic Modelling section). It is essential that the exemplar has faith in his or her body's ability to express unbidden deep wisdom.

- You need to ensure that the place you are working in is sufficiently large and physically safe. The exemplar needs to agree to whoever may witness this expression, which includes permission for video recording. You want to ensure that anything that might trigger self-consciousness is reduced to a minimum.

- An overall goal will be set – say a time frame, a destination point, response to a stimulus, a particular task. The modeller only intervenes should the exemplar become endangered.

2 Exploration

- The exemplar knows that there are no constraints on time or on space. The exemplar is free to make any accompanying sounds as appropriate.

- You maintain critical sensory acuity, watchful of any micro-movements that may be usefully expanded – a tightening of the fingers, a tilt on the toes, a loosening of one shoulder. These could be portals into a whole new world of experience and information.

- You are required to deeply second position the dance that is being created, to feel its dynamics and energy flow, to note the emotions the movement evokes, to gain insight into the relationships between the elements, and to register any occurrences that 'bump' with your own physiology. In this process, you will gain some description of the internal structures.

- You need to stay well back and leave the space free for spontaneous movement. Should the exemplar pause, hold that space without any intervention until the movement continues or the exemplar 'comes back into the room.'

- Insight may emerge during the experience for the exemplar – certainly feelings of surprise, concern, joy, sadness may register. Again hold the space for the exemplar, so that exploration can incorporate these responses and continue to its final resolution.

- You may introduce additional sounds, images or words that relate to the behaviour being explored.

3   Reflection

- The exemplar is invited to make any comment regarding his or her experience, either about the movements themselves, or about their own response to these movements. This new learning may be crucial for the final model, or merely for the benefit of the exemplar. This awareness could become a source for further cognitive exploration.

- You can feedback your own experience of the movement. If you notice inconsistencies or incongruences, seek to enquire further.

4   Intervention

- Any further intervention will depend on the purpose of the modelling activity and the needs of the identified end user. If the acquirer is the exemplar, it may be sufficient to have gained new awareness. If, however, there is an identified third party, and a coded model is required, either the exemplar or you can reduce the movement down into its key elements and label these. A formal acquisition process can then be devised – see Part 6 – The Formal Acquisition Process.

Applications

Business

Outdoor activities are legendary team development activities. If the facilitator takes on a modelling perspective, then useful or unuseful patterns of interaction can be identified and labelled, open for restructuring.

Systems of communication can be analysed through physical descriptions from different consumers of the system. Barriers to flow, and elements contributing to this, can be detected, as well as the emotional response to these. It may be that participants are more free to express this in the 'anonymous' form of actions, rather than words.

This dance/movement approach can be directly applied to team building, and exploring the individuals' contribution, to the team output.

- *Lara Ewing:* Lara offered this exercise. An individual starts off making a movement of his or her choice, which is then repeated and repeated. Then the next volunteers and makes a complementary movement of choice. And then the next, until a complex 'machine' is created of continuous inter-related movement, some big, some small, some quick, some slow, some at the heart of the body and some on the periphery. Not only do the individuals learn about themselves from the movement they have intuitively selected but also the impact they are having on the others, and the effects of the others on themselves.

- *Andy Austin:* in his 'Metaphors of Movement', Austin invites the client to take his or her metaphor literally and explore fully the system it embodies: e.g. if a person is in a pit, then he'll encourage them to try to explore the sides of the pit, or find a way out of it.

Coaching/therapy

Again depending on the outcomes of the modelling process, the modeller has the option of offering a 'generative intervention', which can take the exemplar to beyond their current standard of performance, or Remedial Intervention, which provides strategies to enable the exemplar to reach the desired standard.

- *Generative:*

  - The exemplar could identify those areas within the movement where his or her commitment to the process is less strong compared to others. The exemplar could then re-enter the movement driving commitment throughout the full process.

  - Or the exemplar may question the presence of a state which either could be amplified or reduced, and dance the movement accordingly. The exemplar could even introduce a state to add to what is already there.

  - The exemplar could view the movement on a screen and second position those who experience the modelled behaviour, generating new insight.

  - The key elements of the movement could be identified and labelled, and a model constructed, to create a sequential model of a new strategy, or a process model which can generate new awareness – see Part 5 – The Results of Modelling. This model can then be offered within a bespoke Acquisition process to colleagues or third parties.

- *Remedial:*

  - The exemplar could view the dance as if on a screen and spot those aspects which displeased; come up with suggested alternatives; view the alterations on the screen until satisfied; and then practice the amended dance and calibrate the difference.

  - The exemplar could identify a resource that is needed to take this experience into something rewarding and effective. The exemplar then identifies music that embodies this resource. The modeller downloads/selects the music and the exemplar is asked to 'dance' the exact movement to this music, making any adaptations to the rhythm, rate and amplitude of the movement.

  - The exemplar continues to dance the movement, making incremental changes with each iteration, until the full movement is sufficiently modified to please and generate the desired state. Once the desired movement is reached, it is then practised until it freely enters the system. This practice could involve speeding it up or slowing it down. The exemplar could take on different dancing personalities and complete the dance from these perspectives. These personas could be mentors, or expressions of internal parts.

Training

I have been really privileged to have had some fantastic experiences of personal learning through movement.

- *Michael Colgrass:* Michael Colgrass offered us this experience at the end of one of his performance workshops in Bali. He had already given us some exercises to become aware of the physical space around us. I remember running diagonally across the space and jumping with my arms stretched out. The second time, I actually stretched my arms and legs out, yet I knew I still could have filled the space even more – and there lies the physical metaphor.

  He then put on one of his own compositions and invited us to make our own movement. Possibly, it was a particularly lively thunderous part, or that was just in my imaginings, but I found myself stomping around in a ferocious bundle – just long enough to surprise myself before self-consciousness brought me out.

- *Lara Ewing:* Lara introduced physical improvisation into her workshop on Exploring and Connection. Two exercises stand out. In the first one, we were arranged in an inner and outer circle and, with our partner opposite, we were all given an idea to express – one person was the sauce the other the spaghetti; one person the cup, the other the tea. This really exposed information about relating and how we held our boundaries.

- *Frank Daniels:* Frank, the UK NLP Trainer, provided this experience, 'Running Blindfold'. At one of his trainings there was a field next door. With our eyes closed, we were led out in a line following the sound of Frank's bell. We all lined up at a point 20-30 yards from where Frank was standing. One-by-one, eyes closed, we were asked to run forward full tilt towards the sound of the bell.

  As you might imagine, there were all manner of performances: some very tentative and slow; some distrusting with their hands out in front; some zig-zagging; some thinking they were running flat out but only in fact at half cock; some eyes opening and closing fearing to fall; and others giving up after the first few faltering steps.

  However there was one, and only one, whose performance is seared into my memory. Dave, one of the assistants and who has spina bifida, let out a roar and charged at full tilt and full volume across the space, only stopping when Frank was behind him. If ever we were given a description of total commitment to life, there it was.

- *Judy Delozier:* Blind Man Walking, a process I learned from Judy in Bali, is one I used on the first day of every one of our thirty plus Practitioner trainings. The exemplar is blindfolded and given a stick, and a partner who was only allowed to intervene if the exemplar was actually at risk. They are given permission to go to wherever they wanted in 20 minutes. At our training centre Station House, some never left the room, others crossed the main road or had to be retrieved from the other side of the railway line, or the football pitches. Most managed the steep stairs and took up home in the car park. Some clung to the edges; others felt most comfortable in the open spaces. Their patterns for their relationship with the Unknown were starkly revealed.

  As interestingly, the Rescuing patterns of the 'guide' also showed up, which was to pay dividends later on when refraining from intervening in another's processing.

Ecology

- Naturally, the physical space needs to cater for the activity. However, much can be done with the movement of hands or feet from a sitting position – back to Rossi territory.

- Actual physical limitations of the individual need to be factored in, although check for congruence if the 'bad back excuse' is, yet again, wheeled out as an avoidance agent.

- This public display of internal processing can be alarming for those who spend much of their time hiding their 'truths' from public scrutiny. Such people are likely to be very reluctant or certainly hesitant about entering into such activities. Significant preparation and trance work may be required to overcome reluctance and establish full commitment. Possibly the exercises may be stacked in terms of build-up exposure so that, ultimately, there is full access to learning.

- Strong emotions can be evoked in the process and the modeller needs to be attentive to hold the space for these emotions to be processed usefully.

Coding

Working with movement can throw up lots of information, hitherto unknown. Some of it may be easily accessible to the individual, or may be just outside awareness. In some ways, *because* it is expressed non-verbally, coding and labelling becomes easier.

Areas that can be potentially coded are:

- *Strategies:* repetitive movements appearing throughout the 'dance' can indicate important information. Identifying where they are occurring in the narrative, and what goes before and after can throw up some really useful insight, as can unpacking the actual nature of the movement into its components.

- *States:* the exemplar can identify which movements surprised them, pleased them immensely, shocked them or resonated a familiarity at a deep level. Such movements are ripe for unpacking into their emotional elements and labelled accordingly.

- *Prevailing beliefs:* when the movement is looked at as a system, the relationships between the elements can be explored. This can be sequentially through the movement or across the system. Every perspective can generate beliefs, which can be distilled through meta model questioning.

Concerns

- The exemplar may have total resistance to this form of experience, feeling exposed, foolish and without a 'script'. This, of course, may be the reason for the suggestion to do it. However, should the modeller sustain belief that this approach would serve the overall goal, consistent pacing and leading will be needed.

- Some may dismiss the experience as meaningless, just a physical dance, and have no natural predisposition for exploring the implications of their instinctive movements and actions. If it is a group activity, then the accounts of others may influence such doubters to think otherwise. Or, in the context of therapy or coaching, the individual may need time to let the experience marinate in his or her physiology for the insight to emerge unbidden later on.

- Natural inhibitions can interfere; therefore, it may take three rounds of activity before the individuals let go and open themselves up to what can be possible.

Finally

Modelling through movement can be a truly liberating experience for the exemplar, speaking with no words and through instinctive compulsion.

As a kinaesthetic undertaking the exemplar feels both the internal urges of direction and the external sensations of joining the outside world. It serves as a great way for exemplars to connect with their bodies and ground them in accessible experience. It also provides undeniable evidence of the unconscious mind's message, undiluted by any other form of coding. In our left-brain dominated world, having an alternative to the spoken word as a means of communication can be a cathartic release.

Art Modelling

Background

Art Therapy first emerged in the late 1940s, and a British artist Adrian Hill led the field. He saw that the value lay in completely engrossing the mind, as well as the fingers, so that the frequently inhibited patient could release his or her creative energy and give spontaneous expression from the unconscious mind. The resulting drawing provided symbolic speech.

No experience in art is required, nor is aesthetic perfection. Instead, the aim within Art Therapy – and modelling – is to enable the exemplar to become aware of his or her internal organisation and open the possibility of change and growth through increased self-awareness and self-modelling.

The visual representation could be a drawing, painting, collage, sculpture, photographs, or a mixture of all of these. It is likely, however, that the modeller will predetermine the medium, given the restriction of supplies and environment.

The Approach

From the start, the aim of the modelling process is for the exemplar to produce a tangible artefact which illustrates the exemplar's inner world. There are various options open to the modeller.

1 Set up

- You may provide a range of materials from just a set of coloured pens all the way up to different paints, pens, inks, magazines, materials, modelling materials like clay and plasticine, as well as fixative and scissors. You may offer different sizes of paper to include rolls of wallpaper. The exemplar may work on a table, floor, or wall. You might want to consider protective clothing as well.

- All materials should offer sufficient choice for the exemplar, and be in good condition – no dry pens and ransacked magazines.

- You provide the context for the creation. The exemplar may feel initially inhibited, and as part of the introduction of the outcome and the journey leading up to this outcome, you may find it useful to induce a light trance. Most people will have a childhood reference experience of drawing and be into fully participating.

- The explorer is clear about the outcome and its purpose, the process in terms of timing and permissible size and the location. He or she needs to know that artistic ability is not required, and fine artwork is not expected. They have complete choice regarding what to produce.

2 Exploration

- You may choose to leave the exemplar initially to overcome any possible self-consciousness on the part of the exemplar.

- Once the creation is underway, you want to merely observe, second positioning the creation and also being aware of how the exemplar is proceeding with the creation – where attention was paid to some areas over others, where there were pauses in the process or aspects speedily done, where selection of particular tools was highly considered.

- Various approaches can be taken:

    - Existing images: the exemplar can be asked to select particular images that resonate with their internal experience, or identify within images specific aspects that attract them and subsequently offer their reasons.

– Pre-framed Drawings: here the exemplar is given specific symbols to draw that can be mapped across to the elements within the identified behaviour or system. For example, House/Tree/Person could, in a business context, depict the organisation, its products and services and the staff; or, in a family context, the drawings could depict the exemplar's response to home, its atmosphere, family members. The exemplar is likely to be unaware of the isomorphic nature of this process.

– Free Drawing: here the exemplar is given the topic and visually expresses whatever comes to mind.

3 Reflection

• The exemplar has full responsibility for content and interpretation. However you can direct the exemplar's attention to certain aspects of the drawing, which the exemplar may have overlooked, leaving the exemplar then to provide his or her own comment. You may feedback what you noticed regarding how the exemplar worked through the process.

• Interpretations can be made based on:

– Colour: types, usage, blending, and original use

– Over or under emphasis

– Lines and shapes, enclosure of lines and shapes, ground lines, sky lines; quality of lines, length, space usage

– Reality and abstraction

– Representation of the image in context

– Use of people and/or animals or other metaphors

– Movement portrayal

– Placement on the page

– Omissions

– Relationships between elements.

4 Intervention

• If something the size of a standard sheet of paper is produced then this can be used as a visual anchor, either as a picture posted where the exemplar can regularly see it. If the production is larger than this or not portable, then photographs can be taken.

• The exemplar may now be invited to produce what they would rather have, and make the amendments and adjustments they desire.

• Key elements can be identified, possibly through cutting the image into component parts and moving them into different configurations. These elements could also be coded and labelled.

Applications

Therapy and coaching

From a modelling perspective, the use of modelling through visual representation produces fascinating insight, constructed without the editing by language or influence of the modeller. Certainly, it is a natural methodology to use, in particular where the exemplar is inarticulate, over-rational, has a developed visual representation system or, as interestingly, an underdeveloped visual representation system.

I have used the approach to invite exemplars to draw themselves as they are now, how they want to be, or how they have been in the past. Pretty quickly the blocks and barriers begin to emerge, as does the sensory specific description of the desired outcome. Exemplars are often totally surprised at just how much is unintentionally revealed through their drawing.

I have also invited exemplars to plot their version of events graphically, so creating an illustrated system. Sometimes entering into the realms of psycho-geography and interfacing with kinaesthetic modelling, symbols are placed on pieces of paper that can then be moved, and different dynamics and relationships can be tested. This testing is particularly effective when dealing with confusing systems and exploring the next steps to take.

Business and training

Robert Dilts first introduced me to the use of drawing to support business aims. Working with the Disney Model, in small groups of three or four, the exemplar was to provide The Dreamer description of his or her intended project. The others then drew what they heard and fed back their drawing. This proved an excellent way to reflect filters, detect dynamics and highlight problems. The Critic's punch was softened yet still present. This approach is particularly effective when working within teams, where alignment of perception and interpretation is critical.

Skills Required

- Unlike traditional Art Therapy, there is no requirement for you to have any knowledge of archetypes or be an expert on symbols. As a constructivist, you 'merely' facilitate the exemplar to provide the explanations.

- You need to be able to second position both the exemplar during the production, and what is produced, detecting inconsistences and apparent omissions.

- You have to refrain from offering any verbal or non-verbal feedback during the process of the action which could suggest approval or otherwise.

Ecology

This approach is completely non-intrusive. However, it does beguile the wary to disclose more than they may mean to. So the modeller has to judge just how much attention to pay to the image and how much of the image to code.

As ever, emotions can be aroused and the modeller needs to be alert to sponsoring them.

Coding

Once the exemplar is happy that the production is a complete representation, or as complete as feels right or necessary, coding can begin if required. Coding can be achieved in a variety of ways.

The exemplar can:

- Identify the most significant elements

- Reduce the drawing down to its minimum construction and then label it

- Identify the sequence for getting from A to B

- Identify what has to be true for X to be present, or disappear, because ... This set of conditions becomes the operating belief set.

The modeller can:

- Compare the characteristics of this exemplar's drawing with those of others (provided the context was the same)

- Identify the most significant moments either in the construction of the drawing, or the processing of the interpretation, and draw these out

- Second position the piece through own neurology and determine the key elements

- Invite others to determine the key elements and gain a composite response.

Concerns

- Some may feel that such an approach is infantile, or have performance anxiety of not being able to draw properly. However, even the most reluctant can find themselves regressing into that delightful childhood experience of selecting just the right colour and giving just the right amount of attention to detail. The tip of the tongue just about emerges from the lips!

Finally

When applied to the modelling, I find this methodology a highly productive means of eliciting underlying structure, in a friendly participative manner. The exemplar is given time on their own, without interruption. The exemplar becomes fully engaged, and is given total autonomy for interpretation, and the opportunity to enter into the emergent system to engineer his or her own solutions.

It is highly enjoyable for both parties and the end results can be used as visual anchors for as long as they are needed.

Music/Sound Modelling

Music is organised sound. Noise is disorganised sound.

Todd Epstein

Background

The origins of Music Therapy go back to the Middle Ages, and the connection between music and the soul has been written about for a long time. It has been used to improve cognitive functioning, motor skills, emotional and affective development, behaviour and social skills, and quality of life through free improvisation, singing, song writing, listening to and discussing music, and moving to music.

Found in all cultures, music has the power to touch us in all aspects of our life. It is a universal expression. I was totally moved by a story of a British soldier in the Falklands who had, the day before, held his dying mate and was now entering into Stanley for the final offensive.   They cleared the garrison of Argentinian soldiers, and there he found a cassette player belonging to one of the soldiers, with a tape in it. It was Tchaikovsky's Fifth Symphony.   He took it up the hillside nearby, played it and wept for the power of the music, for his friend, and this connection with the 'enemy'.

Music influences mood – film scores depend on this, as do composers of sacred music, club DJs, joggers, retailers and Lotharios. It also provides a sense of subliminal structure, through the logic of the note sequences and the rhythms involved. Ian Rankin's Rebus and Colin Dexter's Morse used the structure of music to inform their sleuthing. In neuroscience, it has been shown that music can directly affect changes in parts of the brain's cortex.

The Approach

The modeller has many avenues open for personal exploration, which cater for the non-musical and the musically minded alike.

1   **Set up**
   - You can offer a wide selection of equipment to generate sound/music, from formal stringed, wind and percussion instruments, to household objects that can be hit, clashed, scraped and rattled.
   - Again within the context to be modelled, the exemplar is free to use this equipment to create any sounds that reflect his or her internal experience.
   - For naturally auditory-referenced exemplars, this will be a pleasurable and familiar experience, enabling easier access to internal patterning.   Exemplars can 'pick and mix' between equipment, knowing they can make as much noise as they desire, without causing a disturbance.
   - There are no restrictions – the duration, composition, and volume is just as the exemplar feels; the more 'lost' in the process the more spontaneous and revealing the expression. Exemplars may want to introduce movement to the sounds they create so sufficient space for this could usefully be offered.
   - Exemplars need to know that they are not being asked to produce something that could be described as being musical. It is the nature of the musical offering as it relates to their internal system that is important.

- You may need to provide some warm-up exercises so that the exemplar breaks free from an accepted use of the equipment, and finds their own spontaneous 'voice' through the original sounds they create.

2 Exploration

- You can offer the following approaches:

    - Response to a particular piece of music: exemplars can identify music of their own choosing and talk about what draws them to it – rather like BBC Radio 4's Desert Island Discs. This more cognitive approach can highlight emergent themes. Listening to the meta comments made by the exemplar can describe patterns of, say, connection, excitement, loss etc.

    - Musician: where the exemplar is a competent musician, he or she can be asked to depict the experience either through selecting known music and expressing sentiment through his or her playing, or by creating a piece of music.

    - Free expression: having a range of percussion instruments available allows exemplars to choose a particular instrument, or to indulge in the full gamut of their 'drum kit'. The choice of instrument could be telling.

        Similarly a piano can be used, or other any other instrument which is easily accessed and doesn't need skill. The exemplar is specifically not asked to make recognised music as such, just to link to those sounds that resonate within.

    - Vocal expression: vocal sound is a low cost and an instantly accessible vehicle, either in singing, even if there are no words or recognisable tune, or in sequences of sounds such as grunting, shouting, hissing, laughing.

- You need to enter into the sounds that are being made, mindful of the context that is being modelled and gain a sense of where the exemplar is placing attention, the dynamics and energies through the rhythms, and the states expressed through the range of tone and pitch.

3 Reflection

- Once the sound has been satisfactorily concluded, you both can explore:

    - What is its structure?

    - Where does the sound reside?

    - Where does come from? Where does it want to go?

    - What is its message?

    - What would it rather be?

    - How does it connect with the other sounds?

    - What does the sound represent?

    - What comes before and after this sound?

    - What is this sound a part of?

- The exemplar may have been aware of specific words and phrases emerging, already known or unfamiliar. These may have particular significance depending on what is being modelled. Or else musical phrases may have arrived unbidden, which may have historical or cultural significance.

4 Intervention

- The exemplar may identify particular areas which could be developed further, or which could be removed, or adapted using a different piece of equipment.

- The sound could be altered by shifting the rhythm, the volumes, the levels of repetition, the pitch, whilst using the same sequence of notes or actions. Conversely, rattling could be replaced by tapping, for example.

- The exemplar is responsible for telling the story behind the production and offering their own take on what has emerged. You can add personal observation and your own experience as a consumer of the sound.

Applications

Therapy and coaching

This approach lends itself to personal development, especially for the musically and auditorily inclined. It makes a very welcome change to the predominately kinaesthetic or visual approaches more normally selected. For the inarticulate, this could be just the vehicle to give voice to their internal processes.

Business consultancy

I know of Salsa Bands being brought into FTSE 100 Conferences, and in small sections each are taught a series of rhythms before coming back into the full conference hall and playing in unison – an obvious metaphor for corporate unity. Similarly on a smaller scale this can bring about team unity.

In small groups, the individuals are coached to play the rhythms of others, thus experiencing a description of the other at a deeper level. Acting As If this is your rhythm can bring about altered filters and shift perceptions.

Education and training

Music has been used for a long time in schools, especially in primary schools. Children feel free to act out feelings through sound with little or no inhibition. For young or older people, this approach can help them re-access this level of spontaneity with no judgment.

UK NLP Trainer Frank Daniels uses vocal warm-ups as part of the open frame to the day's training. This serves to loosen up the system and stimulate the senses, not least of which because it requires the intake of breath leading to increased oxygen to the brain.

Coding

Once the exemplar is happy that the sound is a complete representation, or as complete as feels right or necessary, coding can begin if required. Coding can be achieved in a variety of ways.

The exemplar can:

- Identify the most significant elements

- Reduce the sound down to its minimum construction and then label it

- Identify the sequence for getting from A to B.

- Identify what has to be true for X to be present, or disappear, because … This set of conditions becomes the operating belief set.

The modeller can:

- Compare the characteristics of this exemplar's sound with those of others (provided the context was the same)

- Identify the most significant moments either in the construction of the sound sequence, or the processing of the interpretation, and draw these out

- Second position the sound through own neurology and determine the key elements

- Invite others to determine the key elements and gain a composite response.

Ecology

- Exemplars may feel naturally inhibited, since music and sound is often a private endeavour. They may also be conditioned to operate within known injunctions – 'don't make noise', 'sing in key', 'don't draw attention to yourself'. The modeller needs to set up a sufficiently altered state within the exemplar to overcome such inhibitions and enable access to free expression.

- Again this can be a highly emotional experience that needs to be supported and held. And the process can be highly revealing. Therefore, there needs to be clear contracting with the exemplar as part of the pre-framing.

Concerns

- Apart from those raised in Ecology, the only major concern is one of logistics. Is there enough space? Will the sound disturb others?

- Individuals may take some convincing that there is a correlation between the sounds they are making and how they are organising themselves internally. The level of commitment will determine how effective the process is. However, it is likely that, should the exemplar have delivered a congruent expression, they will feel a significant emotional shift inside – one of relief, catharsis, and wonderment.

Finally

Modelling through sound is a great alternative to more cognitive approaches. Like visual modelling, it taps into the unconscious mind of the spontaneous child within. Making noise is a delightful pastime for a child. Making legitimate noise is even better. Making legitimate noise to discover more is a revelation! It adds to the modeller's repertoire and serves to meet the predispositions of a small and often overlooked exemplar group – those who have a developed auditory representation system.

Metaphoric Methodologies

Metaphoric Modelling operates at the halfway house between deep structure of uncoded experience and the surface structure where experience is packaged in language. It is expressed in metaphor and symbols as a means of describing inner patterning, without the intrusion of grammar or logic. Each description is a powerfully unique depiction of the exemplar's internal organisation.

This approach, as with the previous modelling methodologies, doesn't require the modeller to put meaning on what is offered, merely to go with what is emerging and let the exemplar perform the interpretation. However it does require the modeller to negotiate and navigate the exemplar's map, drawing attention to specific areas in an orchestrated manner that ultimately brings about resolution and understanding.

It is the third class of methodology to become formalised, initially by the work of James Lawley and Penny Tompkins in 2000, with later approaches developed and identified by myself. Its arrival was much welcomed because it put an end to the either/or debate of intuitive versus cognitive.

In this class of methodology you will find the following:

- *Punctuation Modelling:* a methodology inspired by Lynne Truss and developed by myself. Of the four in this category, this approach requires the least amount of modeller intervention and direction. It is closest to the expressive modelling methodologies in the previous section.

- *Sand Play Modelling:* a methodology that generates 3D symbolic descriptions of inner experience.

- *Symbolic Modelling:* the work of David Grove formalised by James Lawley and Penny Tompkins. This approach operates on a given range of questions provided by the modeller, in order to elicit the representative metaphors.

- *Parts Alignment:* a methodology which holds the Six Step Reframe at its heart, again developed by myself. In terms of language the modeller is free to select from the range of language patterns available within the NLP repertoire.

Some of you might consider that Punctuation Modelling and Parts Alignment are ineligible for serious attention since they fall short of my own strict set of methodology standards. I acknowledge that full details of the practice of Punctuation Modelling and Parts Alignment have yet to be officially published. However, the inclusion of the their respective methodologies in this chapter is the start of gaining such recognition.

Punctuation Modelling

Fran Burgess

My proper introduction to NLP was in 1986, courtesy of Liz Mahoney who was one of the early adopters of NLP drawn to Santa Cruz, Ca. Liz was also the mentor of UK NLP Trainer John Seymour and set him off on his own notable NLP path.

This catalyst served to awaken me from my 'fur lined rut' of Edinburgh living, and bring me to pastures new in Lancashire, England. From there my NLP journey took me to Bristol, London many times, Bali three times, Santa Cruz and twice to Hawaii, until 2000 when the stream of magnificent Mohammeds came to the mountain, namely The Northern School of NLP. Here the bulk of my learning on modelling took place. The NLP influence extended to meeting my future husband Derek Jackson at the NLP Conference in 1992, of all places!

As a child, I was an artist by inclination until I was directed into the sciences by my Biology teaching parents. Even though I railed against this injustice, I connected with the form, structure and sequenced order found within scientific thinking: the Periodic Table in chemistry; the taxonomy of plants, and the classification of invertebrates and vertebrates gave me a working appreciation of logical types and logical levels. I naturally made links between behaviour patterns in animals and human behaviour, recognising the significance of feedback and systemic interaction. Instinctively, I would test a 'truth' by applying it to larger or smaller examples and into other contexts, to see if it held good. I never realised that my awareness of structure would be so useful in later life.

As mentioned in the Preface, my Call to Action came at the end of a workshop on Patterns in the late 90s given by Grinder and Bostic St Clair. I don't know why I heard Grinder's call for new modellers and new models, at such a deep level. I hadn't done much modelling myself and produced a sketchy piece for my Master Practitioner. In fact, when talking with James Lawley about the School's intended inaugural Master Practitioner Programme, he made some basic references that I completely didn't understand. I was a novice, beginning from an almost standing start.

Initially I was overwhelmed at the enormity of the challenge I had set myself – modelling Modelling? Creating models out of the modelling process? Yet my drive and commitment to code the process never wavered. My desire to find ways of teaching it simply has stayed as my mission and is the whole point of this book and the supporting training materials found on our website, *The NLP Kitchen*, and in *The Bumper Bundle Companion Workbook*.

In the process I have extended my own abilities, particularly as a qualified Psychotherapist, and have really appreciated how working through the layers towards deep structure always takes you to the heart of the exemplar, to the magic held in his or her spirit. It is a total privilege. And then in the trainings I can now offer, extraordinary results can be achieved in a very short time.

As a result of my commitment, I am proud to say that I have identified and coded a range of models and frameworks, found within this book, that are proving to offer a simple and believable way to approach modelling. It is an extremely satisfying feeling!

Part 3 – The Methodologies of Modelling

The Background

> Punctuation marks are symbols that indicate the structure and organization of written language, as well as intonation and pauses to be observed when reading aloud.

Wikipedia

Lynne Truss in her book *Eats Shoots And Leaves* (2006) makes a humorous and relentless argument for attention to punctuation. Just taking the title of her book, as it stands it seems to refer to some hungry gunslinger heading out of town, when in fact it relates to the eating habits of pandas.

Truss cites many examples of what has become known as the 'Grocer's Apostrophe' given the number of instances of the absent or wrongly inserted " ' ". However there was one particular example that really made an impact on me:

A woman without her man is nothing.

The lack of punctuation implies that an effective woman requires a man – a statement most often cheered by our male participants and booed by the women. Something very different happens, when the punctuation is altered.

A woman: without her, man is nothing.

That punctuation has the incredible ability to entirely change the meaning and powerfully shift emotions in the perceiver – reversing the boos and cheers!

I considered that anything with that power to provoke a restructuring of internal experience, so swiftly and completely, is worth exploring further. This led to the question: 'what would it be like if we could punctuate our lives?'

Since punctuation removes ambiguity and provides clarity, directs meaning and attention, and requires first and foremost a context, a string or 'sentence' of punctuation is just another form of hieroglyphic language.

Highlighting all the common forms of punctuation, I explored how an individual's perception of his or her life could be described metaphorically through the symbols of punctuation. Here are some of my findings.

- The approach can be applied to different types of time frames – a lifetime, a particular period of time, a day. It can also be applied to past, present and future time frames; the longer the period of time, the more obvious the patterns.

- The individual is required to filter past events and evaluate whether or not they justify being incorporated and by what punctuation mark. For some, actual content and events are important, for others the meaning or relationship with the events is the focus. In particular, if the positive intention behind a negative experience is recorded, then a different story emerges. Actual words are not permitted.

- Once the process is understood and is underway, individuals report that they can go onto autopilot, and their unconscious mind provides the notation.

- Trends and transition are highlighted. A preoccupation with a particular period can be quickly evidenced, just as a chunk of time can be minimised.

- When left to the individual, the strings can be delineated into decades, periods of intense emotion, transitions, marriages, or jobs.

- Often the same combination of symbols appears in both long and short periods of time. The stripped down syntax provides a fractal and coded indicator of inner patterning.

- Some people discover lives full of???, or !!!, others with lots of ... ... or ,,, or a single . . Occasionally individuals create a mark that has specific meaning to them.

- Only the individual can interpret the syntax since an '!' may mean fantastic, surprise, or bad; " " can mean meaningful dialogue or falseness.

- Recurring events can be summed up by enclosing the syntax in brackets, so nominalising and reducing impact. Recurring emotions can be encapsulated in one significant mark. This then allows the other positive elements to come to the foreground and bring the system into balance.

- The process can evoke memories and reveal sadness, or triumph or wonder. It can cause re-evaluation of own contribution and that of others.

- Negative events may have a different configuration, in terms of marks selected, to positive events.

- Whatever the time period, individuals discover that a sense of perspective is gained; good times mingle with bad times; order emerges out of chaos. Events cannot be seen in isolation – for example the origins of Life Decisions can be easily tracked. Some report that whilst the big event is marked out by a strong piece of punctuation, the before and after marks prove to be more significant.

- Out of this can emerge a micro story of one's life, summarised for example by: 'Life is about questioning and discovery; being exposed and growing.'

- Individuals can identify ingrained patterns of response and detect where their lives fell short of their desires. They can even see how they are continuing to project these traits into the future.

- The idea of customising their future by designing their desired syntax produces some strong responses. 'I hadn't realised that I never put a comma in my life. I never pause or stop.'

- As a result of the experience, individuals come away with a strong sense of self-efficacy and being in control of how they punctuate their lives. They report a loosening in their grip of their previous 'reality' and being open and receptive to different interpretations. They find they were invested in the habitual story of their life and were constrained by its 'truth'.

Whilst specific punctuation may differ between languages, the concept is universal. This delightfully simple vehicle enables direct access to internal organisation and these instantly recognisable symbols can resonate emotionally whilst encapsulating some very complex programming.

The Approach

The following range of marks including symbols for the musically minded provides the selection an exemplar can choose from.

$$! \ ? \ ** \ / \ \backslash \ , \ . \ ; \ : \ ... \ " " \ ' ' \ - \ — \ \_ \ = \ \neq \ + \ X$$

$$\div \ \pm \ (\ ) \ [\ ] \ \sim \ \wedge \ \leq \ < \ > \ \$ \ £ \ \wedge \vee \checkmark \ \varkappa$$

$$\flat \quad \flat \quad \flat \quad \flat \quad \flat \quad \natural \quad \#$$

The period of time can either be identified by the modeller or the exemplar and becomes the focus of attention. This could be a full life, a troubled period, a particular good time, a particular type of event like a transition or loss, an instance of excellence, or persistent stuckness.

The exemplar provides the initial coding, the first phase notation, and processes the description through his or her neurology. The hieroglyphic script takes on a life and spirit of its own, stripped bare of content, and becomes an expression of pure meaning. Shifts in the script bring about shifts in meaning whose effects are instantly transmitted through the body's system.

Whatever is produced can then be worked in many different ways. By the end of this process, the exemplar has a very clear idea of what configuration feels good, and what enhances a sense of wellbeing. He or she can access the implications behind the metaphoric structures and can gain a far deeper interpretation of his or her relationship with life experiences to date.

Intervention 1 – Reconfiguration

The following variables can be applied to the produced notation to effect a reconstruction of emphasis and meaning. Some changes will have a strong impact whilst other changes will make little difference.

1   **Substitution:** exemplar identifies the dominant mark, and substitutes it for an alternative less used one, so rewriting the script. This can be repeated and the effects tested.

2   **Removal:** you can ask the exemplar to remove key marks altogether. This can lead to new questions, or a totally revised version of the events.

3   **Submodalities:** you can lead the exemplar through a wide range of structural shifts, asking his or her to be mindful of the somatic response each change creates.

   • *The size:* increasing or reducing the size of a particular mark or marks; or making larger or smaller the entire script so that it might end up with only a few marks per line or page, or be shrunk into one line.

   • *The style:* slanting it backwards or forwards, making some lighter or darker, adding decoration.

   • *The spacing:* from spreading it out, to squeezing it together.

   • *The grouping:* to having it all on a continuous line, or breaking it up into sections, introducing new paragraphs or even chapters.

   • *The orientation:* instead of left to right, writing it downwards in columns or in a spiral, making it wavy, or spikey.

   • *The order:* taking strings of syntax, reordering the sequence.

4   **Homogenise:** how the notation is written out allows you to invite the exemplar to consider rewriting the layout, and construct a flow of strings which have the same 'weight' to them, and which represent 'real' time. This applies to where there is wildly different emphasis on different events, some with much more detail, or the string for two months is the same length as ten years, or size and intensity overshadow what was before or after. This might require some time periods to be unpacked or some to be jettisoned.

Intervention 2 – Perspectives

Once the default version has been plotted, you can also widen the system and calibrate it against other perspectives. This then allows for the exemplar to return to the original and write it anew.

1 **Streams:** the exemplar can divide the string into three parallel streams – one for work, one home and one social. This illustrates levels of harmony, or imbalance between all three.

2 **Mentor:** the exemplar can be asked to think of key people or mentors, and ask how might they punctuate the exemplar's life.

3 **Neurological levels:** the exemplar could draw on positive resources from different neurological levels

   • How would your best talent, your highest value, your Spirit punctuate this period?

4 **Physical and emotional:** the exemplar could be asked to punctuate a period of time through the perspective of parts of the body:

   • How would the heart, the hand, the head punctuate this period?

Or the exemplar could consider plotting from the perspective of different emotions: or from an abstract concept like well being, or contribution.

5 **Different representations:** depending on how adventurous the exemplar is, this syntax can also be converted into somatic syntax and sound, so that the exemplar can sing, make sounds or dance or create gestures. These can be similarly explored in terms of submodalities – rhythm, speed, volume, size and shape etc. Good rapport is required here.

Intervention 3 – Application

It is likely that, in making adjustments to the original configuration, changes will have taken place. Certainly, new awareness will have occurred. This may be sufficient for the exemplar's outcome. However, once satisfied that this metaphorical expression is congruent, you can put the structure to good use.

1 **Reduction:** given that there is a fractal nature emergent in this process, the exemplar is invited to reduce his or her representations to the minimum syntax that still provides meaning. This stark representation reveals the default pattern that the exemplar has to own as being self-generated. This reduction is part of the coding process.

2 **Future plotting:** you can then ask the exemplar to punctuate his or her future, customising it to generate optimum well being. Invite them to calibrate for joy and connection with spirit, creating a future that is a pleasure to live and behold. From a timeline perspective invite them to step into the future with this syntax and experience the possibilities.

The final version is reduced to four or five elements, which then provides the exemplar with their map of the future. The abstract nature of the injunctions contained within the selected punctuation proves to be a powerful and enduring message. Illustrating these can provide a tremendous visual anchor.

Required Skills

• This methodology requires little in the way of developed skills, other than operational levels of rapport, and sensory acuity to pick up exemplar' non-verbal responses, which means this approach is useful in the hands of the most novice modeller.

- Within therapy, you are required to pinpoint the particular area(s) for examination. Once the exemplar has understood the process, and the range of options given – see Perspectives – then he or she can determine where exploration may be most useful.

- The exemplar is responsible for the interpretation of the selection of symbols.

Ecology

Once the exemplar has overcome the rather bizarre nature of your request to use punctuation, they are free to enter into their own world and take full control of the choices they make. This is a highly ecological approach with limited intervention from the modeller.

The modeller needs to emphasise the dissociated nature of the symbols of punctuation and how 'reality' can be reduced into the manageable metaphor of the syntax.

The process may appear to be benign and deceptively simple. However, it does have the potential to touch on sensitive areas which are currently unresolved, and may open the individual up to unexpected emotional responses.

The modeller needs to be aware of this possibility, perhaps preframing the likelihood of this, and judge if it is appropriate for the individual(s) involved – certainly if this is a group endeavour.

Applications

Therapy

Punctuation modelling is useful for throwing up patterns of behaviour that are due for an overhaul. It fits the constructivist mindset perfectly, and since it presents itself in a digital manner, it makes the process of reconstructing or repunctuating really easy.

It can be used to plot the overall life journey of an individual, or a particular aspect, like career, relationships, or marriage. It can be used to model out successful transitions in preparation of a change to come. It can be used to generalise a specific event within a larger overview.

Dominant negative emotions can be identified, and through the process of reconfiguration and crossing representations space can be created to free such emotions and let them go.

Because language is not required, and interpretation is down to the exemplar, this methodology is excellent for those who are not ready yet to put words to their story.

Relationships

Apart from highlighting personal patterns within relationships, working with partners can offer the opportunity to second position another's syntax. This can be done initially with the meaning that the individual brings regarding these marks, and then taking on any specific differing meaning held by the partner.

Laying the strings of punctuation parallel to each other gives the opportunity to look at the corresponding relationship between them and the mutual events in their lives. Shared or differing responses, the levels of intensity, the absence of events, or preoccupation with events outside of the relationship, can all emerge.

By working with this dissociated representation, words can be found to discuss aspects previously avoided or unknown. The couple can then choose how to punctuate their relationship, customise it so that it feels good for both, and then draw up the string for the next five years.

Business consultancy

This can be a useful way for management teams to gain individual descriptions of experiences, say within a project. The similarities and differences can highlight personal responses to arguably what is the same process. Processing everybody's syntax with a common punctuation mark could help to cohere the team approach whilst accommodating individuality.

Coding

- Whilst the exemplar is most likely to be the end user of the resulting syntax, as with other idiosyncratic models, coding is possible once the exemplar, or the modeller chooses to label the symbols.

- Since it lends itself to both processes and states, it has the potential to generate constructed sequential as well as simultaneous models – see Part 5 – The Results of Modelling.

- Once the experience has been reduced to a pattern of four or five marks, these can then be labelled and taken forward into a digitised model. However for personal consumption, it has been found that keeping the syntax in the metaphoric format allows it to 'talk' to the individual at a deeper level.

Concerns

- The credibility of Punctuation Modelling as a bona fide modelling methodology may suffer because of its simplicity. Something with such limited technology could easily be discounted. And with other weightier methodologies available it could be easily overlooked.

  However this would be a loss. The approach really belongs to the exemplar, with the interface with the modeller being kept to a minimum. It is non-intrusive, yet has the potential to reveal inner patterning clearly and without effort.

- Light hearted doesn't mean lightweight.

Finally

This is a very simple yet effective modelling methodology that clearly demonstrates the ability to give form to deep structure – in this instance using the metaphoric use of punctuation marks. And in line with all constructivist thinking, once you have identified the structure, you can restructure it to deliver desired results. Exemplars have reported significant breakthroughs as a result of their experience.

It serves the need to provide structure, opportunity for self-modelling, and the creation of models out of it.

Its very simplicity provides a great, quickly accessible, description of the process of modelling itself and more specifically self-modelling, where all the elements of the modelling process are contained within it. It can be used to great effect as an introduction to the subject.

The Punctuation Modelling application deserves to be applied more widely and written up with case studies providing evidence of its effectiveness. Its time has yet to come.

Sand Play Modelling

Background

Sand Play Therapy is a recognised therapeutic modality for both children and adults, based on the psychology of C G Jung and developed by the Swiss psychotherapist and teacher Dora Kalff. I am grateful to Masha Bennett who introduced it to me and gave me my first experience of its powerful effects and my access to beneficial insight.

It consists of playing in a specially proportioned sandbox – approximately 20 x 30 x 3 inches; floor and sides painted with water-resistant bright-blue paint. Boxes of dry and moist sand are provided.

Exemplars also have at their disposal a number of small figures to choose from. These provide as complete as possible a cross-section of all inanimate and animate beings that can be encountered in the external world, as well as in the inner imaginative world: trees, plants, stones, food, tools, wild and domesticated animals, ordinary women and men pursuing various activities, soldiers, fairy-tale figures, religious figures from diverse cultural spheres, houses, fountains, bridges, ships, vehicles, etc.

The fixed border of the box provides form and shape to the boundless perception of 'reality'. This limitation contrasts with the freedom offered to the exemplar in shaping the sand and selecting objects, albeit from the choice available.

The tactile nature of Sand Play and its creative use of symbols allows for the emergence of a three-dimensional metaphoric landscape, capable of being moulded and restructured as the exemplar shifts attention and moves through time.

Traditionally the Sand Play therapist is required to have a deep knowledge of the Jungian symbols and extensive personal experience of their impact, with the intention that their interpretation and direction can establish resolution to conflict and generate a sense of wholeness.

However, from the NLP perspective, placing meaning on the symbols selected would be an intrusion of personal map and a potential installation. In fact, even assuming physical properties of a selected figure could be utterly misleading – dragons don't always breathe fire and threaten; dragons can be guardians and protectors. The exemplar is completely in charge of attributing characteristics and relationships to the selected figures. In fact, an object might have been selected because the desired one wasn't available, and this one was merely a stand-in.

Using Sand Play as a modelling methodology, the exemplar can reveal, without the use of words, his or her internal dynamics. Gaps in the landscape can invite further exploration. Joys and sadness can emerge. Dissatisfactions and offending relationships can be addressed by adding, moving or removing elements.

The Approach

The exemplar is invited to focus on a current situation or on a desired outcome. He or she then usually starts off marking out in the sand a basic representation of the situation, selecting objects to represent physical realities, usually from a logical perspective. After a period of time, as the 'inner child' emerges, the unconscious mind takes over and begins to direct activity, without the need for logic.

This then develops to reveal and mark out underlying problems, concerns and themes. These can highlight responses to safety and security, isolation and connection, work and relaxation, and stimulation and learning, for example.

During this time you do not comment or interfere with the free choice of the exemplar. There is no implied judgment at any stage regarding the selection and placing of the figures or symbols.

You have to pay attention to any commentary, meta comment or explanation offered by the exemplar, and these can be reflected back as necessary, or explored at a later stage through meta model within the context of the metaphor.

You can also introduce questions of the developed landscape that reflect previously stated issues and desires. Only if appropriate, you may suggest movement of characters around the sand tray; consider the introduction of new characters; or invite the exemplar to view the system through time.

It is useful to take a photograph of the final representation to act as a visual anchor of a significant reference experience. It might even be that you film the process as it evolves.

Skills Required

- You need to create a protected space for the exemplar and have the ability to accompany the exemplar's experience.

- You need to follow sequencing and the selection of objects. These relationships can be explored subsequently, or at any points of impasse.

- You need to stay well out of the process, to exclude any non-verbal sounds or movements, leaving the exemplar to develop his or her narrative intuitively and without pressure.

- And you may need to be on the alert for areas of avoidance and intervene to direct attention to these areas, possibly at the time, but more likely in the review afterwards.

Ecology

This can be a powerful process, so you need to be alert to the possibility that the process can evoke emotional responses, and sponsor and hold the exemplar in such moments.

Coding

- *One exemplar:* you could ask the exemplar:
  - What are the most significant elements?
  - What can be removed?
  - What was important about doing it the way you did?
  - How were you able to remove, introduce, disregard X or Y?
  - What surprised you during the process, in terms of what you produced?
  - What could you have developed further? What stopped you from doing that?
  - What did you pay particular attention to? What was important about that?
  - What insights emerged during the process?
  - What parts of the narrative provoked a strong emotional response within you?

From these responses you can isolate key words or detect recurring themes that indicate the underpinning structures that are operating.

- *More than one exemplar:* if you have a range of Sand Play landscapes to draw from, which address a particular situation, then common characteristics can emerge which can then serve to form a model. These could relate to essential components and requirements for change, to beliefs about significance and relevance. From these, the modeller can detect patterns and construct a model accordingly.

Application

Therapy and coaching

This approach is perfect when working with young children – and world-weary adults.

The exemplar can construct a landscape of the current situation, including all the influences at play. This can then be converted into what would be desirable, with the modeller paying particular attention to the order in which the elements are changed, removed or introduced. Different options, which may already have been aired, can be introduced and rehearsed until the best one emerges.

Business consultancy and training

The modeller could operate a 'goldfish bowl' approach, where individuals take turns at creating the landscape and so offering their own three-dimensional take on what is happening in the team or the company. Working towards a landscape that accommodates the needs of everyone could be an exceedingly useful and cathartic process.

Concerns

- This is not an easily portable process given the number of boxes required to carry all the figures and symbols, not to mention the bags of sand. Therefore the exemplar is more likely required to visit the modeller's place of work.

- This is a one-to-one process, which limits its application.

Finally

From firsthand experience, I reckon that this is a bona fide modelling methodology, and one which holds its own as an example of metaphoric modelling. Its kinaesthetic, tactile approach complements the visual process of the others in this section and serves to bring good practice, developed elsewhere, into our field of practice. It produces a 3D landscape full of meaning and potential for awakening insight, similar to those generated through Symbolic Modelling. It provides an external representation of internal processing in an unequivocal manner. And it is deeply enjoyable to do – even the emotional bits!

Symbolic Modelling

James Lawley and Penny Tompkins

Lawley and Tompkins have achieved a well-earned reputation and their rightful place at the 'top table' of NLP developers. Second generation in origin, they have ploughed a remarkable furrow in the field of modelling, and our understanding of its process.

Arguably late in arrival to the world of NLP, in 1991 they initially met during their ITS Practitioner training in London, and got together during their Master Practitioner training at PPD Learning, also in London. It was this training that sparked their interest in modelling. Tompkins had been a co Managing Director of an oil industry supplies company, and Lawley had previously been a manager within British Telecom.

Then in 1992 they attended NLP Trainers Training in Santa Cruz and made the momentous decision to marry, under the Oak Tree, officiated by none other than the late Todd Epstein. There was not a dry eye in the meadow. I know, I was there boohooing with Gino Bonissone. It was just beautiful, and Todd's service brought home the connection between ritual and trance.

After their Practitioner training, they set up the London Practice Group. At the end of the Santa Cruz training, Tompkins made an impassioned plea about the need to generate an NLP Community to bring collective wisdom of our modality to the waiting world. By 1992 their Practice Group was attracting all the visiting top trainers and taking regular numbers to over 100 before they handed over the mantle.

1992 also marked the establishment of a group of NLP practitioners operating as therapists. As founding members, Lawley and Tompkins were instrumental in the formation of the Neurolinguistic Psychotherapy and Counselling Association (NLPtCA) and then spearheaded its registration with UK Council for Psychotherapy (UKCP).

In 1993 they both attended a talk given by a strange half Maori man, the psychotherapist David Grove. There they experienced the impact of his approach on themselves and on others. They hadn't a clue what he was doing; yet his focus on how an individual's deep structure can be expressed symbolically in metaphor fascinated them.

Tompkins, in particular, never lost the pull she had to learn more. Grove dropped below the radar during 1994, so she had to wait until 1995 to attend her first full workshop. She persuaded Lawley that this was worth pursuing, little knowing just where this journey would take them, and how much of a contribution they were about to make to the understanding and application to modelling. They were not the first from the NLP community to attend Grove's training. However, they were the first to publish their findings, through an interview of Grove for *Rapport* in 1996 and a year later with an article on the Clean Language approach, again in *Rapport*.

Metaphors In Mind came out in 2000, and Clean Language – a label coined by Grove – entered into NLP language. The Clean Change Company became established led, by Wendy Sullivan, and over the next ten years, not only did Lawley and Tompkins continue to explore and develop new materials, they were also responsible for creating a tiered certification programme and an assessment capability, to meet the needs of the ever-growing body of learners.

By 2010 they developed a lifestyle with time equally divided between Australia and the UK. When resident in the UK they continue to hold their bi-monthly Development Group, first started back in 2001, where the gathering of like-minded modellers explore with whatever thoughts and ideas that are currently preoccupying the pair. And they never seem to run out of ideas! Out of this hothouse has come many new models and expanded thinking. You could spend hours on their website http://www.cleanlanguage.co.uk browsing through all the published articles, materials and blogs freely available to all.

Happily for us, The Northern School of NLP has had a very fruitful partnership with them both, coming together through our mutual fascination with modelling. They presented a memorable workshop on the first of our Master Practitioner programmes and returned every year to bring their own clarity and passion for the modelling process and their unique application. In 2006, Lawley headed up the delivery of our remarkable NLPt Psychotherapy Diploma holding therapeutic modelling at its heart. The participants were incredibly fortunate to have had this one-off experience.

At the untimely death of David Grove in 2008, Lawley and Tompkins were honoured guests of his family at his funeral in his native home in North Island New Zealand. They were invited to participate in the five-day Maori traditional ceremony.

Whilst theoretically at the stage of retirement, Tompkins continues to provide the focus and drive and Lawley the intellectual depth and rigour. Together they are a formidable, far-reaching team.

The Background

When Lawley and Tompkins set about modelling David Grove, they sought to work from first principles, clearing their minds of any models and methodologies already existing at the time. Since Grove refused to take any part in the process, they were – probably thankfully – unable to interview him and glean his version of how he did what he did. Instead they sat in on many workshops, recording his transactions with exemplars, annotating the transcripts, and unconsciously absorbing his mannerisms, energy, and attention.

Recalling this time, Lawley says,

> We did hear his many and wonderful explanations of what was happening in the process. It took us a year or so to realise most of these explanations were confusing us and getting in the way of what he actually did, and how the exemplar responded.

Working from these first principles they were able to generate and code Grove's work with metaphors, and devise an approach that became known as Symbolic Modelling. They identified a series of honed questions with its own syntax, initially unfamiliar to the ear; a method of delivery involving repetition, rhythm and intonation; and the start of a methodology whose framework was to grow and become fully established.

The marked-out linguistic patterns became known as Clean Language, because the content of the structured questions is formed around the exact words and gestures the exemplar uses, keeping the intrusion and influence of the modeller's map to a minimum. Working linguistically with the metaphors that emerge, following the prescribed procedures, and replicating the non-verbals as they arise – *from the exemplar's perspective* (this is counter intuitive to the teachings of rapport) – became the territory of Symbolic Modelling.

As constructivists, their methodology is based on the premise that all language and gesture can be taken to be a metaphorical representation of how an individual is organising and conceptualising their inner patterning, without the need for full grammatical coding. Lying midway between deep and surface structure, these natural and ever present metaphors can create a rich landscape of description, which holds a profound logic for the individual, but may appear utterly irrational and nonsensical at face value to an observer.

Furthermore Lawley and Tompkins identified that the symbolic elements within the landscape are organised within an ever-changing dynamic system, which can alter in response to natural or applied influences. The metaphors were found to interconnect through time and through space, operate inside and outside of the body, and be applied to outcomes as well as problems. This shifting structure inevitably invites change and over time, growth and development.

Bateson's assertion: 'When you view a system, you change it.' Is evident within Lawley and Tompkins's approach. Once the amazing and unique symbolic construction becomes known, the exemplar can often spontaneously take over the process, creating impactful change. Through self-modelling, he or she can then begin rearranging and transforming the landscape, and in the process gain a visceral understanding of the nature of the problem and solution.

Initially Grove took a 'traditional' approach to therapeutic change – find the cause of the problem and remove it. When I first encountered him, I experienced the powerful effects of finding the 'redemptive metaphor' that could cleanse (my metaphor) the system and remove the problem. However Lawley and Tompkins have established a future based approach, concentrating attention on identifying and developing the desired outcome as their starting point.

Lawley and Tompkins's significant theoretical knowledge informs their intuitions, and has been of service during the testing and refining of their methodology. In 2011 Lawley published a concise theoretical explanation of the principles that underpin the Symbolic Modelling approach, constructing a rationale of their thinking and their conclusions. He draws on the collective wisdom of other post-modern thinkers, which in turn validates and embraces the practices they have established. No other modelling methodology presents such a conclusive rationale.

They continue to develop ideas and material, and have made unique contributions with their additionally coded models of PRO (Problem, Remedy, Outcome) model, Binds and Double Binds and many others. Lawley is a prodigious reader and is constantly applying the thinking of others to the field of modelling and human experience. Their website continues to be updated with their latest preoccupations, leaving commercial publishing of their work to others.

The Approach

My experience of Grove taught me this profound lesson: Deep Rapport is not about matching and mirroring. It is about coming alongside the deep structure of another, holding it, being curious about it and accepting it.

Slumped in his chair beside you, he paid no attention to you and gave no eye contact, just asked strange questions. Pretty soon you realised that this was not a social occasion – this was a deep impersonal penetrative journey into your inner 'caverns measureless unto man'.

As you quickly became absorbed in this fantastical creation that somehow has its source within you, all outside distractions fade and the realities that are replacing them are more than equal to anything that Alice experienced in her Wonderland! From this deep trance new possibilities emerge.

However if this were not astonishing enough, this man would retain your description with all its detail and nuances, even though he was also working with six or seven others, and even though forty-eight hours had elapsed.

This was extreme attention and sponsorship in action. Having your very inner being caringly tracked for you to see is a powerful experience. His very lack of social engagement made the process even more ecological.

You will find that Lawley and Tompkins have reduced the original complexity of Symbolic Modelling to very clear stages, each with their questioning frames. As the learner advances they will become aware of more distinctions and points to pay attention to. What I am offering here, is a simple overview, which hopefully doesn't dilute the methodology's sophistication, less I violate Einstein's mantra – 'reduce it to the simplest level, but no simpler.'

Lawley and Tompkins's 'Forward Pull' approach means the start and finish of the process is on Outcome. They contend that many people who are stuck have no clear description of the actual outcome they really want, richly described and somatically engaged with.

Through expressing themself in metaphor, the exemplar has no need to get caught up in the rational 'why nots' that normally accompany a stuck person who wants something else.

The process operates in six stages, but not necessarily in a straight sequence, responding as the dynamic system reveals itself.

The Set Up, identified from the metaphors present in what the person is saying, is critical to identify the way into the process. As the modeller, you can choose to zone in on the metaphorical content within the words offered, or on the gestures, body movement, non-verbal sounds, line of sight or the exemplar's adopted perceptual position, each of which is spontaneously generated by your question.

The process is then kick-started with the standard outcome-eliciting question:

And when [entry point] what would you like to have happen?

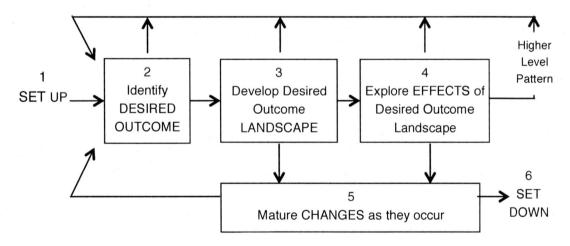

When a Change occurs, go to Phase 5.

When a Problem occurs, go to Phase 2.

Stages in The Symbolic Modelling Process
Reproduced with permission from Lawley and Tompkins

Often an exemplar will dress up an outcome into what is actually his or her idea of a remedy to the problem. This observation by Lawley and Tompkins is pure genius as is their strategy for inviting closer examination.

A remedy is a statement that contains reference to a problem.

> **Problem:** I am overweight.
>
> And when *overweight* what would you like to have happen?
>
> **Remedy:** I want to lose weight.
>
> And when *lose weight* then what happens?/what happens next?
>
> **Outcome:** I will become a size 12.

It is worth noting that problems will be presented during the process and not just at the start of it, so the modeller needs to be alert to this, and address further remedies masquerading as outcomes.

After establishing a clear outcome, the nine basic questions (see next section) leap into life, working through the 'legs' of the answer, attending to each of the metaphoric references contained in it. Actually it might be that only a few of the basic questions are ever required.

The point where the landscape is fully developed is punctuated by the exemplar drawing his or her landscape. This graphical representation highlights where the exemplar is placing emphasis and possibly those elements that might have been omitted. It also checks the map you have been creating internally as well.

The drawing triggers the start of the next phase, where the outcome question is asked again and this time it is followed up with questions to elicit metaphorically what has to happen for the outcome to be achieved, testing if these changes are possible.

As the outcome matures, you invite the exemplar to explore the nature of the identified changes, what their effects will be and if this shift causes shifts elsewhere. Once this final stage is reached, the calm and satisfied exemplar once more draws the new emergent landscape.

Throughout the process the exact words are written down and movement through the process is plotted. This allows you to have a ready reference and source for back-tracking, and to prevent omissions or misrepresentation.

Basic Clean Language Questions

Whilst Lawley and Tompkins identified over twenty regular questions used by Grove, they narrowed these down to the nine that were most commonly used to generate the metaphoric landscape. They have divided these according to their function. The questions are used time and again to track the various metaphors found within the answers and the answers to the answers.

Developing questions

These questions serve to hold time still, and serve to describe the form of the metaphor.

- *Attributes*
  - And what kind of [exemplar's words] is that [exemplar's words]?
  - And is there anything else about [exemplar's words]?

- *Locating*
  - And where/whereabouts is [exemplar's words]?
- *Converting*
  - And that's [exemplar's words] like what?

Relationship questions

These questions provide the links between the various identified elements buried in the system.
- And is there a relationship between [x] and [y]?
- And when [x], what happens to [y]?

Moving time questions

These questions move time back and forwards identifying cause and effects and also reveal the system in operation.

- *Sequence*
  - And then what happens? What happens next?
  - And what happens just before [exemplar's words]?
- *Source*
  - And where could/does [exemplar's words] come from?

These questions may appear to be naively simple, or cumbersome and unnatural, depending on your initial view. But when woven into the slow dance of exploration, they serve to reveal fascinating structure, which offers illogical logic and presents a coherent truth. The emerging landscape holds the exemplar's ever-present wisdom and a reassuring description of the previously unknown, unseen inner organisation.

Required Skills

1 **Establishing trance:** the Symbolic Modelling process requires the exemplar to enter an altered state and become immersed into the hallucination of his or her personal metaphorical landscape. This is achieved through various means.

2 **Syntax:** this following structure gives Clean Language its identity, serving respectively to:
- *Acknowledge:* And (match exemplars words / non-verbals).
- *Orientate:* plus And when/as (match exemplars words / non-verbals),
- *Question:* plus ask Clean Question *of the metaphor*.

3 **Vocal qualities:** here you need to differentiate, in tone, the words used by the exemplar and the words you use to construct the questions.
- *Exemplar-generated words:* match *the way* they speak those words.
- *Facilitator-generated words:* s-l-o-w d-o-w-n your speed of delivery and use a consistent, rhythmical, poetic and curious tonality.

4   **Non-verbals:**   as the modeller, you replicate sounds, gestures and perceptual space of the exemplar, *from the exemplar's perspective.*

You also need to backtrack frequently, stringing the words and phrases together.   This serves to keep both yourself and the exemplar on track: after all you are the one with all the notes, whilst the exemplar is absorbed in his or her inner world.   It can also act as a punctuation point, before changing tack and moving to another part in the sentence or the landscape.   The more comprehensive the backtrack, the easier the lead to a new area can be.

5   **Selecting the question**

 • *Open connection:* knowing what question to ask directly affects the smooth flow of the process. The more you take up residence in the metaphoric landscape and feel the inherent logic within it, the more intuitively you will know the line of enquiry to pursue.   You will gain a felt sense of the dynamics of the emerging system, know where the undeveloped spaces are, and feel where the energy flows or has stopped.

   You are also able to listen to your inner intuition and hear the voice of your internal coach, directing and suggesting, reminding you of loops opened up much earlier.

 • *Significance:* this inner coach also registers those moments of significance, which then determine the direction to take.   These can either result from the attention the exemplar pays to his or her answer, to the emotional impact of its novelty, or to the new connections that are emerging.   You may not respond immediately, but make sure that all of these 'hotspots' are addressed before moving on to the next step.

 • *Step-by-step:* the less experienced may usefully seek to unpack the metaphors within the presented outcome, word by word, including the use of 'I'.   Those who know about parts know that there could be more than one 'I' operating in any system.

Obviously metaphor will follow metaphor as answers to Clean Language questions continue, and as the modeller you alone will decide which one to go for, depending on the 'logic' of the answers, or on the emphasis given to the answer by the exemplar.   They will either reach a 'cul-de-sac', where the answers become repetitive, or bear insufficient energy, or they will produce further new metaphors – metaphors all the way down.

I regard the revealing of these interconnected layers as 'going down the leg' as in a table until the modeller and exemplar come to a halt, at which point they return to the table top or original statement, select another metaphor and work down that leg or look for connections between the legs.

6   **Handling the data:**   personally, as I am writing down the answers, I will circle the original metaphor and link it to all the following layers, with the type of question attached to it.   This means I can track what I have been pursuing and what I have yet to do, or have decided, for whatever reason, not to pursue.

And I will try to have all the legs on the same page so that I can easily connect across with Relationship Questions.   These I mark out with straight lines.

Ecology

With its emphasis on only working with content provided by the exemplar, arguably the ecology issues within this process are minimal – almost non-existent. However since you are in charge of selecting the questions, there will always be a likelihood of bias.

It is worth noting, however, that due to the strong loyalty to this methodology, or lack of familiarity with any other approach, the practitioner may run the risk of imposing an approach incompatible with the exemplar's disposition.

Applications

Target groups

This methodology has a proven track record for being highly effective with those who are:

- *Inarticulate:* those who are young or elderly, people with disabilities, and those dealing with trauma, or those who are naturally wary.

- *Highly cognitive:* those who have reached no resolution through the cognitive route of counselling, CBT, or inner and often circuitous reasoning.

- *Naturally predisposed to metaphor:* those who liberally sprinkle their language with obvious metaphors. The modeller needs to apply a steady hand to the tiller, to keep the exemplar grounded. The more absorbed the exemplar becomes, the more focussed they then become.

Therapy and coaching

The transcripts within Lawley and Tompkins's *Metaphors in Mind* arise from therapy exemplars. You can also find many references to instances with individual exemplars in their descriptions and articles.

Education

Caitlin Walker, one of the early adopters of Clean Language, has pioneered the use of the methodology in the classroom, proving that it has rapid effects on working with unsettled classes. Children have no problem talking in metaphor and have direct access to their internal structures. In fact in some cases they are amazed that grown-ups have come to join them!

Business

It might seem an unlikely place to introduce such a therapeutically based practice, but Clean Language can be played out conversationally, without heavy reliance on the intonation and some of the syntax. This is particularly useful for problem solving more abstract types of problems. Much depends on the congruent delivery of the modeller/consultant.

It has found a place in working with organisational change, in research interview methodology, and in market research approaches.

Non-purist use

I have found that having the Clean Language questions as part of my repertoire enables me to introduce them to ease open an exemplar's awareness, whilst pursuing a different methodology. I don't feel the need to develop a full-blown landscape, merely enable the exemplar to gain a clearer sense of what is lying just below the surface.

I also may use the some of the Developing Questions to identify an operating metaphor, and then work within the physicality of that metaphor and its known logic – roads lead from and to somewhere, bodies have hearts, lungs, legs and arms, gardens change with seasons. Working at this level is coding inner patterning at just below surface structure.

Coding

Lawley and Tompkins operate primarily in the world of therapy and coaching. There is no need to code or produce a digitised model since the end user is the exemplar. However the exemplar may put meaning on the symbols and metaphors that emerge, and relate them to specific instances in his or her earlier life.

Having said that, Lawley and Tompkins have demonstrated how it can be used to construct a digitised model that can be acquired by a third party or end user.

- *Idiosyncratic model:* the interim and final illustrations, created by the exemplar, are idiosyncratic models in their own right. The exemplar as end user can inhabit the model and navigate through it as a three-dimensional space, as it stands.

  Arguably, so can the modeller and any third party, provided each of the elements are accompanied with the developed descriptions as provided by the exemplar.

- *Metaphorical model:* I know during our first workshop at The Northern School of NLP, we were guided towards constructing a model for curiosity, through working in threes, and establishing the common elements within our three landscapes. These processes then became the model that was then acquired by another 'three'. The process/format/strategy technique stayed in metaphorical form.

  - Have a sense of your attention being caught
  - Focus on what is catching you
  - Feel drawn towards it
  - Stay open now to what is happening.

Constructed Model

If constructing a coded model is an outcome, the modeller will be given an illustrated description of the problem, the transition process to solution, and of the solution, as well as the accompanying verbal description. So the modeller can choose which to focus on.

- The modeller can then ask the exemplar to take one of these descriptions, and identify the key elements and what they represent. The exemplar will have clarity about what is significant and what is not. The modeller does not need to be preoccupied by this at this point.

- If a generic model is the goal, then this process can be repeated with several exemplars (provided the context is the same or closely similar). Now it is the modeller's turn to cohere the differing descriptions into a unified model, testing constantly to feel if it delivers the class of experience in question.

- The modeller, of course, may choose to work independently with the landscape, and through his or her own neurology test what is significant within the landscape. The modeller may factor in those moments of discernable significance to the exemplar and possibly come up with a codified model suitable for the third party end user.

For details on how to construct a model, see the section on model construction in Part 5 – The Results of Modelling.

Concerns

- Personally, I lament the day that Grove labelled his language patterns 'Clean'. As a metaphor it immediately presupposes 'Not-Clean', or, more pejoratively, 'Dirty'. If only he had chosen 'Neutral' instead. I have viewed with disquiet the growing band of enthusiasts, many of whom have had no exposure to NLP at large, and who have become almost evangelical around the banner of 'Clean'.

  Starting as an adjective, it serves as the prefix to the activities within the 'Clean Industry'. The word has now become a standalone nominalisation for not just a practice but also a disturbing tone of superiority in the field of modelling and changework, to the point that if you are not 'Clean' then you are outside the fold.

  Now I know that this was never the intention of Lawley and Tompkins, yet any attempts by them or their lieutenants to defuse this thinking have not succeeded.

  As a result we either get followers or mismatching rebels with the odd impartial consumers along the way. Personally I believe the approach is too good to tar with this narrow mindset.

- In essence the word 'Clean' is a poor metaphor, and so, annoyingly, is not code congruent. Whilst the mindset insists that the practice is free of the modeller's map, the modeller still has an influence. The modeller chooses the questions, directs the exemplar's attention, determines the route through the process and implies levels of significance. This last point is particularly so when the modeller marks out personal significance through non-verbal sounds or gestures, or shifts in intonation and energy whilst delivering the set questions.

- On a more grounded note, an interesting dynamic results because all of the focus rests on the emerging metaphorical landscape. The modeller's relationship is with the landscape, as is the exemplar's. The modeller has no need to take on the landscape or to understand the exemplar – in fact this detachment is encouraged. The modeller is dissociated from the exemplar, second positioning the landscape and not second positioning the exemplar. The modeller has no need to find out what it is like for the exemplar to hold this landscape, only to support the exemplar in his or her navigation through the landscape.

  Therefore, practitioners do not need to have high relationship skills. They do need to have a forensic interest in the dynamics of the system they are being presented with.

  Some may say this is a benefit of the process. Others, like myself, may question the faint pulse that can beat through it.

- Not everyone is predisposed to talking in metaphors, even though their language is unwittingly full of them. It may be a concept that is really alien, or too illogical. Their need to keep a tight grip on their conscious mind prevents them from slipping into the meta level of consciousness that is the land of metaphor.

- Not everyone may be receptive to the somewhat unnatural language structures, pace and intonation, and become irritated by this deviation from 'proper' communication. The modeller is required to have a light touch, pacing the level of trance the exemplar is ready to enter.

As a therapeutic approach, Symbolic Modelling requires that the exemplar becomes absorbed in the metaphoric trance. Rapport can be quickly lost should the practitioner insist on pursuing the process, in the face of resistance. The exemplar can sense any frustration of the modeller, should the questions not activate the 'right' response.

It is suggested that this is the fault of the modeller and his or her lack of skill, and not the methodology. Maybe there are just some resistant exemplars, and having alternative methodologies is essential at such times.

- Symbolic Modelling is so thoroughly researched that it can be adopted as a comprehensive answer to any therapeutic or coaching problem. This 'one size fits all' mindset could in fact be its limitation. Where it is the only methodology available to the modeller then there is no fallback approach to step into should this one be non-productive for whatever reason. If a technique will always let you down at some point, as Delozier is fond of saying, then so will a methodology.

Were Symbolic Modelling my only option, I fear I would tire of its prescription, no matter how good the results.

- Over exposure to the syntax, intonation and questions can become wearing, especially when mindlessly offered. It is the one methodology that receives the greatest 'move away from' responses that I am aware of, which does it a huge disservice. 'And what kind of move away from is *that* move away from?'

Having said that, these behaviours are usually found in the new learner, who has yet to learn distinctions and discretion.

Finally

Despite these concerns, I am full of admiration for what Lawley and Tompkins have created and what they have achieved. When I look at my listing of standards for a modelling methodology, Symbolic Modelling and the work of these modellers meet all of the requirements.

Grinder's protestations that no new modellers of note have emerged since the heady days of the1970s, shows how much he is in denial of what Lawley and Tompkins have brought to the field.

Together Lawley and Tompkins have provided a remarkable combination of creativity and discipline in their modelling endeavours, rigorous accountability and impeccable design in their training and development activities, with vision and strategic thinking in their dissemination and marketing.

For a methodology that is just over ten years old, what Lawley and Tompkins have achieved is truly outstanding. Through their ability to sponsor commitment in others, as at 2013, trainings now take place in over sixteen countries and four continents, by a delivery team of qualified trainers. The UK Clean Conference has become an annual event, and additional books and articles have been written by specialist practitioners. Lawley and Tompkins have created a modelling methodology that stands shoulder to shoulder with its older brothers and sisters.

Parts Alignment

Fran Burgess

For biographical details, check back to Punctuation Modelling.

The Background

Parts Alignment is another example of metaphorical modelling using the metaphor of parts. The underpinning constructivist thinking builds on the principle that our identity is composed of facets of our personality, which we call parts which are held in an interconnected system. Their presence shows up in language, voice tone and physiology, each being responsible for particular activities and behaviour. This understanding underpins the statement 'we are not our behaviour', since we are more than any one part which is operating at the time.

The methodology works on the principle that all behaviour is a result of the quality of relationship between all of the operating parts within the internal system. Disharmony occurs when the parts are in conflict and working against each other, and harmony when parts are in agreement and aligned.

When I was in my 30s in Edinburgh, I befriended a troubled adolescent, self-harming and suicidal. I had no formal training. At one point I ask her to draw the different people inside her that she talked about. I can still see the Baby, densely drawn in thick black felt pen. I often wish I knew then what I know now, since I could have come alongside that blackened Baby and found out what was needed to help it grow, and discover the influences the other parts were having on keeping it there. I believe I could have been instrumental in helping her so much further.

The methodology started out with the work of Virginia Satir. She identified the notion of parts that led to the creation of The Six Step Reframe. This seemingly simple process contains some pretty powerful presuppositions, namely:

* We all have parts that are responsible for behaviour

* There is a positive intention behind the behaviour

* We need to be respectful and establish rapport with each part

* Parts can interconnect and communicate with each other

* Agreement needs to be reached between parts before change can be contemplated

* Ecology and congruence is dependent on this agreement.

On learning of Virginia Satir's 'Parts' Parties', I began to explore the possibilities revealed in working with all the parts operating at any one time and not just the one responsible for the behaviour. It is often the case that ten or so parts are operating at any one time. My group work training helped me plot and record the multifarious interactions and relationships in these intricate and often-warring systems.

I was also aware of Jung's work with archetypes and the suggestion that there is a basic population of archetypes within all of us. As a constructivist, I choose not to go down this route, because it would predetermine the outcome, impose labels, risk installation, and limit filters. I hold that only the individual can identify and describe the workings of his or her own parts, certainly their names and their characters and how their personalities express themselves.

The methodology emerged organically as I naturally responded to exemplars' responses whenever parts were indicated and I have records as far back as 2000 of completed casts of parts. By the time the process became formalised and coded, and I was ready to train others, I gave the methodology the name of Personality Alignment that I have now more accurately relabelled Parts Alignment.

As a starting point, I assume that a part takes on the universal metaphor of a human form, so each has a name, gender (male, female or androgynous), particular clothing, job or purpose, and responses to each other. At the same time amorphous representations also can occur having their own less well-defined characteristics. I found it is essential that the process stays metaphorical and unrelated to known events or people, to maintain access to the inner deep structure.

Early on it became obvious that just connecting existing parts and creating conversation between them was not enough. The parts themselves often needed to undergo a change.

So methods of transforming the initial configuration emerged and often provide moments of epiphany. Once harmony becomes established, that triggers an integration process to return once more to a holistic system.

Grinder observes that

> The notion of parts is an imposition by the left brain onto the flow of experience. It is a temporary distinction for leverage in the change process.

Whenever we put words to explain or code internal experience, whether it is submodalities or metaphor, we are removing ourselves from that experience and applying cognition – which serves a purpose for that moment. He then goes on to say:

> They are ultimately fictions, simple punctuations on direct experience … And with all impositions, the notion of parts is useful until you start to believe in them.

Origins of Neurolinguistic Programming (2013)

This is an extremely important point Grinder is making. Parts are *part* of the holistic system, which makes up our identity. They do not operate in isolation, or operate separately from the overall personality. All operations and communication with parts has to be held within this understanding.

The Approach

The approach splits itself into three phases: Identification, Transformation, Integration, although transformation can be activated during the identification process.

Stage 1: Identification

During the Identification phase the whole system is modelled out, to discover which parts are operating and contributing to outcomes – actively or passively. As the modeller, you will already have been filtering for patterns of mannerisms, voice tones, and vocabulary blocks, and will have gained a sense of which parts are already making themselves available.

1   **Elicit the parts:** usually between seven and twelve parts makes up the average operating system. The exemplar may feel that two or three are sufficient, but you've been holding the overall context and can challenge this limitation and encourage the revelation of more.

These are elicitation questions that you can use:

- Which part is speaking at the moment?
- Which part brought you here today?
- Who is ready to come forward now?
- Which part objects to that?
- Who helps you?   Who don't you like?
- Who haven't we met yet?
- Who tells you this?   Where does this come from?
- Is there any part that is hiding, or waiting?

2 **Profile:** once a part has come forward, establish name, age, clothing, job, and relationship with those other parts that are present. You may also establish early on who is standing/sitting where, and who is in a group and who is alone. The exemplar will immediately gain a sense of how each new part relates to the existing ones.

3 **Handle difficulties:** parts don't emerge just because you ask them to, or arrive in ways that you might expect. In the next section, there is a listing of the difficulties you might expect to encounter.

4 **Avoid interventions:** this period in the process is merely to establish the Cast. Only once the full system is revealed can interventions be targeted, and implemented in an integrated systematic way. Anything else is ad hoc. Having said that, I may opt to resource say a child early, by inviting him or her to choose what they would like to wear, instead of the rags or constraining clothes they arrive in. It's a matter of judgment.

5 **Handle emotional responses:** you need to be prepared for strong emotions on the meeting say with a little abandoned part or a loathsome part, or the arrival of an essential missing part.

6 **Backtrack:** backtrack regularly to remind the exemplar of where you have reached. This can highlight gaps and imbalances. It can also deepen your own grasp of the system and the dynamics between each of the parts. You will always have greater clarity regarding all the parts, since often the exemplar is concentrating specifically on the machinations of one or two. Plus it is likely that you are taking notes.

7 **Test:** you are monitoring for gaps, mapped against what you know of the exemplar. When you feel you have come to the end of the process, or when the exemplar has come to a halt, you want to double check before you move on to the next stage.

Invite the exemplar to go to the edge of the system and look on, watching how all the parts are behaving. At this point you ask,

- Is there any other part that we have yet to meet?

It can be surprising how one or two more emerge, often quite crucial to the process. Their reluctance to appear earlier might be significant.   They may have needed convincing through standing back and observing the process.

Problems to overcome

During the process of establishing the cast of parts, you may encounter some difficulties. It is useful to expect these so that you can work with the exemplar and come alongside the part itself. How you behave in these early stages will have a direct effect on how well you are 'allowed' to do later on. Establishing rapport with each part early on is absolutely critical.

- *Difficulty dissociating from the part:* the exemplar will give the part the exemplar's own age, and call the part by the exemplar's own name. Invite the exemplar to really listen to what the part is saying, in particular the tone of voice. Sometimes I even invite them to become aware of the mouth that is speaking. This usually will generate a sense of the age and the gender of the part. And when the exemplar for example says, 'quite young', ask 'how young?' All exemplars need is an experience of this inner conversation, to give themselves confidence and allow themselves to dissociate freely.

- *Discounting a part:* the exemplar may place little value on the actions of a particular part, and overlook its significance, especially if that part's behaviour comes easily. As the modeller you have a lot of information already from your initial interview or previous sessions, so you can specifically call upon the part to emerge who is responsible for say 'getting things done' or 'tasting foreign foods' or 'befriending people'.

This can be an easy way to get the ball rolling, since the exemplar, whilst surprised that such a part is important, has to acknowledge that it exists. However you may find later on that this part has a minor role and the exemplar's instincts were accurate.

- *Hidden parts:* enabling a reluctant part to come forward and state its case, can have a tremendous effect – and require courage on behalf of the part. Time needs to be taken to create a safe environment for it. Asking for example 'what has to happen before you feel able to come forward?' can give you something to work on.

Don't force a reluctant part. Acknowledge that it is there and move elsewhere, holding the intention to return at a later stage, when the system is more established and safer.

You may find that one part is responsible for hiding and protecting a more vulnerable part. This is their job. This can be detected where there seems to be a muddled reply to what their job is, often including the job of the hidden part as well.

- *Alliances:* you need to be aware that each part is part of a wider system. Parts will gang up on each other. Where there are alliances it is useful to identify one after the other. These alliances can explain certain patterns of behaviour, and provide reasons for the suppression of other parts. You can then find out either who irritates them, or which other part doesn't like them. Demonstrating an understanding of the Vulnerable Part or the Feared Part's world could be all that is needed to entice it forward.

- *Loners:* there may be a part that is set aside from the others, in a different room even. This could be because it has been banished by the others for their safety reasons; or there is a self-imposed exclusion and a sense of not being part of the whole system; or it feels unsafe in the larger group; or it doesn't know how to get in.

Again, avoid forcing this part to join the group. Find out what is keeping it where it is and what needs to happen before it is ready to come in. Waiting until the system is known and a bit more stable might be required. Or possibly one of the existing parts needs to sponsor this part and go out and bring the outsider in.

- *Commentary:* very often a question of one part will be answered by another, or provoke a meta comment. Don't be fooled that this is the intended part speaking. This can highlight a deeper level pattern of one part taking responsibility for another, or prevailing antagonism one against another. Acute listening needs to detect this, to avoid misunderstanding. An Intellectual Part may provide dissociated commentary, talking *about* the process or a part.

  Log these interactions in your mind or on paper, since this is information about the system and can be referred to later.

  Should interruption occur, then firmly say to the intruding part that their time will come, or that they have already had their turn for the moment; and that it is important for this part to have his or her say. You are the shop steward for those parts who don't have their voice heard.

- *Blanks:* the modeller may come up against a seeming brick wall. Instead of accepting this and retiring defeated, just realise that there will be a part responsible for this behaviour, usually for protection. Pace the desire to protect – and wonder what had just happened which called on the need to protect – and then find the conditions that need to be in place for this part to hold back from triggering the blank response.

  Often when you identify the system that generates the blank, the exemplar will recognise that this is something that happens, to a greater or lesser extent.

- *Naming:* initially parts may be given pejorative names, which describe the nature of their behaviour, not their intention. For example, a truly critical Bully Part might prefer to be called George.

  Instruct the exemplar to ask the part directly and wait for the answer. This sends a meta message to the part that you are on its side, and that it is worthy of respect.

Plotting the System 1: once the full cast is established, the exemplar is left alone to draw the scene. This requirement provides a punctuation point and confirms the key players, clarifies the relationships and the exemplar's perceptions. You can also check how closely your internal representations line up with the exemplar's.

This illustration will provide the calibration point for the future outcome. It also provides an explanation for the current situation, which can bring tremendous relief to the exemplar. Give time for the exemplar to absorb the impact of this external expression of what's been going on for him or her.

Once the illustration has served its purpose, it is useful to turn it over so that the exemplar's attention can return inwards once more, and move forward.

Stage 2: Transformation

The current combination of parts is responsible for the unsatisfactory system; therefore, the nature of these parts needs to be reconfigured so that they complement and support each other. This is the process of Transformation.

Ideally, you wait until all the parts have appeared before any changes are made. This is not cut and dried. As mentioned earlier, it may have been appropriate to offer a change to a part so that they become more resourceful, or as a way of removing a blockage preventing a part from coming forward.

There is no set procedure for this, and it is best to tap into the natural wisdom of the system. Letting the parts know that change is possible and outlining the options, can allow the exemplar or a part to volunteer for change. Certainly you should be in no rush to 'convert' a seemingly 'difficult' part just to generate comfort. Often such a part needs to gain confidence that the altered system can deliver before it commits to conceding its current functioning. Opting to do this as part of a comprehensive process, offers the various parts an understanding of what's involved whilst experiencing the benefits that arise. Sometimes change will happen spontaneously once the part knows what is possible.

Whatever the shifts, the ecosystem has to align and reach agreement with the new structure. If there is any dissension, then this needs to be addressed.

Change options

- *Function:* it could be that the job allocated to the part is not suitable because of its age: a 3 year old cannot protect the system, or a 9 year old is not able to be fully heard by the adult world. Or under a revised system that function is no longer required, but another one might be more suitable.

   On identifying the positive intention, you need to detect what attributes are presupposed within the role, and how these could be applied more usefully. For example a young part that rails against injustice could use this energy to become The Defender, or The Spokesperson. Or the part who wants people to like it could become The Lookout, or PR part, since it already has a high level of social awareness. Often the part will come up with its own suggestion, once it knows that it can choose.

   The part needs to agree to the new job. You need to listen out for any incongruence, since often such changes threaten another part who possibly fears that it will become redundant.

- *Naming:* with the change in function can come a change in name more suited to the emergent role. Again this is down to the exemplar/part to determine.

- *Clothing:* changing what a part wears, and inviting that part to choose for itself what it would rather wear, can make a significant difference and radically shift energy. Should a part be wearing a cloak or armour for example, shedding this could reveal a very different appearance. If a Little Girl part is wearing shabby clothes, which is most often imposed upon her, she can choose a pretty party dress or freedom-seeking dungarees.

- *Aging or regression:* parts can become older or younger, sometimes in surprising directions. Children can become babies and vice versa. Ancients can become even older, middle aged, or teenagers, and in the process the energy shifts.

   Where there is a high number of young parts, say under the age of 15, it is unsurprising that the system is not able to cope with the adult demands placed on it. This is a fairly common occurrence.

   Sometimes when considering changing age, the part splits into two aspects, and some characteristics stay with the original part, and the emerging part adopts the other characteristics to deliver the new role.

- *Gender:* genders can be altered. Giving the option to shift from male to female or vice versa can remove distortion in energies and contribute to a greater sense of completeness. There is no prescription regarding the balance of genders, or being all of the same gender.

- *New part:* you may consider that there is an imbalance of function and invite the system to identify what part is missing. Such a part can then be invited in. All parts have to be fully in agreement.

They need to agree what this part will look like, how it will behave, what its role is and if its presence will be temporary or fulltime.

Once the part is introduced, it needs to connect with each of the other parts, acknowledge its roles and desires, and agree how it will work with them.

- *Departure:* parts should *never* be asked to leave just to suit certain other parts or yourself. This just perpetuates non-alignment. However, sometimes a part may realise that its role is now redundant and its work is done. It has no further contribution to make. If this is the case, the other parts need to bid it farewell, and thank it for the work and energy it has been offering up until now. Or it might choose to wait in the wings in case it is needed.

  Alternatively, the part may choose to adopt a different role within the system and 'make a new life' for itself.

At the end of all of this, it might become evident that another part is now ready to emerge, so you need to make a final check.

Key Parts

Whilst I don't subscribe to predetermined archetypes, I have found that certain key parts need to be present. If they do not already exist, they need to be created out of the existing cast, or introduced.

- *Essential*

  - *The Director aka the General Manager, the Conductor, the Junction Box, the Controller:* this part is responsible for coordinating the actions of the other parts and set direction. How it holds its power is down to the individual. It might be quite authoritarian, or operating through consultation. It is the first port of call for The Child (see below) and is therefore responsible for responding immediately to any concerns The Child may have. It also is likely to be the main contact for The Spiritual part, should it be present.

    Often this Director emerges from a young part that may have had a job 'to keep everything together' or 'to bring cohesion and stability.'

  - *The Child:* this part may have started out as a baby, or youngster, or it may be a lost adult part. It may have been given a job that only an adult can do. Whatever its origins, its new job is to play, to be free of all responsibility, just to 'be', whilst becoming the emotional lightning conductor, with a direct line to The Director, alerting feelings of danger, sadness etc. These are signs that the system is not operating well on all fronts and something needs to be done.

    On the very rare occasion that The Child is not sourced from within the existing Cast, it has to be invited into the system from outside. This need's to be a very gentle process.

- *Optional*

  - *The Spiritual part aka Chairman, Mentor:* this part connects to a higher wisdom and provides The Director with the sense of direction and overall purpose. Its inclusion is often dependent on the age of the exemplar – more likely in 40+ exemplars, or when exemplars report that they 'have lost their way'.

  - *The Nurturing part aka Nurse, Carer, Nanny, Mother:* this part is crucial if the system has a history of not looking after itself, possibly paying more attention to the needs of others.

- *Frequently found:* no finished collection of parts can be predetermined. Having said that, in my experience it is common to end up with some of the following:
  - Defender, Protector
  - Scout, Learner
  - Archivist, Intellectual, Planner, Problem Solver
  - Socialite, Fun part, Lover
  - Spokesperson, Activist, Rebel, PR part
  - Worker, Organiser, Practical part, Doer
  - Artist, Creative part, Dancer
  - Coach, Moderator, Balancer, Cheer Leader.

Note: This listing may be a result of my personal filters. When mapped against a full listing of archetypes – about 80 in all – the are many that don't feature here.

The Process

It is hard to have a set procedure for this stage in the process since literally everyone is different, with a unique system of parts, and their own responses to the process itself. As the modeller, your sensory acuity needs to be really sharp.

1   **Provide the reframes**
    - 'Your dominant part has had to be like this because your other parts weren't doing their jobs right.'
    - 'Some of your parts are doing the wrong jobs, or aren't equipped to do the jobs they have.'

2   **Explain the options:** let the parts know what is possible for them. Some may volunteer straight away. These are likely to be the lesser parts.

3   **Trust your exemplar:** ask which part would make, for example, the best Director. The system is likely to know and the right part may actually volunteer for the role. You need to test the ecology with all the others and gain agreement.

4   **Listen to resistance:** if your exemplar seems reluctant, or a part expresses a concern regarding a suggested change, pay attention. Even it you are convinced that this part is destined to become The Director, or The Lookout, or whatever, listen to the wisdom of the system. The exemplar will prove you right every time.

5   **Pace the change:** some parts may quickly attain the desired age – usually to become the age the exemplar is now. Others may have to grow incrementally, spending time in teens or twenties, with the exemplar testing the shifts in clothing, attitude, and relationships. Sometimes a part will revert back to the original age, which might suggest that some work hasn't been done yet on its behalf.

    Some parts may wish to stay in their teens or twenties. This would make sense if their energy or youthful enthusiasms or strength are needed.

6   **Leave big changes to the end:** big changes are likely to be -

- The rehabilitation of a 'nasty' part
- The establishment of The Child part
- The introduction of a significant missing part.

The system needs to have a strong degree of stability to be able to hold these changes. The other parts need to feel safe and secure in their new roles. And the part in question needs to feel that the system is now safe enough to trust.

7   **Epiphany:** one change may be particularly significant. Be prepared for a strong emotional response – often when you least expect it. It could come when a part takes its rightful place, or the introduction of, say, a Spiritual part or Nurturing part. It could be the emergence of a part that has been long hidden.

Let the exemplar fully experience the moment and give them all the time they need to complete the journey through their emerging awareness.

8   **Be prepared for a new part:** once the system is ordered, then it is not unusual for a totally new part to emerge from within. Sometimes this arrival makes complete sense and finishes off the picture entirely.

9   **Calibrate:** increasingly, the system will become quieter and quieter and exude a level of contentment and peace, particularly after a significant change. Other changes can happen quickly and fall into place. The exemplar is likely to become more animated and laugh. They will comment about feeling much better, lighter, different, and look at you wonderingly. After all it is a pretty amazing and powerful process. When you feel the system has come to rest, the exemplar is ready for the second drawing.

Plotting the System 2: once the new arrangement has been finalised, the exemplar then once more draws the system.

Or the exemplar writes the names of each part on bits of paper and lays them out in the preferred arrangement – an approach that accommodates changes in thinking. This is then plotted onto paper, and the exemplar can take away the slips of paper as well.

There should be a significant difference between this model and the interim illustration. The finished representation will be symmetrical.

- It is highly likely that on the central line will be The Director with The Child below. The Spiritual part if present will be above The Director, or embracing the whole system.

- If the illustration is deeply aligned, then the rest of the parts will be on both sides of the central line, either in a circle or a square, will be matched in pairs of complementary activity.

Combined with this symmetry will be a calm, quietened, expansive state. The exemplar may report feeling safe and secure, or grounded and stable, ready to take on the future.

Stage 3: Integration

Once the aligned cast has been finalised the final two-part integration process is ready to begin.

Photograph: the exemplar takes a photograph of Team [Exemplar]. This serves to anchor the freeze-frame now: the exemplar feels really good at seeing such a committed team of parts rooting for him or her, full of energy and a collective sense of purpose; the exemplar sees the gathering, who's on the front row, sitting, in the middle; and hears their comments plus hears and feels the click of the shutter as the picture is taken. This provides a strong reference anchor.

The exemplar then moves into the centre of the gathering and views the future that the parts are seeing. You can perform a future pace at this point.

Taking up residence: for full integration, one-by-one the parts are invited to enter into the exemplar. The more associated the exemplar is in the process, the more likely they are to take charge of the sequence. I call this 'The Night John-Boy' moment, as the lights are switched off in the Walton's *Little House on the Prairie* TV series, and the home beds down to sleep.

At the point of entry each part is asked:

· What is your promise?

The modeller records this promise on the final illustration.

· Where do you reside?

The exemplar will indicate whereabouts in the body the part moves to. Any future sensation from this area could be interpreted as a signal from this part and a conversation can ensue.

Again the location is recorded on the illustration.

The exemplar then takes away his or her illustrations and you may choose to keep a photocopy for the record.

The Skills

This methodology draws on all the modelling practitioner's NLP skills.

1   **Work with Meta Model:** fluency here helps to prise open the system and shine a light on the nature and characteristics of each part and the relationships between them. Each part will have its own meta programmes and beliefs. Recognising and responding to these will ease rapport and deepen credibility with the exemplar's system.

2   **Attention to rapport:** this is at the heart of the process. Your task is to sponsor each part equally, without bias, to enable each to have its voice. Gilligan's Tender, Fierce and Playful approach comes into its own here. Through maintaining rapport with the parts, you establish deep rapport with the explorer. In fact time flies by.

3   **Attend to meta comments:** no word is merely a throwaway comment, especially those that are chucked in by another part. Where possible use the words your exemplar's part gives you, or to demonstrate that you understand, paraphrase them whilst keep close to their meaning.

4   **Have strong sensory acuity:** this is essential to detect nuances, shifts in tone and energy – and to judge when to slow down and sit in the space, or to move onto another part in the system.

5   **Respect resistance:** handle resistance with a gentle touch. It is worth remembering that the process is staggering and at the same time fascinating for the exemplar. And it will always be a particular part that is resisting. Pace it and all will be well.

6   **Note taking:** you may feel more comfortable noting down the key points for each part. I have found that the more engrossed you, the modeller, becomes with the unfolding soap opera that you have been presented, the less you will need your notes. These become 'real people' as vibrant as any social gathering, and your attention becomes naturally focussed.

7   **Recap:** regularly cover name, purpose and relationships at different stages to maintain and support the hallucination. The exemplar is lost in the experience and won't have metacognition of all that is going on. Your recap serves to regroup the process and ground progress.

8   **Pace intrusion:** avoid going directly for 'problem' part. Let it be until the dynamics support a supportive response to its presence. One way to ensure this is for you to deal with and manage any constantly intruding part – to do what the other parts have failed to do. In the same vein, remember to return to any unseen parts.

9   **Increase association:** judge when to talk to a part directly or via the Exemplar. Going directly to a part ensures accurate unedited response and full recognition of their presence. It also allows for the part to bypass any interference. However this can make the part feel exposed and vulnerable.

10 **Think systemically:** all the parts interconnect in a relationship that is supportive or otherwise. Their energies influence the behaviours of each other. One shift to one has the potential to create a shift in others. You need to second position the group and experience the relationships, to gain an understanding of the vulnerabilities and concerns that are operating.

There's always a part there. Whatever is happening is down to a part.

Ecology

- I have encountered a strong resistance in those who fear the concept of parts and see it as a process of dismantling identity. For a psychiatric nurse, this was akin to schizophrenia that in her mind merited strong medication. Another couldn't allow the phrasing of 'a part' since she saw that as being an embedded instruction to disintegrate. She would grudgingly accept the concept of 'a facet of personality'.

  It is essential to provide a congruent preframe, highlighting the natural presence of parts in language, and in the different personae that we adopt which show up in our greetings, choice of dress and even our walks.

  It is also essential to remind the exemplar that the main directive of the unconscious mind is to keep us safe, and if it feels threatened, it will withdraw from the process.

- Integration is an essential stage in the process and not an optional bolt on. No exemplar should be left without a formal integration process. Whilst most individuals will naturally accommodate the information and bring it back into their system unaided, there may be one who might not. This person cannot be left with the idea that they are not a fully integrated holistic being.

- No parts should be banished – even though the modeller or the exemplar or both might think it a good idea. It is essential to sponsor and re-integrate the energies, and acknowledge the positive intention.

- Suggesting that physical sensations could be attributed to a part might cause the exemplar to discount the symptoms. Should a 'psycho-active' conversation not produce any diminishment, the exemplar is advised to follow mainstream remedies.

Coding

- *Exemplar as end user:* it is sufficient for the exemplar to go away with his or her final illustration, including the comments and location of each part. As with the metaphoric landscape produced through Symbolic Modelling, this illustration is an idiosyncratic model as it stands.

  The exemplar can refer to the element and dynamics within the illustration to explain behaviours, or to open up conversations. The exemplar is now aware of the process and can continue to self-model.

- *Third party end user:* if the modeller has a particular end user in mind, then appropriately selected exemplars can provide details of the Parts that are involved in producing the desired behaviours. The modeller can then extract the beliefs, meta programmes, or values of each Part; or establish the necessary conditions that need to be present for the relationships between each of the parts to be operating at their best.

  The modeller is then able to construct composite 'archetypes' each with its own make up and required interactions. The Disney Strategy is an example of the type of coded model that could emerge, although it was derived in a different manner.

Applications

- This approach is primarily used for therapy. It is most suited when an exemplar refers to parts in his or her opening remarks – 'being pulled', 'indecisive, one minute saying X, the next Y'; 'negative voices'. etc. Whilst the modeller has other methodologies to choose from, the exemplar is saying that he or she is already predisposed to talking in parts.

- This methodology is a good way of 'clearing out' the system to establish a solid foundation for further exploration. Where there is a lot of turmoil with the exemplar becoming distracted by his or her internal dialogue, this is a great way to quieten it all down. Reference can be made later to certain parts.

- Irrespective of the severity of the presenting problem, because this approach takes as a founding principle that there will always be a part responsible for the behaviour, the part that is, for example, abusing drugs, displaying irrational anger, or succumbing to deep depression, can be identified, sponsored and supported.

  Often such a part is isolated and banished by the other parts out of real fear. There may be huge reluctance to even let this part come forward. However this part exists *because* the system is unaligned and insufficient to meet its needs. Holding the space to enable this rapprochement is a very powerful service to offer any exemplar.

  The meta message offered by the modeller is that no part of an individual is 'bad'. All aspects of behaviour have a positive intention. This matter of fact thinking really supports an exemplar in what can be quite a difficult exploration, and bring him or her to a new level of self-acceptance.

Concerns

- The full process in its entirety takes about 2½ to 3 hours, which is fine provided the time is available and the modeller has the ability to concentrate for that length of time.

  I had a concern about splitting the session, between the Identification and Transformation stages, since this would mean that the parts were left 'bare'. However during the training process, this was unavoidable with a day being allocated to each stage. Provided there is an interim integration process where the unconscious mind is invited to 'Reintegrate the parts and make them ready to be available the next time we meet, so that the system is safe', then there is no cause for concern.

  With this evidence, I have felt comfortable splitting therapy sessions. Sometimes this gap gives opportunity for reflection and clearer understanding of the emergent parts and the conditions they are working under.

- This process does require good NLP skills and sensitivity. It is not for the untrained novice. Yet I have a belief that under such circumstances the exemplar's unconscious mind would quickly kick in and the unskilful modeller would be greeted with a lot of 'don't knows'.

Finally

Parts Alignment provides a highly personalised description of an exemplar's inner structure in a manner that is highly effective for bringing about change. Exemplars become fascinated to discover their Cast, and have a clear wisdom about how the various parts are cohabiting, becoming more and more fluent as the process continues.

It fundamentally adheres to the notion of Sponsorship, where everything is fine and acceptable, seeking to reunite what Gilligan calls the 'Disidentified Self'. Not only does it alter old programmes and reconfigure internal parts, it allows for the introduction of missing pieces, in a profoundly reassuring and caring way.

What the methodology has yet to do is produce a written up account with detailed case studies and published references to support its rationale. This account however, is a start.

Part 3 – The Methodologies of Modelling

Cognitive Methodologies

Cognitive Modelling is the last of the four classes of modelling methodologies, and, as its name implies, uses language as the means of eliciting underlying structure.

Whilst the Intuitive and Expressive approaches tend to be more holistic, operating from creative thinking and unconscious processes, the Metaphoric and now Cognitive methodologies work applying the conscious thinking of logic, and working procedurally as opposed to simultaneously. By this stage the methodologies clearly have an external starting point then progress to working internally as opposed to the other way round. Instead of operating in a childlike fashion, the modeller is dissociated from the action and applies an adult rationale to the process.

Happily for us, once more we are given choices about which methodology we can select from this section. And one of the major benefits for the modeller is that cognitive approaches are most familiar to the exemplar. We understand communicating verbally. Little or no introduction is required. And provided the modeller uses linguistic skill and precision to steer the exemplar to the most useful part of his or her inner experience, the modelling process is the nearest approximation to a conversation that we can have.

Because the responses are already coded in language, it is a small step to convert them into fully digitised models that can then be activated to generate new and targeted reference experiences.

In this class of methodology you will find the following:

- *Experiential Array – David Gordon and Graham Dawes:* a comprehensive framework and questions, driven by the operating criterion and supporting beliefs, and incorporating strategies, emotions and observed behaviours.

- *Analytical Modelling – Robert Dilts:* eliciting a wide range of information which can then be scoped into familiar frameworks, the most common being Neurological Levels, as well as other neurological/linguistic frames such as time and perspectives.

- *LAB Profile – Rodger Bailey/Shelle Rose Charvet:* an ingenious means of detecting the meta programme traits an individual is running in particular contexts.

As mentioned earlier, I had considered including John McWhirter's *Developmental Behavioural*

Modelling (DBM), since he is a modeller in the full sense of the word. Starting from within the world of NLP he has moved on to develop his own independent modality that stands alongside the practice of NLP. DBM operates outwith NLP and is its own study.

The Experiential Array

David Gordon

David Gordon is a feisty, funny and loving individual, with a rapier-like mind, a love for debate, a heat-seeking-missile means of detecting incongruence. He also has a legendary reputation as a storyteller. He is deeply committed 'to participating fully, and helping others to participate fully, in life's variety of experiences.' He is a self-confessed experience junkie, which explains his continued pursuit over the last thirty years of developing the practice of modelling.

> Every human being I meet teaches me how experience works. I enjoy the experience of experiencing someone else's experience – it's fun, enriching – I enrich my own experience.

While the first stirrings of what was to become NLP began in Santa Cruz, Gordon was part of the vital body of learners who tried and tested the discoveries and propositions created by Bandler and Grinder. We can remember the time when conversationally Gordon mentioned the point they 'invented' Change Personal History.

> We were sitting around talking about how we felt bad about things, and one of us said 'I never feel bad about what's happened'. Immediately the rest of us swooped onto him and asked 'how do you do that?'

Well before any tools and techniques had been developed, learning was through pattern detection, sensory acuity, testing, evaluating feedback, reworking questions, never assuming the outcome, being up for surprises, and endless fascination and curiosity. In the beginning was modelling.

By 1977 enough material had been formalised and developed to begin certificated trainings. Taking over the work of Leslie Cameron Bandler, under the auspices of DOTAR (Division of Training and Research), Gordon was in charge of the very first Practitioner Trainings held in Santa Cruz.

A natural storyteller, unsurprisingly his first book was *Therapeutic Metaphors* (1978), written whilst he was practising as a therapist. He then went on to co-author with Marybeth Meyers Anderson *Phoenix* (1981) that is a highly accessible account of the basic patterns of Milton Erickson. He then co-authored with Leslie Lebeau (previously Cameron Bandler) *The Emprint Method* (1985) and *Know How* (1986), two fairly technical books on the process of modelling.

Modelling continued to fascinate him, which led to his most recent collaboration with Graham Dawes. Together they developed their unique modelling methodology into what has become known as *The Experiential Array*, presented in their book and CD *Expanding Your World* (2005).   They continue to refine their work through a series of thorough essays on their website www.expandyourworld.net, and in early 2014 they produced an interactive eBook of *Expanding Your World.*

As a modeller, Gordon's interest lies only in helping the individual. He is not motivated by money or commercial practice. It never occurs to him to take his modelled information further and construct Product models and make a business from marketing these. His sole focus is on the modelling process and helping the individual. He is only fascinated by the experiences of another individual – and of course self-interest. Whenever he discovers something he would like to do better, he sets off to find an exemplar.

In addition to his contribution as one of a small number of thoughtful, rigorous human experience modellers, and as well as being a therapist and writer, Gordon has also spent time as a scriptwriter, primary school teacher, trainer, house builder and loyal friend.

We are forever grateful not only for his constant support of The Northern School of NLP and our pursuit in understanding the nature of modelling, but for our introduction to the card game Casino.

Graham Dawes

Graham Dawes was the founder of the UK Training Centre for NLP – the first centre outside North America, an academic and exponent of the Self Managed Learning (SML) approach.

The Background

Gordon's understanding of experience drives his modelling endeavours. Here are some of his statements which underpin his thinking.

> Experience is all we have. It is a constellation of senses and their submodalities.

> People understand experience. We need and seek shared experiences. If we didn't we wouldn't have books, films, music – there would be no community and no relationship.

> Word is the medium to make sense of our experience. If we don't share the language we don't know if we share the experience – it becomes mind reading. Without shared meaning through words, we may have to rely on our intuitions.

The Belief Template and Experiential Array, to give it its snappy full title, is based on the premise that whatever the ability, there will be a *simultaneous* interaction between beliefs, strategies, emotions and behaviours that naturally and automatically gives rise to that ability.

The Array

The Array is a framework that addresses the identified ability in its specific context. As an information gathering tool, it allows the modeller to plot the range of information as it's being gathered. Once the targeted ability is established, there is then a natural progression through the framework. However, it is not essential to pursue this progression as a fixed procedure. The more familiar the modeller is with the components and dynamics of the Array, the more able he or she will be to spot which element the exemplar is offering as and when it arrives. The modeller's job is then to fill in the gaps.

The Array captures all the information available because the modeller doesn't know ahead of time what's going to be significant. Only afterwards, once away from the exemplar, does the modeller begin to work with what's been elicited and generate his or her model that satisfies the requirements needed for the ability.

The framework covers the following elements, usually pursued in this given order.

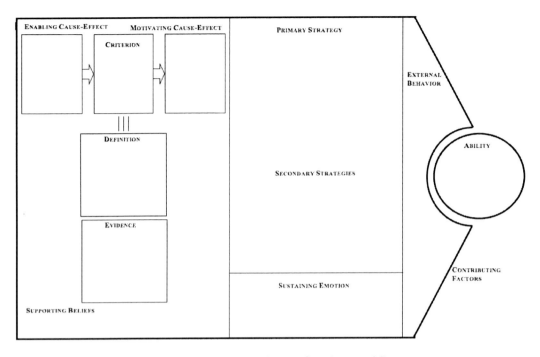

Experiential Array Template – Gordon and Dawes

Criterion

The Criterion is the beating heart of the experience. Gordon and Dawes are unique with their identification of the significance of the operating Criterion. Within any context and behaviour, the exemplar will always be concerned that the operating criterion is satisfied. Fulfilling and maintaining this criterion is essential for successful operations. The exemplar's choice of criterion is the *cause* of the excellence since it provides drive and focus.

It might be 'Understanding', or 'Balance', or 'Security', or 'Pleasure'. Whatever it is, the exemplar's attention is focussed, consciously or more often unconsciously, on whether or not this need is being met and all strategies are directed accordingly.

Change the criterion and the whole experience changes. Similarly change the context and the criterion might change. Being context specific, the criterion differs from values, which are important across contexts.

- Elicitation Questions: when doing [ability] what is important? When doing [ability] what are you evaluating?

Belief template

These relate specifically to the criterion. This is a fascinating powerhouse of discovery, separated into four components:

• *Definition* – what the exemplar means precisely by the criterion, to remove any ambiguity and misperception on the part of the modeller.

- Elicitation Questions: what is [criterion]? What do you mean by [criterion]

- *Evidence* – a sensory specific description of how the exemplar knows whether or not his or her criterion is being satisfied – good basic NLP here.

  – Elicitation Questions: what do you see, hear and/or feel that lets you know there is [criterion]?

- *Enabling Cause and Effect* – to give the exemplar's rationale for the essential conditions required to generate the criterion. This belief provides the route towards gaining the criterion.

  – Elicitation Questions: what must be true for there to be [criterion]? What is necessary for there to be [criterion]?

- *Motivating Cause and Effect* – to discover why this criterion is so important to the exemplar. When taken to its full extent you will find the very Purpose of the exemplar that runs through his or her marrow and informs excellence irrespective of context. This prime motivator provides the leverage for change, and will be different for different exemplars of the same ability.

  – Elicitation Questions: why is [criterion] important? What does [criterion] lead to or make possible?

Gordon suggests that when you lose sight of your enabling and motivating C-E your behaviour loses meaning and connection.

There is also an additional box of miscellaneous beliefs that support the behaviour as well. These will be offered conversationally.

Strategies

These are the internal processes that operate and generate the behaviours, so that the criterion can be fulfilled. Gordon and Dawes usefully divide these into two categories Primary and Secondary Strategies – what the exemplar does when all is going well, and what the exemplar has to do when there are difficulties to overcome. This distinction matches Grinder's requirements of a complete model.

I have always maintained that the Secondary Strategies hold the key to the exemplar's excellence since they demonstrate deep understanding of the operating context and call upon flexibility and dexterity of skills.

It is worth noting that within this section, you will never find a string of K_i^+ -> A_{id} -> V^{ac}/A^r -> K^{+++}. Gordon strongly rejects any notation that he considers diminishes the marvels of experience. 'You don't see people doing this! I hate labels because you never see the person any more.'

  – Elicitation Question for Primary Strategy: what do you usually do to fulfil [criterion]?

  – Elicitation Questions for Secondary Strategies: what do you do when [criterion] is not sufficiently satisfied; is not at all satisfied; cannot be satisfied?

Emotions

Emotions either support or generate the strategies. Again Gordon and Dawes divide these into Sustaining Emotion, which is the constant one that serves the criterion, and Signal Emotions that are in response to success or lack of success of the strategies and can be ignored. These will be offered conversationally.

It is worth noting that this is the only modelling framework that incorporates emotions as a core component. For me, this essential piece of information indicates the *manner* in which the exemplar is performing the ability. It lets us know *how* a person is conducting his or her performance. A sustaining emotion of Love will produce a very different performance to one founded on Pride, or Frustration.

- Elicitation Question for Sustaining Emotion: what is the background feeling that enables you to continue pursuing [criterion]?

- Elicitation Question for Signal Emotions: what other emotions do you experience?

External behaviours

These are the actions that others can see and hear whilst the exemplar is in the pursuit of his or her ability.

- Elicitation Question: what are you doing on the outside when you are responding this way? What can others physically see, hear and possibly feel?

Contributing factors

These elements establish the viability of another's ability to deliver the performance. Being dextrous, having perfect pitch, being highly numerate may be a significant requirement of a future acquirer. These will also be offered conversationally.

Elicitation Process

Gordon and Dawes have identified specific questions, outlined above, that they believe will generate the desired information for each of the elements. The novice modeller would be wise to follow this prescription. Otherwise, they may gain information totally irrelevant at best or misleading at worst; information that would then highjack success.

When modellers *fully* understand the target of these questions, and what each is designed to retrieve, then the questions can be reworded, should the exemplar not respond. At such times modellers need to pay particular attention to the quality of answer, to test if it is delivering the information they were looking for.

Modelling Methodology

The Array in itself is not the methodology although the relationships between its elements generate an active dynamic that underpins the ability. The developers have done much of the work already for the modeller, so you can just step into these shoes and hit the track running.

Idiosyncratic and Generic Models

Gordon and Dawes make a clear distinction between: the model you can generate from one exemplar, which they call an Idiosyncratic Model since it has the specific characteristics of that exemplar; and a Generic model that is a composite model supplied from the data of various exemplars. As they put is in their Essay on Generic Models:

> A generic model is created by looking for, and making generalizations about, patterns of structure shared by several exemplars of the same ability. The process of creating a generic model is one of

stepping into and comparing your exemplars' Arrays for similarities in either content or structure, and resolving discrepancies. A potential weakness of a generic model is that the process of generalizing may 'wash out' details that are particularly useful or compelling for some individuals. The strength of generic models lies in their ability to winnow out idiosyncratic elements belonging to particular exemplars, leaving a model that better reflects the essential patterns of the ability, and is more generally accessible.

Going Deeper: Working Models: Generic Models Essay – Gordon and Dawes (2014)
www.expandyourworld.net

The essay goes on to cover the process of combining the sources of information and deal with those pieces that don't seem to fit – using the vital ability of 'Stepping In' which is essential for any modeller.

Note: In the Classification of Models in Part 5 – The Results of Modelling, I have used the term Idiosyncratic Model for something similar, i.e. a model produced from one exemplar.

Basic Principles

The following is some fundamental thinking that informs the construction and application of the Array, and modelling in general.

- Reference experience informs our map and gives it meaning and significance.

- Modellers will NEVER have the experience of the exemplar.

- Maintain a desire to understand; otherwise you risk becoming judgmental and superior.

- Questions need to be neutral and precise.

- Evidence needs to be specific so it can generate an experience of it in the modeller.

- If it works for me it will work for everyone since we all have access to pretty much the same range or variety of experience in our personal histories.

- Competence is having ways of organising skills and knowledge.

- Start at the level of your own competence and chunk up from there.

- Modellers need to have a secure sense of self.

- When acquiring the model it needs to operate from the individual's own Motivating Cause and Effect.

- Integration occurs when the behaviour starts being used in the world.

- The Acquisition process needs to be sufficiently powerful to provide a strong enough experience to drive change.

The Approach

1 **Identify the exemplar:** this exemplar demonstrates a particular ability that you wish to understand, or wish to offer to another. Or it may be that your coaching or therapy client is your exemplar and you are seeking to find out what's going on underneath.

If you are selecting an exemplar because you want to produce a model, then choose one whose behaviour is on the edge or just beyond your map.

2   **Identify the contexts:** the exemplar is required to identify three occasions where they performed the particular behaviour, each time to the same standard with the same results. This context determines the criterion.

You will be continuously testing the answers you are receiving in your experience. Therefore, using your reference experiences, you are testing as Gordon puts it, the 'systemic efficacy and importance of the information'. You need these three occurrences to help you sort out what are patterns and what are not.

3   **Gather the information:** be prepared for the exemplar to start off with a chaotic information dump. They want to be helpful. They think they know what you need to know. Don't trust the exemplar to know what's right for you.

Work through the Array, writing up the answers preferably on a flip chart or somewhere the exemplar can see. This, (a) lets exemplars know that you are listening to them and using their words and, (b) gives them the opportunity to reflect and correct any answer.

When you offer your assumptions of what you're hearing, do so with the intention of being wrong, to be open to the exemplar correcting you, 'not this, it's that'. Exemplars will correct you since they don't want to be misrepresented.

You need to be alert to receiving information out of sequence and recording it in its appropriate place.

4   **Identify patterns:** as you are receiving the information double/triple check if this information applies to each of the examples given. If it does, then you have unearthed operating patterns. This stage and the Testing stage that follows becomes intermingled as the process unfolds.

5   **Test:** you have to run the ability through your own system to know if the pattern you have detected has any usefulness. The 'Stepping In' process is where you the modeller take on the exemplar's structure, and in doing so experiences shifts in your own behaviour towards that of the exemplar. Testing each contribution within your own experience allows you to manifest it and reproduce it. If you can't, discard it. If it does, write it up on the flipchart.

Be mindful that discarded material may become useful later on, as you begin to know and understand more about what is going on.

'Stepping in' is about gaining empathy and identifying with the other's system. However should the empathy become overwhelming – for example if the exemplar is an abuser – then you need to step out and shake yourself and get back into your own skin.

Always be asking yourself 'can I do this?' You have no intention of becoming the exemplar, merely the desire to be able to do the ability. You the modeller are no longer there. Instead you are resonating with the exemplar's experience. You'll know you're on track when you find yourself saying, 'I'm getting it. I know what's going on. I recognise the pattern I'm giving myself'.

And you exit your TOTE when you can replicate it within yourself in the context of your own goal – real or imagined.

6   **Tidy up the model:** strip out any duplication. Test if by removing an item, your own internal sense of being able to do the ability diminishes, or stays as strong.

Devise the process of third party acquisition. When preparing to offer your model to a third party, it is important to remember that there is always someone 'in there'. So whatever you offer will be assimilated through his or her neurology and the resulting behaviour will reflect the acquirer's uniqueness. The acquirer needs to apply the model through his or her own Motivating Cause and Effect.

The completed Array might constitute the finished idiosyncratic model, and acquirers are invited to take it on and explore the results within their own neurology. Adjustments might have to be made. There may be elements that the acquirer doesn't have yet and which might have to be installed. Or it may be that the acquirer doesn't have the physical capability required of the exemplar.

Skills required

- For this approach, you need to have a familiarity with the Array, its dynamic and the quality of information expected for each of the elements. You need to know the eliciting questions – have a hard copy of the Array with the questions to hand. You need to know the distinctions between what constitutes a definition, or evidence, or the enabling cause and effects.

- You need to be constantly aware of the relationship between yourself and the exemplar. Productive rapport is essential. This will build as the exemplar gains more and more evidence that you are not just seeking to understand, but you are actually gaining a felt sense of the exemplar's inner processing.

- You need to be skilled at extracting the criterion from the midst of the data coming forwards. This could be the opening question, or it could be some way into the process. It is essential that you 'try on' the criterion and notice how your own physiology shifts to a new level of awareness. If it doesn't then it is likely that you are not there yet.

Derek Jackson and I were extremely fortunate to be invited by Greg Laws, an NLP Modeller, and advocate for the San Bushmen, who are living in the Kalahari Desert of Botswana. The San are renowned trackers which, of course, is *the* fundamental metaphor for modelling. We had gathered a whole range of information – what they did, what they knew, how they knew it. After a considerable amount of time observing, following and asking questions, I eventually asked 'what was important in tracking and hunting?' 'Success' was the succinct and somewhat self-evident answer. When I next asked 'what does Success bring?' – I was expecting (bad modeller me!) something like 'a good reputation', or 'a warm welcome' or some such western reward. So I was utterly unprepared for, 'Connection with God'. When I took that in, it made such sense. Everything these legendary hunters did was to do with God's world, God's creatures, and God's spirit. Success would bring them to being at one with God. This information shifted my perceptions radically, and created a far deeper channel of appreciation and understanding. And led to a powerful model!

As Gordon says: 'When information is counter intuitive, then you know you are onto something. It is going against your assumptions.'

- You need to be able to ask clear and concise questions, with awareness that precision with language is essential. You are directing the exemplar's attention and are therefore responsible for the quality of response you get. Clumsy questions wear down rapport, undermine your credibility and challenge the exemplar's self-belief that they can offer what is required.

- You need to demonstrate flexibility if the exemplar is having difficulty in responding, without losing sight of the goal, by maintaining the context and keeping your exemplar fully associated. Check chunk size and bring references back to this level of operating. Offer a suggestion that you know will require a correction – 'Not that, it's this.' – which re-activates the exemplar's connection with the ability. And check how well formed your questions are.

Applications

This multi-purpose approach lends itself to revealing the structure responsible for a desired behaviour, leaving little responsibility on behalf of the modeller for making decisions regarding what direction to take. Once the ability and context is determined, the modeller is off!

Business

Being presented in language, this cognitive approach lends itself to easy assimilation, relatively speaking. The obvious application is through identifying what works in a particular way, and generating a model out of that. Exemplars can be key employees who are consistently successful within the company, and common patterns can be identified and generalised across operators in similar areas.

Or the Belief Template can formalise the criterion and beliefs of a Leader within the organisation, as a means of opening up discussion regarding the desired culture. This can be particularly effective at times of amalgamation or team change.

Therapy and coaching

- The approach is as useful for finding out how someone is able to be so excellent at being consistently stuck. The structure revealed within this can throw up the Motivating Cause and Effect, which can then be used as leverage for change.

  So if someone who is consistently depressed and his or her criterion is 'Survival' because that gives a 'sense of being Me', then the therapist/coach could ask, 'so how can being depressed give you a sense of being you?' and 'how else might you gain a sense of being you without being depressed?'

- Where an exemplar is in a low state of resourcefulness due to a particular problem, he or she can identify something they know they can perform well in. Modelling this out will generate an effective system of beliefs, strategies and emotion that are already successfully operating and delivering benefit, along with strong reference experiences. The exemplar can then be invited to test out what would happen if this structure were applied to his or her current situation.

  For example the exemplar might be being bullied or abused. Working in this context and applying the Array for 'Survival', and 'sense of being Me', the exemplar can be offered a really useful home grown resource.

- And when a structure has been proven to be consistently effective in the context of an unwanted behaviour for one exemplar, it can be applied to a similar, more desirable class of behaviour.

For example you can take the undesirable behaviour of say 'not doing the housework and letting the dust build up'. Here the exemplar is able to 'resist the ought's and should's imposed by others' – the desirable class of behaviour. This could be a really useful resource for someone who wants to develop the ability to stand up for oneself.

As a coaching approach, Jenny Thomas invited her dyslexicexemplar to 'act as if' she had already written a great academic essay, and then took her through the Experiential Array framework as this Excellent Writer. The process provided her with a rich reference experience. The exemplar wrote a well-structured, remarkably fluent essay without a hitch, and it was highly commended.

I worked with a consultant who was struggling to get the wording for her new website. We identified what it was that she does particularly well and it was 'Find the Gaps'. Using the Array we extracted a whole wealth of language that addresses her particular service and she was able to identify many examples to illustrate her claims.

Ecology

Apart from the usual requirements of contracting with the exemplar and the need to maintain rapport, I see no areas within this approach that could jeopardise ecological practice.

Coding

Gordon has said that in any elicitation process, there are usually three to five pieces that fall into place and make the whole structure meaningful. It is like waiting for the second shoe to drop.

However, Gordon has a strong reluctance to reduce the final contents of the Array to a point that removes the essence of the individual and provides a reference experience for the beholder. He is certainly not up for summating a vibrant Array into four or five elements. He does not consider that model construction is part of the modelling process.

I don't have such qualms! And with all respect to this wonderful modeller, I feel that holding all options can lead us to squeezing as much mileage as possible from this modelling process. I believe the Array can throw up a range of models, not just one. This versatility is one of the reasons it has been selected as the methodology of choice by most of our Master Practitioner learners.

For example:

- A sequential model based on the strategies.

- A system of beliefs that can be kept in its extended language format, or reduced to macro labels.

- A composite model that pulls out the 3-5 key elements. With the San Bushman of the Kalahari Array, for example, I derived a simultaneous model of Activity, Energy, Life Themes, Talents, which has the emerging property to generate a sense of Connecting with God.

- I have also found mileage in working with the Sustaining Emotion and Motivating Cause and Effect (MCE), to provide a turbo charged Identity. Take the MCE and identify an archetype that would hold this Purpose, then add the emotion as an adjective: when I do X, I am a Loving Warrior, or a Fascinated Sorcerer. This adjective really sets the mindset and approach of the archetype.

Concerns

- This approach does require a certain fluency of language on the part of the exemplar to respond to the questions. The questions in the array are designed to elicit specific information, which the exemplar may have difficulty putting into words. High levels of rapport are required to keep the exemplar confident and productive. Provoking correction could prove to be a major tactic.

- Finding where 'to pitch the flag' is critical for this approach, since it is so specifically focussed on a finite ability in a particular context. Being woolly about where in time, or the degree of complexity to drill down, or up to, could miss the sweet spot where the key information lies.

  If the modeller is not gaining a sense of cohesion and congruence, this is a clear sign that the flag is in the wrong place, In which case, the flag has to be taken out and nudged into a more fertile place – no matter how far into the information gathering process the modeller and the exemplar have already undertaken.

  Commonly the modeller is operating at the wrong place in the sequence of the ability. The identified criterion is the motivating cause/effect, or vice versa.

- The modeller needs to chunk to the level of his or her own competence. Any higher and the information will be assuming an ability that doesn't exist. Any lower will not bring in sufficient news of difference. Much can also depend on the modeller knowing the level of competence of the end user. The smaller the chunk and more specific the ability, the further away you take the exemplar from his or her immediate mission.

- Questions arise regarding the place for meta programmes and representational systems and submodalities, sometimes as a way of invalidating the comprehensive nature of the Array. These Gordon suggests, are embedded within the experience. Personally I regard these frames as an additional category of scoping, and don't feel the need to include the kitchen sink. If the ability can be acquired without them, then so be it. The modeller can choose to pursue them in addition, or opt for a different methodology.

- It has been suggested that the Array is 'merely Neurological Levels laid on its side.' After resuscitation, Gordon would answer that Dilts's model isn't constructed in experience and determined by a specific experience. Nor does it have as its starting point the founding flow from beliefs, through strategies and emotions, to ability.

- This methodology, again because of its specificity, relies on the accurate questions being asked. This renders the process somewhat vulnerable to novice practitioners, who may or may not notice the subtle differences in the types of answers they are getting.

- Establishing the Criterion is critical to the success of the information gathered. It is the focus for the beliefs and provides the raison d'être of the performance. Therefore, much hinges on getting this right. Too often fledgling modellers are unaware that they have not identified a criterion at all.

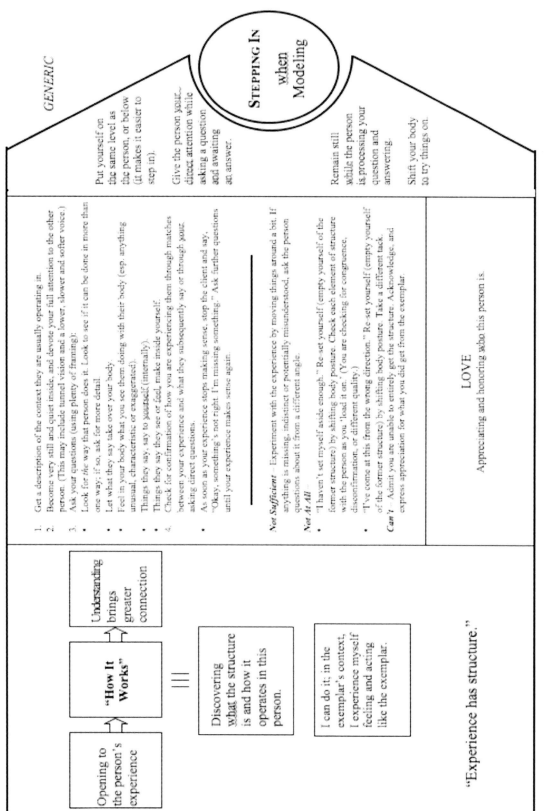

© 2002a David Gordon and Graham Dawes

Finally

This modelling tool was the approach of choice for the vast majority of our learners, who were specifically tasked to produce a model and then an acquisition process. It naturally paces our predisposition to cognitive enquiry. It is clearly laid out, provides a simple step-by-step process, instils confidence in the new modeller, and provides a means of navigating through the range of information an exemplar is likely to offer.

Once completed, anyone can step into the information and gain a felt sense of the activity in action plus an understanding of the processes involved, for that activity, in that context.

The Array also provides huge potential for constructing reduced models, due to the comprehensive range of information gathered. It is simple. It is comprehensive. And it is effective.

Analytical Modelling

Robert Dilts

Ever since his involvement back in 1977 in the feeding frenzy of learning that was the hallmark of Bandler and Grinder's early days, Dilts has been steadily developing and pioneering a wide range of applications of NLP thinking and modelling. Whilst others have fallen by the wayside, or indulged in ™ed side lines, Dilts has preserved the mainstream of practice and promoted the efficacy of NLP to a worldwide audience.

A polymath, his studies covered physics and calculus, animation, economics, psychobiology, anthropology, computer programming, hypnosis, therapy, politics, language and linguistics. His default state is fascination. He is a consummate learner and so the whole process of modelling was a natural experience for him.

In 1977, Dilts and Gordon put together the first certificated trainings under the auspices of DOTAR (Division of Training and Research). He then co trained first with Jim Eicher and then Terrence McClendon, delivering Practitioner training in Colorado for Steve Andreas. In 1982 Dilts co-founded the *Dynamic Learning Centre* with the late Todd Epstein. In 1991 he and Todd, together with Judith Delozier and Teresa Epstein, established NLP University, based at Santa Cruz campus amongst the red woods, where NLPU continues and thrives today. In 1992 I was wonderfully fortunate to experience Trainer Training and NLP Presenting in this fantastic environment, overlooking the meadows down to Monterey Bay, whilst Todd was still alive.

In 2013 NLPU sponsored the activities of NLP Planet, a web based initiative set up to present top NLP trainers from around the world through week-long webinar conferences.

Throughout his time, as well as the twenty plus NLP related books, many articles and developed software programmes, Dilts has maintained a consultancy practice working with top international organisations, and providing private therapy and coaching sessions. He also finds time to jog each morning!

A prolific writer and modeller, he is notable for his modelling from the written source. His *Strategies of Genius* (1994/1995) series give us the wisdom of Aristotle, Conan Doyle, Walt Disney, Mozart,

Einstein, Da Vinci, Freud, Tesla and Jesus of Nazareth, which led to the Sleight of Mouth Patterns. However Dilts will always be remembered for his formulation of the Neurological Levels – Environment, Behaviour, Capabilities, Beliefs and Values, Identity and Spirituality, which are now as he says 'an integral part of many modern NLP trainings'.

Dilts knows the value of partnering with other people as a means of growing and developing, both personally and for generating new ideas. His strength lies in this collaborative process.

> What happens in this sort of co-working is that there is a really deep kind of intuitive modelling that you get out of being with somebody. It could be working with clients (or colleagues). You begin to incorporate more of that person to the second position and you both become enriched.

> Interview at The Northern School of NLP (2004)

He often quotes Thomas Jefferson: 'If two individuals get together and exchange a dollar, they each walk away with one dollar. If the same individuals get together and exchange an idea, they both walk away with two ideas.'

His collaboration has brought us many milestone works:

Todd Epstein	*Tools for Dreamers, Dynamic Learning*	1991, 1995
Tim Halbourn and Suzi Smith	*Beliefs: Pathways to Health and Well Being*	1991
Gino Bonisonne	*Skills for the Future*	1993
Robert McDonald	*Tools of the Spirit*	1997
Judith Delozier	*Encyclopedia of Systemic NLP*	2000
Anna Deering and Julian Russell	*Alpha Leadership*	2002
John Dilts and Ian McDermott	*Success Factor Modelling*	2005
Steve Gilligan	*The Hero's Journey*	2009
Judith Delozier and Debora Bacon Dilts	*NLPII The Next Generation*	2010

The Northern School of NLP was really fortunate to have Dilts visit us on two occasions, specifically to major on the process of modelling. Both times we brought in an exemplar for Dilts to model, and to produce a model (all within 48 hours), whilst we had the opportunity to intuitively model him and his process and then cognitively ask questions.

On the first occasion, Lawley and Tompkins were also invited to model his modelling process, which they subsequently developed and published on their website – see section on Modelling Skills.

These workshops were amazing experiences, full of insight and learning. It was particularly special for me to have the man, who had given me so much, there in front of my family of learners, offering us his wisdom and humorous truth.

No one has done more to provide focus to the application of NLP. Whilst NLP has at times lurched into dubious territory, Dilts has consistently steered a description of practice, both ecological and credible. He has provided us with our moral compass. He has given us leadership through example, and not through headlines.

We, the NLP community, are extremely fortunate that he took up this mantle. Without his energies and commitment, I doubt that many of us within the community would be living the quality of life we now have. He truly has provided us with the opportunity to create a world to which people want to belong.

The Background

Dilts has not devised a modelling methodology per se. Rather his wizardry lies in his elegant integrated application of all of NLP's skills, thinking, and processes, and all that he has learnt through the accumulation of the many models and exemplars he was immersed himself with.

What does set him aside from other modellers is the range of beliefs he holds about the process. The following statements were taken from his workshop with us. Stepping into this listing offers huge learning in itself.

- *General:*

  - A Model is a process structure, independent of the exemplar.
  - The world of subjective experience is not literal.
  - Bateson: 'Everything is a metaphor for everything else.'

- *In the modelling process:*

  - It is impossible to separate model from own experience.
  - Seeds can bear fruit in months from now.
  - The exemplar needs to benefit.
  - Awareness is transformational. Incomplete awareness can diminish. Having a consciousness creates dissociation.
  - Once you have the sketch, you have a general idea of where a piece needs to be.
  - The words are cues, or labels to try to express the process.
  - It's not about getting the words precisely – it is about getting the process precisely.
  - There is a relationship between the goals and the processes – the Why and the How. Your notes form the What and seek their respective headings.
  - The art is to stay in the analogue – not removing the components out of their context otherwise you lose the relationship and the metacognition of the field.
  - Each element within the experience has its own reality that I connect with and relate to.

- *Modelling:*

  - Isn't a description of what someone does.
  - Is at least 50% you – you can't separate observer from the observed.
  - Is a creative dance. It should flow.
  - Deepens connection.
  - Is about producing something that is meaningful and which will make a difference – finding that difference held within the exemplar.
  - Is not about getting something; it is about finding jewels.
  - Is a TOTE.

- *When I am modelling:*

  - I am pulled into the space, into openness for places of surprise.
  - I can fill in the gaps myself if I know how to do something.

- Connecting is important to me.
- I don't want to share. I want to be like you.
- I make it up if I can't get at the information.
- I WANT TO KNOW.

The Approach

State

Dilts is very clear that the modelling state is singular and you need to prepare for it. Whilst the state of fascination and curiosity is key, he knows that for this to flow, there needs to be openness of the Centre and connection with the exemplar – otherwise the key feelings are lost. As he says: 'When the exemplar feels safe and heard, things will flow into the field'.

His awareness and attention is all over, with his peripheral focus in the background, and single attention in the foreground. For him: 'Attention is on the exemplar while in the background there are all the different screens and the cocktail of information'.

Even while Dilts is creating a reference experience from the material the exemplar has given, and is testing it within his own neurology, he is committed to staying present. And as the fascination develops this state of fertile awareness grows, unplanned. It is determined by the quality of connection between the modeller and the exemplar and the modeller and the modelling process. He comments: 'My body is much less active when I'm in the exemplar.'

Skills

From Dilts's perspective, the skills are very simple!

- *Develop interplay:* between your cognitive and somatic mind so that significance can be detected. For Dilts, this takes the form of a radar bleep bleep!

- *Listen:* to what is repeated in order to find the leverage point that will lead to something that's useful. The intensity of the signal tells you where the emphasis lies.

- *Backtrack frequently:* Dilts encourages you to use your own words to demonstrate the precision of your understanding. This process:
  - Narrows the deletions, distortions and generalisations
  - Tests what is still significant.
  - Tests if the pattern has been captured
  - Distorts on purpose to test 'truth', and near or far from the truth
  - Identifies missing bits
  - Allows the modeller to hear their own congruence regarding the emerging processes
  - Rehearses for future instructions and teaching
  - Validates the exemplar and deepen the levels of trust and relationship with the exemplar.

- *Record:* what is significant. These become the external markers of the process synonymous with Mozart's humming. This form of anchoring allows you easier tracking of the flow of information.

- *Hold systemic awareness:* and the flexibility to move attention from foreground to background.

- *Store information:* within different spatial locations, rather like keeping windows open on a computer, where each has its own reality, allowing then for parallel processing. This allows you to balance attention between end user and exemplar.

- *Pursue associated ad hoc responses:* and ignore dissociated comment. Instead of talking about a key word, find out what it is and its place in the process. As Dilts says 'push out the space – go for richness held within examples'.

- *Listen to your internal dialogue:* this could be the wisdom of the unconscious mind coming through.

- *Be mindful of the relational field:* between yourself and the exemplar, so you don't crowd the exemplar's processing experience, thereby allowing them to process and explore questions unimpeded.

- *Punctuate:* by touch, those meaningful and necessary points offered by the exemplar.

Preparation

Once the particular activity under question and the end user have been confirmed, you need to start off knowing the exemplar's present and desired state so you can become clear of the exemplar's operation, and the direction you are travelling in.

You need to establish boundaries with the exemplar so that they know what to expect. And whilst you may have a plan of questions prepared, be ready to respond spontaneously to what is coming.

Sorting/Scoping Frames

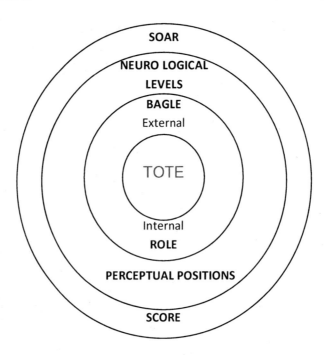

This is the overall framework that Dilts uses for categorising the information he is receiving, incorporating the following models of experience. These can be the windows you open on your internal 'computer'. Amongst them all, the Neurological Levels provides the dominant filters.

- TOTE – Test, Operate, Test, Exit.
- BAGLE – Breathing, Anchors, Gestures, Language, Eye Accessing Cues.
- ROLE – (Strategies) Representations, Orientation – Int/Ext, Linkage, Effect.
- Neurological Levels – Environment, Behaviours, Capabilities, Beliefs and Values, Identity.
- Perceptual Positions – 1st, 2nd, 3rd.
- SOAR – State/Operator/And/Result.
- SCORE – Symptoms, Cause, Outcomes, Resources, Effects – Time orientation.

Primary acquisition (aka Informal acquisition)

- *Somatic acquisition:* during this period you are connecting with what is said and matching it with your own experience, getting a somatic sense of what you're hearing, and discerning the essence behind the words. By repeating the exemplar's gestures and physically practising the spoken metaphors by hand, you embody them. Through taking notes, the hotspots become highlighted on the pages, to reveal emerging connections between them.

  Once you have reached saturation point, the time has come to let the information settle. This uptake phase is a prelude to the process of cognition. You need to be alert to new thoughts and ideas that arrive unbidden.

- *Cognitive acquisition:* at this stage, you are seeking to find if the details 'fit'. This is more of a cognitive than somatic process. With the end users firmly in mind at this point, you may already have the intention of teaching the process.

  On the inner eye, you play what the exemplar is saying he or she is doing, finding the edges of the beginning, middle, and end of the process, without the need to focus on those elements you can already do. Within this process of rehearsal you are focussing on the submodalities needed for performing the ability successfully.

Model construction

The end user will determine what needs to be 'in the box', and you need to avoid the temptation to overfill the sandwich. Whatever data is left over, you can use it as part of the acquisition process or contribute to another related model.

The Model construction process can take six or even twelve months. I know this is true for some of the frameworks I've come up with – even longer in fact. If it does indeed take this long, you need to keep the faith and trust that something will emerge.

Dilts talks about 'being prepared to receive the muse' since it is a process of creativity. Once the filters are set, other things start 'floating up'. He says it is important to be Open to balancing our conscious reason with the musing and ad hoc thoughts emerging up out of our unconscious mind – drawing on the powerfully important information gleaned through unconscious uptake. As the modeller, you add to this rich mix thoughts and ideas from apparently disconnected explorations from elsewhere.

Then it is a process of chunking up, down, and across through the data until a level emerges that resonates. Different classes of data may appear as dominant, and the data becomes organised under each category heading, on the understanding that these categories can shift and change, amalgamate and divide, causing redistribution of the data each time.

You then go through a testing process, looking out for any missing links, gaining feedback, staying open to the experiences being generated, and taking care not to over-evaluate and slip into the critic phase too quickly. You may have to return to the exemplar if the gaps can't be filled, or if your own references experiences are drawing a blank.

Whatever results, Dilts reckons it will be something beautiful.

> There will be organic symmetry holding beauty in the relationship between the components.

Model acquisition

This is the stage where you activate the model within a technique – either drawing from or adapting one that is already known, or creating something original. Whatever you come up with will then have its own life evolving from the acquirers' experiences and responses. This means that whatever is produced is likely to need reworking and rewriting until the process settles down and produces a consistent class of behaviour.

According to Dilts, whatever is delivered will be at the higher neurological level than the level the exemplar was operating at.

Applications

Dilts has operated extensively within industry and commerce, as well as privately as a therapist and coach. He is a prolific reader and writer. He is constantly seeking to understand, through instinctively applying his modelling nature.

He would suggest that any NLP practitioner, armed with the repertoire of NLP skills, could be operating as a modeller in whatever context they find themselves. This may be 'merely' to bring about understanding, or with the ultimate intention of producing of a model that is of service for an identified purpose.

One of the features of Dilts's work is his ability to make his models work for him, and so for us. He demonstrates just how flexible and creative we can be if we put our minds to it. This was a big wake up for me when I realised that one model can deliver so many techniques just depending on how I work with it: thinking which resulted in *The NLP Cookbook*; see Part 6 – The Formal Acquisition Process in the section onTechnique Construction.

Working with Disney Strategy

The model *Dreamer, Realist, Critic* is probably well known to most of you. It is used to process an idea through planning and rigorous criticism, until all 'why not's go quiet. This is usually a spatial exercise, with or without content. Very effective – it got me to Bali and launched me on my NLP career.

However many people just stop there and don't appreciate that it can deliver so much more. Working on the principle that these three energies need to be involved before an idea can be acted upon with some belief in its success, the model can be used for:

- *Building the Creative Team:* knowing that creative thinking needs all three energies, on an individual level, those that are less well developed can be strengthened. Or in a group, additional people can be recruited to bring balance, and the virtues of each can be emphasised.

- *Team planning:* this can be used to generate future planning, drawing on the resources within the team. Either divide the team into its naturally occurring roles, or have them work collectively through each of the stages, preferably in different locations.

- *Testing an Idea:* working in small groups, have the Dreamer come up with its idea and possible plan for its implementation. Then invite the others to draw what they think they've heard, no doubt bringing in metaphors and symbols. The Dreamer just listens and gathers the feedback and goes off to modify thinking.

  This approach was offered during our Trainer Training in Santa Cruz, and I unashamedly incorporated it into our Trainer Training for lesson plan design.

Working with Neurological Levels

This must be Dilts's favourite model since it is the one he returns to again and again.

Most of us have gone through Neurological Level Alignment – and if you haven't I strongly suggest you find an experienced person to take you through it. It is one of those special NLP experiences. You may have had an experience of Co-Alignment where two would-be collaborators move up their respective levels, joining at the top and coming down the centre rather like a zip fastener bringing their shared aspects with them.

The Neurological Levels can be used as a spatial exercise, or used cognitively in conversation or written questions. It can be detected through language and emphasis, and its elicitation patterns can be interlinked with other models.

- Dilts uses the framework frequently as an alignment process, often within a series of questions, or as a guided trance, to establish and strengthen understanding and purpose: for example as a means of exploring personal Charisma as part of his *Art of Authentic Charisma* workshop.

- Dilts has used the NLL framework to develop new techniques. He offers a wonderful experience, moving upwards through the combination of the Levels and physically with the chakras, using binary hands to explore a dichotomy – me at my best/at my worst, present me/future me. Just delightful!

- He uses the Levels to make greater connections with other systems, for example linking it with the different operations of the brain and nervous system (see Hierarchy of Neural Systems, NLP II), as well as the system of chakras.

- Dilts uses the NLL framework to create new models, for example *Coach To Awakener Model*, which identifies the ascending roles involved in guiding personal development from Caretaker to Awakener.

- *Ego and Soul Model:* as part of his sustained attention to the role of Leadership, Dilts has developed this all-embracing model to explore the dichotomy between Entrepreneurial Leaders and Bureaucratic Managers, between Soul and Ego, with the suggestion that we can operate on both sides of the line depending on context and task. The complementary relationship between Soul and Ego is the human balance between our expression of 'an unfolding connected self' and 'the development and preservation of our sense of being a separate self'.

At each Neurological Level, the individual will be focussing on particular aspects: for example for Soul, Environment will offer opportunities, whilst Ego at the same level will present constraints and dangers. It is useful for us to notice where we are, and if this position is serving our outcomes. When these elements are out of alignment, we will be feeling profoundly dissatisfied. Dilts concludes: 'Optimum performance comes when the ego is in service of the soul'.

Ecology

Because there is no prescribed modelling methodology, this approach is possible ultimately the most ecological of all the approaches, certainly the most flexible. In skilled hands, no exemplar is 'shoehorned' into a predetermined framework or mindset, and all intervention is in response to the feedback the modeller is receiving.

Alternatively, the less-experienced modeller may feel insecure by the lack of direction, and uncertain of what steps to pursue. Unfettered by any constraints, there may be a danger that this modeller becomes susceptible to imposing his or her own map.

Coding

A coded digital model is always bubbling away under the analytical processes deployed by Dilts. The distillation of the material into discrete elements is the hallmark of this approach. Once categories are determined and labelled a coded model can arrive.

Concerns

- Some modellers need the imposed frameworks and mindset to give them direction and to reduce the potential overwhelm the 'blank canvas' can present. Without this, the modeller can be easily daunted and give up. This is reduced to a degree by the clarity set by the end user's needs. The 'options' people have a field day.

- This approach does rely on trial and error as a means of growing modelling competence. Whilst this is a great way of building up the somatic recognition of what is working, it does rely on sustained commitment from the modeller to keep on in there with the process, and with his or her faith in the process. Good intentions can so easily fall by the wayside.

- There is a reliance on the modeller having a naturally developed sense of structure, systemic thinking, and the ability to process logically. Which again may be a reason for drop out.

Finally

Dilts has said clearly that: 'If something takes me 100 days and I find a way of doing it in 10, then of course I want others to know about it'.

And that is what Dilts has been doing all these years. He has taken his modelling abilities to many corners of human experience to find models to simplify what's involved and to offer them to us so that our lives can be enriched. His work on Beliefs was particularly fruitful. He always works with the end user in mind – which means that he starts already anticipating creating something for others to consume.

I have come to the conclusion that Dilts models at behavioural level. Modelling is what he does. In fact, he cannot not model. However, his identity is not one of a Modeller. Undisputedly, he is a Learner, a Creator, a Sharer, a Builder of a Better World. At some stage in his development, he morphed into the identity of Leader, and has channelled his energies in this direction.

Modelling is a means to an end for him – in service to his end users. He does not actively focus on training modelling. His reputation is not centred around teaching modelling, after all his book *Modelling with NLP* was published as far back as 1998. Instead his reputation is for all the many fabulous experiences he has generated as a result of modelling. Year on year, for over twenty years, he has introduced new models and processes – the fruits of his latest passion and collaboration.

He has been prolific and in fact has done much of the work for us. Perversely, this could be the cause of some of our laziness – ready-made meals to microwave versus raw ingredients to prepare and cook ourselves. Many of us within the global NLP community may have been lulled by this convenience. We lose sight of the pleasure which total engagement in the creative process can bring. We have either forgotten or never discovered the joy that comes from coming up with innovative results through using our own skills and knowledge.

If we want to stay active Modellers, we need to resist becoming total consumers – or know the difference and operate at choice. To keep our modelling skills alive, we need to know that we always have an alternative to the off-the-shelf models and ready-made techniques. As modellers, we need to be continually flexing our skills of enquiry and Not-Knowing, if we are to keep our modelling thirst alive.

Having said that, Dilts has done much more than his fair share towards demonstrating just how much can be delivered to a world to which people want to belong – through modelling.

Language and Behaviour (LAB) Profile

Leslie Lebeau (Cameron Bandler)

Leslie Lebeau (Cameron Bandler) was part of the original group of pioneers exploring and developing the ideas of Bandler and Grinder, also journeying with them to Phoenix to meet with Milton Erickson. Married briefly to Bandler, she was the original instigator of DOTAR (Division of Training and Research), the first NLP training company to formally disseminate the emergent field of NLP. During her time working with Richard Bandler, Lebeau became fascinated with the concept of Meta Programmes, so called because she considered that these characteristics were somehow the 'programs which ran the programs' in people's heads.

Bailey recalls:

> I heard from Leslie was that when she and Bandler were debriefing after client sessions, she would ask questions how he decided to use (or not use) a particular technique or approach. He would respond that the client was, 'away from' (for example) and that tactic requires a 'toward' mindset.

> Leslie said that after the second time Bandler said that kind of thing, she started listing those labels. After she had a long list of these kinds of comments from him, she came back to him with the list and started asking for more in-depth information about these labels.

As Lebeau developed her understanding, she compiled a list of about 60 distinct patterns, roping in

David Gordon and Robert Dilts to work on sorting out and specifying the distinctions, and then experimenting with them. Leslie gained a lot of information about the mental patterns of people based on each pattern and was beginning to establish examples of what their language patterns might be. She was able to clearly state, for example, that an 'Away From' person will use avoidance language and will live that avoidance attitude as well. As part of her training on this work, she devised a Question Grid, which provoked a lot of response from the exemplar, and out of this she would search for the patterns she knew about.

Lebeau let go of her fascination when she realised that meta programmes were not the 'universal' answer to behaviour. She reluctantly became aware that their configuration was dependent on context.

> For ten years I'd been looking for what are the patterns that tell me about the person and for a long time I thought it was Meta Programmes and then it turned out not to be, cause they change by context too, so always I'd been looking for 'What's the essence?' ' What's the core?' because that's what I want to be able to touch.

> From tape 6 side A of Empowerment: The power that produces success, courtesy of Inspiritive website.

Leslie is the author of *Solutions* (1985; originally titled They Lived Happily Ever After, 1978) and is co-author with David Gordon and Michael Lebeau of *Know How* (1985), *The Emotional Hostage* (1986) and *The Emprint Method* (1985). Her method *Imperative Self* was one of the first applications of the distinctions and the principles of NLP to identify and expand the personality patterns.

Rodger Bailey

Rodger Bailey graduated with degree in Anthropology, and completed an MS in Educational Counselling where his studies in Transactional Analysis led him to an interest in NLP – the latter whilst working at IBM as a Staff Programmer/Analyst. He was drawn to NLP in his fascination to understand the links between his understanding of humans and our psychology, his understanding of technology, and his understanding of our evolution.

Initially training in New York in 1977, he took his learning to Santa Cruz, being a participant in the first Master Practitioner DOTAR training: 'My certificate is #5'. It was during this training he was first introduced to the notion of Meta Programmes.

> When I was exposed to metaprograms. I thought I had uncovered the Holy Grail. I saw it as the most useful and impactful application of NLP for business.

In '79 and '80, he and his co-collaborator Ross Stewart took up the baton and worked out their original set of patterns. Theirs was a fruitful partnership because they were opposite in many of the patterns, which enabled them to refine the process of elicitation by identifying precise questions and also identify the range of Influencing Language mapped against each of the Traits.

Bailey and Stewart formed BioData and worked together in teaching and consulting what they called their IPU Profile until '84. During this time they added to the research carried out by Lebeau, and Bailey's staff-work at IBM, interviewing 'thousands of folks'. This led them to come up the remarkable distribution figures for each of the Traits. This research is all the more noteworthy considering that NLP is not known for its thoroughness in producing evidence to support its claims.

> I believe that Ross and I with the BioData Profile and later me with the LAB Profile were the first to

216

make metaprograms come alive and become useful for everyone to understand and recognize and utilize.

When I asked how they selected their thirteen patterns out of the sixty or so identified by Lebeau, he offered this prosaic answer:

> Ross and I narrowed down what we had available to thirteen patterns because we wanted to actually do knowledge AND skill transfer in a two-day workshop. The thirteen patterns we ended up with all had value in business decision making and in business communications, and were easy to learn.

Bailey continued to refine his thinking and practice independently of Stewart, creating the LAB (Language And Behaviour) Profile that is well-known today. Over the last 30 plus years, he has modified how he sees the profile and some of the language, expanding some of the Traits further and lessening the importance of others. His latest incarnation, *The Bailey Profile* is available in 2014 as an online training programme.

Living in Uruguay, he and his wife went on to solve the problem of developmental issues for children – Attention Deficiency Hyperactivity Disorder (ADHD), autism, Asperger's, dyslexia, etc. – where he mapped the LAB Profile archetypes to the infancy-to-maturity developmental process. Now he is specialising in working with amateur and professional athletes wanting to improve their coordination, timing, speed, reaction time, accuracy, concentration, attention, focus, visual field, and mental stamina.

Bailey is a remarkable man and a true pioneering developer, consistently seeking to make a contribution to the world. He has applied his discoveries to be in service to the individual, and not as a changework tool for general consumption. I have found him to be very generous with his time and consideration.

> For me, utilization is about helping someone find the patterns they need for their success within their repertoire of patterns across all their contexts. I show them how to use those patterns to achieve their outcomes.

Shelle Rose Charvet

Shelle Rose Charvet is one of the most charismatic trainers in our field. I can still see her padding around the platform as the Keynote Speaker at the ANLP Conference in her pyjamas and slippers offering us incredibly funny and penetratingly insightful comments on the current position of NLP. She is a pint-sized ball of energy with a wit that is a compound of Jewish, Canadian and European humour.

Graduating in Social Sciences from the University of Ottawa, which she completed in her second language, French, she gained her first NLP learnings at the Institut Français de PNL and Institut-REPERE in Paris. It was there that she came across Meta Programmes, introduced by Brian Van Der Host who had the licence to deliver this training in Europe. Rose Charvet undertook to translate the materials into French and so began her fascination into the possibilities that meta programmes could afford.

> The material was very practical and based on linguistics and language – a love of mine. At the time I was a trainer and consultant working for a French training firm and then I set up my own firm with my then husband.

She became a Certified Trainer of Neuro-Linguistic Programming. She is also a Certified Speaking

Professional from the Global Speakers Federation and a Certified Life Skills Coach since 1983.

Under a licence agreement with Rodger Bailey, she went on to market, promote and train the LAB Profile, writing her ground breaking book *Words That Change Minds* (1995) which we at the Northern School of NLP then gave to each of our Master Practitioners as a basic text.   I first saw her at a workshop sponsored by Frank Daniels in 1999 and was instantly attracted to the LAB Profile's thorough logic.

Rose Charvet also developed the Consultant/Trainer program, the Master Consultant program, the LAB Profile Online Practitioner, in which there are a lot of new ways of using the LAB Profile; Culture Change, Coaching, Strategic Marketing, Context Painting (developed by Bill Huckabee originally), utilising combination patterns, identifying the below-conscious shifts in large group customer behaviour, developing the LAB Profile software *Libretta®* which automatically detects the patterns in text, the *HusbandMotivator™* iPhone app, Guess and Test methodology, the 4 Step Motivation Method and The Macho Test.

Consultants from around the world attend her annual LAB Profile® Consultant/Trainer Certification Program. By 2013, close to 400 learners in about 30 countries have met the certification standards and are certified Consultant/Trainers. But out of all of this what she is most proud of has been her ability to: 'Make this technology and processes easy to learn for many people around the world who use it to make communication and relationships better.'

While Rose Charvet teaches the modelling applications, she works more with how the language patterns can be used to improve 'below-conscious communication' through understanding what drives people to do – or not do – things, outside of their awareness.

Working in English, French, Spanish and improving German, her great skill and contribution has been in her vision of how the LAB Profile patterns can be used in so many different situations. In the unionised auto parts industry, she helped negotiators avoid an expected strike and sign the first 5-year contract in the history of the company. For an Enterprise Resource Planning software company, she helped a marketing department increase direct advertising response rates by uncovering the hidden Motivation Triggers typical of their target market Chief Information and Chief Executive Officers, in the different phases of the buying cycle. Another high-growth software company asked her to help create and implement their international Customer Philosophy and Customer Transaction Processes based on identifying the Motivation Triggers for happy and unhappy end-users.

Her second book, *The Customer is Bothering Me* (2010) decodes how customer motivation shifts when there is a problem, and how to deal with it. Her chapter in *Innovations in NLP* (2011) tracks the complex motivation shifts that occurred during Arab Spring. Her fourth book is 'min-ebook, *Wishing, Wanting & Achieving* (2013); a quick self-modelling process to help people use their own meta programmes to best achieve their goals. She was an early adopter of the marketing potential that social networking brings and her website http://www.successtrategies.com is full of useful practical learning materials.

Background

- How is it that you can explain something to someone until you are blue in the face and they don't understand or seem to refuse to understand?

- How is it that some people are easy to work with especially when thinking strategically yet, with others, it seems a frustrating uphill struggle?

- How is it that people appear logical, rational and task-orientated one minute and then the next are all over the place?

These behaviours are all down to a set of unconscious filters we use: these filters dictate our preferences for certain types of information, determine the ways we like to receive our information, and the terms of reference we apply to the information we receive. We will instinctively respond in the presence of information that matches our pre-set structures. Similarly, we will not recognise or code information coming our way that lies outside them.

These filters are called Meta Programmes and, added to our other sensory filters and our beliefs, contribute to our relationship with the world we perceive. With two or more patterns for each category, they are powerful determinants of our likely response to given situations or contexts. Having access to each of the dimensions of a meta programme may sometimes provide multiple descriptions and a balanced perspective.

Sources

The roots of Meta Programmes lie in different places, depending on whom you are listening to. James/Woodsmall (1988) would suggest that they arose from the three core Jung *Personality Types* (1923) further developed by Myers Briggs. Dilts and Lebeau would say that Meta Programmes evolved from the work of Noam Chomsky in his 1957 thesis *Transformational Grammar*, where he identified the three major filters of Deletion, Distortion and Generalisation by which we create the model of our individual worlds.

Personality versus Context driven

James/Woodsmall would suggest that Meta Programmes do offer personality profiles, in line with the Myers-Briggs approach and mindset. They support the Jungian archetype theory. With this thinking, they suggest that it is hard for the individual to change these patterns. These patterns are hard-wired and learned at some point in the past, possibly in a traumatic situation. Accordingly, any change in them would require serious interventions to achieve rewiring. This thinking puts people at effect not cause – and being at cause is fundamental to all NLP thinking.

Dilts sees Meta Programmes as distinctions relating to patterns and trends in cognitive strategies and that they are not rigid and unchangeable features of identity. These patterns are flexible and evolving, they describe a general trend in a particular context.

Bailey and Charvet promote the context-based nature of Meta Programmes. We have the possibility of having all the traits – it all depends on the circumstances we find ourselves in. Even if there is a trait that we consider we never use, then it may just be that we haven't found ourselves in the situation that would trigger it. As Bailey says:

> Everything changes by context. On the other hand, most of us have some context under which we operate most of the time. So, metaprograms are a powerful predicting and influencing tool, and they are a moving target at the same time.

Personally, I believe we know we all have the ability to behave and respond differently in different situations – thank goodness sometimes! And we know that flexibility and options are critical for influencing others and ourselves. However, the inconsistences in our behaviour can be confusing to ourselves and to others. Meta Programmes explain these contradictions because they provide us with a picture of how we interact with different environments and contexts.

I would go one step further. Given my predilection for Parts, I suggest that the context dependent nature of meta programmes is down to the dominant part(s) operating in that context. It is the meta programme profile of the part(s) that determines the responses. A strongly dominant part will operate accordingly in a variety, but not necessarily all, contexts.

Knowing what our default patterns are can enable us consciously to rationalise and explain our own behaviours and those of others, allowing us to adopt consciously a different approach more suited to achieve the desired outcome.

Importance of activity and process

There are no good or bad meta programmes – some are just more useful in certain contexts than others, even within the same process.

With planning it is useful to be 'future orientated', 'big chunk', 'through time', and it is irrelevant whether the drive is as a result of 'move toward' motivation or 'move away from'. However chunking down, there comes a time in the planning process when action plans need to be drawn up, and tasks and staff allocated. Here it is important to apply 'small chunk thinking', and focus on 'what' and 'who'. How someone goes about delivering the operation will be influenced if the end point is 'personally' determined or involved 'others'.

Similarly, the approach will differ if the operator is 'proactive' or 'reactive' by nature; 'involve others' or be 'independent', be 'task-orientated' or 'relationship focussed' The tests the operator sets to confirm if their evidence requirements have been met, will be dependent on the meta programmes they are running in that context. For example, if the test focusses on 'similarities' as opposed to 'differences', or if it is 'general' in nature and not 'specific' in description, the evidence that they go looking for will differ significantly, and the rest of the data will be deleted accordingly.

Other developers

It is worth noting that work continues to be done in exploring the nature and applications of meta programmes. Patrick Merlevede a specialist in Emotional Intelligence in Belgium has developed a proprietary computer based *iWAM Test* (internet Work Attitude and Motivation), based on the LAB Profile, and adhering to the testing standards set by the American Psychology Association.

Other tools include *Identity Compass* by Arne Maus and *Mind Sonar* by Jaap Hollander.

UK's Bruce Grimsley is completing his PhD looking at gaining credibility for meta programmes within personality psychology literature. He is seeking to identify those patterns that are relatively stable through life, and those that are more situational.

Meta Programme listings

Meta Programme Filter or Trait		Dilts	James/ Woodsmall	Bailey/Rose Charvet
Hierarchy of Criteria		✓		✓
Level of Focus	Who/Why/How/What/Where/When	✓	Primary Interest Filters	
Direction of Movement	Towards/Away from	✓	✓	✓
Chunk size	Large, global/Small, specific	✓	✓	Scope
Locus of Control	Self/Other	✓	✓	Attention Direction*
	Proactive/Reactive	✓	✓	Level*
Comparison	Similarities, Matching/ Differences, Mismatching	✓	✓	Decision Factors
Problem Solving Approach	Options/Procedures	✓		Reason
	Self/Other/Context	✓	✓	✓
Source	Internal/External		✓	✓
Organisation	Things/Systems/People		Work Preference Filter	✓
Style	Independent/Team/ Management		Affiliation Filter	✓
Stress Response	Associated/Dissociated/Choice		✓	✓
Rule Structure	My:My/My:O/No:My My:Your			✓
Convincer Channel	See/Hear/Do it/Read about		✓	✓
Convincer Mode	Each time/Once/2 –6 times/ Over a period		✓	✓
Intensity	Satisfied/Apathetic/Active/ Inactive		✓	
Modal Operator	Possibility/Necessity		✓	Embedded in Options/ Procedures
Thinking Style	Vision/Action/Logic/Emotion	✓		
Time Frames	Short/Longterm	✓		
	Past/present/future	✓	✓	
	In time/Through time		✓	

* Rose Charvet: 'Not convinced that Attention Direction and Level are about Locus of Control. I think Level is about needing to reflect/act. Attention Direction is about verbal/non verbal awareness.'

The LAB Profile

The LAB Profile contains Motivation Traits and Working Traits, each with its Eliciting Questions to reveal the various categories within each Trait, their respective Pattern Indicators and the Influencing Language matching each of these categories. This proves to be an exceptionally useful tool, able to be applied in a wide range of contexts. It is offered in a framework that is coherent and logical, and therefore easy to be taught. It has a flexibility and a simplicity and is extremely practical: Rose Charvet can cite endless uses and give examples of its effectiveness in many different contexts.

For all these reasons, I promote this approach above others. However, since the process appeals to those who have a preference for Proactive, Away From, Procedures, Specific, Thinking, Thing, this is no surprise!

The Framework

The following framework, which I came up with in 1999, outline the Traits, their sub categories, the Eliciting Questions, the Indicators and the Influencing Language. As with all the other methodologies, this coverage only touches the surface but hopefully sufficiently intrigues to inspire further learning.

CONTEXT:			
Criteria/Values	What do you want in (context)?		
MOTIVATION TRAITS			
Trait	Eliciting Question	Pattern Indicators	Influencing Language
Level	Arising from general comments	**Proactive**	Do it, go for it, jump, get it done, don't wait
		Reactive	Understand, think about it, consider, might, could, would analyse
Direction	Why is *that* important to you?	**Move Towards** – attain, gain, achieve	Attain, obtain, get, include, achieve
		Away From – avoid, problems, exclude	Avoid, steer clear of, get rid of, exclude, not have
Source	How do you know you've done a good job? (made the right choice)?	**Internal** – I know	Only you can decide, you know it's up to you, your call
		External – others will tell me	X thinks, you'll gain brownie points, others will notice
Reason	Why did you choose ...?	**Options** – values	Break the rules, choices, opportunities, expanding, possibilities
		Procedures – story	Step-by-step, tried and tested, failsafe, first, then, next, the approach is …
Decision Factors	What is the relationship between ……… and now?	**Sameness** – same, no change	Same as, in common with, traditional, exactly like, as you always do
		Sameness with difference – comparisons	More, less, improve, incremental, evolving, same except, progress
		Difference – new, unique	New, totally different, completely changed, switch, shift, unique, brand new
		Difference with Sameness and Exception	Mix of above

WORKING TRAITS			
Trait	**Eliciting Question**	**Pattern Indicators**	**Influencing Language**
Scope	Arising from general comments	**Specific** – details, sequences, exact	Exactly, precisely, specifically, give lots of detail
		General – big picture, overview, random order	The big picture, essentially, the important thing is, in general, concepts
Attention Direction	Cough, drop something, sneeze	**Self** – flat, short monotone responses. No response in concern for others	Use language as for Internal. Only you can decide, you know it's up to you, your call
		Other – animated, automatic responses. Instinctive response to other's needs.	Influenced by depth of rapport
Stress Response	Tell me about a (context) that gave you trouble.	**Feelings** – stayed in feelings	Empathy, happy, intense, exciting, mind boggling, wonderful
		Choice – in and out	Empathy, appropriate, makes good sense and feels right
		Thinking – never goes in	Clear thinking, logical, rational, cold reality, hard facts, statistics
Style	Tell me about a (context) that was (criteria)? Write down the answer What did you like about it?	**Independent** – alone, I, sole responsibility	Do it alone, by yourself, you alone, without interruption, total responsibility, control
		Proximity – in control, others around	You'll be in charge, around others, you'll direct, delegate, their responsibility is
		Co-operative – we, team, shared	Us, we together, all of us, team, group, share responsibility, do it together, let's
Organis-ation		**Person** – people, names, feelings, reactions	Personalise – use people's names, feelings, thoughts feel good
		Thing – tools, ideas, process, systems, no names	De-personalise – things, systems, process, task, job, goal, organisation, company
Rule Structure	What is a good way for someone else to improve?	**My/my** – automatic response	You should, they need to, I would do
		My/ O – me OK/others I don't care	Let them sort it out for themselves
		No / My – I don't know/I know for you	Advise yourself
		My/Your – I know/others are individuals	Different strokes for different folks
Convincer Channel	How do you know someone has done a good job?	**Hear** – Tell you	Reported conversations, discussions, interviews
		Read – Show you	Written reports, certificates, references
		See – Present to you	Demonstrations, presentations
		Do – Work along side you	Work together, experience for myself
Convincer Mode	How many times do you have to (see, hear, read, do) to be sure?	**Number of times**	2-6 (av 3) examples of performance
		Automatic	One-shot, immediate, straight away
		Consistent	Can't assume, situations change, need to check every time
		Time Period	Trial period, over time, prove himself

Evolution

How the Eliciting Questions were devised has always intrigued me. From what Bailey says, much of it was derived in true modelling fashion, through trial and error, responding to feedback both confirming or rejecting their thinking. Rose Charvet also tweaked some of the questions. Here are a couple of their fascinating responses:

- *Bailey:* I was always intrigued with how the connection was made between a story could indicate the trait of Procedure, and values indicate Options Trait. Here is the answer for you!

  Ross and I had recorded and videotaped many folks responding to our profile questions. When we were trying to develop the Possibility/Necessity pattern questions and figure out how to interpret responses, we started by searching for the use of those modal operators in the language.

  We struggled with that pattern for a couple of years. It turned out that the Options/Procedures question, 'Why did you choose …?' cannot be answered by a Procedures mind. The reason is that there is no 'Why' in that thinking process. So, the person distorts the 'Why' to a 'How' (which is about following the procedure) and they answer the 'How did you choose …?' The answer they provide is the story and not the reason.

- *Rose Charvet:* whilst Rose Charvet accepted the LAB Profile in its given form. she also added her own spin.

  The original Towards/Away From question was: What would that [criterion] do for you? I found this question mostly gave Toward answers even when it appeared the person was in an Away From mode. So I changed it to Why is that important? And it got a more even spread between the patterns, that when tested was more accurate.

  Also I moved the Stress Response question to be asked before Style and Organization to make sure that people with Feelings Stress Response could be moved back to a positive state more easily.

The Approach

1 **Confirm selection:** first of all you need to be aware of how selecting the meta programme approach is going to be the appropriate intervention to meet the exemplar's outcome. It might be that:

   - The exemplar is confused about his or her responses in given situations, and can't understand the apparent paradoxes in their behaviours.
   - Or the exemplar is reporting on-going conflict with another party or organisation, and has a requirement to establish a useful working, even supportive, relationship.

2 **Your outcome:** be clear of your own outcome as the practitioner, and I suggest be really clear that it is ecological and ethical. Ideally your outcome is to enable the end user achieve his or her outcome.

3 **Context:** confirm with the exemplar or end user the context that is the focus for the intervention, and their specific outcomes. It may be that you need only focus on say on the Working Traits, and keep the Motivation Traits on the back burner.

4 **Existing information:** if your exemplar is available to you, then lead them into conversation. If your filters are in place and your sensory acuity is alert, many of the patterns and traits will have

already become apparent, without any direct elicitation on your part. If it is a work context, for example, you can glean significant information from the environment under their control. If you are working with an organisation, then much of the information will be held in their marketing materials, and reports, and how their culture is being expressed.

5   **Identify gaps:**   identify where the gaps lie and artfully introduce Eliciting Questions. Your exemplar may confuse this with a conversation – though happily not an interrogation, whilst in fact you are fishing for the key pattern indicators. I love the fact that these questions really highlight and reinforce that structure and not content interests the modeller! The questioner will often know the pattern within a couple of words or a sentence.

6   **End user:**   once you have established the required profile, you then work with this information to meet the end user requirements.

- If the exemplar is the end user, then the traits can serve to explain the behaviour and the options of alternative responses can be explored.

- If the exemplar is seeking to improve relationship, then he or she can be coached regarding the impact of their traits on the other. Similarly the traits of the other can be determined to highlight the cause of the impasse. The exemplar can then be coached to select Influencing Language to match the other's traits.

- If the end user is a Third Party, then communication directed towards this organisation or individual can then be consciously selected to effect rapprochement and establish working levels of rapport.

Skills Required

Part of this methodology's elegance is the fact that it can be learned fairly easily. Specific skills lie in the following areas.

- *Familiarity with the framework:* you need to know what you are looking for. You need to know the contents of the Framework, the traits, the eliciting questions, the indicators and the influencing language. If you are doing phone work, then having the framework in front of you could be a good crib sheet.

- *Sensory acuity:* your job is to sort for structure and not content. Your filters have to be sorting for the Trait Indicators offered, verbally and/or non-verbally.

- *Fluency:* as you gather your information regarding your exemplar, you will be responding with the matching influencing language. Similarly you could usefully develop your skills so that you are able to mix your language and address multiple patterns – whilst still sounding coherent and sane!

- *Congruence:* you need to be able to monitor your own internal congruence signals to ensure that your practice is ecological.

Applications

This would appear to be one of the most versatile approaches available, since fundamentally it addresses communication at its most stripped back. Rose Charvet has demonstrated wide-scale applications, particularly in the business world. The following examples have been provided by Rose Charvet's website.

Business and Consultancy

- *People management:* you can train managers to identify the LAB Profile Patterns and thereby the strengths of their team members, so they can adjust assignments to suit what staff members naturally do best at work.

- *Recruitment:* you can do a LAB Profile for a position and corporate culture to create an advertisement that will be irresistible to those who fit and turn off those who do not fit. You can the screen the selected short-listed candidates to find the best match. (Note: The LAB Profile does not measure skills, knowledge or attitude; rather it measures whether the person has the Motivation Traits and Internal Processing to fit the tasks and the environment; in other words 'fit'.)

- *Implementing organisational change:* you can diagnose the present and desired organizational cultures in LAB Profile terms and determine the appropriate change methodology for maximum sustainable results.

- *Marketing:* having a clear idea of your target market and its predominant traits enables you to address this audience directly, through selective use of language and images. This also helps when tailoring products to meet specific traits – viz bespoke holidays, restaurants etc.

Training and Education

- *Skills training:* learning the LAB Profile will enable people to develop finely tuned abilities in the following areas: Influencing & Persuading, Negotiating, Leadership, Conflict Resolution, Sales and Customer Service.

- *Consulting and problem solving:* Rose Charvet has developed an easy to use LAB Profile methodology to diagnose and develop solutions to any communication problem. This is a favourite amongst business leaders and consultants.

- *Team building:* when you do a team LAB Profile, you can determine the team's strengths and weaknesses with regards to their mandate. You can also identify communication patterns within the team and between this team and others, as well as determine the ideal patterns of the next person to recruited to the team.

- *Teaching and learning:* teachers and students can easily identify the LAB Profile Patterns that facilitate or cause difficulties in learning for individuals and whole groups. Minor adjustments can then be made to the teaching/learning methodology to correct any problems. Rose Charvet gave a workshop to the National Indian Education Conference in Canada, for teachers on Native Indian Reservations, on how to prevent dropouts using this methodology.

Therapy and Coaching

- *Behaviour change:* using the LAB Profile you can choose activities which will create the desired behaviour changes for any target group, first by decoding the Motivation Patterns for the group and then understanding which LAB Profile patterns are addressed by any given activity.

- *Modelling:* the LAB Profile Patterns can be applied to a modelling a skill, and appear through the beliefs the exemplar holds; 'I hate mistakes' implies a 'move away from'; and the strategies deployed 'I get people together' suggests 'cooperative'.

- *Developing relationship skills:* this approach could work really effectively for those on the autistic spectrum, where there is an inability to recognise social cues to inform their relationships. Constructing relationship 'by numbers' using the influencing language could significantly improve their relational skills.

Ecology

The LAB Profile is an excellent methodology for revealing and explaining to the exemplar the sources of their behaviours, and then opening up alternative actions through awareness of language.

However, where the practitioner seeks to fulfil their own personal outcomes through using his or her knowledge to influence an unwitting audience, then ecology issues become a concern for me. Similar to the effects of Milton Model language, Influencing Language patterns deliberately target directly the unconscious mind of the receiver, and by definition this influence is outside of the receiver's awareness. Once an individual's traits are accurately identified, and appropriate language is offered to match these traits, the individual will find it hard to resist whatever is coming his or her way. Unless incongruently delivered, the receiver will not be alerted to the fact that they are being 'worked'.

Deployment of this information calls upon huge integrity on the part of the practitioner. I'm not aware that this aspect is highlighted overmuch in training.

Bailey's response to the question is:

> Almost any communication approach has the possibility for inappropriate influence. And much of that inappropriate influence is probably unconscious. I think it is an ethical paradox and I have mixed feelings about where the inappropriate aspects of it are based and how they are identified. For me, communication is communication and that involves many pitfalls. But, where would we be without it?

Whilst Rose Charvet pragmatically says: 'Yes it can be [manipulative]. It's very powerful and can be used negatively or positively – just like most of NLP, so using it with integrity is important.'

Finally I go with what Dilts offers: 'Knowing someone's Meta programmes can help you closely predict his/her actions – without any value judgement. Use your knowledge to make other people's lives better.'

Coding

The LAB Profile provides the most coded outcome of all the modelling methodologies. People, situations, organisations, processes can be summed up in a view succinct words, all of which carry a clear meaning. For the recipient that may be sufficient.

It can be that out of all the available identified traits, only three or four contribute significantly to the outcome. These can be packaged to form a model for that particular behaviour in that context.

Rose Charvet has also been able to identify different combinations of patterns that can form a strategy to follow, for example her Suggestion Model:

> Here is the formula we used when we wanted a participant to change something that he or she was doing:
>
> 1. Make a suggestion using the Influencing Language for the Internal Pattern.
>
> 2. Give two reasons why you think it is a good idea: one reason states what the suggestion

would accomplish (Towards Pattern), and one reason would state what problem the suggestion would prevent or solve (Away From Pattern)

3.   Make an overall positive comment about the person, his/her abilities, etc.

Here's an example:

I was thinking that when you are asking a client about his needs, consider repeating back his key words. This would allow you to make sure that your client knows you got what was important and also avoid any misunderstandings on the deliverables. You already acknowledge what is important to people by nodding so this should be do-able.

Concerns

The concerns I have are centred in the area of application. Since the practical use of the LAB Profile is one of its major selling points, then application is inextricably part of the methodology package itself.

- *Ecology:* as I have already mentioned, the possibility of abuse is very high. It is no wonder that this material is significantly favoured in the Sales world, because it gets results. In my limited interface with LAB training and reading, I haven't noticed much by way of HEALTH WARNINGS and ECOLOGY ALERTS, so that every practitioner consciously carries the awareness of their ecological responsibilities.

- *Outcomes:* it is essential that the practitioner is clear about the outcome of the end user target audience; otherwise the process could be used solely to deliver the practitioner's outcomes. Ecology can only be attended to if all of the intervention is focussed on enabling the declared outcome of the end user.

- *Robotic:* for those 'people' and 'options' people amongst use, application of the LAB Profile might be seen to be robotic, with its mechanical step-by-step process. Its usage does tend to depersonalise the interaction and the relationship, although according the individual with such bespoke attention is a mark of respect. But this may be the means that delivers the desirable end.

- *Incongruence:* I have seen too many marketing brochures and mail shots saturated in trait specific language – all very clever and all very manipulative. I just wonder about the congruence being communicated in the meta message. As the provider of, say, a service, I will have my own preferred traits, which are likely to consistently show up in my language. 'Who I am?' and 'who they are buying from?' will emanate off the page. And it is likely that I will attract those people who resonate with how I present myself – a good matchmaking strategy. I know that the receiver will delete everything that doesn't fit, and so will not necessarily notice any loss of relationship. However, I feel such engineering is contrived, and accept that I am probably missing a trick!

  Having said that, when all else has failed, and the outcome to communicate effectively remained, I have called on this knowledge and achieved great results. I can hear someone ask 'what took you so long?'!

- *Wrong context:* compared to the other points, this is a minor detail. One of the issues can be to assume that the profile you have identified will apply across the board, and you don't call upon your flexibility to adjust to the altered context. This can create a bit of a jolt with the receiver who thought you were totally on their wavelength.

Finally

The evolution of meta programmes is a story of modelling at its best. The supremo modeller Lebeau gained a whiff of something and pursued it and pursued it, testing and verifying until she became convinced that previously undetected meta programmes were a reality – indeed one that shone profound light on all our respective realities. This exploration into a total hitherto unexplored unknown is the hallmark of a true modeller. I have such admiration for her and her achievement, which I think is certainly on par with the creation of the Meta Model.

Bailey then took the concept and the data, and whittled it down until he constructed his robust model., the LAB Profile, which was now portable and easy to access. He focused on the exemplar being the major end user, offering control to the exemplar and offering options regarding his or her behaviours.

Rose Charvet took as her end user the awaiting Third Party public and modelled out many formal acquisition processes. In doing so she brought the inherent wisdom within meta programmes to life.

Without doubt, meta programmes – a methodology to reveal the hidden 'architecture' upon which all behaviour results – has its place amongst all the others. And because these patterns lying in the deep structure are rapidly brought to the surface, the resultant information arrives ready coded and ready to be used immediately. The application of the complementary Influencing Language is icing on the cake.

Rose Charvet is handing on the baton to others around the world, as well as developing new technologies using the LAB Profile: www.weongozi.com. Her work within organisations, groups, roles, and cultures, as well as individuals, demonstrates what a universal construct meta programmes have turned out to be. That glimmer that first ignited Lebeau's interest has truly developed into a practical and versatile contribution to improving communication and understanding.

Summary

Now you have some idea of just how many options are open to you as a modeller in terms of the approaches you can take, I hope you have broadened your understanding of what's possible. You may find that you can adapt and modify what you are already doing, or you may now have an agenda for future skill development and seek to sign up for further training.

What I do want to have achieved in this chapter is the strong message that there is no one way to model and no one methodology which is better, or more worthy, than any other. Each have a strong contribution to make and approach the underpinning structure in their own way. Whilst some are more developed than others, and some are more widely promoted, each is in service to our constructivist principles.

Whichever approach you select is all a matter of personal predisposition and taste, of knowing your outcome, knowing the nature of your exemplars, and knowing what you ultimately want to achieve. Hopefully your selection is not down to the narrowness of your experience and limitation of your skill. You may think that you have done just fine with the tools you have already. Just consider how flexible you could become if you have more options.

However, elegant results aren't just down to having lots of approaches at your disposal. It's how you use these approaches that matters. Whilst the skills introduced in Practitioner training and developed during Master Practitioner training are your starting point, it is the advanced skills of modelling which make all the difference between a constructive meeting with your exemplar and a speedy(ish) understanding of their situation, and a long drawn-out clumsy exploration, which asks a lot of your exemplar and of yourself.

The next chapter introduces you to the thinking behind the additional skills all modellers need to have at their fingertips.

Part 4

The Skills of Modelling

Introduction

Whether or not you use a formal methodology, or you model using neurological and linguistic frames, you still need to develop the repertoire of skills that will take you from being someone who is being merely effective and proficient to a higher level of operation. You want to aspire to becoming elegant where your skills have become second nature and responsive in the moment to what is happening. This is the domain of the expert.

In most Practitioner trainings you are introduced to the skills of outcome setting, sensory acuity, rapport, multiple perspectives, anchoring, and flexibility, plus working with Meta Model, Milton Model and some reframing. In Master Practitioner learners are possibly offered advanced Sleight of Mouth reframing patterns, and maybe some pattern detection. Few, if any, Master Practitioner trainings teach extensively the skills involved in modelling itself. Only by Trainer training or Therapy training is there likely to be any serious integration of previous NLP learning.

This chapter covers many of the advanced skills required of a modeller. None of it is rocket science and I'm offering you a simple yet comprehensive description of each. However, skill development comes from a total commitment to this pursuit, and from practise, practise, practise, understanding, testing and refining. The *Bumper Bundle Companion Workbook* provides nearly one hundred exercises to help you test and develop your applied understanding.

Hopefully what you find here shines the light on the direction you want to travel.

Basic Skills

It goes without saying that, throughout the process, you will need to draw on your basic NLP skillset and demonstrate flexibility as required. Only through a modelling filter do these skills now make sense and provide an unarguable rationale for their importance.

- Setting Outcomes

- Establishing and Maintaining Rapport

- Applying Sensory Acuity

- Operating Multiple Perspectives

- Demonstrating Flexibility

- Using Meta Model.

Advanced Skills

To become an expert modeller, you need to develop your competence in the range of advanced NLP Skills. If you are fortunate, you will already have received training in this area and been given the opportunity of supervised practice. However for most NLP practitioners, these skills remain a mystery and possibly many out there are unaware of their importance.

The modelling process calls upon these skills at different times. In the following framework, you will see which skills are required for each stage in the modelling process. Obviously, it is not so clear-cut in practice, but it does suggest where the skill is required the most. Additionally, it is inaccurate to suggest a cut and dried timeline, since there will be blending of borders and functions. However, hopefully, the following illustration gives you some idea of what you will be needing skill-wise for each of the stages.

Basic skills

Set Up	Gathering Data	Model Construction	Acquisition
Outcome Setting, Rapport, Sensory Acuity, Multiple Perspectives, Flexibility, Use of Meta Model			

Advanced Skills

Set Up	Gathering Data	Model Construction	Acquisition
Modelling State			
Contracting			
Pitching Your Flag			
Handling Meta Messages			
	Monitoring Outcome		
	Second Positioning / Stepping In		
	Monitoring Systems		
	Holding Multiple Attention		
	Shifting Focus of Attention		
	Asking Questions		
	Detecting Significance		
	Tracking Vectors		
	Recording Data		
	Thinking Systemically		
	Detecting Patterns		
	Scoping		

Range of Advanced Modelling Skills – Burgess 2013

Set Up Phase

This is the period of planning the project, identifying source exemplars and negotiating your relationship with them.

However from the start you need to have ready access to your modelling state so that you can draw on it at will, and notice quickly should you have lost it.

Modelling State

Whether you are a modeller with an exemplar, a coach, a therapist, or a consultant, a trainer, a parent, a manager, or anyone who is embarking on a process of seeking the structure that is driving behaviour, success requires you to enter into a Modelling State.

Judy Delozier's West African friend Titos has a couple of stories of when he brought a troupe of dancers and musicians from his tribe to perform in Europe. They had never been out of their forested region before. When they then travelled over the grasslands and saw elephant in the distance, they marvelled at how small they were. And experiencing the foyer of a hotel for the first time, they were fascinated and somewhat fearful when they saw two men being eaten up by a hole in the wall, and only to re-emerge as a woman.

A Not-Knowing state enables you to experience as if for the first time, to use unaccustomed filters, see and hear anew. It allows you to park your map, and let go of your pre-existing labelling and generalisations. It quietens down your certainty and opens you up to new possibilities.

You do not know this person in front of you. You have no idea of what is happening on the inside. His or her model of the world is a glorious mystery to you. There is no expectation that you ought to know in advance, and that you ought to have preformed theories and solutions to address their behaviour. You do not have a clue until you begin to detect some of what you're being offered.

For me this process can be summed up by the fantastic lyrics of 'Something's Coming' from *West Side Story*: 'Something's coming, I don't know what it is, but it is going to be great!'

Acquiring the State

I offer you a range of ways of thinking about the Modelling State and approaches you can take to access it.

As you read each one, do yourself the favour of stopping and 'trying on' each approach, so that you can evaluate for yourself the effects of each – and notice the similarities and differences between them. This is NOT an intellectual pursuit. This has to be done at a somatic level, experienced, integrated and anchored so that you can switch it on at will.

At the same time, apply each of these approaches to those modelling experiences where you became frustrated, with yourself and possibly your exemplar, or with the process you are working with. Like as not this was because you had lost your modelling state and taken on another (more familiar perhaps) unresourceful state. Rerun the relationships adopting the approach in question and see if it makes a difference.

Strategies

- *Richard Bandler:* is attributed with the description that NLP is an attitude of curiosity, a sense of adventure and a desire to learn.

- *Robert Dilts:* talks about the Nerk Nerk state of a Martian who has landed and who has no idea of how to interpret the world around him. The Martian has to start noticing reoccurrences and begin to put meaning onto these patterns.

- *Judy Delozier:* makes much of cultural modelling – the idea of landing into an unknown culture and having to abandon existing generalisations about habits, values and respectful behaviour. 'Don't try to make known the unknown' was the mantra she would repeat at the trainings in Bali.

- *John Grinder:* talks about the three-part Tracker State, which is an on going process throughout the modelling encounter:

  - Maintain soft focus.
  - Notice and relax any muscle tension.
  - Quieten down any internal dialogue – sing a song internally if needs be!

This state seeks to bring the unconscious mind to the fore whilst reducing the noise of the conscious mind. The modelling state is a state of trance, where the modeller lives at the conscious/unconscious interface.

- *David Gordon:* when 'trying on' the information he's being offered by 'stepping in', Gordon's sustaining emotion is *Love* for the individual, and his overriding criterion is a *Desire to Understand*. Seeking to understand lovingly assumes Not-Knowing and the pursuit of discovering.

- Personally when I am working with an exemplar, I am aware of shedding my own map and becoming just a collection of senses. At its most intense, it's as if I disappear and become just a mass of energy. My focus is complete and my concentration and retention can last for an entire two to three hour session.

- *3D pictures:* another road in is to adopt the way of seeing required for viewing three-dimensional pictures. I love this metaphor since it is so congruent with modelling – you need to look for the picture behind the picture, always knowing that there will be one. And this hidden structure is revealed because of its tiny differences within a seemingly repetitive construction.

This is an image created by one of our students Andrew Reid. You should see a large NLP&.

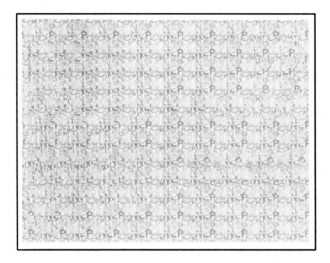

- *Lief Smith:* is the Director of the Explorers' Foundation and has no direct links to our NLP world. He talks about 'creating Magic', and for him this is generated by the combination of wonder, sensitivity, intensity and integrity.

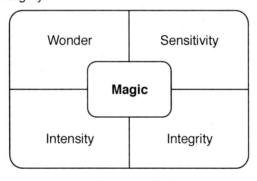

Magic – Lief Smith

When I tried on these descriptions I realised that this generated the sense of *Presence* – the definitive modelling state.

- *Wonder:* not curiosity, which has a much narrower focus. Wonder includes a sense of awe and amazement, deep regard and respect, all essential ingredients in working well with someone.

- *Sensitivity:* having the lightness of touch to know when to press on, when to hold back, when to acknowledge and when not to interrupt, and when to laugh and rejoice!

- *Intensity:* maintaining your focus on your outcome, whilst manoeuvring the information you're getting; keeping your motivation and focus high and resisting deviations and doubt.

- *Integrity:* remembering that it is not your right to gain access to this information; it is given to you as a gift that needs to be cherished and honoured.

This is a powerful model, and one which can help you notice and self-correct should your state slip. I love the shifts and flexibility it offers, and how it can accommodate the frailties of the modeller. I urge you to try it on yourself and gain a somatic description of the state that emerges, so that you can anchor it.

- *Steve Gilligan:* to my mind Steve is The Man where the modeller's state is concerned, more notable since he hasn't been operating from an NLP perspective. From his work as an hypnotherapist and with his passion for Aikido, he developed a process of what he calls Centring which he maintains is essential before even beginning to connect with an exemplar. He has further

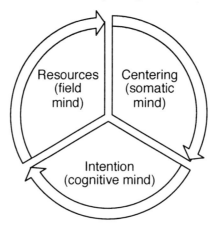

Connection with Another – Gilligan

developed this into the process of Generative Connection, which allows for the ability to hold multiple attention, which we look at later in this section. His sensory specific instructions provide us with a step-by-step strategy, and as NLPers we can't ask for more than that.

1   **Centering:** this enables you to open the Somatic Mind – the unconscious mind. It involves:
   - *Relaxation:* physically, mentally and emotionally, opening to the possibility of becoming even more relaxed.
   - *Opening yourself to possibilities:* the energy emerging from your 'belly' mind and expanding out to include the other person and the space in between.
   - *Absorption and Detachment:* a sense of being connected with the other whilst being clearly separate.

2   **Setting intention:** this enables you to open the Cognitive Mind – the conscious mind. It involves:
   - *Creative Acceptance:* acknowledge what is present and what is not present.
   - *Letting Go:* breathing out any unuseful thoughts and states.
   - *Acknowledge Intention:* for self and for other person.

3   **Inviting resources:** this enables you to open the Field Mind – the joint mind that you create with the other. It involves:
   - *Dynamic Field:* bringing in awareness of family, friends, ancestors.
   - *Unconditional Awareness:* the person you are here to be.
   - *Nurturing Energy:* the sense of universal acceptance and support offered to you.

Signal States

Writing a book is the process of modelling out your internal understanding. I remember when I was working on my first book, I had sent off my initial draft to David Gordon for editing, convinced that I had found the meaning of life and he would heap praise on me. Instead he came back with what is referred to as constructive criticism, but in my mind was total devastation. I was gutted.

Coincidentally that weekend, I was exploring with Master Practitioners the emotions we can experience during the modelling process and realised that I was 'just' at that point when essential feedback has arrived like a wrecking ball scattering the chickens of certainty and causes you to doubt the very basis of your thinking.

Take my word for it, you will welcome and relish these moments. They remove the **** of your thinking and strengthen your accountability – to yourself and to your model. In fact I no longer wince at these inevitable displays of my naivety, accepting that they are an inevitable part of the process.

The process of true modelling does not run smooth. If it does you're deluding yourself. It can be a highly frustrating process, and calls upon tenacity, resolve and the ability to bite the bullet and revise thinking. When new information arrives unexpectedly, your modelling state can go out the window!

It is useful to be aware of the possible emotions you will experience, as a means of letting you know what's happening, reassuring you and gearing you up for the next phase. I call these signal states, following Gordon/Dawes' thinking. These are the states or emotions that arise when your strategies are not working and you have to find alternative responses. They can powerfully let you know to boost your modelling state, or find it again and reactivate it in readiness for the task in hand.

This is a simplified plotting of the emotions you can expect. There will be little eddies and flows, with mini feedback loops along the way. By and large, however, there is a pot of gold at the end of the rainbow.

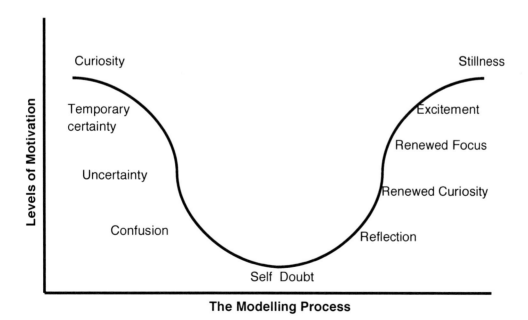

The Modelling Process

Signal States in Modelling – Burgess 2008

Contracting

The idea of Contracting in a therapeutic and coaching relationship is part and parcel of good practice, and the elements of boundaries, confidentiality, nature of approach, referral, marketing, payment etc. would be covered in training relating to Clinical Practice and Ethics Policies. Therefore in this section, I am only referring to the exemplar/modeller relationship.

Most exemplars have no idea of what is involved in the modelling process. So it is useful for the modeller to be able to preframe the meeting with the following contracting points, offered either in writing in advance to save time, or as part of the start up of the initial meeting.

1   **Appreciation:** your exemplar is doing you the favour in the first instance and not the other way around. Accordingly, you need to express your sincere appreciation.

2   **Purpose:** provide your exemplar with your intended outcome, your identified end users and how you see yourself working with whatever model emerges. Let your exemplar know where he or she fits into the overall process and what they might expect from you.

3   **Benefits:** let your exemplar know that no one is more fascinating than ourselves! And you are about to offer your undivided attention so that they can spend quality time with themselves.

It has been suggested that modelling generates self-consciousness in the exemplar and can run the risk of acting as a pattern disrupt to the natural ability. However, by far and away the consistent reports from exemplars is one of gratitude: the interviews heighten their own awareness of what they do, increase their own self belief in their skills and effectiveness, and shed new light onto areas which could be further developed.

All of this is because we rarely completely know how we do what we do. It takes someone from the outside, preferably trained with the sensory acuity to detect significance in seemingly insignificant comments, to illuminate the wider system responsible for delivering the skill or behaviour.

4   **Logistics**

-   *Time:* you need to negotiate how much time your exemplar is able to offer, and see that you work within these timescales. If your exemplar is unable to offer you more than an hour, say, then you will want to consider having others lined up.

    You need to confirm that your exemplar is available for a follow-up conversation, to fill in any gaps you subsequently realise that you have. Take care that you don't overstay your welcome.

-   *Type of interview:* ideally you want the opportunity to see your exemplar performing the identified skill as well as being able to interview them after. This way you can see what actually happens as opposed to his or her account of what happens.

    Again face-to-face interviewing is preferable since all the non-verbal gestures can be available, but the advent of Skype can work as second best and phone contact can also serve a very useful purpose.

    You may also like to reference any of their published materials that you are going to draw on. They may supply you with additional resources, video or sound recordings and texts.

- *Recordings:* you need to gain permissions to record the interview and establish that the exemplar is happy for sound or videoed recording, as well as the range of notes that you will be taking. You can offer them a copy of whatever is produced.

- *Interruptions:* seek to contract that the time given will be without interruption, phone calls or texts.

5 **Scope:** you need to confirm from the outset the area of behaviour that interests you. However, you need to alert your exemplar that, as a result of the answers you're getting, you may switch your attention to a different aspect within the overall performance.

6 **Content and structure:** let your exemplar know that you are interested in finding out what lies behind what they do, to find out *how* they do what they do. For this reason you are likely to be using a range of questioning frameworks, which may not seem immediately relevant to the exemplar. Let them know that some of the questions may seem strange and possibly illogical. Should this happen, ask them just to trust you! Assure them that they will gain access to information that would otherwise have remained hidden. Should, however, the exemplar feel awkward with the direction the experience is going, you have to backtrack to safer ground.

Your exemplar is likely to want to help you and give you what they think is useful. Let them know in advance that you are not being disrespectful if you choose to pursue a different line of enquiry. After all, you are responsible for the outcomes of this investment of time and resources.

7 **End result:** you need to explain that whatever conclusions you come to, and whatever model you devise as a result of this engagement, is by definition a product of your own creation. You will not be reproducing a replica of your exemplar's responses. This is particularly true if you are engaging several exemplars.

You may like to use the metaphor of portrait painting – how different artists would produce very different images of the same sitter, and that the sitter may decidedly prefer one to others. Therefore, whilst you are happy to share your findings with your exemplars, you need to warn them that they may not agree with the conclusions you come up with. On the other hand, you may find yourself providing them with a piece of extreme enlightenment! One modeller confessed to having 'two sets of books' – a model that the exemplar would appreciate and the actual model.

'Pitching Your Flag'

Gordon talks about experience being a three-dimensional 'soup' – level of detail, type of detail and place in time. When a modeller is going after a particular behaviour, then the modeller needs to carve out his or her particular sector within this 'soup' and set the parameters for exploration.

As a modeller, you meet with your exemplar and you don't know yet where the key information is going to lie. You know the behaviour that you want to pursue. What you don't know is, where the actual drivers of that behaviour are located within the exemplar's model of the world.

You may think it is to be found in one place, and there you pitch your flag, burrow in, ask your questions: only to discover that you come up with not a lot. Now you have to be prepared to take your flag out and pitch it somewhere else – *no matter how much time you have taken thus far!*

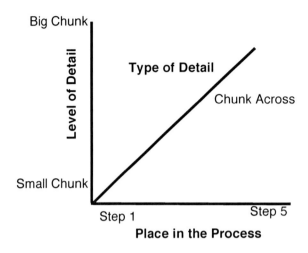

3D Experiential 'Soup' – Gordon

1 **Place in the process:** a modelling group at the Northern School of NLP wanted to model Gordon's wonderful ability to tell stories. Anyone who has been on the receiving end of his 'Science Fair and The Planarians' story, or his 'Halloween Computer Costume' know this to be true.

So he asks, (because he is helping us): 'Do you want to know how I identify stories to tell? How I construct the stories? How I choose which ones to tell? How I deliver the story? How I evaluate its effectiveness?'

Without his guidance, we would likely have ended up with a real hotchpotch of data covering all the bases, some in more detail than others, depending on our respective interests, but with no clear specific idea of what had been delivered. And, more than likely, we would have become swamped, overloaded and demotivated in the process.

As a modeller I may start out thinking I want to know how Gordon tells his stories. But after some time, I realise that the real power house to his story telling abilities is in how he constructs his stories, where he puts his emphasis, how long he gives to each bit in the narrative, how much detail he puts in. So I may shift my attention from his performance, to this earlier stage.

Dilts would say that, if he already knows how to do something satisfactorily, then he wouldn't bother modelling that piece from the exemplar. He will focus on the areas that he is less familiar with, which he can't replicate and deliver in his mind's eye.

2 **Level of detail:** there is a presupposition that the structure behind a high level, 'big chunk' piece of behaviour will be repeated down in the small chunk details; that behaviour is a fractal and replicated at different levels of operation. So what moves me whilst watching a film (small chunk) is likely to be the criterion that drives my purpose in life (big chunk).

Too much detail, and the overlying pattern can become lost. Too little detail prevents distinctions being detected. However if actual replication is required, then attending to the minutiae is essential.

3   **Type of detail:** you want to keep focussed on the methodology you are using and the categories of detail you are gathering, otherwise you will end up with a pile of apples and oranges and pears. This can easily happen if the exemplar wanders off onto a different train of thought. So you need to be mindful of what you are getting, and elegantly steer your exemplar back onto your track.

Handling Meta Messages

'We cannot not communicate', is one of our fundamental NLP Presuppositions. 'What is going on on the inside is likely to make itself known on the outside,' is another way of saying this.

As a practitioner, we have to be aware of the messages we are offering beyond what we are saying. We will always be saying something more than our words and our gestures convey. We are transmitting a higher-level message, a meta message, which in fact could reveal more about us than the actual message itself. The secret is anticipating accurately the filters the exemplar might be operating.

Turning up with your Mont Blanc pen could transmit a message of success, or quality, but could be received as flashy or superficial. Having the latest technical gadgets could be seen to be professional or intimidating. Using jargon could suggest greater familiarity with the process, or alienate and exasperate. To detect this as second nature, we need to be able to second position those who are making the judgments.

The Sender

As a modeller, you need to be aware of the meta messages you are sending out to your exemplar(s), directly through your presence and actions, and indirectly through your management of the modelling process and relationship. How you dress, respond to comments, receive difference, operate as a learner, and commit to your pursuit, will send strong messages that may be warmly or coolly received.

Basic incongruence speaks volumes – the tone not matching the words, the gestures not matching the facial expressions. At its most simple, incongruence is a meta message that you are not believing or are not comfortable with what you are saying or doing. If this is the case, your exemplar will not trust you and be on guard.

Conversely your exemplar could be the sender. Detecting whiffs of incongruence in what is being said is a great signal to delve a little deeper and allow the exemplar to explore just that bit further.

The Receiver

At the receiving end, these meta messages can be misinterpreted. We have all heard of the millionaire who is discounted in a top-of-the-range car dealership because he or she turns up looking as if they don't have two pennies to rub together.

When you find yourself responding contrary to how you would expect to respond, it is because you are tuning into the meta message that you are detecting behind the given message.

Or you could be putting a totally different meaning onto what is being transmitted, at odds with the sender's/exemplar's intended meta message. In moments like these you are operating from your own map. Alert! Alert! Wake up and back track, and go back to the last point where you had established common understanding.

Gathering Data Phase

Monitoring Outcomes

Given that there are so many systems operating, at any point in time you need to be aware of what outcome is driving your own behaviour. This can be at a big chunk level concerning identifying the specific activity to be modelled, or it can specifically relate to the forming of the next question.

The expert modeller is able to say at any point in the process what outcome is determining this or that action. Without this level of awareness and discipline, you are not able to manage your TOTE.

The following points apply to the modelling process where there is a separate end user in mind. It differs from that of coaching or therapy, where the modeller's outcome is to enable the exemplar to achieve his or her outcome.

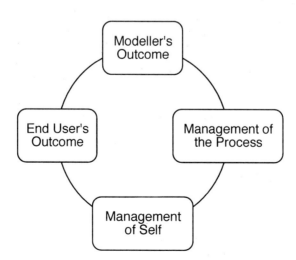

Range of Outcomes Operating with Modelling Process – Burgess 2008

Modeller's Outcome

Fundamentally, when with the exemplar, your main outcome is to gather sufficient relevant data, efficiently and effectively, which contributes to the description of the underpinning structure. Be prepared for up to 90% of your information to be irrelevant.

So you stay within the TOTE until either time runs out, or until you can construct an internal sense of the ability and your successful attainment of it. This informal acquisition process allows you to exit your information-gathering TOTE.

Then later alone with the data, your outcome is to create a model that will serve the end user's purpose. At times like this you need to stay focussed on what you want to offer your end user, since it can be all too easy to lower the bar and produce something that might be merely 'good enough'.

All of this, however, will be determined by how well you manage the other outcomes.

Management of Process

Your outcome here is to place attention on the many aspects of the process. It may be on practical issues like ensuring the physical environment supports the meeting, or if your means of recording the session will hold up as reference later on, or you have sufficient thinking time and space to lay out your data. Many a kitchen table has been cleared and precious notes swept in time for tea.

When with the exemplar, your primary outcome is to gather information effectively and efficiently, maintain relationship, and gain understanding through clarification and backtracking.

Your outcome is also to consult the wisdom of your unconscious mind, to determine significance, double check it, and test the information you're getting. And then your outcome is to identify what you still need and what question to ask next. Every time you ask a question it will be framed within your outcome for that moment.

You may feel pressed for time, a real or imagined constraint, self-imposed or part of a commercial contract. Whilst the process takes as long as it takes at one level, it is really important to know when to stop tweaking. You will never get your model absolutely perfect. You will be continually find ways of improving it. But you need to know when any alterations may not make any material difference to your results, and get out of your TOTE fast!

Management of Self

Here your outcome is *to stay in the modelling state*, or return to it once you've realised that you have ceased to be curious.

This applies to time spent with the data and the emerging model, as well as the time spent with the exemplar. Looking back at the previous section, you will find the various states that can alert you to the need to re-engage with your modelling state.

If you are becoming bogged down, or have just been hit by the wrecking ball of inconvenient feedback, walk away. Go and do something different and allow your unconscious mind to make sense of it. Changing to a neutral state allows for focus to return renewed.

End User's Outcome

You have to always keep in mind what the end user needs and wants. More than one model can emerge from a modelling process. There may be one that may be prettier, fancier, more sophisticated than the others, or one that echoes your current pet theme. At times like this you have to guard against the lure of your ego and give your end user what is required. Your end user won't thank you for something that is not fit for purpose, no matter how wonderful it is.

Second Positioning/'Stepping In'

Twenty years ago, I was a visiting assessor for an NLP Practitioner Certification weekend. Lovely group of people and good trainer. Things were going well until I spent time with one woman – who refused point blank even to contemplate the idea of going second position. She was convinced that she would lose herself and had a profound and understandable ecological argument against it. No matter what I offered as we walked round the garden – and I recognise that my own understanding of the dynamics of second positioning was limited – she wouldn't budge. I had to refuse to her a certificate.

The ability to go second position is absolutely essential for whatever you're doing within NLP. It is essential for establishing rapport, determining what reframe to offer, guiding someone through a process, and it is absolutely essential when you're modelling – not just when with your exemplars, but also when you are with your data, your model, your acquisition process, and even your written instructions.

Having the ability to let go of your own map, and enter into the map of the other, or into the structure of a system, is the quickest and surest means of connecting at deep structure level. No amount of question and answers will take you to the same place. You have to fully engage somatically with the source and process all information through this. What is revealed often totally surprises, being hidden to outside view. First-timers are often shocked at the words that emerge from their mouths, unbidden, when they step into another, or a mentor, or even a metaphor. Yet somehow the words and their essence are a revelation yet make total sense.

As a modeller, the ability to second position is essential.

McWhirter's Degrees of Second Position

As an NLP trainer, I used to be at a loss to know how to respond convincingly in words to a learner's concern of 'losing sense of self'. I would often get 'How do I know I'm not making it up?' 'How can I possibly know what he is thinking and feeling?' Rather impatiently I would say – 'Just try it and see what happens.' Therefore, when I came across McWhirter's thinking about second position I fell upon it gratefully.

McWhirter explains second position in terms of how much the modeller stays in his or her own map to how far the modeller moves into the map of the other. I wish I had known this when I was with that learner in the garden.

		Self Only	Illusionary
-3	Make Up		Illusionary
-2	Put Onto	⬆	Mind Reading
-1	Move To		Moved over but still experiencing from own system
0	IDEAL	**Self and Other**	Moved over and experiencing from system of other
+1	Take On		Acting
+2	Take Into	⬇	Unconscious Uptake
+3	Be	**Other Only**	Psychotic

Degrees of Second Position - McWhirter

Self to self and other

- Moving not at all, and with absolutely no idea of what is happening for the other, the modeller can only make something up based on no information.

- When the modeller recognises the other's situation but stays put and processes solely through their own map, they are guilty of intensely irritating mind reading: 'I know what you're thinking.' This is where the modeller would be making it up.

- Then the modeller can be deluded into thinking that they are entering the map of the other, because they believe they have taken on the other's situation. However, they process what's happening as if it was happening to them. This is a mistaken form of empathy, and equally irritating: 'Oh how awful for you. I would have been terrified.'

Self and other

- Only when the modeller lets go of their own map and takes on the map of the other, experiences the situation through the other's eyes and ears, can any real understanding become available. The modeller stays aware of his or her own system, their conscious/unconscious interface is active, and they can step back into self at any moment.

Self and other to other

- When the modeller consciously adopts the mindset of the other and acts as if they are that person, then the modeller has crossed the line, leaving their own self behind, albeit temporarily.

- The modeller might have become totally unaware of the fact that they have adopted the mannerisms and responses of the other. This unconscious modelling occurs through intensive immersion with that person, sometimes through choice, sometimes through unconscious emulation, and sometimes because their own sense of ego is weak and the charisma of the other is strong.

- Finally the modeller becomes lost within the psyche of the other person. They have 'gone native'. This can happen to method actors or undercover agents who need to have a mechanism to ground them and bring them back to who they are.

Gordon's Stepping In

In the modelling context, for Gordon the key to second positioning, or 'stepping in' as he prefers to call it, is to be fully committed to wanting to understand how the particular behaviour works, what it is and how it operates within the person. This commitment brings for him greater connection. By being fully open to this person's experience, he gains his own experience of how to do the action in the exemplar's context, all because experience has a structure.

To achieve this end, Gordon will become very still and quiet inside, and devote his full attention on the other, almost in a dissociated way with tunnel vision and a slowed voice. Listening to responses to his questions, he will let what they say take over his body, especially anything unusual, characteristic or exaggerated. He will say what they say to himself internally and internalise what they say they do or feel. He will then match his experience with theirs, seeking confirmation. When there isn't a match, he will stop and ask another question.

Any difficulty in finding out how it works may come from him 'not having set myself aside enough'. So he will shift position and possibly take a different tack, always mindful of keeping his sense of love, appreciation and a desire to honour who this person is.

Second Positioning Systems

Second positioning people is a well-known practice for an NLP Practitioner, and is an obvious skill when with an exemplar. However, using our kinaesthetic sense to gain information from seemingly inanimate objects can be equally revealing. Have a go at second positioning company logos and find out if the experience maps your actual experience as the consumer. Second positioning a shop layout tells you where the 'hot' and 'cold' areas are, the rate of traffic, and the key decision making areas. Second positioning a hall or training room, mindful of the location of doors and windows and the layout of the seating, lets you know how well the energy flows.

When it comes to working with data, then this skill once more comes into its own. Taking time to enter into the words on the pages of your notes, feeling the rhythms, the relative pressure of the handwriting as you re-hear the words being said, can take your attention to where it needs to be. As you are reducing all the redundancy down to the key elements, you step into the dynamics of these elements and their relationship with each other. Through your body, you are looking for balance and a natural unimpeded flow. You are looking for a sense of 'yes that fits'. Any niggling corner tells you you're not done yet.

Monitoring Systems

Any relationship is a system; it is a flow of cause and effect. It can get clogged and it can be energised. And it can come to a complete standstill. Within the modelling process, there is a range of systems operating simultaneously, and attention needs to be given to each of them.

Again, the professional therapeutic and coaching relationship has specific requirements regarding the management of the relationship, and attention needs to be given by the therapist and coach to their respective Codes of Practice and Clinical Practice training.

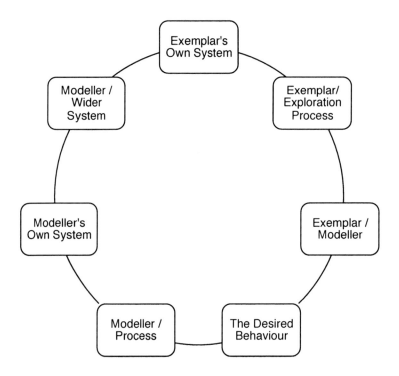

Systems Operating Within Modelling Process – Burgess 2008

Exemplar's Own System

The exemplar may be stuck in what he or she thinks you need to know and seek to 'teach you' as opposed to 'submit' to your line of questioning. Your exemplars may not be freely articulate, especially since you are taking them to a place where they haven't been before. Gently handle the 'Don't Knows' with 'Guess' and 'If you did know …?' Pay real attention to gestures and throwaway meta comments. All of this will serve to reflect back the exemplar's internal experience to themselves.

Your exemplar may be feeling self-conscious and embarrassed, or highly dismissive of the significance of a particular behaviour. When we are naturally good at something we very often discount its value since it came easily to us.

Exemplar/Exploration Process

If you have contracted well up front, and pre-framed the process so that the exemplar has a reasonable idea of what to expect, then you should have few problems regarding executing the process. If the exemplar does find something awkward, you can always refer back to the contract, offering that what is happening is an indicator of why they get the results they do, and suggesting that this novel approach could be the key to gathering vital information.

Exemplar/Modeller

Rapport is essential for a free flowing interview. Guard against being too task focussed, whilst keeping your eye on your outcome. The sooner you demonstrate some understanding of the exemplar's model of the world, the quicker you will gain credibility. Just the process of back-tracking, or, more usefully, using your words to describe what has just been said, lets your exemplar know you are operating within his or her map. The quality of questions you offer as follow up to the information your receive will demonstrate your commitment, integrity and fascination for who they are.

Guard against being in awe of your exemplars, even though they may be serious experts. Go in there knowing you are a modeller and this is the skill that you are bringing.

Manage time efficiently. It is very precious. Keep chat to a minimum and stay focussed. Remember your relevancy challenges!

The Desired Behaviour

The desired behaviour rests within a much bigger context of skills and behaviour, to include the chunk size and the stage in the process. You need to be aware of what information belongs inside or outside the area under exploration. Gordon talks about 'pitching the flag', and Dilts about the 'Box' that the end user will want.

It is essential for you to spot when you have become distracted, or risen to too high a logical level of abstraction, or drilled too far down into detail, or strayed into a different time zone or stage in the process.

Modeller/Process

You may become lost in the three-dimensional nature of the exemplar's experience. Back track, back track and back track. This gives your unconscious mind space to offer up direction. It also allows the exemplar to offer something more that might be crucial.

You may have lost your place in the modelling process itself. You may find yourself scoping out the data before you have fully gathered it. You may be putting yourself under 'Hurry Up!' or 'Be Perfect!' drivers, and become anxious if the process is not smooth and plain sailing. You may become concerned that you are taking up your exemplar's time. Breathe, check out with your exemplar regarding available time left, and quieten your internal dialogue.

You may be concerned that the methodology you have chosen isn't working for this exemplar. This is more a concern if you want to choose the same methodology across the board. Trust your instincts, be flexible, and adjust your approach to suit the individual. So use somatic syntax for example, instead of cognitive questions, or Clean Language. You can find the patterns across all systems later.

You may not be fully competent with the methodology you have chosen. Unless you understand the dynamics inherent within the framework of each methodology, you will have difficulty interpreting the data you are getting and not know what's missing or misplaced.

Modeller's Own System

It goes without saying that the modeller comes with a highly developed map that needs to be parked. Why come to meet this expert merely to confirm what you already know?

What is your relationship with Not-Knowing and with Learning? To be a competent modeller, it is essential you are aware of your patterns when confronted with ambiguity, uncertainty, failure, and the need to look good and get it right. As soon as you notice the urge to 'prematurely evaluate' because of your own personal discomfort, you need to reconnect to your modelling state and keep your attention on the outside.

One fabulously discerning modeller I know confessed to having a default pattern of five: she would rarely stop at four questions, or add a sixth one. Noticing this allowed her far greater clarity about where to put her attention next.

Modeller/Wider System

You may be feeling pressed for time. Resist assuming knowledge as a short cut. This is a time to be really aware of the messages your system is giving. Don't waste time on aspects you already know how to do. Go for the pieces that are unfamiliar to you.

Make sure all your technical equipment is working. You don't want to distract your attention to changing batteries in your recorder.

Resist seeking connections between what this exemplar is saying and others that you have interviewed. Put all your attention here with *this* person for as long as the interview lasts.

Throughout, you will be checking against the needs of the end user. If you realise that the information you're getting isn't suitable for the end user, then be prepared to bring the interview to an early end.

Holding Multiple Attention

Jugglers start off with one juggling ball, and then get used to working with two, then three. By this time, they start to learn a variety of moves with increasing complexity focussing on catching and not dropping. Then the number of balls is increased, and different objects are introduced, whilst even more complex patterns of movement are developed. Then the Juggler may choose to work with fellow Jugglers and coordinate his or her actions with those of the others. All the time he or she is building on their bank of skills and seeking to extend and expand them, as their earlier learning stacks up within their muscle, building instinctive response.

Gilligan talks of the Sensei Master who first of all teaches his students the basic moves, working with single opponents. After about three years the student is invited to contend with multiple attackers, since by now the basic moves are instinctively accessible. Attention can now be given totally to the assailants. Finally mastery comes when the student can be equal to all the permutations of attack, whilst reading the posters on the wall!

The San Bushmen tracking in the Kalahari move this way and that through the bush, looking. Looking for spoor – markings in the sand and droppings. They can not only identify what the animal is, they can tell when the track was made, they can tell the speed of the animal, its next intention, and its state of health – all from the footprint. Again the droppings identify the animal, its recency, where it has been. They also look for damage to branches, to the grass, holes in the ground, and bark rubbings at different heights on the trees. They also smell the wind, the ground, the bark. And they know where the sun will be at any point and where the moon would have been the night before; therefore, they know the likely grazing path and resting place each animal will have taken.   All of this is conveyed to their fellow trackers through signs and grunts. When asked, 'what does your apprentice need to learn?' the answer was 'to start at birth'; to learn the stories; the dances depicting the movements of many animals; learn the plants, the trees, the roots and where they grow; learn all the different footprints; eating and sleeping habits of all the animals; and understand their likely responses to events; and watch their fathers.   In short, incrementally gather layer upon layer of integrated knowledge and test it, test it, and test it, so that they can 'read' the environment at a glance.

Developing the Skill

Dilts may say that all of us who drive can hold multiple attention. But that doesn't explain how to become the rally driver that he is.

I have spent time looking for the model to accelerate the skill of holding multiple attention which, to my mind, is one of the major skills required for elegant modelling mastery. I wanted to find the model that could be the key to this magical art.

I am now reluctantly coming to the conclusion that, for this particular skill, there is no short cut. This is an instance of the 10,000 hours of practise required for mastery, raised by Malcolm Gladwell in *Outliers* (2009). The increasing ability to Hold Multiple Attention is no different from that of the Juggler, or the San Bushmen. It comes from the combination of Deep Commitment and Embedded Learning and Application.

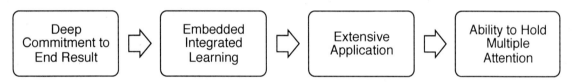

Developing Ability to Hold Multiple Attention – Burgess 2012

However, the more you practise and expose yourself effectively to increasing volumes of information, through extended time periods, the more you will embed your skills of managing this information. The more aware you are of your signals which indicate significance, the more you will be able to switch your attention to where it matters.

Maintaining your open state, and trusting that the information is going in and that your unconscious mind will offer it back to you when you require it, removes the pressure of keeping everything in the conscious domain.

The more experience you pack into your muscle, the more you can rely upon your learned intuitions.

Robert Dilts's Model

It is fair to say that Dilts, with his nearly 40 years in the modelling field, has the ability to hold multiple attention.   So as part of our modelling workshop at The Northern School of NLP, Lawley and Tompkins modelled his ability to *Gather Information* and revealed that Dilts runs six major streams of attention simultaneously when working with an individual, which he maintains everyone can do. 'After all everyone who drives a car is doing it all the time.'

They identified six different elements, with a seventh, Relational Field generated between the modeller and exemplar, added after another visit to the School.

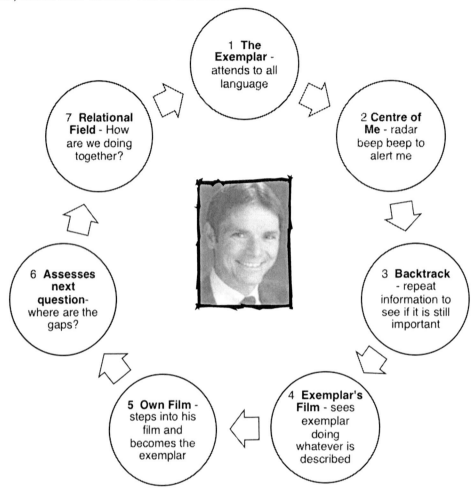

Dilts's Model of Information Gathering – Lawley/Tompkins 2006

David Gordon's Model

Gordon has a simpler approach, kinaesthetic as opposed to auditory/visual. You can almost feel when he switches on and 'morphs' into you in his deep desire to make sense of what you have just said, just asked or communicated. From the outside, he goes very still, closes his eyes, lowers his breathing, and occasionally nods and moves from side to side. Understanding is a critical need for him, coming from a place of love and deep respect for his fellow human beings.

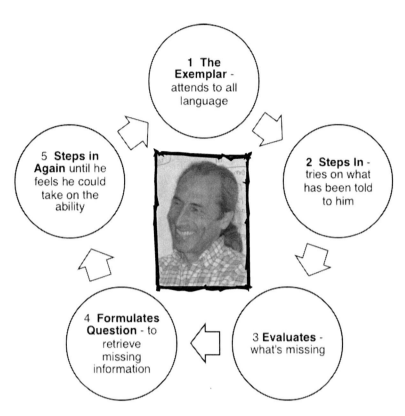

Gordon's Model of Information Gathering – Gordon

Shifting Focus of Attention

Given that Dilts has integrated so many of his modelling skills which he has developed over the years, and built upon his own layered banks of knowledge and experience, it is understandable that his strategy for identifying what is important operates at a fairly high chunk, non-specific level. There is much that is assumed.

Because there are so many systems operating at any one time within the modelling process, *and* we have to manage a range of outcomes, *and* hold multiple attention, we have to develop the flexibility to shift our attention from one system to another. We have to be able to: come out from focussing on one outcome and gain clarity about another; allow our unconscious mind to hold all the information that is outside of the seven-plus-or-minus-two items our conscious mind can hold; check out what system we are operating in and which system is causing the blockage to understanding.

I am assuming that by this stage, you will have been introduced to most of the information gathering skills involved in modelling. You will know the sources of information that you can seek. You will have an understanding of what you need to do and how you need to manage this. So there will be some processes and practices which are now hard-wired within your muscle and neurology which you don't have to think about, whilst there will be some elements which are still clunky, or have dipped below the radar. There may also be some requirements that are new to you.

You have reached the stage where you need to embed all your skills and knowledge so that they form an invisible integrated web of expertise that you can draw upon instinctively as you pursue what needs to be done to deliver your outcomes.

The following listings offer you an inventory of all the aspects you could possibly be paying attention to. Notice any sense of overwhelm: this is just a sign that you want to improve. And with any task worth doing, mastering the elements bit by bit is the way to success. You may choose to say: 'Right I'll focus on this and that one and concentrate my attention on them.' If you want to get good, practise, and you will get good! You'll remember how you managed to recover from the overwhelm first experienced when you were introduced to meta model – and how you have been able to accommodate the different patterns into your responses. (If you haven't then practise some more.)

I've provided a checklist and against each entry you could usefully consider instances when you have done this – in a formal modelling situation, naturally at work or home, or informally socially. You may also like to consider occasions that would have benefited from paying particular attention to one aspect instead of another.

Attention on Exemplar

EXEMPLAR		Evidence
Exemplar's first words or gestures.		
Language Used	Meta Model Patterns	
	Metaphors	
	Sensory predicates	
	Temporal predicates	
	Spatial predicates	
Physiology	Breathing	
	Facial movements	
	Eye accessing	
	Physiology	
	Hand gestures	
	Congruence	
Patterns	Displacement activity	
	Meta comments	
	Gestures, spatial markings	
	Strategies	

Attention on Modeller

MODELLER		Evidence
Management of Self	Level of personal relaxation	
	Personal congruence	
	Internal dialogue	
	Shifting focus of attention	
	Access to unconscious mind	
Management of the Process	Focus on exemplar's outcome	
	Intrusion of own map	
	Flexibility of approach	
	Evidence requirements	
	Ecology checks	
	Awareness of own outcomes in the moment	
	Calibration data	
Management of the Relationship	Second positioning exemplar, landscape, relationship	
	Monitoring and responding to rapport levels	
	Strategic reframes	
	Levels of resourcefulness	
	Adoption of different perspectives – self, both	
Management of the Technology	Level of understanding of received data	
	Construction of precision questions	
	Emergent patterns	
	Nature of underpinning structure/system	
	Detection of route(s) to pursue	
	Range of appropriate techniques available	
	Possible blend of neurological frames	
	TOTE	

I hope you find this list is a useful means of clarifying the 'experiential soup' that you, the modeller, operate within. You certainly will have identified elements which are well established 'in your muscle', outside your awareness and ready to be called upon as and when. As usefully, this listing may have flagged up some activities that you have either deleted, or are currently working on.

You can also use the lists as a diagnostic checklist, to explain where some relationships turned out less than satisfactorily. Rehearse what might have happened if you had shifted your attention elsewhere and see what might have happened differently.

Trust that your unconscious mind will let you know when to shift attention, otherwise your behaviour will become stilted, stressed, and unproductive. Equally, it is important to contract with your unconscious mind to pay attention to the signals it offers to alert you. Personally when confused, I stop, go still and listen to my inner voice saying 'try this', 'go to that'. This usually serves me well and removes the strain of having to consciously monitor and track all the balls that are dancing in the air.

Asking Questions

We've all been asking questions since the time we first learnt to ask 'Why?' It's as natural as breathing. So what's so crucial about them, that requires special attention? Well the difference between blurting out a spontaneous 'Why did you do that?' and a precisely worded 'What happened just before X to cause you to do that?' is like comparing a spray of shotgun pellet with a well-aimed sniper bullet, or to use a less brutal metaphor, a floodlight with a laser beam.

Questions are our means of gathering information, of clarifying current understanding, and taking stock of the point reached in the exploration. The purpose of a question is to direct the attention of the exemplar to a particular area of his or her internal experience. This can be either because you, the practitioner, need particular information to fill your internal construction of your exemplar's map or, you are inviting the exemplar to access this information for self-exploration.

PRO RATA Model : Criteria for 'Good' Questions

If these criteria are met, then you have come up with a good and useful question. The better you are at constructing these, the easier the relationship and the greater the quality of information you receive. I offer the mnemonic PRO RATA to help you remember.

1   **Presuppositions:** the question's content holds knowledge that can be 'true' for that exemplar, yet possibly outside of the exemplar's awareness. These presuppositions direct attention to the exclusion of other details. 'What is particularly interesting about that?' suggests that there will be more than one element of interest to comment upon.

2   **Rapport:** the question should sustain or deepen rapport, because it paces what is already known, makes accurate assumptions, and points to what the exemplar needs or wants to know next. The questioner has to ask the question from inside the exemplar's world. 'How do you manage to overcome any embarrassment?' might be met with a blank look since the concept of embarrassment never entered your exemplar's thinking.

3   **Outcome:** the question should always be serving the exemplar's outcome. Questions are not there to satisfy nosiness or the self-purpose of the questioner. You need to always be asking yourself 'What is my outcome for this question? What do I want to find out?'

4   **Response:** a good question generates a quality response of wonder, in the form of new information, an inner truth, a never-before stated desire. All of these can bring the exploration to a

satisfying conclusion or ignite a further one. However don't be seduced by streams of revelation – such floods could sweep you away in a totally different direction to the one you intended.

5 **Awareness:** the question takes the exemplar to somewhere new, often measured by how long the exemplar stays 'inside' before reconnecting and putting his or her discoveries into words. The question might initially be met with possible meta comments of 'I've never thought of that' or 'No one has ever asked me that before'. Because of the newness, instinctively the exemplar might say 'Don't know', so after some time follow it up with a gentle 'Guess' to ease the path.

Such a question often earns a thank-you from your exemplar, since you have offered the gift of a new doorway into insight and learning.

6 **Target:** the question is carefully constructed so that it directly targets the precise source of wanted information. One question instead of ten is the sign of the lightest touch and elegance. The less ripples you create through the flow of questions you offer, the deeper your levels of rapport – and the smoother the information gathering process becomes.

7 **Artistry:** the question should cause the minimum disruption to the exemplar's desire to explore. It can disturb the flow of well-worn information, but is pitched to make the alternative exploration much more desirable.

Modelling Frameworks

The following modelling frameworks hold their own structure of questions, which have been designed to deliver precise information. By taking the discipline to learn these, you are demonstrating respect for the hours of work, refinement and testing undertaken by their developers. And by widening your linguistic repertoire, you give yourself the freedom of flexibility and choice, either to pursue the established format of the methodology or selectively mix and match to pursue your own path.

Modelling Framework	Language Patterns
Symbolic Modelling	Clean Language Questions
Belief Template and Experiential Array	Dawes and Gordon Questions
Neurological Levels	5W&H Questions
Belief System	Meta Model Questions
Personality Traits	Meta Programme Questions
Timeline Elicitation	Sensory, Temporal and Spatial Predicates

Modelling Frameworks and Respective Language Patterns – Burgess 2010

Outcomes of Question

Gordon reveres questions. He loves answering them, and he considers constructing them an art and a science. He has a mantra that directs his enquiry:

- *'What have I got?':* this causes him to evaluate how far into his TOTE he is, and how close he feels he is getting to the desired state or not. Sometimes he will take time out to marshal all the data and not just the most recent responses. He will step into the material and lose himself in thought. All of this is really respectful to the exemplar – it is a measure of the person's importance to him. This stage heralds the next one.

- *'What do I want to know now?':* here he will respond to what he doesn't have, and what he feels would serve him to know next. In the moment, he is framing his outcome. He then sets about forming the question, rehearsing it in his mind, checking how it might be received. He may rework it, pinning down the precision even further. And then he'll ask it. This leads to the next stage.

- *'Did I get it?':* this is when he evaluates the significance of the answer he has been given. This is feedback on the quality of his question. It is also information about the exemplar's current internal experience. And possibly about the relationship between the two of them.

As ever, critical to this process is pinpointing the outcome. 'What's your outcome?' is the question to precede all questions. Before you open your mouth, even before you form the words, you need to know what it is you want to know. This can change a meandering or lurching exchange into a purposeful, rewarding pursuit.

The better you are at knowing precisely where you want your exemplar to go, how to construct your questions to achieve that, and the impact the questions are likely to have, then the more efficient and elegant your interaction will be. The fewer the questions, the better the process.

Purposes for Questions

Try as I might, I couldn't create an mnemonic to make these pointers easy to remember. However to make it slightly easier I have arranged them alphabetically.

1 **Awareness:** every time you ask a question, you are directing the attention of your exemplar. Hopefully you have constructed it so precisely that you have predetermined the desired target area. You want to encourage your exemplar to self-model, and make connections within his or her own inner structure. You may have no need to hear the answer yourself.

Many of the questioning frames are designed to expand the exemplar's awareness; for example Meta Model reveals belief systems, Clean Language reveals metaphoric landscapes, reframing questions reveal new beliefs. Using a contrast frame question brings into sharp relief what the exemplar might rather have.

2 **Clarification:** your clarifying question could be to check out your exemplar's level of understanding about a process, or some information or theory you have offered. Or you could be checking for any deletions – the Who or the What of the story.

You may be building up an internal representation of what the exemplar is saying, and then something comes in which doesn't match. This could be because you have misheard earlier, or made the wrong assumption. I remember hearing my exemplar saying 'a dog' and in fact it was 'a duck'! Bit of a difference and completely shifted my internal construction.

Your clarifying question could be a means of double-checking something that has been said, so that the exemplar re-hears and has a choice to change what they've said. A relevancy challenge may be to bring the exemplar back to the point of departure, or to reveal the genuine purpose for the deviation

3   **Confirmation:**   you have a good idea of what is happening, and through summarising you want to establish that you are on the right track.   This is the purpose of a tag question in trance, used to gain a 'yes' ideomotor response.

You also want to check again the signs of congruence, to be really clear about the significance of what you are detecting.

You want to provide a punctuation point in the process of enquiry.

4   **Information:**   you may be seeking an update covering an intervening period.   You may choose to go for more of the story, which will give you more material to sift through for patterns and the underlying structure.   Or you may be following a specific modelling methodology, say with Clean Language, Meta Model questioning, or meta programme detection.

5   **Leading:**   Lawley and Tompkins always start off a therapeutic session with the standard question 'What would you like to have happen?' by way of initiating the overall outcome of the exemplar, or else starting the process towards determining it.

You may want to lead the exemplar to a new place, possibly physically to stand up, move, or sit down.   You may want to check out if the exemplar is ready to move on to the next piece.

You want your exemplar to come up with his or her own solutions, using the universally effective question of 'What has to happen for that to happen?' followed by 'Can it/you/they?'

6   **Relationship:**   asking easy-to-answer questions, even closed questions, (psst! – closed questions start with a verb), is a way to get the exemplar speaking, and a great way to help them overcome nerves, hear the sound of his or her own voice in this context, and the possible strangeness of such an 'intimate' relationship.   I may ask about the journey, or go through the Personal Details documentation.

Going for specific detail to demonstrate that you are interested, and you can refer to say the dog's name, or colour of the kitchen, later on.   You may just be giving the exemplar a space to talk and settle into the session.

7   **Retrieval:**   this is the major purpose of Meta Model.   It seeks to retrieve the missing information that underpins the patterns within deletions, generalisations and distortions.

If you detect that the exemplar is still inside even though, possibly through politeness, you're told they are now ready for more, then asking 'What else?' 'Why else?' can bring out the next layer of information, which at the time may not have seemed relevant to the exemplar.   Often this is really significant and your acuity is to be congratulated.   Going to meta position and asking 'What's missing?' can be a really quick way to gain missing pieces.

8   **Resourcing:**   you may want your exemplar to access a significant reference experience to provide needed resources.   'Can you remember a time when …', 'What does this remind you of …', 'What other occasions were good for you?'

The 'As If' questions of 'Guess' 'And if you did know …?' 'Who else might know?', plus the call on mentors, could be your means of catalysing access to deeper structure.

9   **Testing:**   you may be seeking to establish an inventory or the starting point of a process for calibration purposes.   'On a scale of 1 low to 10 high, how confident are you feeling?'

You may be seeking means of future pacing events, as a means of generalising change. 'As you consider having had this outcome for some time, what is now possible?'

10 **Not on the list – nosiness:** this can be another name for curiosity. You can risk abusing your (arguably) more powerful position, and coerce your exemplar to answering. You could be putting your exemplar into a very difficult position, where they may find it difficult to refuse to answer. Thank goodness for 'Don't knows'.

Detecting Significance

At one stage in my life, I qualified as a BS5750 Lead Assessor. During the training, we learnt how to prepare for an audit. We were told how the team would look at previous audits and seek to follow up non-conformances. They would anticipate possible areas that might be usefully scrutinised. And they would devise the audit plan, allocating particular elements to each member of the audit team. On arrival they would set off on their prescribed route.

> You would ask a question, and feel the whole building shake. You would pull the monster by the tail, and if it came away in your hand, you would continue with your plan. If it didn't then you knew there was much more there. You would tear up your plan and track down the monster.

'Feeling the whole building shake' was that auditor's way of knowing that he had landed on something really significant, which had to be followed up.

Judith Delozier talks about spending time hanging out at the racetrack paddock, where the horses walk round before going to the starting line. She would discuss with fellow cognoscenti the form sheets, appraise the configuration of the animals, eye up the weather and the track conditions. And after all of that, the ol' timer turns to her and says 'If you've got a hunch, back a bunch!'

Within our system we have the means of processing incoming information and detecting what's important and what isn't, what to pursue, and what to leave by the wayside. Developing our natural antennae is essential if we are to provide a ripple free transition through an exemplar's journey. It will determine our direction of enquiry and the importance we will place on the answers we're getting.

However, significance is such an individual judgment. We can be trained to notice significant elements. But the perceiver of this information is you and not everyone. You will always be the determinant of what happens next. No two practitioners will follow identical lines of enquiry, although you both may end up in or around the same end point. This is why it is so important that you are in charge of your internal enquiry system and use it to its maximum effect.

Much will depend on what your outcome is, or you may be operating multiple outcomes. 'What's important to me?' will set your filters. So will your adopted methodology. For example, if you are alert to meta model patterns and predicates, you will quickly notice and place significance on these specific language patterns.

Significance can also come from the seeming importance placed by the exemplar as they are answering. However, don't be blinded by these filters. Remember, the exemplar is having his or her own experience, and serving their own personal outcomes. You need to check out if a strong response is as a result of the reference experience you have activated or, perhaps to something completely independent of what is happening in the room – remembering a phone call that should have been made, or even a reaction to you, the modeller.

When these strong responses are evident, you want to notice them, and should they reoccur, you want to attend to them in the moment.

Significance for yourself

Dilts talks about his radar going Beep! Beep! He then has a second check-in, when he tests if he can perform what has been described. Alert signals go off if he finds pieces missing.

Personally, when tracking patterns, I have a visual radar screen with its scanning beam. When something comes into sight, I test it for the same shape that is already on my screen. I also monitor the amount of movement going on inside my body: the more relevant the information, the slower the movement, until all becomes settled. Or conversely, if a piece of information comes in, which disrupts the movement causing eddies, then I know this is something to pay attention to and pursue.

Significance for exemplar

At the same time, you need to be alert to signs that something significant has occurred for the exemplar. Remember, whatever is happening on the inside will show up on the outside.

- *Changes in skin tone:* flushing, going white
- *Shifts in breathing:* big breath or sigh, holding the breath, audible shallow breath
- *Tears:* from increased moistness or shininess to crying
- *Sounds:* snorts, laughter of joy or hysteria, meta comments
- *Gestures:* clenched fists, movement against body, pushing away
- *Eyes:* fixated, narrowed, open eyed.

You need to notice and register these. You may choose to take your foot off the pedal for a bit, to evaluate what has just caused it, or you may wait to see if a pattern emerges. You may also need to acknowledge the importance of whatever is happening inside. At this point, it is now your call to know when to stay with the moment and pursue this particular line of questioning or let it pass.

It is worth remembering that something significant for an exemplar could be some fabulous breakthrough, new insight or tremendous surge of resource. Or it could be the intimation of something troubling and delicate, which may require some really sensitive and sustained handling.

Remember, too, that your exemplar may not be tuned into his internal system, and may not register that something important has just occurred. It may be that it happens so frequently that the exemplar is inured to it. Your external sense can provide external feedback, not only of what has just happened, but also, if you've been tracking this for a while, the possible triggers that set off the response. The exemplar can choose to recognise the worth of it, or not. If the answer is not to pursue, this is more significant information for you, and you can tuck this knowledge away, to bring it out at a later point.

- *Incongruence:* when I am with an exemplar, I pay close attention to incongruence. Incongruence for me poses some good questions:
  - Has the internal processing reached new territory and the exemplar hasn't found the answers yet, or suspects that the answers may be too telling?

- Is the old territory no longer providing reliable answers?

- Are the incongruent behaviour changes, or language changes from a different part, which has kicked in to 'save the situation and provide protection', since the behaviour doesn't add up with where we had been?

- Am I being given a standard response, or one the exemplar thinks ought to be offered?

- *Emotional response:* I will also pay attention to eyes glistening or tearing up, knowing that tears can be tears of relief as well as pain. They may be the 'tears of truth' that Steve Andreas talks of, when the words have touched an important place deep inside. Or there may be a longer than usual period of internal processing, and I detect a stilling in the air as if the pause button has just been pressed on our relationship. Often I will find myself holding *my* breath! Obviously the more I am in second position, the more quickly my own intuitions will alert me.

- *Displacement:* alternatively, if the exemplar launches off into some seemingly unconnected story, or repeats some earlier reference, or simply closes down, I may well check out what had just happened to cause that. I may put importance on gestures or over-emphasised words, but I may also suspect that these are signs of a rehearsed story or a response that the exemplar either habitually has, or believes ought to have. Still I may check it out.

Testing

As with Dilts, you need to check out and update your understanding of what is or was significant. It could well be that in the short time you've been with your exemplar, he has moved on and that issue is no longer the issue. Or what you were offered was just the precursor to something even more important. Again it is your call as to where you go to next.

It is often useful at the end of a session to ask the exemplar what had been the significant moments during the encounter – note the presupposition here. You may well be surprised by the answer. It might even be something that you hadn't even noticed and certainly didn't zone in on! Food for thought.

Tracking Vectors

Lawley first introduced me to the notion of vectors in relation to the process of enquiry. I had come across them in the dim distant past of my maths and physics days. Here he was using the metaphor to describe the shifts, intended or otherwise, in the direction an enquiry is taking. If you want to learn more in depth application of this concept, then check out *Vectoring and Systemic Outcome Orientation* on the website www.cleanlanguage.co.uk.

With an exemplar, the modeller seeks to go from Point A, the current situation, along the pathways within the system to arrive at Point X, the end point, having touched on all the points in between. Whilst it is unlikely that a direct path to successful conclusion is possible, or even desirable, arguably the more efficient the line of enquiry, the fewer points and deviations there will be in between.

The concept of a question as a vector is expressed as an arrow, drawn from A to B, and defined by its magnitude and direction. In our context of exploration, the magnitude or length of the arrow denotes the amount of time spent pursuing a particular line of enquiry. The magnitude depends on the quality and quantity of questions the modeller is asking in pursuit of particular train of thought. It will be a short arrow if the modeller alters tack after one question.

Given the shifts in direction, what becomes of particular interest is what is happening to trigger the new direction.

Direction

The modeller determines the direction and the deviations of an enquiry. The modeller decides what is significant and what is not. You are the one who picks up the meta model patterns, the metaphors, the throw away gestures, the signs of incongruence, the calibration evidence, and all the other pieces of information you're receiving through the responses you're getting. You are also testing this information within your own system to see what fits, what is missing, and if you are getting what you want. And you are evaluating where you have reached within the overall process. All of this will inform your next question.

So you determine the start of the vector, its direction, and its magnitude, to good effect or not.

Taking time to discover the pathways you have taken through your lines of enquiry can prove to be extremely rewarding. What do you pursue? What do you body-swerve? Recording and then transcribing a session is a fantastic way of offering yourself feedback on your practice without any coach in sight. You will inevitably discover your own patterns that work well for you, and you can marvel at your genius. Or you can reveal those patterns that don't serve your practice and divert you off to backwaters of inert information. You will also alert yourself to where you place too much emphasis or too little emphasis, your favourite patterns, and possible vanities.

This form of self-modelling will indicate the reasons behind your levels of effectiveness, and can plot your own journey towards elegance. Remember the hallmark of mastery is asking the fewest questions to yield the most relevant information.

Contributing Factors

The interesting piece is where and when you decide to change tack. No two practitioners will plot the same vector patterning, since each of you will be filtering for different things and responding to different cues. In fact, it has been proven that the efficacy of therapy is not down to the modality, but to the effectiveness of the therapist, *irrespective* of the modality they are working in. A good therapist will pursue the most appropriate line of enquiry to bring home the desired outcome.

So it is worth considering the influencers that would affect the direction your enquiry might take.

1   **Outcome:** keeping the same outcome in mind will inform the continuing direction of your vector. Changing your outcome, for whatever reason, will start up a new vector. It may well be that you will return to a previous vector, should the current one harvest no useful information or cease to serve your overall outcome. Conversely, you may choose to abandon forever an earlier vector, given the relevance of the information you are now getting.

2   **Formula:** you may be pursuing a particular prescribed line of questioning as part of a modelling format, which is likely to implicitly hold its own pattern of vectors. Symbolic Modelling, Meta Programme Elicitation, Experiential Array, for example, all hold preferred questioning patterns that determine the direction to take.

3   **Focus:** the tighter you control your own sense of direction, then the more controlled and focussed you will be in your enquiries.

Hold your outcome too lightly, and you will find yourself flitting from one topic to another, without any clear sense of what you're doing and where you're going. You may be using this approach as a starting point for your exploration, skirting round all bases as a means of detecting what is significant. Or you may just be demonstrating insufficient focus, no matter how you dress it up. Your signals for significance need to be raised higher.

In this condition, you risk being seduced by the exemplar's content, possible displacement activities, emotional susceptibilities, or attention-seeking behaviour. You also risk being distracted by your internal processing, unuseful internal dialogue or the fascination of your own map. At worst you may just enter into a conversation.

Hold your outcome too tightly, and you run the risk of deleting some relevant information, and denying the exemplar his or her own right to self-determination. Happily, if it is important, this information is likely to return to give you a second chance. And exemplars are notoriously forgiving – except when they are not.

4   **Acuity:** you may simply not notice a particular cue, emphasis or word pattern. Your attention was elsewhere, possibly testing what you've just received, attending to inner processing, or constructing your next question. More to the point, we can never pay attention to everything. We will always miss something that is offered. Again if it is important it will return.

So you may continue in a particular direction where pursuing a different one could have paid larger dividends, or resisted the temptation to pursue something else and stayed where you are to mine the seam further.

Because of this, going through a transcript can be telling. This process gives you huge, guilt-free opportunity to spot, a second time round, what was missed the first time. You can't turn the clock back, but you can learn from it. It might be that you will have another opportunity to open up the conversation. It is amazing how fertile an opening of 'I was just thinking about what you said the other day, and it made me wonder …' can be.

5   **Shared maps:** this is fascinating when it occurs. Where you share maps, hold the same values, have the same beliefs, operate from the same complex equivalences, etc., you are less likely to detect these patterns and bring them to question. You will glide past them without a pause, probably internally agreeing with the wisdom of this exemplar in front of you!

It takes great commitment to stay sufficiently alert to question your exemplar's map whilst possibly leaving your own unexamined.

6   **Circumstances:** you may simply have run out of energy. Your ability to concentrate fully on what is being said has peaked. Or, it may be that you are coming to the end of the session, or the meeting, and you have to curtail the process. These are all plausible reasons for cutting short the process prematurely.

7   **Habit:** we are all a package of our own patterns, and basic filters, each essential for our navigation in the world. You may have some favourite models that direct your thinking and which have proven to be amazingly effective in the past. Or you may have some strong generalisations that have served you well, and you have consistently found the evidence to support them.

You may remember the story of Fish in Dreams, of a therapist who was convinced that everything could be encapsulated in the symbol of fish. And so all his enquires sought to establish that fish featured somewhere in the exemplar's experience.

It is really important that you stay mindful of the sieve through which you process your exemplar's stories. Staying alert to what is really being offered and initiating a new line of enquiry will be the best teacher you have ever had.

8   **Pattern detection:**   as a result of your general line of questioning, you may come to the point when you feel you have spotted the key patterns operating in the system, and you are ready to up the anti and pursue the structure that holds these patterns. Here you would see the vectors becoming longer and steadier in direction as you zone in towards the centre of the system, and go for gold.

9   **Reviewing:**   you stop the enquiry in its tracks in this moment, and either review through using the Backtrack Frame, or both of you step into third position and view both your contribution and the relationship between you. From this meta position, you can gain a clearer view of the pattern of vectors that you, the practitioner, have been creating.

10   **Indulgence:**   as a relationship-building outcome, you may indulge your exemplar by encouraging content, since you judge that he of she would benefit from hearing the story said in this moment, in this situation. Your questions may not deliver any immediate pertinent information to promote a clear line of enquiry, and your contribution would be more comment, and encouragement. At this point, the pattern of vectors would be temporarily interrupted.

11   **Your sensitivities:**   this is a really interesting and fruitful cause of vector deviation. The exemplar may well touch on a topic that you instinctively shy away from. In such moments, you will find yourself taking a different tack, often as far away as possible from the one just touched upon, and you will be able to come up with perfect justification for this.

Such hotspots could be any aspects that are currently unresolved within yourself – for example the desire to leave a relationship, abuse, sexual issues, parental issues, bullying at work. Or it could be an emotional area of anger, fear, shame, or guilt. If you have difficulty finding the language to work with such topics, then you know that your modelling results will be circumscribed.

12   **Your exemplar's sensitivities:**   finally, another cause for deviation or avoidance occurs when your exemplar becomes really upset, or you suspect this is going to happen, and you pull your punches. You make it easy for your exemplars and you rescue them from their distress. This is akin to the cause above, because your sensitivity is avoidance of distress. However, at such moments, it may be even more essential for you to keep your finger on this pressure point, holding the space firmly and rock-steady for your exemplar, so he or she can navigate their way through it. This may be the first time he or she has ever been able to face whatever it is, and they may be eternally grateful that you were sufficiently steadfast to assist them through it. This is true sponsorship in action.

Recording Data

With the best will in the world you will not retain, verbatim, all the content of an interview. With practice you may retain quite a lot, but not necessarily enough to serve all your purposes. Therefore you will need to have some method or methods of recording the dialogue and the process that went on.

Recording Purposes

1 **Credibility:** taking notes sends out a meta message that what they are saying is important to you, that you want to make sure that you cover all that is offered. This is particularly true for exemplars you are modelling for specific behaviours.

2 **Attention:** it is unlikely that you will be writing everything verbatim. So you need to know where your attention can most usefully lie. The more experienced you become, the more you know what to record word-for-word, and what can be summarised.

You will detect what is important to them, through the emphasis placed, repetition, time taken to respond, or emotional response. These would be useful to record, but possibly more interestingly, what you asked prior to the response.

Some modelling practices require verbatim accounts. Symbolic Modelling with Clean Language, for example, require you to use *only* the exemplar's words. However Dilts prefers the line that says: 'If I paraphrase accurately what a exemplar has said, then they know that I know and understand them accurately. It also gives them a chance to correct me.'

When your exemplars see you writing, they know they may have said something significant, which can help divert their attention away from their story, and more to how they are creating the story.

3 **Review:** having tangible evidence enables you to review much more accurately and usefully, when you are away from your exemplar. You can pick up points you glossed over at the time.

Within a session itself, you can backtrack from your notes, possibly following the sequence of events, or providing a cohesive summary of what has emerged. Again it lets the exemplar know he or she has been heard and lets you know if you have left anything out that is significant. You also give yourself the opportunity to spot any patterns of language, responses, or recurring themes.

4 **Evidence:** as a modeller, you may find yourself presenting your model to the contracting customer, and your notes can serve to bolster your findings and indicate the journey you have taken. In truth, it's the model that is all the evidence you need of success, yet your source details can support you further.

If you are also a trainer, keeping records of learner progress is essential for certification purposes. Furthermore, having good case notes allows you to draw upon the details for case studies and scenarios, provided the exemplar's identity is not known. If you are pioneering a particular approach and seek to write up for publication, then you most certainly want to have a bank of clearly annotated examples to draw from.

From a modelling perspective, you may use your notes as a case study to illustrate the journey towards model construction.

Logistics

Recording a session comes under the walking and chewing gum category of multi tasking – becomes easier with practice and daunting to begin with.

1 **State:** you may not feel comfortable about taking your attention away from your exemplar. But exemplars would expect you to be recording the session. Otherwise they may think that you are wasting their time, or that they are not important to you.

2 **Contracting:** as part of the contracting process, you need to say that you will be taking notes or recording the session. You need to gain agreement for this. And if you have any intention of going on to publish any of the content, you need to let them know that you will ask their permission first before going further with your project.

For exemplars, you can offer them feedback on the model or models you come up with. However be aware that the exemplar may feel that they are not being truly represented within your model – how often does a sitter like the artist's portrait? Explain that the model is for specified end users and that you may be accessing multiple sources, to come up with a composite model.

Media

We have a variety of recording methods at our disposal. It will depend on how intensive and long lasting you intend your enquiry to be. A modeller will want to have as much data as possible to refer to. A researcher will want to have on record the data supporting the research findings. A committed student therapist will want to have good sources for feedback and learning.

1 **Written:** you may have document templates that you are required to complete. These are useful to guide you through the process. They are also useful for comparing apples with apples later on. Guard against squeezing your exemplar into this particular shape. Be alert to those bits outside the pre-set boxes, and be up for empty boxes. Know that the box doesn't determine the quantity or quality of content.

You may have developed your own style of handwritten notes, with your own symbols and shorthand. You may also have layout characteristics to highlight particular types of content – beliefs, predicates, meta programmes – so that these can be easily accessed during and after the session. Make sure you number the pages, so that you can keep track of the process.

It is useful to transcribe your notes onto computer – certainly saves a lot of space. This way you reconnect with the content and its context, and possibly gain a meta cognition through connecting emerging patterns.   You will of course lose the visual impact of your handwritten hieroglyphics. You may need to code this a different way through different font size and colour. You can also begin to order the data if you already have some scoping framework – although if modelling you need to be prepared to rearrange it.

2 **Visual:** as mentioned earlier, always have coloured pens and sheets of paper handy so that your exemplar can create a visual representation of his or her internal processes. One of the great advantages to using this medium is that you can check out your own internal representations against theirs. You could be in for significant surprises, enough to learn that it is highly unlikely that you are intuitively replicating their map in your own mind, no matter how deep the levels of rapport and second positioning.

3   **Audio recording:** there are many options now available for audio recording, including your mobile phone. Technology has simplified the process that makes the process accessible to even the strongest technophobe.

This is by far the best method of accurate recording, especially for modellers and for fledgling therapists. It keeps you free to attend completely to the exemplar. However, I suggest total dependence on this loses the punctuation points your own note taking creates, and the visual/kinaesthetic anchors you are setting up for yourself. But knowing you have this back up completely removes any stress you may feel about 'not getting all of it'.

Unless both you and your exemplar are miked up or, if you have a particularly powerful device, your questions and your exemplar's responses during a special intervention may not be picked up. This might also be the case if you have opted for a trance intervention.

Audio recording is in real time. So, to make use of it, you will need twice as long, if not longer, to go through it and make any meaningful sense of it. You may find yourself taking further notes as you listen more intently without the need to maintain relationship.

If you are intending to transcribe the material, then either give yourself three times the length of the session, or out-source the job to trained transcribers. Once you have the full transcript, you can mine it endlessly for the information within it.

With a transcription, you cannot delude yourself with your deletions, generalisations and distortions. It is there in black and white. You may be totally surprised to discover chunks that you have completely deleted or certainly minimised. Again this is great learning for you.

4   **Video recording:** what audio recordings don't provide is the visual evidence of non-verbal physiology, gestures and location of attention. As NLPers, we know such communication is of critical importance.

For modelling purposes, having a video recording of the exemplar actually performing the identified skill is the ultimate source of information, especially if you have the chance to study it before your face-to-face interview. The details that lie outside the exemplar's awareness can be evident, the tics and mannerisms, the positioning and gestures can be tested for their essential contribution, or indicators of inner processing.

For face-to-face modelling, a video recording can be exceedingly useful to give feedback onto the effects of your questions, your responses to answers, and your relationship. For this to be effective and avoid the downsides of video, you will ideally have THREE cameras; one on yourself, one on the exemplar and one on both of you – a tall order for most modellers.

There are downsides to using video. It can create self-consciousness both on the part of the exemplar and the modeller. This can be overcome through familiarisation. Where the modeller is limited to one camera, movement can be restricted and this fixes the activity to one point in the room.

Storage

This is a quick comment on the protocols of storage of data records, particularly relevant for therapists. However should you want to put your findings forward as part of a research project, you will need to be able to consult your records and produce them if required.

Good practice suggests that records should:

- Be maintained for each exemplar and each exemplar session

- Contain contact agreements, initial interview and follow up interviews

- Include any notes and drawings, etc. which should be attached to the interview summary

- Be available for the exemplar to see, and other legitimate parties

- Be kept in a locked cupboard or filing cabinet

- Maintain anonymity if that is part of the contract

- Be kept for a minimum of seven years, if part of a professional personal development activity

- Conform to the Data Protection Act.

Part 4 – The Skills of Modelling

Handling Data Phase

Whilst placing these advanced skills within this phase in the process, it is important to know that the skill of systemic thinking operates throughout the process of gathering data, handling it and the acquisition phase. Similarly detecting patterns operates during the investigation phase, since they can drive questions.

Thinking Systemically

We are constructivists. We believe that all behaviour has a structure, which is not linear, but multi dimensional. As a modeller, your focus is on discovering this structure: exploring the system that holds it, in its entirety; up, down, throughout, to the edges and into its depths. This is systemic thinking. Your focus is not on pursuing the distraction of the content or story that embellishes it.

When you were first introduced to Meta Model and were set up in small groups to practice, it's most likely that you found yourself wanting to comment on what was being said, and to add your tuppence worth. It was quite a quantum leap to realise that you were being asked to listen to *how* the speaker was telling the story, and pay attention to the key words they were using. It was those key words – 'can't, should, means', etc., which were providing the vital information that you wanted to work with, not all the fluff around them.

Task and relationship

A pursuit of structure means you can cut to the chase, cut out loads of unnecessary time, and in the process, provide a pattern disrupt to the exemplar's trance. That's the upside. The downside is that you may forget to maintain relationship in your forensic pursuit, and lose sight of the fact that the content has meaning for the exemplar.

Your exemplar is going to believe it is the story that you want, and will be keen to offer lots of evidence. As the modeller, once you have the pattern from two or three examples, you may be ready to move on. If you have clearly explained to your exemplar about the importance of structure over content then your exemplar will not be offended. He or she may find themselves becoming equally fascinated by this meta level approach.

On the other hand, balance this with remembering that you are in relationship, and that your exemplar may need to be heard. You may have to curb your impatience, maintain rapport and lead more gently.

Structure of structure

Structure is a three-dimensional system of logical levels and logical types, moving from detail up to overview and across different associated topics.

If this idea doesn't have meaning for you just yet, then the next section takes time to explore just what a Logical Type, and a Logical Level are, and the relationship between them. When you gain a real understanding of how these connect you have the key to bringing order to a seemingly chaotic system. You are at the threshold of bringing clarity and stability into your thinking.

Logical Types

Gregory Bateson expanded on the thinking of Bertrand Russell and his thoughts on Logic. Seeking to explain the complexities of communication and behaviour, he developed the notion of Logical Levels and Logical Types to frame how we think and how we make sense of information we receive. As significantly, this approach demonstrates how we can think differently from another and how misunderstandings, tensions and conflict can be created.

It has taken me a bit of time to feel really at home with the dynamics of Logical Levels and Logical Types sufficiently enough, to offer a lucid explanation for you. I can only say that gaining clarity regarding the relationships between them and recognising how they are operating within a complex system eases confusion and quickens the process of generating order. For me, to grasp the essential simplicity of these two concepts opens doors to sanity.

In weaving there are two types of threads: the main vertical threads that run through the entire fabric – the warp, and the horizontal threads that are woven across – the weft. So Logical Types, like the warp threads, provide the major strands and classes of thinking, and Logical Levels like weft threads connect elements that are operating at the same level of complexity, either within the same Logical Types or across Logical Types.

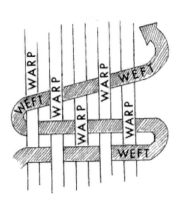

	Logical Type	Logical Type	Logical Type
Logical Level 1			
Logical Level 2			
Logical Level 3			

Basically, Bateson suggests our mind is made up of pigeonholes or labelled boxes, to which we have allocated specific meaning and generalisations – experienced or imagined. This way we can predict and act instinctively. Our labels set up our potential ability to respond appropriately and accurately with others – provided our labelling system has some form of commonality with those around us.

These labels can be referred to as categories, codes, classes or Logical Types, and the process of allocating these labels is referred to as sorting or scoping.

Generally speaking we are able to communicate with each other because there is an unspoken consensus with labelling: an apple is a fruit, or a food. When this is the case, little or no further clarification or explanation is required. But for some an apple may represent a bribe (apple for the teacher), a health remedy (an apple a day keeps the doctor away), a sexual lure (as in the Garden of Eden), a record label, or an international IT company. And for the orchard farmer it may equal currency.

It is the rare speaker who doesn't wander a bit, especially when he or she is struggling to make sense of something. Their confusion is *because* they haven't sorted the issue into an orderly system. The issue hasn't found a home in one of the labelled boxes, or else a new box has to be created for it.

Misunderstandings occur when the speaker is operating from one logical type, and the listener is coding the words under a different logical type. Often when this happens, there will be a stutter in the conversation and pretty quickly either the listener will seek clarification or the speaker will check understanding – otherwise a heated debate at cross purposes may ensue.

Strong arguments relentlessly hound the logic inherent in the logical type and hold fast to it – terrorists and freedom fighters. Without this focus, the argument becomes flaccid and easily dismantled. Mixing logical types immediately weakens the train of thought. Robust debate depends on maintaining the inherent logic of the selected category, and holding at bay any attempts to derail and destabilise through introducing information under a different category. Conversely altering the logical type with the same data becomes reframing and a means of looking at the situation anew.

Sometimes there will be wilful switching of logical types to deliberately confuse and throw the other off balance. Teenagers are renowned for this. Parents think they are discussing the time to be home, which is about safety and wellbeing, when they are quickly highjacked as the discussion becomes one about the parents being too old, injustice, or bullying. No wonder the parent is left impotently speechless as the door slams. The inherent logic in the argument has gone up in smoke!

Speakers, ideally, are aware of the logical type they are operating from and remain constant within it – or else mark out when they are switching. This coherence aids understanding. The listener may not agree with what is being said, but at least understands 'where the speaker is coming from'. Confused speakers, however, are not often aware of their own inner logic, and so are unaware when they are shifting the categories of their thinking. They have no way of monitoring the flow of their argument and so can become frustrated at the lack of understanding in others. This is where cause and effect, or complex equivalent patterns come into play.

Listeners excel when they not only can identify the logical type being worked within, but also as and when this type changes. The first signs of their own internal confusion are the first signs that the logical type has likely been switched. At such moments the switch can be challenged. Sometimes, the switch is to the listener's advantage because it helps to understand the generalisations the speaker is making.

Bateson was fascinated with how people think and how different people think differently. He wanted to know what was causing misunderstandings and subsequent conflict that would arise from discussions. He realised that much was dependent on how people were labelling the information they were getting, and then comparing it with or against labels they already hold. This process of labelling is key to how we make sense of the information we receive.

Logical Levels

Note: Logical Levels are not to be confused or substituted for Dilts's model – Neurological Levels. Here he has named a particular set of ascending logical levels, placed in a hierarchical framework. Neurological Levels is an application of logical levels. You need to be clear to always make this distinction.

You may have come across the idea of fractals – a pattern repeating endlessly, regardless of scale.

The classic example is the cauliflower. Looking at the cauliflower head it has a recognisable shape and form. Break off a large floret and it looks the same as the head. Now from this break off a smaller floret, and it has the same shape and form. And so on.

The following diagrams are an excellent illustration of the geometric regularity of fractals since it also shows the patterns for these four different shapes (Types) and iterations of fractals to 5 levels of complexity (Levels).

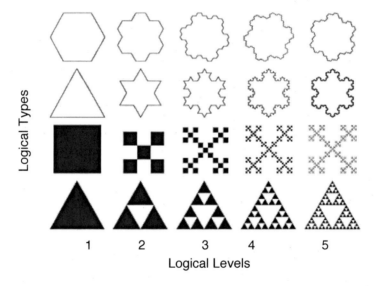

Interestingly, the distinctions in level 5 seem pretty indistinct, to the point of being indistinguishable from level 4. The only way to verify this is to get up really close with the magnifying glass – an interesting metaphor for how easy it is to delete significance.

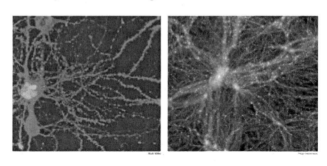

Brain Cells   **The Universe**

Logic, therefore, is not only strengthened by maintaining the structure of logical types, it also requires the speaker to be mindful whether or not the examples being offered by a speaker are from the same logical level, and therefore of the same scale and level of complexity. Jumping up and down the scales of complexity can be confusing to the listener. At the same time you prove the presence of a pattern by citing instances of its occurrence at different scales – for example feeling threatened in a one-to-one conversation, at a family gathering, and in a large crowd.

Sometimes the speaker is unaware of the connection between seemingly different and disparate events, or thoughts, or actions. It takes the modeller first of all to be predisposed to consider that these behaviours are part of the same pattern and so reveal what each of these examples have in common. The emergent theme that the modeller has detected (which another might not) becomes the operating pattern that underpins all the behaviour. Erickson was a master at detecting similar structures within disparate accounts, which would lead to him tell stories that reflected this structure or set tasks that mirrored the structure.

The danger here is that the modeller may have some pet themes and be predisposed to funnelling all information into his or her favourite categories – Dilts's 'fish in dreams' story of the psychiatrist.

Another way of experiencing the importance of maintaining consistency regarding your choice of logical type and level comes from this example.

Case study

Imagine the following details is data that you are gathering from an individual, who is talking about diversity within farming, specifically in the area of crop production. As you're listening you are trying to make sense of what he's saying. To do this you have to construct some sort of framework in your head to understand how each element connects with each other. So you go through a process of finding out the similarities and differences between them. Finally, and it may take no time at all, depending on how familiar you are with the subject, you come up with some construction which seems logical to you – see the framework. (Worth noting that someone else may come up with something different.)

So you identify the three major areas of crops he mentioned, and focus on fruit since he gives most information in this area. You're not sure about Lapins – French rabbits didn't seem to have a place here – so you leave it to one side. Or you may start obsessing about Lapins and delete everything else, which might not be useful. Worth hanging on until Lapins either fits your existing map, or you have more information that is similar to Lapins and you can revise or reconstruct your map. You could always ask 'Where do Lapins fit in?' But all is well. He mentions casually that Lapins are types of cherries, whereupon you thankfully slot it in to a prepared place without any bother. Notice how the stress arising from confusion drops – it may be minimal but it is a sign of reaching further understanding.

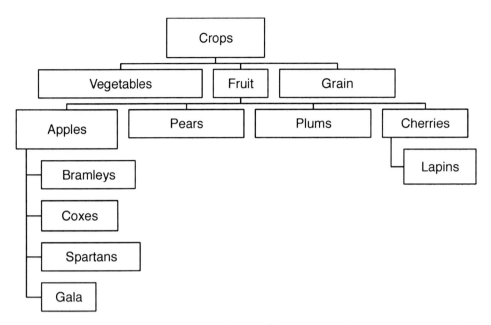

You continue following the conversation fine until he starts talking about pears, Lapins, plums and Bramleys. All of a sudden you become confused and have to work to make sense of what you've just heard. Happily you have your framework and can refer to the place of each. You may find yourself querying how come he had mixed them up, since there may be a connection between them that you didn't know about – a connection that in fact is crucial to your understanding of this man's concerns. He may look at you blankly because he hadn't realised that he had done this, or he may say that he was distracted by something else, or he may say they are all the same colour.

And then he put Coxes, Bramleys, apples and Spartans into the same sentence. This doesn't feel right! Apples don't belonging here. You are aware that all the others are types of apples, and 'apples' covers all of them. The incongruity is because 'apples' is the class that the others belong to, which violates the obvious rules of logic. It has to stay at the level above.

A class at one logical level cannot also be a member of itself at a smaller level.

As the one working on making sense of this, you need to be alert to the mixing of logical levels, so that you can choose which level to pursue, especially if he starts talking about cherries and plums.

Detecting this incongruity is a great intuition to develop. It helps you query the data you're given to regain balance once more, steering the investigation along logical lines. But if the incongruity continues, then you may have to consider going back to the drawing board and starting from scratch.

Relationship between Levels and Types

The category or class of information needs examples to illustrate and define it. So by chunking down, we will find various examples of that category, at different levels of scale and complexity. Establishing at least two levels of logical levels – the lower one more detailed than the one above – within a framework, you can test the pattern of the inherent logic within it.

The higher logical type drives, organises and controls the nature of the examples below it.

As you are searching to make sense of the details you have, you will experiment with the boxes, or logical types, that you are sorting your information into. This can be a challenging process. You may find that most of the data fits, with some irritating 'odds and sods' which are left over. You have to think very carefully about turning your back on these inconvenient pieces. It might just be that these are key to a whole new way of looking at the picture. The theory on Chaos was discovered this way!

Case Study continued

Imagine now you are alone, away from your fruit farmer and you are mulling over your conversation. You are wondering if there are any other patterns beyond the obvious one of crops, which could usefully be explored. So you consider another way of looking at the data and decide to sort it under 'Nutrients' instead of 'Crops'. This makes a huge difference to distribution of the information.

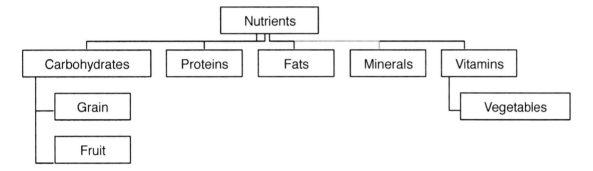

It makes you realise that you had gathered no information about the other food types. If you had wanted to gather data on nutrition, then you should have taken more charge of the investigation and not left it to the farmer to tell you what was obvious to him. Instead of seeking to make sense of his world, you actively need to gain precise information to support your needs – and the person you are writing the report for.

Change the logical type and your change the meaning of the data. You reframe it

You could also have considered other logical types or sorting categories could be 'Diets', 'Colours', 'Types of Farming', 'Land Use', for example. Notice how this would make a difference to what you're paying attention to. Just notice what happens to your relationship with the data when you change the type. At times of stuckness and confusion, it is well worth just sitting back and considering that, just possibly, a different logical type would suddenly reduce this nonsense into a new clarity. Your farmer may not have been talking about farming at all – he may in fact, even unwittingly, have been talking about his relationship with his wife, or the vagaries of climate change.

The more creative you are about the possible logical types that you could consider, the greater the access to different possible permutations. This explains why one modeller may come up with a fairly limited model, and another can produce something revolutionary.

Your outcome determines your filters. Your outcome determines the ultimate Logical Type.

It's at moments like this that the 'odds and sods' become essential to you. What you have dismissed as being insignificant could now emerge as your biggest clue. Resisting the temptation to try to shoehorn these pieces into your tidy model or discarding them as being unimportant, you have to have the courage to face up to the fact that your tidy, well thought out model, just isn't holding up. A stressful realisation. You are now contemplating going back to the drawing board. I know how desperate this moment is, but I also know that what emerges subsequently is something much more profound, unique and useful.

> **'Inconvenient' information requires you to chunk up and consider a new common logical type at a higher logical level, which satisfies the similarities and difference of all the data.**

The conversation takes a turn and your farmer starts talking about milking and the huge price of setting up a milking parlour. You've lost it. You don't know where he's heading. So you have to ask 'What's the connection between milking and fruit farming?' (the last point where you were certain). He says he is considering diversifying. This is a totally different topic now – different logical type. In your current framework of understanding there would be no place for 'Milking' or 'Parlours'. What you would rapidly have to do is chunk up, think 'Cows', think 'Dairy' cows specifically, think 'Cattle', think 'Livestock', and group livestock and crops under 'Types of Farming'. And if you wanted to test your thinking, you could fill in 'Sheep' 'Pigs' and put in some examples. This tells you that this framework at least still holds up.

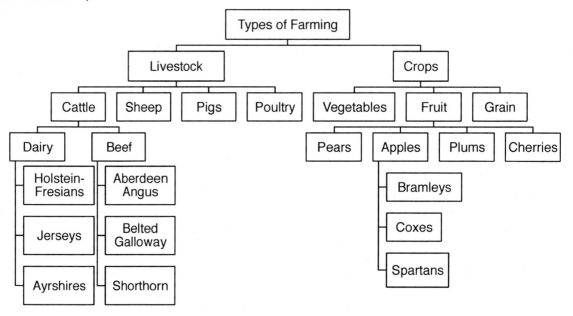

> **Chunking across should operate at the same logical level.**

> **A diagonal link is an indication of lesser/greater distinctions in one type compared to another.**

But you still don't have somewhere to put 'Milking' or 'Parlours'. These don't come under 'Types of Farming' – at face value, one is an activity and the other is a farm building. So you would put these ideas to one side saving them until anything similar emerges. Suppose you heard 'Jams', 'Wool', 'Cheese', you might turn your thinking to what is produced. A lesser person might then be tempted to alter tack a bit and start to look at end products of farming and consider something like this:

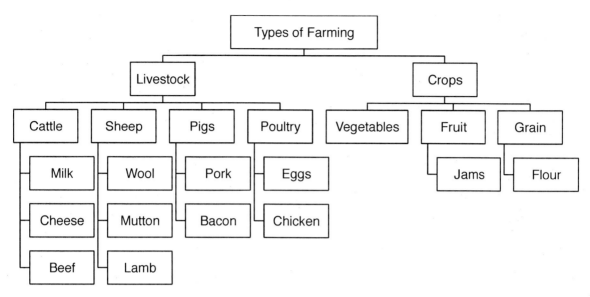

But you realise that 'Milk' and 'Jams' are not Types of Farming and so don't logically fit within this logical type. You would also realise that Milk and Bacon whilst at the same logical level – one is naturally found and the other is processed. It's likely you find yourself now focussing on a very different framework of thought.

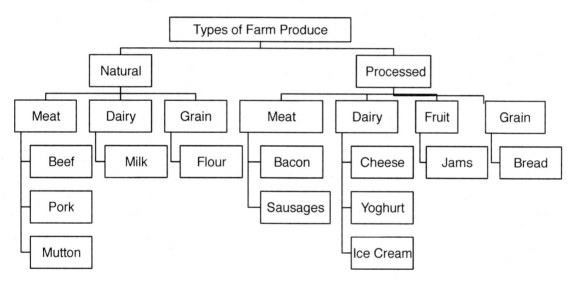

You cannot add a different logical type further down the 'leg'. All lower levels serve the higher one and stay within that type.

If you don't go down this route, instead you may become aware when the conversation turns to 'Tractors' and 'Combine Harvesters' you now have a category of 'Types of Farm Equipment'. Notice how you have already let go of your original labels of 'Activity' and 'Farm Building'. If you had clung onto them, you would either have deleted the references to products and equipment, or set up new headings and not included 'Milking' or 'Parlours'.

You have to be prepared to abandon your labelling in response to new data, and redistribute your data accordingly.

You conversation with the farmer is now over. You are happy that you have understood his world and could respond appropriately with what he was referring to. And that might be that. Or else you continue thinking about what you had covered and this set you thinking about what else you could consider. This may be part of your remit with the farmer, as part of an overall outcome 'To Explore Areas for Diversification.'

You have established your farmer's starting point. You've become interested in what else might be connected. You now need to develop your model further. Sometimes leaving the safety and familiarity of a vouched for model can be a real wrench, and as a modeller you may be prepared to pull your punches and merely tweak around the edges. As a consultant however, you have to examine the full system.

If in doubt, chunk up, chunk up, chunk up. Chunk across. Then chunk down.

Staying with the thinking, that livestock and crop production are the only sources of income open to a farmer, really limits the possibilities open to you. Your job is to explore all the viable sources of agricultural income. You may go back to your farmer and question him some more, or your enquiries may take you to other authorities, or you draw on your existing expertise. Voila! You have come up with very different ways of milking the resources available – apologies for the pun.

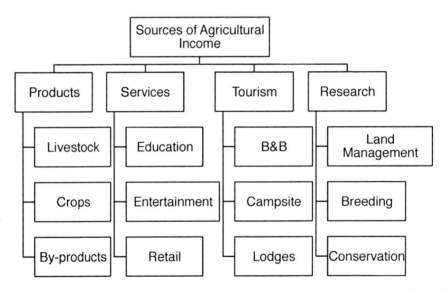

The more you chunk up, the more the parallel categories come into view. Possibilities become apparent. Creativity is generated by the ability to dart around the wider system, free of any need for logic until you are able to create your own. This way you find out where stray pieces of information fit, and then you're at choice to discard them, or zone in. This way you can discover that there are many possible models emerging out of your exemplar's system.

The person who is able to travel freely and quickly up and down logical levels, and explore similar levels in different logical types, will be able to demonstrate understanding of how grand ideas can operate on the ground, and how day-to-day events can influence policy. This is the key to ultimate flexibility.

Comment

There is a fair amount of debate regarding the classification of thinking, going back to Bertrand Russell and still current today within our own community. I know I could be accused of going down a 'cheap and cheerful' route of description, one that may lack rigour in the eyes of some. But when I start to read accounts by others, my eyes glaze over and I nearly lose the will to live. So as with all models, if this works for you then go with it; if it doesn't, there is other thinking out there.

In some quarters the terms logical level and logical types are not seen as separate distinctions. I suggest that there can be two reasons for this.

- All the individual elements within the same logical level will be of different logical types. If, say, two elements appear to be of the same logical type, then the following possibilities need to be considered.

  - The two similar elements are operating at a lower logical level, containing less information than their fellows. Therefore what they represent becomes the logical type that now sits alongside the others at the higher level.

  - Or a totally new logical type is created at a higher level which accommodates both, and may cause other fellow elements to be discarded or raised to a higher or lower logical level.

- A standalone element becomes the logical type. Only when other elements, similar in structure, appear alongside it, does the presence of a different additional logical type emerge at a higher logical level.

Finally

Having a clear understanding of the framework of our thinking helps us stabilise our thoughts, fill in the gaps and notice inconsistencies or even plain errors in reasoning.

Similar configurations of elements become Patterns. Patterns reveal similar configurations of logical levels and logical types. Using our abilities to detect inherent logic within a system allows us to detect patterns. And reccurrence of these patterns takes us to the Holy Grail of the structure operating within the exemplar's system.

Detecting Patterns

> The most desirable scientist is the rare scholar, a nomad-by-choice, who is essential for the intellectual welfare of the settled disciplines.
>
> Benoit Mandelbrot (1924 – 2010)

Mandelbrot, the scientist who first identified the startling beauty and structural uniformity of fractals, began by exploring the tiny inconvenient deviances that occurred in some previous mathematical thinking. Instead of brushing them aside as anomalies and too small to be significant, he gave these pieces relevance and sought to find out if similar occurrences could be found elsewhere. He took his head out of conventional thinking, and Fractals and Chaos Theory emerged. 'I started looking in the trash cans of science for such phenomena (fractals), because I suspected that what I was observing was not an exception but perhaps very widespread.'

Euclidian geometry, which had served for over 2000 years, could not explain the irregularities found in nature. 'Clouds are not spheres. Mountains are not cones,' he would say.

Having a totally different view on the physical world, his thinking took him beyond the reasoning that had previously been used to find the answers, and took him and his colleagues to a higher, more expansive system where the apparent chaos turned into beautifully explicable order. The quote of his that I love the most is:

> When I came into this game, there was a total absence of intuition. One had to create an intuition from scratch. The old intuition was misleading. Intuition is not something that is given. I've trained my intuition to accept as obvious shapes which were initially rejected as absurd, and I find everyone else can do the same.

Chaos: James Gleick 1987

And as Mandelbrot would have it, we need to clear ourselves of our pre-existing maps, on which we have been basing our generalisations, and be prepared to think afresh, ready to create a new intuition and a new way of appreciating the complexity. Only then will familiar information take on a new light and be open to new interpretation.

Human beings are riddled with patterns – structures bearing the same shape and nature, our programmes. However we are institutionalised by these instinctive patterns, which in turn drive our behaviour. To have any hope of changing them we need to spot them first.

For example you may have patterns of:

- Getting irritable before the visit of your mother-in-law
- Choosing inappropriate partners
- Expecting the worst outcomes
- Getting angry with yourself when something goes wrong
- Becoming excited at the thought of an audience.

Sometimes these patterns are disconnected from each other, or else are indicators of a more significant pattern operating at a higher logical level, even more deeply within our system. It might be that:

- Getting irritable before the visit of your mother-in-law
- Getting angry with yourself when something goes wrong

are examples of:

- Needing to be perfect; believing failure is unacceptable; believing only the good are loved.

So as modellers, it is essential that we can nose our way into a system, detect patterns, and sniff out the underlying pattern that is consistently driving unsatisfactory behaviour.

Thinking about Patterns

Patterns are always present. Some may be obvious and easily accessible, and some may require some precise excavation.

A pattern generates a predictable behaviour in response to certain triggers – actions, contexts, states. It lies within a cause and effect system. It only becomes useful for change and development once it is identified.

The more experience you have of the maps of others, the easier it is to be open to difference. If you are familiar with a particular culture or tribe, then you will be able to interpret the behaviours and recognise what is expected much more quickly than someone who finds the culture totally foreign and has to create generalisations from scratch. Having said that, care has to be given lest a pattern of behaviour is being assumed too quickly.

Definitions

A pattern is a systematically repetitive event in the world.

Christina Hall

A pattern is a configuration which has coherence and continuity.

Philip Harland

A pattern holds constant while other variables change.

Robert Dilts and Judith De Lozier

A pattern is an aggregate of events or objects that will permit in some degree (better than random) guesses when the entire aggregate is not available for inspection.

Gregory Bateson

Purpose of Patterns

We live our lives by patterns. We have unconscious internal patterns that instinctively control our behaviours and unconscious external patterns that provide ritual and familiarity. Without such unconscious generalisations, we would have to think through every behaviour before we act.

Patterns help us navigate our often chaotic and hostile worlds by offering us points of certainty to organise our experiences – and those of others. As you know, a book which is well laid out, with clear chapter and section headings, following a consistent layout and font formats, with clear contents pages, and comprehensive index, makes it much easier to use and follow.

By grouping repetitive and familiar experiences or patterns together, we have the freedom to direct our attention to areas of difficulty and unfamiliarity. Knowing that doors tend to open inwards or outwards saves us having to work out each time what to do with a door. We can then pay attention to what is on the other side of that threshold.

The Nature of a Pattern

* Individual patterns are unique, composed by the sequence (syntax) of their components and the relationship between them.

* Patterns draw on our ability to connect what we are experiencing, with previous generalisations.

* A pattern needs to repeat itself at least twice to establish itself as a pattern. For its perceivers, the third occurrence acts as confirmation.

- Patterns repeat through time and space. In fact so much of our behaviour is based on a few basic deeply embedded patterns.

- Patterns generate a specific outcome.

- The perceiver creates the pattern. The perceiver is selective about what is perceived from all the information available.

- Most patterns lie outside our awareness. We are aware of patterns when we are in a state of conscious learning. Reviewing allows unconscious patterns to become revealed.

- Patterns can combine and generate new patterns.

- Patterns can be useful and serve us. They can also be responsible for all the detrimental behaviours we run in our lives.

Pattern Detection Process

Detecting Patterns requires a state of Not-Knowing, or being prepared to revisit the meaning made of previous experiences.

Grinder spent 10 months 'working hard not to understand' during his study of Erickson's behaviour. He needed to build circuits for classes of this behaviour but wouldn't inspect these circuits until he had enough evidence that he could generate new patterns.

Pattern detection is dependent on your filters and frames, the selected logical level you are focussing on, and the perspective position you are taking.

Ellen Herber Katz was conducting a series of tests on a particular strain of mice known for their remarkable tissue regeneration abilities, to develop a compound for Rheumatoid Arthritis. These mice were identified by an ear puncture. After four weeks, she noticed that the puncture had disappeared, and learned that others had noticed it and discounted it. Not Ellen. She recognised the pattern and shifted her attention which resulted in her discovering that the compound she was working on also dissolved crusts and rejuvenated tissue. A whole new avenue of possibility emerged.

We recognise patterns because they reconnect us with previous generalisations. When we are tracking a pattern in someone else or in a system, we run the great danger of prematurely predicting a pattern lazily we will say 'oh this is just like …' or 'I know what this is about …' or 'this is always the case when …' This is the risk as Grinder would put it, of 'premature evaluation'.

The critical pattern that may be operating below or beyond the commonplace become noticeable when we are aware of mismatches to our generalisations. We need to be attuned to detecting such seemingly inconvenient mismatches, because here is the doorway to the new information. At the point of noticing the mismatch, we need to let our intuition come into play to offer insight into what we might next expect. Otherwise we will learn nothing new, stay within our own existing map, and dangerously deepen our conviction that we are right.

Delete, distort and generalise

We have an overwhelming drive to make meaning of our experiences. We do this by mapping events – or, more accurately, the information we filter from these events – against our previous experiences. Where there is no convenient match, many people will choose to delete the inconvenient information, or distort it to fit existing knowledge, or be selective and generalise those aspects that fit with what is known. NLP practitioners know that the moment there is a mismatch between known and new information, they are on the threshold of discovery. Here is the opportunity to learn something new.

1 **Development:** animals live by patterns and habit. Humans add the extra dimension of noticing, internalising and making meaning out of patterns. Humans have the ability to construct patterns out of the unknown, which has enabled our evolutionary development. We have developed the capability of harnessing technology through discovering patterns and applying them in different contexts across the sciences and the arts at macro and micro levels. In fact NLP was born out of the commitment of the Dean of the UC Santa Cruz campus to interdisciplinary study groups, for the very reason that patterns could emerge from seemingly unrelated sources.

2 **Context:** there is a need to establish the context of the pattern. The context gives us the appropriate filters and removes the ambiguities.

Once a pattern is suspected, it needs to be tested to pare away unnecessary information, until the bare components are revealed. Remove the noise. This is through discovering what happens if you delete certain components of the pattern. Do you still get the same outcome? We need to find the edge of the pattern.

As Grinder says: 'Detecting a new pattern is to have your expectations foiled.' Once we think we have identified a pattern, we need to look out for the exceptions. The more useful pattern may lie within the similarities between these exceptions than in the pattern originally detected.

We can overgeneralise a pattern. A child will learn through mimicry to say, 'I went to the shop.' Once the child learns grammar and linguistic rules, she will start to say 'I goed to the shop.' She needs to learn the patterns within exceptions. Welcome to the world of irregular verbs and inconsistent spellings.

3 **Consequences:** once you detect a pattern, you can scan laterally for at least one other instance of its occurrence. Then you have access to the next level of thinking. You gain a meta-cognition, learning about the effect of the pattern, not the pattern itself.

Identifying new patterns in oneself or others produces new filters. This can radically alter our perception of reality. Creativity is born out of working with patterns through mixing and matching them.

You gain the ability to predict future events. Once you see the pattern begin, you know where it will go. The outcome will be inevitable. However this brings its downside. If you predict too early, you may lose valuable information about an entirely different and possibly more useful pattern.

If certain patterns generate desirable results, then you can map them and acquire them for yourself and others. If the pattern generates unwanted behaviour, then through this prediction, you can choose where to intervene and disrupt the pattern, so preventing the natural progression of the outcome. This intervention is essential for changework. Business Re-engineering was all about viewing established patterns with new eyes.

Scoping

Whilst you are going through the process of gathering your data you are already seeking to make sense of it. However, if you have multiple sources you will need to wait until you are away from your exemplar to give structure to what you have received.

Sorting your data into a logical format is the process of scoping. Finding the categories to box your data – or to box the patterns and themes emerging from the data – is the process of labelling your boxes into your selected logical types.

Personal Endeavour

First of all it serves you to understand that no two modellers will arrive at the same descriptions. Modelling is a completely individualised process, and the results are totally dependent on the nature of the modeller.

As with portrait painting, a range of artists can paint the same sitter and come up with a range of highly original and dissimilar portraits. Whilst it is likely that there will be some recognisable similarities between the images, this can't be assumed. It all depends on the artist's perception, what the artist sees when he looks at the sitter, what the relationship is like with the sitter, how the artist experiences the sitter, and what the artist wants the final viewer to experience when viewing the end product. It also depends on the artist's level of skill and stage of development, what the artist considers to be important and worthy of emphasis, and also the artist's trademark, which makes that portrait a 'Lucian Freud', and that one an unmistakable 'Hockney'.

Picasso was asked by a man on a train, why he painted such unrealistic portraits, and why he didn't make them true to life. Picasso asked what the man meant and the man produced a photograph of his wife.

'Like this!' he exclaimed, 'How she looks in real life.' 'She is small, isn't she? And flat,' was Picasso's reply.

This is also true for the process of modelling. I have sat with a group of fellow modellers and marvelled at how different our focus of interest is. Sometimes I was so grateful for where their questions took the exemplar and the information this brought forward. I wished I had thought of that. At other times I was frustrated with the 'trivia' that appeared to be invited, or the attention that was taken to what I considered to be the 'wrong' place. And do you know what? My fellow modellers probably had the same response to me!

This is what makes the process of modelling so interesting and never a foregone conclusion. Where each of us place our attention will deeply influence what we notice, and what we delete. Our filters are crucial for our success.

Your Personal Influencing Filters

It is useful to know the filters you are likely to be operating, so you can notice if they may be getting in the way, or causing you to delete information. However, I advise you to keep to who you naturally are. This way you will achieve consistency. Thinking you ought to be taking a different perspective might be difficult to sustain and lead to a mishmash of data that is hard to bring together later on.

Here are some pointers to keep you focussed:

- Keep your end user in mind, and maintain this focus throughout. Otherwise you risk becoming sidetracked and shifting emphasis towards an unproductive area.

- Manage your resource state. Notice when you have lost your modelling state and stop; either walk away and come back refreshed, or re-access combined wonder, sensitivity, integrity and intensity.

- Know your preferred meta programmes in this context. A general big chunk thinker is likely to be reluctant to go for strategies and minutiae within a process, and will need a bolstered resolve. Conversely specific small chunk thinkers may recoil from the thought of the wider system and be tempted to keep their head in the trough of detail. A 'feelings-based' modeller may go for state, whilst a 'thinking' modeller may want to explore belief systems.

  You need to know if your own meta programme traits are getting in the way of your enquiry and blocking the information you really need to be getting your hands on.

- Be mindful of your own preferences and current fixations. Whilst it is totally legitimate that much of you goes into the melting pot, be aware that you could be approaching the modelling process as an extension of yourself.

  You may be in the middle of pursuing a particular theme, and find that everything turns up flavoured by this theme. For a while I was really interested in the nature of Acceptance; another time it was Connection. Surprising just how often my conclusions took me into this territory!

- Make connection with the bigger picture. You may find that your interest is drawn to a particular behaviour, for the very reason that it *does* resonate with the overall direction your modelling practice has been taking. This piece could add to your overall understanding. The larger the system that you are tracking, then the more you can find potential in any modelling opportunity open to you.

Limitations to Thinking

When we are confronted with a plethora of data, we can become transfixed like a rabbit in the headlights. We can feel overwhelmed and unequal to the task. Often this knee jerk pattern is a default behaviour when faced with a situation that has no apparent rules, no signposts, or no familiar solutions. It is all 'too difficult' and requires too much of us. It can be shocking to discover just how much we limit our own thinking when approaching a conundrum.

At The Northern School of NLP we would offer our learners a task to think of a range of ways to describe an object – a thick line for example. The average person began to get stuck after about ten ideas. Here were some of the common reasons for this:

- *Reliant on easy accessible answers:* going for the most obvious ideas.

- *Narrow focus:* using the same labels time and again, or certainly in preference to others.

- *Instant gratification:* looking for immediate solutions. Not wanting to give time and handle the doubt and confusion.

- *Doubt in own ability to think differently:* leave complicated thinking to the 'brainy' ones.

- *Easily put off:* if the answer didn't come quickly, wait for others to come up with the answers.

- *Laziness:* questioning of relevance, lack of practise.

- *Avoidance of failure:* believing there are right answers required. Not realising that there are no rules to thinking. You can go anywhere you like to find out if it brings results.

- *Insufficient imagination:* never crossed your mind that someone could categorise in such a different way.

Thinking is a skill and improves with practice. Going outside the famous 9-dots and widening the system allows for different ways to experience a familiar object.

Generalised Sorting Categories

Here is a suggested listing of possible sorting categories that might influence your thinking and imagination. These are just my thoughts and I am sure you will be able to come up with others. You may find yourself asking of your information:

- What are its **dimensions**?
- What is its level of **complexity**?
- What is this **a part of**?
- What is this **an example of**?
- What is this **similar to**?
- What is **made of**?
- What does this **do**?
- What are the **benefits** of this?
- What is the **purpose** of this?
- What is the **need** for this?
- What does this **represent**?
- What does this **symbolise**?

- What does this **infer**?
- What are its **aesthetics**?
- What does it **cater** for?
- What is it **associated** with?
- What is held within? (**contents**)
- What is on the outside? (**surface area**)
- What does it **become**?
- What has it been previously? (**history**)
- What can it be **made into**?
- What **era** does it belong to?
- What **sources** does it draw on?

Go back to the thick line and what ideas do you now come up with? By applying the above categories, your list of possibilities should go well beyond the requirement of ten, and your answers will be far more imaginative and creative.

Scoping Frameworks

Whether you are applying these frameworks to pre-determine the information you are seeking (Cognitive Modelling), or you are retrospectively applying them to work out how you intuitively replicated the behaviour (Intuitive Modelling), or you are using them to interpret and label symbolic expression (Expressive and Metaphorical Modelling), you will find that from these general categories – or any others that you come up with – you are able to construct a fully coded, digital model.

Working purely from the first principles of logical types and logical levels, you can generate your own totally unique take on a particular class of experience. This allows you to work from first principles, and opens up the possibilities of something totally original emerging.

You may already have a sorting or scoping framework that you favour, and find yourself instinctively classifying the information under its headings. You may even remain aware that, by definition, you will be deleting something else. Having a range of scoping frameworks available means you can always shift your scoping categories should you fail to gain any meaningful information through one set of filters.

However since many roads lead to Rome, working with the ideas of others can save you from reinventing the wheel – the whole purpose of modelling. Our modellers of subjective experience have come up with a range of frameworks that serve to sort information into a meaningful cohesive format.

Here are some developed existing frameworks to consider:

VAKOG Submodalities	A means of modelling the structure of a state.
TOTE	A means of plotting the cause and effect strategies.
Skills Map *NLP Encyclopedia p804*	A means of mapping all the elements of a skill.
Meta Model *Bandler/Grinder*	A means of mapping out the operating belief system. Also the means of tracking limiting beliefs.
Neurological Levels *Dilts*	A means of sorting data into who, why, how, what, where and when and who else.
Meta Programmes *Bailey & Rose Charvet*	A means of working at identity level to determine work and motivation traits
Belief Template *Gordon/Dawes*	A means of mapping beliefs that nest the key criterion supporting a behaviour. This can be used independently of the full Array.
Experiential Array *Gordon/Dawes*	The complete mapping of a particular behaviour, to include state.
Sorting/Scoping Framework *Dilts/Delozier*	A framework of 'sorting boxes' for categorising received information. For more details of this framework go to the Robert Dilts' Analytical Modelling section in Part 3 – The Methodologies of Modelling.

Summary

Without developed skills we, are all dressed up with almost nowhere to go. Our skills enable our technology to come alive and dance. Having an understanding of what to do, and why to do it is insufficient for advanced practice. We need to have the flexibility, creativity and initiative that access to our developed expertise can give us.

However, whilst actual practice is the only way to develop a skill, having the understanding of what is involved with it is crucial. The underpinning thinking that I've offered here can help you make sense of the results you're getting and give you greater clarity of where to put your attention next. You may like to use this chapter for reference, as a diagnostic resource to highlight points you may have forgotten or which are now ready to become part of your natural practice, or as a starting point for further training and development.

I obviously realise that, for many of you, what I've covered is not new ground, but it may have been presented in a new way. If that has given you further inspiration, then I'm pleased. And should you like to put your learning to the test, there are the wide range of innovative and intriguing exercises designed just for this purpose in *The Bumper Bundle Companion Workbook*.

Onwards and forwards!

Part 5

The Results of Modelling

Introduction

There would be no point having a well thought out philosophy and highly developed technology if the fruit of the labours was not beneficial to those involved and the world at large. Happily, modelling time and again proves to deliver fantastic results in a practical, unobtrusive and personalised manner. Whether modelling for self-development, working with a client, or constructing a model that can then become part of a formal acquisition process, the practice can effect change in so many ways.

In this chapter, I explore the nature of an intervention, which goes beyond the narrow technique versus modelling methodology debate, and then provide you with loads of real examples of how modelling can be practically applied in the fields of business, education, therapy, and coaching. Because my recent background is predominately in the area of therapy, I am able to draw on my own extensive case notes. If I operated in business or in education, I know I would have been able to give you more by way of firsthand experience. But I work on the belief that whatever your area of specialism, you will be able to take these ideas and adapt them to your own situations.

Not content to be a means of primary intervention, the results of modelling come into their own with the subsequent production of models – coded descriptions of the modelled behaviour – which, in turn, can be converted into interactive techniques to be consumed by the end user. In fact, traditionally, this was seen to be the main purpose of modelling, with less focus being given to the benefits of the process of modelling itself.

Yet if producing a model was the raison d'être of modelling, little consideration seems to have been given to exactly how to do this. 'Now turn this data into a model!' doesn't quite work. This could explain why there are relatively so few new models around, and why many practitioners don't consider themselves to be modellers. Part of my journey was to fill this gap and demystify the construction of models. Starting with the Classification of Models and then zoning in on Constructed Models, I offer design criteria and essential features that are required for a model to deliver in different contexts, with different treatments, built upon the skills of systemic thinking and pattern detection.

It is essential that we are able to promote and trumpet our successes and demonstrate just how practical and beneficial the results of NLP application can be. Unfortunately, in some quarters NLP has earned a poor reputation, where its technology has been put to dubious use. Therefore, we are required to be accountable to the all important notion of ecology.

Ecology

Time now to address the major complaint against NLP; its power to manipulate and lead unsuspecting people to follow the practitioner's outcome and not their own.

Sadly, there will always be those who feel the need to exert power over others. I have formed the opinion that NLP is not useful in the hands of a strong alpha personality. I also subscribe to Maggie Scarf's view in *Unfinished Business, Pressure Points in the Lives of Women* (1980), when she identifies that men define themselves through their achievements and women through their relationships. Accordingly, from this perspective, men will instinctively seek to use the NLP tools for attainment and accomplishment, while women will use the same tools to enhance relationship with themselves and others. Obviously, this is not a black and white distinction and there are many shades of grey between, yet I just find it curious that, overwhelmingly, the field of hypnotherapy is male dominated and the field of counselling is populated in the main by women. Just a personal observation.

NLP is profoundly about relationship – relationship with the exemplar, client or customer, as well as relationship with the hidden structures. NLP seeks a balanced focus between task and people. I believe that NLP began to gain a respected re-position once the feminine natures of Dilts, Gordon, Gilligan and Delozier were infused into the mix, and able to offset the more macho energies of earlier times. We cannot debar certain learners. Hopefully, through example, we can demonstrate an alternative way of being with another. Happily, more and more often, NLP is attracting those who do want to pursue the long-term benefits of developing relationship. The 'Instant Change!' marketing claims seem to be becoming less frequent, and modern sales methods are no longer about 'hit and run' but about growing advocates and return business.

I further believe that NLP without a modelling perspective can be a recipe for disaster. When the practitioner is compelled to lay aside their own map and lovingly seek to understand the map of the other, without preconception or preconditions, they can only be in service to the exemplar and the exemplar's desired outcome.

Without the commitment to use all the neurological and linguistic resources we have to model, the practitioner is left using this powerful technology merely to meet his or her own needs, operating solely from their own model of the world. How many learn the lesson 'just because you can doesn't mean you have to'?

A modelling perspective is the salvation of NLP. Personally it is my saving grace since it protects others from my 'shadow side'. If in doubt about any decision or course of action you are about to take, always ask yourself 'What is my outcome here?' and if your answer is anything other than 'Serving the exemplar's or end user's outcome', then you know you need to pause for thought, possibly regroup and shift focus.

Delozier has a delightful cry: 'Map Alert! Map Alert!' accompanied by a mock flashing light on the forehead, at the whiff of an intruding map!

The Modelling Route Map

In the Introduction, I presented what I consider to be the meta model of modelling – my version of it at any rate. In *The Modelling Route Map* I believe I have found a niche for all the aspects that need to be considered in the modelling process. Many of these aspects will be familiar to you and some may be a surprise considering that they may fly in the face of perceived wisdom. And I suspect you might find some elements you've never thought about before. I also wonder if you had previously imagined the whole endeavour of modelling encapsulated in quite this simple way.

The gift of a new model is the beauty of modelling: how it can simplify and sum up what has seemed to be something complex; how it can take you to corners you haven't considered before; how it signposts where you are and where you might go next; and how it sets you up thinking about where else you could apply it. A model seeks to simplify the complex, expand awareness, provide navigation and offer transferability.

By this point in the book, we have covered much of the elements within the route map. We still need to look more closely at the types of Interventions available – when and where to use them and what happens when we do. In Part 6 – The Formal Model Acquisition, we take working with the model to its next stage, involving familiarity with the technology of the neurological and linguistic frames.

Working With The Modelling Route Map

The Modelling Route Map framework is a great model to help you navigate through the processes and options available to you. It can help you to:

- Consider wider possibilities, beyond any possible habitual practice

- Clarify your outcomes from all the options available

- Plan the approach you want to take so that you are not sidetracked

- Test the decisions that you've made, confirming that the other alternatives are not appropriate

- Detect causes for stuck thinking, where you were in danger of veering off in an inappropriate direction

- Consider alternative paths of action should circumstances change

- Explore further options available to you with the material you have gathered, once you have completed the prescribed modelling process.

Part 5 – The Results of Modelling

Application Area	End User	Focus of Enquiry	Source(s) of Information	Types of Intervention	Types of Outcome
Personal Development	Third Party	Structure of Desired Behaviour (DB)	Self	Product and Process Models	Exploration / Identification of Structure
Therapy / Coaching	Self	Structure of Unwanted Behaviour (UB)	Exemplar	Modelling Methodologies	Remodelling of Structure
Consultancy / Training	Exemplar		Exemplars	Neurological Modelling	
	Host Organisation	Relationships between exemplar / DB / UB	Literature and other media	Linguistic Modelling	Model Construction
Others				Combination of above	
			Systems		Formal Acquisition

The Modelling Route Map – Burgess 2013

Take the following scenarios and notice how the modeller starts with the end user and make their way across each of the categories.

1 **Scenario One:** you are a commercial trainer [Application Area] and have identified a need for 'Management of Meetings' training [Third Party end user] for those who need to improve performance. You opt to go down the route of identifying at least three people to model [Exemplars] – people already known to you, or introduced through recommendation. They are noted for their ability to get through an agenda, drawing out maximum discussion and opinions, and finalising action points, all within the prescribed time period [Desired Behaviour]. You elect to work with the Gordon/Dawes Experiential Array [Modelling Methodology] that lends itself to gathering key information about the operating belief system and strategies involved. Several models [Model Construction] may emerge, some which can be introduced conversationally and others that can be acquired through constructed techniques [Model Acquisition], delivered as part of a resulting training programme.

This is the traditional perception of a modelling project and highly effective in the world of business and training.

2 **Scenario Two:** alternatively, as a Coach [Application Area] you have been called by a Training and Development Manager [Host Organisation] to raise poor performance levels [Unwanted Behaviour] of certain members of staff regarding managing across-site teams. You are tasked to find out what is limiting them and then coach them to raise their game. Since this is going to be an individual relationship, more accurately you are working with single exemplars, because it is likely that you will find that each of them has their own individual responses to this task [Exemplar].

However it may be that there are some common logistical barriers to performance which you can feedback to your contracting manager [Systems]. In which case you might present your findings in

302

the form of a modelled out diagrammatic system [Identification of Structure]. Either way, you come up with an idiosyncratic structure for each exemplar and set about finding the route towards restructuring [Remodelling of Structure].

In the process, you may find that there are some common personal traits that are inhibiting performance – a set of unsupportive beliefs, an absence of a particular resource state, an inability to plan through time, for example. From this data you can come up with a listing of supportive beliefs, key resource states, and planning strategies [Model Construction] – great models that you can test and develop, and then promote and market. A new product has emerged to add to your portfolio!

If this is the case, then for your next client, you may find yourself cutting down on the modelling phase and promoting your ready-made, tried and tested techniques, as your proffered solution.

In *The Bumper Bundle Companion Workbook* there are some other scenarios to test your understanding of this model.

Interventions

The human system has an amazing potential for reorganisation and self-reorientation. Traditionally, for many, an NLP intervention has been synonymous with applying a technique. And given the relatively few numbers of techniques available, this approach gained a bad press. The one-club-fits-all mindset led to over zealous use of applying a favoured technique to 'cure' all ills. However, such limited thinking can be a thing of the past. In fact, not only do we have lots more available techniques designed for more precise purposes, we have fantastic choice of other interventions to choose from, some highly developed and technically complex whilst others can be as simple as offering a few words.

So what is an intervention?

It is something that leads to change – preferably desired. Any form of exploration has the potential to bring about change. This doesn't necessarily have to involve deep processing. A question can be an intervention bringing about new awareness. Establishing an outcome conversationally may be all that's needed to bring about clarity and resolution. The effects may not be immediate or obvious, since the intervention can worm its way into the system and slow-release its effects over time, as feedback strengthens resolve.

Technique versus Modelling

In the early 2000s, Lawley and Tompkins pioneered the concept of therapeutic modelling, to challenge the narrow application of techniques as the NLP therapist's stock in trade. They sought to pursue the practices of the original exemplars – Perls, Satir and Erickson, that of discovering the exact way the individual was holding the problem. This led to the suggestion that technique-driven practice was an unsophisticated form of intervention favoured by novice or beginner learners, whilst modelling was the intervention of experts. Lawley coined the phrase 'Top Down' (technique-driven) and 'Bottom Up' (modelling-driven) approaches.

'Top Down' Approach

This technique-driven approach has been regarded as simplistic, where the practitioner demonstrates little discernment and sees a technique as being the changework solution. It is suggested that the practitioner doesn't take into consideration the peculiarities of the exemplar or the exemplar's circumstances. It is often regarded as a 'cookie cutter' approach to changework, where it becomes an externally imposed solution applied onto the exemplar's experience, within a freeze frame perspective. The technique's original intentions or the reasons for its particular design are often unknown to the practitioner, and therefore there is a danger of a robotic shoehorning of the exemplar into the constraints of the technique. This practice is exacerbated with NLP's sloppy claims of 'quick fix' and 'speedy' resolutions.

As I see it, these claims may only be justified when levied at the novice or beginner practitioner (see the *NLP Competence Development Model* in Part 1 – The Nature of a Modeller), who is selecting from a shallow pool of technology. The subtleties of bulk of the NLP syllabus are overshadowed by the impact of these powerful set techniques. In these early days of learning, everything may seem able to be sorted with Swish, Phobia 'Cure' or Six Step Reframe. As part of their development, these practitioners need to learn when a particular techniques isn't the answer, or have the emerging confidence to modify what they are doing in response to what is happening.

There is richness in the basic repertoire of the most commonly known NLP techniques, which is excellent except when it's not. There will always be learners who arrest at the point of their basic training, who are not motivated to learn more, and who only have this restricted range to choose from. We just hope they go on to deliver these processes with great skill.

However, such occurrences shouldn't throw the technique baby out with the bath water. Techniques do have a part to play in the pursuit of precise intervention. There are many more techniques now out on the markets that are designed to target specific needs – many of them dependent on the process of exploration and discovery by the exemplar. At least eighty new ones are found in *The NLP Cookbook* and on *The NLP Kitchen* website – www.nlpand.co.uk. There are also many unpublished techniques designed around the many models created from the worlds of business, education and personal development.

As the serious NLP practitioner becomes very clear about what each technique can or cannot give, and understands the nature of its 'engineering', they can more accurately match the needs of the explorer with the potential of what the technique can deliver.

I consider it is imperative for any practitioner operating at a professional level, of therapist coach and most definitely as NLP trainer, to have a complete understanding of the engineering of every technique they work with. They need to be able to deconstruct any technique into its individual components and to describe how the process achieves the results that it does. This level of tradecraft, to my mind, is essential. It also deepens appreciation of the wonders that are available within our modality. In the *Bumper Bundle Companion Workbook*, full consideration is given to this process as well as the ability to deconstruct the language of questions.

When a technique's technology and structure is mapped against the exemplar or end user's needs, the technique is legitimately in full service of assisting understanding of the exemplar's internal model of the world.

'Bottom Up' Approach

This modelling-driven approach works from within a formal modelling methodology, and starts from within takes the exemplar's map of the world, and strives to make known the hidden underlying structure. It builds a model from scratch that will be idiosyncratic to that exemplar. Working from inside the exemplar's map makes it more organic and less intrusive, therefore more ecological and arguably more code congruent.

At the time, Lawley proposed that this is the domain of the more advanced practitioner, who has had more training and development, who has more practical experience testing and applying their learning, practised their skills and reached the levels of Competence and Proficiency.

Yet a new learner may have discovered the magic of submodalities or timeline without fully realising that this technology is in the service of modelling. They may have discovered the real delights afforded by working with the Meta Model, or exploring with Sleight of Mouth patterns. They may not have developed any expertise in a formal modelling methodology, but they instinctively seek to work as a modeller, divining the exemplar's inner structure. Because they aren't producing models or devising subsequent techniques, they may not class themselves as modellers at all.

As a committed 'Bottom Up' modeller, I began adding to my repertoire of modelling methodologies: at which point I realised the danger of operating narrowly from such a seductive moral high ground. I realised that in this purist pursuit, I was liable to delete and discount the other fantastic opportunities that are also available. I also admitted that, on occasions, I was 'secretly' not applying a known modelling methodology with my clients, and that this occurrence almost merited a confession at supervision! It took me a while to sit down and re-examine what this technique-versus-modelling polarity was about.

The Third Way

First of all I distinguished what both approaches hold in common. Both will have been designed and constructed by an unseen developer and passed down to the practitioner. The construction and intentions of both approaches may have become distorted through this passage of time. Both hold a prescription of what is expected from the process, the steps involved and in some instances demands on specific language use. Both actually come with built-in inflexibility – heaven forbid!

What neither a named technique or modelling methodology seem to cater for is responsiveness to an individual's reactions, as they happen. So often there is the danger that the exemplar has to fit in with the prescription of the modeller and not the other way round. I know that some of the most rewarding experiences I have had with a client have been those instances when I have gone 'off piste' and made it up on the spot, weaving my knowledge and experience to address the moment.

When I fully examined my own practice, I realised that I use quite an eclectic mix of interventions, and in fact a formal modelling methodology is not necessarily my first port of call. I have some fantastic techniques based on process models that I often use, and the client can freely explore a particular class of behaviour. Occasionally, I opt for a more prescriptive technique say, Meta Mirror or a Neurological Level Alignment, because it is just the right tool to use. I often find myself exploring through ad-hoc modelling using submodalities, perceptual positions, metaphors, time and mentors – all examples of putting the neurological frames to good use; Neurological Modelling being my term for this. I definitely rely on the magic of, similarly labelled, Linguistic Modelling, using meta model to unfurl nested beliefs and patterns of thinking and occasionally meta programme questions to reveal behavioural traits.

This led me to review my understanding of the nature of an intervention and what is available to the NLP practitioner. Seeking to classify the range, I formulated that there are quite a few additional types of intervention, which go beyond the polarity of the Top Down and Bottom Up approaches.

The Framework of NLP Interventions

TOP DOWN
Introducing external structure into explorer's map

Combining both approaches

BOTTOM UP
Revealing underlying structures within the explorer's map

1 Applying a product technique to a specific problem eg: Phobia 'Cure'

2 Modifying a technique in response to feedback

3 Applying a process model to generate an Relational Field

4 Applying a specific modelling methodology eg: Symbolic Modelling

5 Modelling with neurological frames eg: Submodalities

6 Modelling with linguistic frames eg: Meta Model

7 Processing the newly coded model through an existing format

8 Devising a new technique based on newly coded model

Prescribed   **Spontaneous**

The Framework of NLP Interventions – Burgess 2012

This framework, to my mind, covers all bases open to a modeller when working with another. Each intervention is appropriate when specifically selected to meet an identified need, or line of enquiry.

Starting from the top and working towards the right the first three interventions, based on techniques, are as follows:

1   **Product techniques:** a Product Technique is a straightforward technique, which is designed to do a specific job. It is usually based on a sequential model, where the steps follow on in a given sequence or hierarchical model where the next level is greater than the one before. (For the Classification of Models, see Part 5 – The Results of Modelling) These deliver a predetermined end point. These are the most common variety of prescribed techniques, of which Phobia 'Cure', Swish and all the early techniques are great examples. Meta Mirror and Neurological Alignment are also classified here, as are many of the techniques found within *The NLP Cookbook*.

2 **Product + techniques:** here the modeller adapts the technique in response to the exemplar's feedback. Since exemplars don't always conform to the expectations of the original technique, the modeller needs to have the flexibility to deviate from the standard process. You may find yourself adding a new bit of your own choosing, going off in the direction of, say, neurological levels, or triple description, in response to what is actually happening within the process with your exemplar. You may return to the main thrust of the technique and still exit your TOTE on the known point of calibration. Or you may end up somewhere else entirely! Much will depend on your confidence, integrated experience, and versatility.

3 **Process techniques:** this is a term I first heard from McWhirter, to describe those models where each of the elements have equal significance and can be approached in any order. These elements are placed in such a way to create an enclosed space, within which a relational field forms and enables meta cognition to emerge from the combination of each of the elements.

This is a very dynamic and organic process, where the end outcome cannot be predefined, other than saying that it will be within a certain class of behaviour and determined by the elements of that particular model. The exemplar is free to move on and between the elements to make contact with the information as it emerges.

I have come up with several powerful original process models, two of which are in *The NLP Cookbook* – 'Stuff Happens' and 'The Balance of Power'. These I've found to be really effective as they create space for spontaneous exploration.

Now going to the bottom of the framework, and working towards the right, these modelling approaches vary in degrees of prescribed design and procedure:

4 **Modelling methodologies:** in Part 3 the wide range of Modelling Methodologies are covered, moving from Intuitive Modelling relying on unconscious uptake by the modeller, through Expressive and Symbolic Modelling working with metaphor, to Cognitive Modelling operating primarily with the modeller's conscious mind. Here you can select an approach and use it in service of discovering the specific nature of the exemplar's internal structure. This is a bespoke approach and operates from within the exemplar's deep structure of experience.

The more methodologies you have to hand, the more responsive you can be to the needs of the exemplar and the exemplar's outcome, as well as your own levels of resourcefulness and skill.

5 **Neurological modelling:** here we are working informally with the wondrous basic building blocks of NLP, the natural models found within all of us that determine our subjective experience, namely: submodalities, time, space and multiple perspectives, metaphor, parts/archetypes and neurological levels. We can use these tools to explore structure in a freeform manner, outside of a prescribed 'recipe', fully in response to what is emerging from the exemplar's map.

I delight in working with submodalities to reveal to the exemplar just how they are configuring their reality, especially when used within a contrast frame. Plotting a timeline metaphorically, or again with submodalities, provides a totally benign and fascinating way to explore a troubled past or empty future.

With these neurological frames we can externalise internal constructions and reveal unexpected nooks and crannies in an unscripted responsive manner.

6   **Linguistic modelling:**   in NLP we are blessed by some spectacular linguistic frames, which enable us to reveal deep structure through precise language use, with for me the Meta Model framework head and shoulders above the rest.

Just the precise selection and use of questioning or phrasing can be intervention enough. I rely on the Meta Model's fantastic potential for mapping out a belief system and zoning in on the specific limiting beliefs contributing to the behaviour. Meta programme questions can provide a profile of traits and Sleight of Mouth questions can loosen tightly held belief systems. The outcome frame alone can be sufficient to indicate what has to be done to achieve the desired scenario.

I contend that all serious practitioners need to be totally fluent not just in the range of specific language patterns, but also in detecting the cues that can trigger them. This requires commitment and practise. Such conversational interventions are powerful whatever the circumstances – provided there is an explicit or implicit contract to activate this form of exploration.

By now the distinctions between technique application and modelling are becoming blurred, since both approaches are responding to the presented feedback from the exemplar.

7   **Newly coded model + known technique:**   by this stage, you distil your modelling data into a model constructed on the spot, and then process it through the structure of a technique you are already familiar with, with perhaps some modification.

This may sound a bit improbable, but if you look at the different ways to achieve coding suggested throughout my coverage of the modelling methodologies, you will see just how easy this can be. Your exemplar will be telling you what's important through the emphasis they are giving, and you can immediately test your emerging model and go back for further clarity if needs be. Knowing this is possible, and that model construction doesn't mean a six-month project, takes you way beyond the obvious and into the realms of bespoke creativity.

8   **Newly coded model + original technique:**   you may find that there isn't a ready made technique that you know of, or those you do know of don't fit with what you've now got. So there is nothing to stop you for devising a new technique on the spot and integrating the details you've gathered and feeding them back into your exemplar's neurology. This provides an utterly awesome fit for the exemplar from start to finish.

This intervention, arguably, is at the pinnacle of a practitioner's expertise. Here all the NLP tradecraft comes together and dances in service of the exemplar. You need know the simple formula for technique construction and an understanding of how to select and use your neurological and linguistic frames. Such skill is not beyond the ambitious practitioner. After spending time in Part 6 – The Formal Acquisition Process, you can discover just how simple this is – and joyous as well!

At the end of this chapter you will find a detailed description of this intervention in the 'Inside Out Process' that I have devised.

Modelling Interventions

Now's the time to cut to the chase. What specifically can NLP do? How can modelling be used to generate positive results and justify the claims it makes – certainly the claims I make? In this section I am offering you examples of how I and other practitioners have used a modelling approach to meet the needs of an identified end user. I have sorted them under operational categories of business, education/training, therapy, and coaching. You will notice examples of different types of intervention, different sources of exemplar, a focus on desirable and unwanted behaviours, and different end results.

In Part 3 – The Methodologies of Modelling, for each methodology I have already offered examples of how the approach could be applied in each of the application areas. So here I've not gone over the same ground again, and I've not included specific reference to particular methodologies. You may want to go back and check for relevance in the suggestions offered.

In each application area, I have exchanged the universal 'modeller' and 'exemplar' labels, where appropriate, for those more realistic terms commonly used in that world.

Business Consultancy

Modelling within an organisation enables the consultant to produce something that is bespoke for that culture in that context and in that moment. It takes in the interplay of relationships and personalities. It can factor in the political dimensions and consequences of external pressures.

These models can then be generalised and formalised into generic models, packaged into an attractive tried and tested processes, and applied to other organisations either in the same industry or across the board as a very nice income earner. There are some consultancy businesses that have made a lifetime practice of peddling the same product in various disguises.

I would like to think that, by the next edition of this book, I will have been given lots more examples of the excellent applications of modelling within business. I know they are out there, but unfortunately I wasn't able to penetrate this rich seam too deeply.

1   **Reshaping Internal communications:** efficient internal and external communications within any organisation are crucial for success, certainly through periods of change. NLP modelling lends itself to identifying the prevailing systems, the possible blockages and especially the key leverage points. For example:

•   *Developmental solutions:* Gino Bonissone, a vice president at Fiat in Italy, collaborated with Robert Dilts on an extensive leadership project in Fiat. They also worked together on an organisational development programme with the Italian Railways, amongst others. As a result of their modelling approaches and involvement with systems, they came up with many models that could then be incorporated into the developmental solution of the organisation. One model was their diagnostic tool, the Communication Matrix, which plots the range of influencers that affect the quality of communication, under the logical types of People, Message, and Medium.

•   *Cultural congruence:* I was invited into a large established public sector organisation, whose customer-facing activities were shortly to be sold off. Those who were to continue working in the newly privatised company needed to become prepared for the differences in culture that shareholder accountability would bring.

The Internal Communications Manager gave me the task of working through the last twelve editions of their sizeable monthly newspaper, to discover if the values promoted on the pages were compatible with the new culture. He had nothing to worry about, since my trawl clearly demonstrated through the types of printed articles, their subject matter, chunk size and focus, that the move towards privatisation was being supported through emphasis on teamwork, innovation and efficiency, amongst others. The spread of articles provided illustrations of these values at Board level, down to a group from the shop floor who had completed a sky dive for charity.

2   **Providing Initial assessment**

•   *Diagnostic template:* Dilts in his design of the SCORE model produced an excellent framework for establishing a comprehensive and dispassionate method of enquiry into the current situation with a clear understanding of what the desired scenario can be – *plus* identification of the actions needed. Applying it cognitively as an information-gathering tool, either individually or in a group, the consultant comes away with a freeze-frame description of the perceptions of those involved. Out of this, development policy can be formulated.

It's unfortunate that the mnemonic is inaccurate – an excellent example of indulgent model labelling which invites confusion. The sequence ought to be S-ymptoms with an outline of the presenting problems, then O-utcomes and a sensory-based description of what ideally is desired, then E-ffects, once more sensory-based description of what life becomes like having lived with these outcomes. Arriving at Effects at this point is an essential part in the process, because, (a) it acts to strengthen resolve, (b) it is a future pace to test the realism of the identified outcomes and, (c) it provides the resources required to now face the harder part – namely looking at the causes.

So now comes C-auses. Traditionally a consultant will be deluged with all the 'ain't it awful' litany of complaints, blamings and general dissatisfaction, usually provoked by the question 'what's happening?' This plummeting of state is not useful for constructive exploring of what might be. However, with this process, coming to Causes after Effects enables the explorers to have a more dispassionate attitude about how the current situation came to be. By listing all the causes, under the headings 'Can influence directly', 'Can influence indirectly' and 'Can do nothing about', an action plan begins to emerge. Should spirits wane, re-accessing the resources within Effects, usually gets motivation picking up once more.

3   Revealing culture

- *Consensus through metaphor:* as a consultant to a large department, I worked with the management team when it was undergoing shifts in its corporate responsibility and positioning. I opened up with providing three metaphors – I think they were car, a high street retailer, and a holiday – and asked them the question 'If this department was an X, which one would it be?' Once they had identified their individual answers, they had to identify the attributes each of their examples stood for. These were then pooled and a common description began to emerge. Consensus regarding meanings behind the words materialised and before long five nominalisations became established that represented the body they wanted to be known for. The rest of the workshop was the exploration of what each of these values would mean in actual behavioural terms and how the similarities and differences between them could be managed. Branding and in-house training followed on.

- *Exploration through metaphor:* Dilts showed a novel way of working with metaphor in his *Strategies of Genius* workshop. He would take an everyday object – a plant, a motorbike, a mobile phone – and then invite the participants to map the elements operating within their company, their team, their network of suppliers to the various parts of the object. And then the metaphor could continue isomorphically – exploring the plant's ability to grow and flower, the bike's need for oil and fuel, licence and rider, the phone's need for a sim card, apps, protection and insurance. Such metaphors can take attention to areas little visited and highly relevant.

  From his modelling of Einstein and Mozart, Dilts discovered that: 'The use of metaphor allows the genius to focus on the deeper principles and not get caught up in the content of the constraints of reality.'

4   Developing teams

- *Determining development outcomes:* at one point I managed a countywide training provision, with a small team of full time trainers and many associates. I had just come back from Grinder's *Metaphor* workshop and sufficiently inspired, decided to apply my learning at the next team meeting, to explore what our individual and team development outcomes needed to be.

  'What metaphor describes where you are at the moment, and what one describes where you would like to be?'

  'What metaphor describes how we are as a team and what one describes where would you like it to be?'

  I have to say that a tremendous amount of honesty was revealed, possibly unwittingly, which would never have come forward through mere question and answer, certainly not publicly. The responses gave huge cause for reflection. I can still remember many of the answers. One in particular sticks in my mind. In answer to the second question one guy said: 'It is like being part of a bobsleigh team. Fran's the driver. I am the brakeman. I push the car down the track but never manage to jump on in time.'

5   In house development

- *Successful partnerships:* Helen Platts, a notable facilitator, has considerable experience working as a consultant within Local Authorities. One project was developing the effectiveness of Partnerships involving eight individual organisations. She wanted to identify what were the core ingredients responsible for successful partnership working. After interviewing some key managers she came up with a fledgling model which she tested out in two workshops with selected participants – a process, which by its nature, generated awareness and ownership amongst those involved. The finished model became the basis of a programme that was rolled out to all participants and became established in their training calendar. She also was able to market this approach to other Partnerships elsewhere.

6 **Devising commercial models:** there is huge potential in developing new models. Some NLP modellers have been highly successful in taking their innovation and disseminating it widely as a commercial package. For example:

- *Cold calling:* As part of her NLP Practitioner training, Bernadette Doyle set about finding out how some call centre operators had a notable high success rate for making appointments through cold calling. She sat in and listened to many calls and from this she devised a listing of beliefs that these successful operators held in common, plus noticed their instinctive flexibility at matching the voice tones of the various people they were put through to. This apparently simple piece of work became the foundation of Doyle's highly successful communications consultancy.

- *Modelling key exemplars:* UK trainer Dave Shepherd has been successful in creating useful training workshops, arising from modelling key exemplars. His series, *A Date With Excellence*, resulted from his modelling of Steve McDermott, a European Motivational Speaker Of The Year, which led to the *Stand Up Stand Out* workshop; his work with Gavin Ingham a Sales Expert was responsible for *Selling From Nothing*; and Greg Secker a Millionaire Trader resulted in *Master Trading Psychology*. He has successfully marketed these workshops to in-house audiences as well providing open programmes.

- *Effective goal setting:* Claire Smale has written an inspiring book *Transform your Goals with Vision* (2013), which firstly explains the difference between having a goal and having a vision and then it takes the reader through a seven-step process that she discovered is common to the 'visioneers' she modelled.

Training

1 Workshop development

- *Training programme design:* I design my training programmes and presentations on PowerPoint – a fact that often surprises. I have an idea of the topics I want to cover (the logical types) and these might constitute the day's content, or the sections of the day or individual weeks. I may have modelled out a rough mind map in advance by way of a brainstorm, but the real work goes on at the computer. These become the section header slides.

I see the slides within each section as a mini model, with every bullet point being an element of that model. In turn each slide needs to make an equal contribution to the overall topic and be on the same Logical Level as the others in that section. I will click back and forth from slide to the overall coverage to test for balance. If one topic has too many slides this would suggest the topic needs to be subdivided, or I have gone into too much detail. I may have drilled down further into one aspect of a topic more than another and I need to remove those slides but make reference to this content in the lower logical level of my bullet point descriptions. Slides can be easily moved around, deleted, or their content given different emphasis.

Throughout, at slide level or at the overview, I second position my audience, testing their levels of attention and understanding. Reluctantly, I may end up removing or rewording slides.

By having the overview, I can 'try-on' the programme to determine the flow and balance of energy, and the smooth and logical passage from beginning to end. I can test the balance between presentation and activity. I can get an overview of the mix of activity types. This is how I know that the programme will work.

- *Preparing manuals:* the need for structure occurs in the process of producing a manual as well. Coherence between the groupings of all the specific subjects, both into an overall picture and between themselves, not only provides an accessible route into the field of study, but also suggests a deep understanding of the subject by the writer. Pitching the details as subsets of higher logical levels helps the learner navigate between all the new information and tune into the meta-cognition the structure provides. The Table of Contents becomes the model with its Headings and Subtopics.

- *Writing handouts:* as will be illustrated in Part 6 – The Formal Acquisition Process, a handout is a model as well. Each instruction or stage is an element of the overall model, and bullet points are subsets of that stage. Once more the designer has to ask: 'What specifically does this stage contribute to the overall process?' If in doubt take it out. The overall impression should be one of natural progression and resolution.

2 Training room activity

- *Room layout:* as the trainer, I need to step into the training space and model out the energy flow, evaluating the connection between the learners and me. Any disruptions to this connection need to be removed. The flipchart and the projector both have to be strategically placed, mindful of technical constraints. The seating needs to be able to corral the energy towards the front of the room, with no empty seats to allow energy to escape. Ideally the seating is symmetrical with the trainer located on the central axis.

- *Group rapport:* as the trainer, I can experience the participants as one homogenous body, or subgroups, or individuals, at any one time. In the process of establishing group rapport, the trainer is monitoring the learning system as the individuals become knitted up into one body. Any resistance is met with an internal enquiry 'What has to be true for this behaviour to be here?' and to pace that need.

- *Unblocking learning:* someone once told me, should a group not move when it is given an instruction, for example to divide into small groups, it's because there is some information they don't have. My job is to find out what's missing. Individual learning blockages come under the heading of coaching or possibly therapy. Happily the repertoire of NLP can accommodate this as well, without the immediate need for referral.

Teaching

1 Managing Classroom Activity

- *Dynamics of successful teaching:* Michael Grinder, brother of John, has spent a lifetime modelling the dynamics of successful teaching, particularly in order to make improvements in the areas of classroom management, confidence in learning success, and teacher competence in the classroom.

- *A range of somatic gestures:* In his book *ENVoY* (1993), Michael Grinder has identified the importance of a range of non verbal signals, which not only call upon the class to pay attention to the teacher and subliminally take instruction, they preserve the teacher's energy and voice and save considerable time. This practice involves spatial anchoring, the freeze position, the pause with downward hand gesture, obvious slow breathing, pointing to item rather than using its name, stop gesture, and many others.

- *Teacher/individual/class triangle model:* In *A Healthy Classroom* (2006), Michael Grinder explores this model and the dynamics that are held within it. Here the experienced teacher can place attention on all three points mindful of the effects of the others. Additionally the model accounts for the relationship between individuals and the group, and the teacher, and the group's relationship with individuals and the teacher. He spends much time supporting the teacher's familiarity and management of these dynamics, from the formation process to maturation of the class, incorporating 'disruptive' individuals and sub-groups.

2 Constructing Questions

- *Sensory specific language:* Nick Kemp, an international NLP trainer, worked with a group of science teachers, specifically looking at influencing and sensory specific language. He noticed that many of the staff would start sentences with: 'We'll try to ...' 'We'll aim to ...' 'Hopefully ...' 'All being well ...'

In taking up his suggestion to consider using these suggestive predicates, they achieve a significant shift in attention and energy levels in the classroom:

Are you aware that ...?

Has it ever occurred to you that ...?

Have you noticed that ...?

Have you ever wondered ...?

How would you feel if ...?

How do you know that ...?

3 Achieving Full Association

- *Second positioning:* Nick Kemp also introduced the idea of second positioning and challenges the teachers to second position the many processes involved in their science teaching, so that the teachers become fully associated inside each process, and are able to engage more deeply and describe more graphically. They become so animated with this idea that they find it easy to sell it on to their students, who in turn enter the realms of DNA, blood circulation, and even egg fertilisation. The potential to apply this process across the board is immense.

Therapy

Most of the case studies and anecdotes offered in existing publications have come from therapeutic interaction between exemplar and modeller. Each modeller is likely to have their own favoured methods, using modelling both as an information gathering tool and as an intervention (same thing really!). They may use formal methodologies, or a loose combination of NLP strategies.

As a psychotherapist, I delight in the modelling approach to changework, rarely feeling the need to go outside our modality. So I have opted to select some of my own case studies to illustrate the rich variety of available modelling approaches. Hopefully, some of these examples will give you new ideas of what's possible.

I have not included any case studies centred round any of the specific modelling methodologies since these applications are covered elsewhere. Instead I offer a range of examples to illustrate how simple modelling principles can be applied using different basic neurological and linguistic frames – for a full exploration of these, see Part 6 – The Formal Acquisition Process.

1 **Self-modelling:** an individual can take many techniques and achieve insights and greater awareness without having a guide to assist the process. *The NLP Cookbook* was designed to meet this precise outcome. Content free work is an invaluable way of enabling exploration without any interruption or conscious or unconscious influence by the modeller. The explorer can access deep structure without having to put this experience into words, or edit the words for the benefit of the receiver.

   - *Content free questions:* Christina Hall came up with a fantastic set of questions, full of temporal predicates, embedded suggestions, and tag questions, which has the ability to achieve profound change. Half way through this content free process twenty years ago, I put out my last cigarette – for which I am eternally grateful.

   - *Well Formed Outcome Framework:* can enable the exemplar gain real clarity, especially when it is content free, since the unconscious mind can work far more quickly than the left-brain conscious mind. There are many versions of it. Personally I favour the twenty questions I have compiled through combining many of the other sets on offer.

   - *Insight Cards:* I came up with a set of 100 questions from trawling through all the language patterns within the linguistic frames. These are grouped into three major sections: the Past that explores how the current situation arose; The Present that stretches out perceptions of the current situation; and the Future, that develops what might arise from the current situation. There are also ten Wild Cards which help should the explorer get stuck.

     These cards have proven to be an invaluable tool for individuals, providing a means of exploring independently with the best technology, or as a 'filter for the day'. Cards can be chosen at random, or a particular time frame may be taken. They have also proven to work really well as a team building and planning tool, since they take individuals to places within the system that they may rarely visit.

2 **Identifying strategies:** here are very simple examples of an approach familiar to many practitioners – identifying the strategy that is responsible for an unwanted behaviour. Identify the trigger for the K¨ and reconfigure the sequence – pure constructivism first principles.

   - *Phobias:* Client B was strongly spider phobic, recoiling into foetal position on sight of these eight-legged beings. I was new to NLP back in the '80s so all I had was eye accessing cues and strategies. She would see the spider (V^e) and she would hear herself going 'Aagh' (A^i_d / K^{i-}) then scream A^e and curl up K^e. However I had noticed that between seeing and the internal response, her eyes moved to a visual construct, so I asked 'What bit of you are you seeing?' To her astonishment she was seeing herself place her foot on the spider, (V^{ic}) with possible repercussions of it going up her leg. This was the trigger for her distaste, not the spider itself. She then practised a variety of responses at this critical point: the spider running off to hide; her laughing; having curiosity about the wonders of nature; turning her attention to something else. Just this rehearsal broke the pattern and she was now at choice with her response.

- *Stage fright:* Michael Colgrass worked with many musicians and singers who would suffer from stage fright. He would determine their individual strategies for tumbling into uncontrollable $K^{\cdots}$. He would then have them identify what was happening just before this, which was triggering their unresourceful state. Individuals would come up with: 'I hear my father's voice saying I wouldn't amount to anything', 'I see the audience looking bored and impatient', 'I hear a voice saying I am a sham and they will see through me', 'I hear a voice saying I don't deserve to be here'. Colgrass would then invite them to select from the many instances in their lives where they have heard things said about their ability, or times when their performance has been really well received. Isolating the most powerful one, they insert this different tape or video of genuine appreciation and rehearse the outcomes of this new strategy.

3 **Sponsoring state:** sponsorship is the process of coming alongside and befriending an unwanted state, as opposed to seeking to remove it. This is often a new concept to an exemplar, and the last thing they thought they would find themselves doing. And as ever, the thing that is feared is never as scary as imagined. Using multiple perspectives/triple description widens the system, provides deep dissociation, provokes reframes, confirms positive intentions, activates resources and resolves fear and hopelessness.

- *Pain, grief and loss:* Client F came to me devastated at the breakup of her marriage, which came out of the blue. She was finding it really hard to cope with the pain that was eating her up, and she only found respite when she was busy and preoccupied. She could describe the submodalities of the pain, which in turn became the primary calibration point. This description was then converted into a metaphor – taking the Symbolic Modelling question 'And that is a pain like what?'

  Externalising the pain in its metaphorical form and placing it in a separate location not only gives the client respite from its effects, it allows for dispassionate examination. Further dissociation comes with giving it a name and physical description. First looking on to it, and then second positioning it brings a whole dollop of insight. By going to third position this relationship can be viewed even more clearly, with more understanding emerging.

  The next piece is to find out what happens metaphorically at those moments when the state lessens or disappears, which provides another physical description 'a light is switched on', 'a barrier goes up'. Second positioning this new resource, going third to view the relationship between this resource and the client, and between the resource and the state, lets the client see the positive intention of the state and gain a means of controlling it.

4 **Working with submodalities:** submodalities are the most wonderful concept to work with. Not only can the therapist gain rapid access to one description of the structure, the very process of responding opens up the client's connection with his or her unconscious mind. If this is a new experience it can be quite startling yet exciting. It certainly provides details that only come from the

client's inner experience that are then readily owned and worked with – and these remain vivid many years on.

- *Moving on:* Client R reached the stage when she was ready to look at the nature of her relationship. I invited her to establish a big screen up in front of her and select up to seven images covering the passage of her eight-year relationship. Starting from when they first met and moving through to the previous week, she then saw these images in terms of their respective submodalities.

  Her partner was vibrant and larger than life to begin with, but over the years to her horror she saw her partner becoming more and more shrunken. For herself there was a moment when she flowered and she too became shrunken. She was astounded to realise that the relationship itself had not been healthy and sustaining for some time. She had been putting all the blame on her partner for leaving her but now she could see not only why this has happened, but also see that she had been totally passive throughout. She had been taking no responsibility for her contribution to the outcome.

- *Gaining resourcefulness:* Client H had reached a stage in her late 60s when she felt absolutely lost and alone. Her husband had ceased to communicate, and her children were living their own lives away from home. She had retired from teaching and seemed only to be at her husband's beck and call.

  I invited her to see herself on the screen as the teacher, the wife and the mother – which became the faded mother of today and the strong mother whilst the children were growing up. Understandably the submodalities of the wife were not vibrant. However the submodalities of the active mother were powerfully dynamic – great state change whilst activating this image. So this character then sponsored and held the wife, and in an unexpected instant Swish, became the wife she needed to be.

5   **Working with time:** I love working with time, often as a basis of clearing out the client's system and aligning it in readiness for further exploration. I delight in clients' inevitable surprise when they discover that they do have a somatic representation of time and that their hands seem unerringly to offer information that their conscious minds have difficulty computing! Having so many case studies, I offer here a generalised overview.

Modelling out the client's unique way of holding time provides hard evidence of the wisdom of the unconscious mind and the client's access to it. Working spatially, with somatics, submodalities or metaphor, or a mixture of all three, clients can gain a three-dimensional experience which astounds and serves to explain their behaviours and thoughts, *without entering into content.* This approach is a classic illustration of being able to restructure once the structure is known.

If there is no Present to start with, one can be built that enables the explorer to feel safe, secure and able to breathe freely. If the Future is really short, then it can be extended; any gaps between Present and Future can be filled in or addressed in some way. If the Past is murky with gaps, different colours, huge or narrow, very long or wrapped round the explorer, it can be ironed out and homogenised so that any gaps or blockages can be merged with the whole, and in a colour that adds resources and feels good.

6   **Working with beliefs:** Meta Model can be used just as a straightforward framework of questions in response to client statements. It can reveal the system of beliefs influencing the current situation and preventing future actions. To a susceptible system, this can provide a light bulb moment and

provoke a whole train of new thinking.

- *Shifting unhelpful Beliefs:* One very promising young athlete would clock up good times in training, yet when it came to competition, he would come in second or third, seemingly tiring within the final twenty metres. On examination using meta model, it became obvious that the athlete was uncomfortable about winning, as if it was wrong to make another feel bad. Once the belief was identified and acknowledged, it was then easy to remove it and reprogramme the system positively – with gold medals to prove it!

7   **Working with Meta Model:** I like using the Meta Model patterns to create unfinished statements that ask the client to come up with their own unique, often irrational answers. Each pattern holds its own presupposition. This lets me drill down and find the key limiting belief that is the old familiar golden thread that's been running through the client's system for a very long time. Personally I believe this is an enormous gift to give the client, even if at the moment of awareness it often throws up an emotional response. That irrational belief can easily be re-worked using *Time Line Therapy* devised by Tad James.

Discovering the deep rules that are controlling a system is easy. Instead of hearing a Lost Performative that says 'It is wrong to be selfish', statements can be offered for completion like: 'Selfish people deserve what ...', 'The downside of thinking of others before ourselves is ...' And the responses can be quickly followed up with: 'Which leads to ...', 'Which means ...'

Other statements you can offer for completion can be 'It is essential that ...' 'To succeed you have to ...' 'My problem is that I am more/I am less X ... than other people.'

Sometimes I may offer some of my own possible responses to one of these statements, to illustrate how the client could be directing their thinking, or to find out which particular nuance fits their bill, or to nudge them towards the belief that is lurking just outside of awareness. This is always accompanied by the preframe of 'Please chuck back anything I say to you if it doesn't fit.' while watching closely for any incongruence in their reply.

8   **Clarifying the system:** when the client is already self-aware, and open to exploration, he or she can be really receptive to directed questions. Very often just by clarifying the prevailing system, insights can emerge unbidden within the space created:

- *Panic attacks:* Client J was developing panic attacks once again, triggered by financial negotiations within his divorce settlement. Through working with meta model questioning and following the logic of his thinking, the deep structure of his system became revealed. He was able to understand the constraints he was imposing on himself – irrational because he had plenty of evidence to prove otherwise. He also recognised the unsubstantiated fears that were holding him back. He realised that not only would these *not* happen to him, again with evidence to support him, he also could see that the beliefs he had been running in fact belonged to his mother and had little to do with himself. All of this was over the phone, and the call ended with him being full of relief and strong resolve.

9   **Exploring relationship:** modelling is a great approach for helping clients to understand the nature of their relationships. It provides the opportunity for dissociation and safe exploration of second position. The nature of the relationship itself, as an entity in its own right can also be discovered and shaped:

- *Exploring commitment:* Client S was uncertain about her choice of partner, and even though engaged to him, she still could not make the final commitment. She also had career issues. Her story seemed to be one of co-dependency, and, as part of strengthening her own path and sense of self, I took her through a timeline process, by which time her future became something substantial and desirable.

I then invited her to allocate a parallel timeline for her partner, going from when they met and through into the future. From first position, she could feel the claustrophobic nature of the early years, and as she progressed she could feel the sense of independence yet proximity. In second position, she could feel his continuing commitment and his support for whatever she took on. And by walking up between both lines, *becoming* the relationship, she could feel the freeing up of energy and the strengthening of the bonds between them. This insight strengthened her commitment to the relationship and left her predisposed to ploughing her own furrow and trusting that this would bring its own rewards.

- *Dissociating through metaphors:* Client P was stuck in her dissatisfaction with her husband and their marriage. We established different metaphors for each significant stage in the relationship. By second positioning each of these nominalised metaphors, the exemplar was able to gain a clear somatic description of what the relationship was like at that point – feeling the freedoms and the constraints, the tight and loose areas, the flows and the blockages of energy. This removed the trigger to blame and opened the system sufficiently to allow insight to emerge.

I then extended the process by introducing her and her husband, and she positioned them within the metaphor for each stage. By asking 'What is your outcome here?', 'What are you/your husband contributing positively?', 'What could you be doing more usefully?', she was able to understand the nature of the relationship between her and her husband, and with that stage in their marriage.

10 **Applying process models:** these are techniques based on simultaneous models, which are models whose elements have equal importance and there is no set sequence to follow. The exemplar can choose which element to explore at any time, and in any order. There is no predetermined outcome. Instead the model creates a space for exploration and provides a means of conjuring up emergent awareness out of the relational field created by the influence of the combined elements. Because it is a system, each insight with one element affects the functioning of the others, so that over time new awareness and reconfiguration of relationships emerge.

I have devised several simultaneous models that allow for modelling out the space bounded by the identified elements. One in particular which yields really fertile results is 'The Balance of Power' model that I introduced in *The NLP Cookbook*. The elements are Power, Control, Safety and Vulnerability, each scaled -10 to +10 where 0 is the optimal point. I also devised a powerful model for *Life Tracking*, based on my modelling of the San Bushmen. Here the elements of Energy, Activities, Life Purpose, and Talents, can connect to deliver a sense of Life Purpose.

11 **Devising models:** *Stuff Happens*, a technique in *The NLP Cookbook*, is based on a model that emerged during a session with an exemplar.

- *Anxiety:* Client M reported high levels of stress. He cited three recent scenarios at work when he was really anxious about outcomes because of events outwith his control. Although he was either not directly responsible for the outcomes or he couldn't have done anything more, he still felt the consequences would reflect badly on him personally. His desire to look good was running the show despite acknowledging that this outcome was outside his locus of control.

From this, I got modal operators of necessity – must/ought/shoulds, external referencing, lack of permissions, and bad feelings. This reminded me of the OK Corral in Transactional Analysis and I came up with the following coordinates: Stuff Happens and I'm OK, Stuff Happens and I'm Not OK, Stuff Mustn't Happen and I'm OK, and finally Stuff Mustn't Happen and I'm Not OK. We then explored spatially both for work and social situations, which led not only to a mantra to steady the ship but also a route to regaining state.

As the process subsequently developed, a Personal Charter emerged and tapped into a latent source of personal power. This has proved to be a really valuable process for subsequent clients.

Coaching

Coaching as a profession has taken off over the last ten years, and seems to fit a niche in the personal development market for clients who don't feel they are in need of therapy, and for practitioners who don't want the rigour of psychotherapy training and supervision.

There is a very fine line between therapy and coaching and the easiest distinction is that generally speaking coaching is future orientated and therapy is past focused. Clients can be relaxed about exploring what might be and how to attain it, rather than delving into past pathologies and invasive explorations. However, an inability to move forward is often rooted in the past, and an exploration of the future is all part of the rehabilitation for a therapeutic client.

I don't think of myself as a Coach and don't market myself as such, but a session may sometimes turn into a coaching process and a modelling approach can serve exceptionally well. As ever the presupposition that 'We have all the resources we need.' comes into its own.

1   **Shifting state:** as a form of first aid, explorers have the power to reconstruct their pain, anger, shame, guilt or any other emotion that interrupts their wellbeing. Through discovering the submodality composition, and how the state intensifies and reduces by altering this structure, the exemplar has the means of stepping in and actively setting the direction for submodality shifts, with subsequent shifts in kinaesthetic response.

   • *Anger:* Client B described her anger as a red heavy solid ball, which rolls inside and when it gets bigger, it loses some colour and becomes lighter. She was then able to 'play' with these submodalities, discovering which structure minimises the emotion, and what the physical triggers are. Through stepping into the situations that trigger the anger, she could test and practise what strategies were the most effective.

2   **Restructuring the system**

   • *Resources:* Client C was suddenly bereaved and came wanting to find the resources to enable her to speak at the funeral service of her dear friend. I invited her to write out on bits of paper all the elements currently operating within her system. She included people, range of emotions, gains and on my suggestion she added Sense of Self.

   Through shifting the different bits of paper around, she then worked through how she could keep the gains previously derived from her departed friend, from resources within her own life.

She added other friendships and extended her family. She instinctively reframed the gaps and sought the benefits. She began to realise that her friend's going could free her to consider wider options. She left able to decide calmly what her next steps were and what she would say at the memorial.

3   Planning the future

- *Prioritising:* Client J was exploring options regarding decisions for the future. Operating on the mantra of 'No options = Dead, One Option = Robot, Two Options = Dilemma, Three Options = Beginnings of Choice', again I invited her to get creative and write down on bits of paper all the options she could think of, including staying the same. I also added a couple of my own, with a bit of explanation; just to widen the system further.

By moving the individual pieces on a sliding scale towards 'Most Desirable' she was able to gain clarity regarding her priorities and her preferences, the possible barriers impeding progress and also the strength of any connections between the choices. Patterns could be detected, new options emerged and subsequent actions planned for.

The process had given her the language she needed to express her needs and to give support to the decision she was finally ready to make.

4   Working with strategies

- *Tracking a relationship:* Client S had a history of unproductive relationships and had now entered into a new one with great hope. But she didn't want to sabotage this one as well. She also 'ran at the mouth' and it was very difficult to rein her in to slow down her thinking. So once more using bits of paper she plotted out the customary pathway her relationships would take, and added the complex equivalences she was making at each stage: 'Going Well = Not going to last', 'Freeze = He'll see through me', 'Test him = I deserve him leaving me' etc.

It became obvious that the relationship took a downward spiral quite early on. She removed the stages she didn't want and instead of saving up her 'negative' emotions for the grand finale, brought them forward so that she could feel free to express her emotions early when they arose. She then underpinned each stage with the mantra 'I am free to be me'.

Once the new sequence was established, she set up spatial anchors and walked each stage going for a see, hear, and feel. She summed up her resource state at the end – Loving Acceptance, and finally did a walking edit based on this resource, moving through the stages about five times.

5   Working with submodalities: much has been made of modelling using submodalities. Ever since Bandler's original story about the baseball batsman seeing a huge ball coming his way through clear air, NLP coaches have been eager to discover how the sporting client configures their preparation state. Teaching the client about the nature of submodalities and enabling them to become acutely aware of their specific configuration at key points can create optimum conditions for performance.

- *Optimum state:* the golfer Greg Norman waits 'until the fairway gets wider' before he takes his drive. Another golfer reports tracking the golden light like a gunpowder trail to the centre of the hole on the green before taking the putter's back swing. Similarly, the snooker player quickly recognises if the pocket has shrunk and sets about widening it before he takes his shot; the footballer taking the set free kick just outside the penalty box widens the net as the goalkeeper makes it really small; and the show jumper can slow down time and create space for every stride and turn.

- *Rituals and anchoring:* become critical for ensuring optimum state. A ritual is a process of stacking established anchors, culminating into a 'super' anchor. As a result of modelling out natural repetitive behaviours, rituals can be built up to deliver the desired state, hence you will see the sprinter on the blocks looking down the track, touching jewellery, and stretching each leg in sequence. Every tennis player has their own routine for receiving new balls, the number of bounces before each serve, the stance preparation to receive a serve. The habitual chalking of the snooker cue, and Jonny Wilkinson's famous stance prior to taking a kick between the goal posts, are other examples. It can be fun to watch.

Model Construction

We have now arrived at the nitty gritty of modelling's technology – the production of a model. Out of all the data, gathered from a variety of possible sources, we are now tasked to shake it all down and come up with a stark set of labels, which powerfully manage to encapsulate the desired richness of experience. Seems an incredibly tall order! Yet amazingly, it is possible and says much for the wisdom of our internal representations.

But before I go into this process, it is important to have an idea of the range of model types at our disposal, so that we are able to recognise them in their 'raw' format. This way we will avoid reinventing wheels and going over old ground. Much of what is around us are models of something. It serves us to discern if they could be applicable to influencing the structure of internal experience.

Classification of Models

Models can operate at every level of chunk size. Starting at the top and taking subjective experience at its highest level, we have the system of 'map and territory', where all our past experiences, beliefs, filters, internal representations and physiology all combine to form what we know to be our 'model of the world'. A modelling methodology is a model which combines the principles and practices required for its delivery. A connecting system of beliefs is a model in itself. Similarly a connected series of behaviours in the form of a strategy can be called a model, for example The Spelling Strategy. A somatic gesture or a phrase can be regarded as a model for what it represents.

> **Each of these models is a combination of its elements, which when taken together, represent and describe the logical type they represent, ultimately the whole system. Each of these elements have to be identified and coded in order to bring them into the language of surface structure.**

Models don't have to relate to organic experience. The same thinking applies to objective appraisal of inorganic systems. I realised that working out the chapters of this book was a process of modelling – and I have to say much remodelling – identifying the key elements of this vast subject, grouping them meaningfully, so that the Table of Contents becomes a coherent representation of the material held within. In the same manner, a PowerPoint presentation is the overlay model of the topic, each section the elements of that model, each slide an aspect of that element, and each bullet point a feature of that aspect. I suspect if presenters thought like modellers, presentations would be far more logical, coherent and easy to access.

The London Underground map is a model and not a literal depiction of the tube network. Flight paths over an airport become a three-dimensional model of safe aerial passageways. Floor layout plans are a two-dimensional representation of a building section. The Periodic Table is a classification model for Chemical Elements.

> **A Model is a simplified description of a far more complex system, with all the key elements within that system represented. It may be fully coded into a few specific words, or retain some of the analogue and be expressed in phrases or sentences.**

Note: In many descriptions of modelling, the source of the information is called the model, as in an artist's model. This only adds to confusion that may be around, which is why I've adopted Gordon's naming of 'exemplar' to identify the source of the identified behaviour.

Classification Criteria

1 **Degree of investigation required to identify them:** this acknowledges that some models are naturally occurring within all of us irrespective of our experience and 'take' on reality, whilst others are highly personalised expressions that we arrive at through a process of investigation.

2 **Degree of attachment to source:** this covers how much the model is dependent on the exact source for its interpretation, or whether it operates independently and can be consumed in a variety of contexts and by different end users.

3 **Degree of coding required to express them:** this relates to how much description is required to bring the model alive.

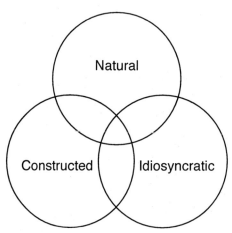

Three Classes of Models – Burgess 2012

Natural Models

Natural Models are those models that reside within all of us, irrespective of lineage, culture, personality, or experience. They are part of our human condition and internal experience. These fundamental models are directly responsible for how we experience the world and how we construct the meaning we make from these experiences.

Types of Natural Models

Natural Models can be sub-classified into three types, according to its level of complexity.

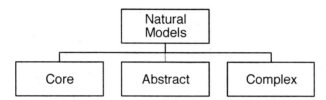

Types of Natural Models – Burgess 2012

1 **Core Natural Models:** these are the fundamental structures of subjective experience which Bandler and Grinder identified really early on, and formed the basis of Classic Code. They are so simple that they tend to be overlooked in favour of the more 'flashy' patterns. Yet within them, they hold the DNA of our inner processing.

Type of Model	Expression
Senses	Submodalities
Time	Past, Present, Future
Space	Multiple Perspectives, Association/Dissociation

2 **Abstract Natural Models:** these are next in the rankings of simplicity/complexity. These models are abstract expressions of sensory experience, covering both the VAK representation systems and the cognitive abstraction of language.

Type of Model	Expression
Visual	Symbols
Auditory	Sounds
Kinaesthetic	Movement
Cognitive	Punctuation

3 **Complex Natural Models:** these complex models are common to all and have the represent internal patterning.

Type of Model	Expression
Metaphor	Images, Descriptions
Parts	Mentors, Archetypes
Neurological Levels	Mission, Identity, Values, Beliefs, Capabilities, Behaviours, Environment

Functions of a Natural Model

I had been spending considerable time tussling with what actually constituted a model, and therefore how to classify them. I remember one of those breakthrough moments, when I was out in the garden weeding, when pieces came together and my mind ricocheted with all the implications.

I became aware of just how special and unique these particular structures are and how they can be applied in a variety of ways of increasing complexity. This awareness began to draw in other strands of my thinking and an overall model took form. I realised that these highly versatile models have the power to operate at three very distinctive areas of application serving serve three very different functions.

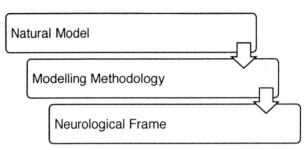

Functions of Natural Models – Burgess 2012

1   **Model:** firstly, a Natural Model is a model in itself – a simple description of subjective structure, and as such can be applied universally regardless of context and content. All subjective experience can be diagnosed, defined and packaged through these Natural models. Some techniques are only expanding the Natural model they contain: e.g. VAK and Circle of Excellence.

2   **Modelling methodology:** secondly, a Natural model has the potential to be used as a means of revealing structure. It can be used as a tool: e.g. modelling out submodality configurations, generating a metaphorical landscape, or revealing a timeline structure.

3   **Neurological frame:** thirdly, a Natural model can be used as the basis of a technique. These models appear as neurological frames which when added to a constructed model, can bring that model to life: e.g. applying multiple perspectives to a state.

Whilst Natural models are basic to all, the next two Classes are *only* revealed as a result of the modelling process.

Idiosyncratic Models

Idiosyncratic models are personal representations of an exemplar's internal experience. The end user in this case is the exemplar, and this form of self-modelling is a highly effective intervention in therapy and coaching. As illustrated in Part 3 – The Methodologies of Modelling, because these models retain a high degree of analogue description, they often require further digitisation and reduction to make them ready for consumption by third party end users.

Idiosyncratic models are generated through using Somatic, Expressive Modelling approaches and the Metaphorical Methodologies of Symbolic Modelling, Parts Alignment and Punctuation Modelling.

The Gordon/Dawes Experiential Array differs as it is derived through Cognitive modelling, yet the content retains a high level of analogue information. Arrays are usually still connected to their source exemplar, where only one exemplar is used, and the exemplar's personality still remains within the descriptions.

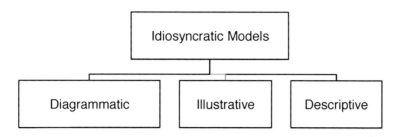

Types of Idiosyncratic Models – Burgess 2012

Types of Idiosyncratic Models

1 **Diagrammatic:** diagrams can plot the flows of energy, blockages, connections and disconnections, and points of leverage all within an internal system. Working somatically and spatially, the dynamics within this system can then be brought into life as a technique, without having to reduce and code further.

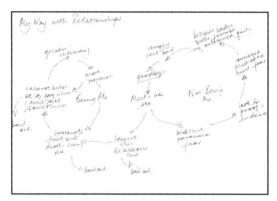

Diagram of a Relationship

2 **Illustrative:** Symbolic Modelling, Parts Alignment and Punctuation modelling incorporate the production of drawings to depict the modelled structure as part of the final calibration process. For more details about these methodologies, go to Part 3 – The Methodologies of Modelling.

- *Punctuation profile:* this is another modelling methodology of mine, inspired by Lynn Truss's book *Eats, Shoots and Leaves*, and uses the metaphor of punctuation as a means of revealing internal processes and structures. It is remarkable how people can respond to this form of description, and feel happy to strip away any content and merely go with their response to the content.

Punctuation for Understanding

- *Metaphoric landscapes:* these are the wonderful, literally fantastic, creations arising from the process of Symbolic Modelling developed by Lawley and Tompkins. Entering into these descriptions reveals a very logical, coherent system, which naturally illustrates the dynamics that deliver the 'thing' modelled, be it a relationship, a skill, a belief, whatever.

  For subsequent use as the basis of a technique, only the modeller and the exemplar are likely to know the significance of the symbolism to enable useful coding. However these landscapes lend themselves to narrative and guided visualisation. The elements may be further labelled in terms of what they represent to the exemplar.

- *Parts profile:* this illustration is the result of systemic modelling of internal parts, in my Parts Alignment process. All the parts currently influencing performance are identified and harmonised to remove internal friction and generate aligned focus. Again the exemplar draws his or her own representation of the final arrangement of their parts.

A Metaphoric Landscape

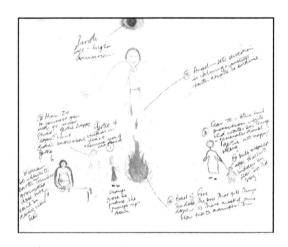

A Final Parts Alignment

3 **Descriptive:** this can be a series of statements, phrases or fully formed sentences. In the Gordon Dawes Experiential Array, you will find lots of words and phrases, all of which refer directly to a pre-identified ability. You can step into this array and take on the information it contains, or you could draw out key components to form into a fully coded model.

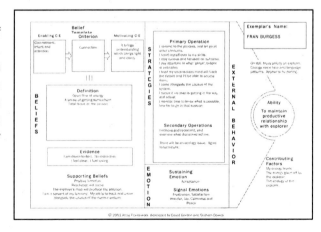

Constructed Models

We now come to the models that are most commonly recognised as being NLP models; those most often constructed for use by a third party. These models are independent of the exemplar, and their structure arises from the creativity and logic of the modeller. The source exemplars are long gone, and you may have added data from your own experience or elsewhere, so your exemplars may not recognise their own behaviour within your description.

These designed models are fully coded and digitised descriptions of an identified ability. Their elements are the precise shorthand of the analogue experience, and they collectively hold the ability to generate something close to the original experience. Their construction is the final stage of the modelling process, after gathering the information from the exemplar, scoping this information through your choice of filters, and reducing it into a minimalist composition of labelled elements.

Types of Constructed Models

The following classification of Constructed Models illustrates the options open to a modeller in terms of the type of model he or she can create.

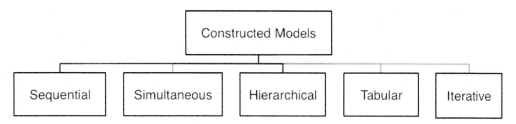

Types of Constructed Models – Burgess 2012

1   **Sequential:** elements are arranged in a direct sequence of steps, the following element influenced by the previous one. Completion of the previous step is required before movement onto the next one. Such models often arise through strategy elicitation, most commonly applied to skill development. The relationship between elements is one of cause and effect, leading to the predetermined outcome. They are *Product* Models.

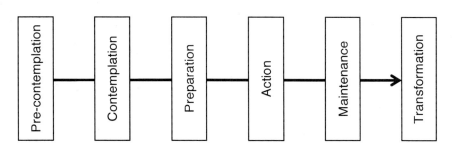

Stages in Change – Prochaska 1994

2   **Simultaneous:** this is where all the elements of the model have the same importance as each other. There is no implied progression from one to the other, and entry can be at any point. Here

all the elements are representations serving a common logical type, whilst being fully discrete logical types themselves within the model. They will all operate at the same logical level, sharing the same labelling format, to generate the requirement of coherence.

These are *Process* Models. Instead of a known end result, the relational field arising from within the model's combined elements provides a transformative emergent property. The specific nature of this outcome cannot be predetermined.

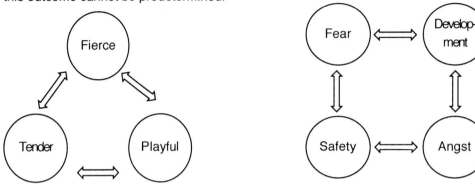

Sponsorship Model – Gilligan　　　**The FADS Model – McWhirter**

These models lend themselves instinctively to the kinaesthetic delivery methods – spatial anchors being the most popular with somatic syntax and sliding scales also working well here. However, these models are more versatile than this, and with some imagination you can harvest many techniques from them.

3   **Hierarchical:** this is where an element is subsumed by the element above it. In turn the higher element is dependent on the presence of the lower one. Each has a direct influence on the operations of the one below and above it. The elements will be all of the same logical type and represent a fractal. The gap between each chunk size is ideally evenly distributed, or else proportionately different.

These can be worked into a spatially or cognitively delivered technique. You can create some fabulous guided visualisations taking your explorer from the specific to the general and back again. You can invite your explorer to come up with collages or pictures of his or her inner journey. Again the options available to you are huge.

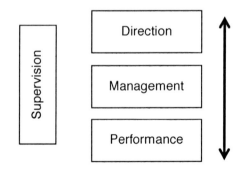

Improving Performance – McWhirter

4   **Tabular:** this is more a technical cognitive model, where the key elements are encapsulated in a table or represented in bullet points.   The sets and subsets follow the same logic and are of the same level of detail. There is often room for additional description and definition.

The table headings are a model in themselves and could lend themselves to becoming a simultaneous model, or if there is an implied progression between them, a sequential model could be constructed.

Meta Model		
Deletions	**Generalisations**	**Distortions**
Simple	Modal Operator of Necessity	Lost Performatives
Comparative	Modal Operator of Probability	Mind Reading
Unspecified Verb	Universal Quantifier	Cause and Effect
Referential Index		Complex Equivalence
Nominalisation		

Meta Model Framework – Bandler and Grinder

5   **Iterative:** this is a sequential model that is looped – the last stage leads to the next stage at a higher level of awareness, based on events in the previous one. This continues until a conclusion is reached or sufficient information has been revealed.   Being a sequential model, the entry point is at the start of the sequence. With these examples, the entry is at the top of the diagram – *Own* and *Acceptance* respectively.

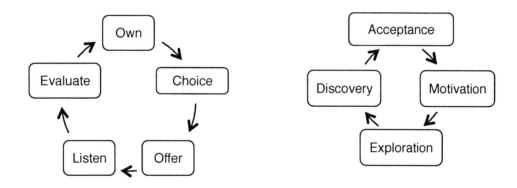

Repairing a Relationship – Burgess   **Unsticking Stuckness – Burgess**

333

It is always possible that the explorer bails out at any of the stages. With *Repairing Broken Relationships*, the explorer may decide that once arriving at 'Own' that it is too painful or the differences are too extreme to continue. With *Unsticking Stuckness*, the explorer may consider that she isn't sufficiently motivated to carry on, or doesn't accept what has been discovered.

As the modeller, you can predetermine the levels, as opposed to leaving it to the explorer to determine the number of iterations. You could specify say Time1, Time 2, Time 3, or apply specific hierarchical models – Self, Other, Family, Company, Industry, Country; or Performance, Management, Direction; or the Neurological Levels. With this choice, you can generate different processes and outcomes.

Working with Iterative Models

These models can be given various treatments, which directly affect the impact and results.

- *Linear:* this is where the levels are set out in a continuous line. The explorer progresses to the next level, leaving the previous one behind.

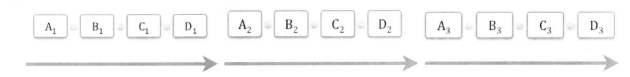

- *Spiral:* the model now becomes a process model with the ability to build up an increasingly impactful relational field, as it is surrounded by the energy generated by the model's elements. There are two possibilities here – the spiral in or the spiral out, creating two distinct arrangements.

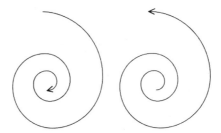

This structure can be further subdivided into:

- *Conical shape:* where the journey spirals in from the starting point on the outside and the circles become progressively smaller until the explorer comes to a halt in the centre. This works really well if you want to arrive at a conclusion and possible final goal. From the side, this takes on a rounded conical form, with Round 1 at the wide based bottom and the conclusion at the top of 'the hill'.

- *Basket shape:* where the journey starts in the centre and spirals out in ever increasing circles. No limit needs to be set regarding how many spirals or iterations the explorer goes through. This format can incorporate Hierarchical Models that expand on the breadth of the ascending levels – e.g. Self to Country. This version of the Spiral works really well if you want to explore a particular issue from various chunked up or wider perspectives, to deliver satisfactory amounts of new information, without necessarily coming to a finite conclusion. From the side, this takes on a basket shape with the relational field building and building in the central axis.

- *Columnar:* this treatment involves combining the Iterative Model with a Hierarchical Model and chunking up incrementally the highest level is within the scope of the lowest – e.g. Performance, Management and Direction, and the Neurological Levels. With the iterative model at the base, the column is ascended gathering the information and then descended with the lower levels now being informed by what has gone on before.

- *Segmental:* this two-dimensional treatment occurs when the chunked out/chunked in levels are predetermined, but instead of working progressively through the iterative model, each element of the model is able to be explored at different levels of thinking, with the ability to work across elements operating at different levels. This creates a pie chart effect holding the dynamics of the model within an exploration space.

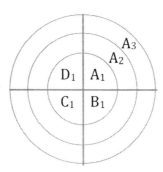

- *Combination:* this chunking up process can be derived from the combination of a Sequential or a Simultaneous model with a Hierarchical Model. Through the combination, a progression is generated which becomes iterative. The models themselves are not iterative.

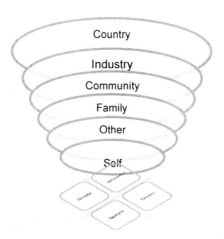

Summary

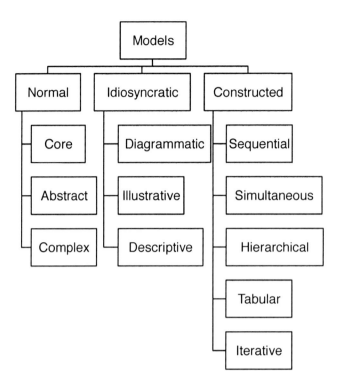

Classification of NLP Models – Burgess 2012

Choices

Knowing that there are different types of constructed models gives you choice about the model you finally produce. Out of the masses of information you have gathered, you may find that you can harvest several models of different types, giving attention to certain aspects of the ability and so providing a multi-dimensional description of the desired experience.

Plasticity of a model

Models don't have to stay in a fixed format. After all it is the elements within the model that carry the 'DNA of experience'.

You may start off thinking you have developed key stages in a process, each with their own label, all leading to the build up of the final experience. And in the process, you may wonder what it would be like to remove the stages and let them 'talk amongst themselves', allowing a hitherto hidden property to emerge.

You may choose to take your sequential model and keep it open-ended, allowing the awareness to ripen and deepen at every meta level of cognition.

Conversely you may choose to take the elements within your simultaneous model and see what would happen if you converted it into a sequence where the next element is dependent on the preceding one, and in turn will influence the next one. Staking these anchors builds up the energies and allows the end result to burst through.

Filters

This classification helps to set your filters, so that you can spot models occurring in other people's work. Some may be obvious, as are many management models that we can 'NLP-ise' and put to good use. Others may be nested within a presentation or a paragraph of a book.

Having greater acuity regarding the presence of a model opens the floodgates to the creation of fantastic techniques, way beyond personal limitations. Having a lively grasp of the nature and shape of models can lead to an amazing platform for the development of human potential.

Technique design

Different types of Constructed Models lend themselves to different types of techniques. Sometimes once the model's structure is determined, the technique falls into place. For example, if you have a simultaneous model, this would strongly suggest a spatial anchor process to build up the relational field.

Coding

In Part 3 – The Methodologies of Modelling, the range of modelling methodologies was classified on the basis of how much the approach ended up with a digitised coded model. With Unconscious Uptake, the process stayed in the deep structure of analogue. Metaphoric Modelling operated at mid-structure using the language of symbols, and Cognitive Modelling brought description of the deep structure to the structure using cognitive language, sometimes more precisely reduced to discrete words or phrases.

Coding is the process of turning the analogue expression into a digital description, and this reduced description becomes the constructed model. I contend that all the expressions arising from each of the methodologies can ultimately become digitised descriptions, even though their originators were more than satisfied to leave the expression in the analogue. Gordon is adamant that experience is never boxed off into a digitised notation; it is always an analogue process.

For those who may consider digital models to be a soulless and futile endeavour and even an insult to the magnificence of the spirit of experience, I offer the following arguments for the digitisation of experience. I see a range of benefits that add further to the contribution the modelling process can make.

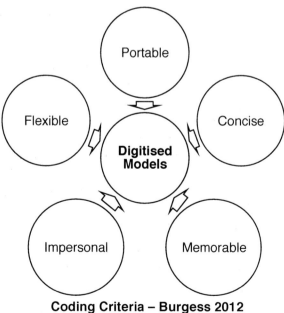

Coding Criteria – Burgess 2012

Coding Criteria

1 **Portable:** the key words that encapsulate the experience provide a lightweight structure that is portable, non-cumbersome, and easy to apply across the board.   It is not context specific and can have the potential to be applied in a variety of areas of activity and at different scales of complexity.

2 **Concise:** akin to Einstein's thinking, a model is reduced to its most simple elements and no simpler. There are no wasted words. There is a precision to the selected label given to each of its elements. And each element earns its place and contributes equally with its fellows to re-activate the desired experience.

3 **Memorable:** this reduction to a few key elements, sometimes expressed in a mnemonic or alliteratively, makes the model easy to remember. This is theory simplified and accessible for a wide range of users coming from many different levels of experience and education.

4 **Impersonal:** models, especially those composite models that are created from multiple exemplars, leave the personalities of the exemplars behind. Any influence exerted by the exemplars is removed and the model has become an objective expression of the modeller's understanding.

5 **Flexible:** because of the reduced nature of a model, it can be further expanded through exploring the individual elements, separately or together in various combinations. It may have the ability to be reconfigured in a sequence or taken simultaneously. It might usefully be combined with other models, to create a higher-level framework.

Whilst I fully recognise that there is a place for a metaphoric landscape to stay in its illustrated form, or for profound experience to be represented in somatic gesture, or for the exemplar's words and descriptions to intimate the nature of the underpinning structure, I do firmly believe that, as modellers, we miss an enormous trick if we don't become equally skilled at model construction. Having said this, I am clear that there are strong requirements of a Model, and the process of digitisation brings with it its own discipline.

Model Design

By now you have determined why you want to create a particular model – you have identified a need and end users who will benefit. You have also developed your skills of detecting structure and pattern detection, possibly using a known scoping framework or following your own intuitions. Now you have the task of not only reducing the information you have gathered but also creating out of all of this data a model that is fit for purpose. The model is the end product of your modelling pursuit. You want it to work. You want it to deliver your intended experience consistently.

This is the area that causes the greatest difficulties for most modellers – certainly, this is the case, judging from the number of our learners who postponed their certification because they had still to come up with a model. And this inability to convert researches into a workable model is the biggest frustration, sometimes even causing them to consider giving up and walking away.

Of course, as is demonstrated in Part 3 – The Methodologies of Modelling, many modelling approaches have no requirement for a digital model to be produced. In fact for some of them, and I have David Gordon in mind when I say this, digital models are almost the spawn of the Devil (my words)! He is likely to say: 'People do not *do* four or five words! People live experience in all its richness.' However, as an independent modeller, you want the option to create something that is portable and able to be easily offered to another.

So if you are going to go down the route of original model construction, then once more you want to draw upon your knowledge and understanding of logical levels and logical types. These provide you with a three-dimensional up/down/across plotting system, which not only sorts the data, but also allows you to test it as well.

Before you undertake the exciting and demanding job of making sense of your data, you need to understand what a model is required to achieve as a model: you need to be clear of the Criteria for Model Design. These criteria, identified in our Explorers' Club at our School, serve to steer you in the right direction and limit instances of frustration and reworking.

The Purposes of a Constructed Model

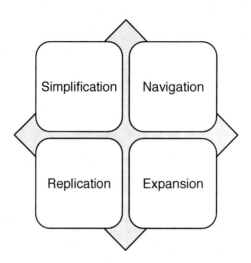

Purposes of a Constructed Model – Burgess 2008

For a model to take up its rightful place, it needs to meet the following requirements:

1 **Simplification:** a model seeks to simplify and reduce a complex system to its basic elements. This process of reduction is tested by removing elements, one at a time, to see if the model falls over, fails to hold up, or ceases to deliver.

I hold that no model should exceed a maximum seven elements, otherwise it becomes too cumbersome. If there are more than seven elements, then this could indicate a need for further refinement. It may be a sign to chunk up and operate at a higher level, so that some of the elements become subsets. Some of the detail can be incorporated in explanatory definitions, or subsequently in the content of the technique's instructions.

2 **Navigation:** a model serves to let you know where you are in the particular process, and so reduce or even remove confusion or anxiety from Not-Knowing or feeling lost. It might be that you are experiencing a strong emotion that can then be explained by identifying with elements within a model – 'Oh that's just my Dreamer feeling attacked by my Critic.'

Or you may be wondering what to do next, or what information is missing. You can then select the relevant model and see what elements you haven't covered and those you have. Arguably the more models you have to hand, the easier navigating the unknown becomes. Those who are highly procedural love working with loads of models since it reduces the ambiguity and provides tried and tested order.

3 **Expansion:** the elements within the model set the edges of the model and its resulting dynamics provide the channels for energy flow. These boundaries may take the explorer beyond his or her current awareness, through offering new territory that hadn't previously been considered. Often the unique combination of elements and their emergent properties takes the explorer to a higher level of connection.

The relationships between the elements can highlight the dynamics within this microsystem to indicate where energy flow is blocked or excessive. As an information gathering frame alone, without the likelihood of change, the model serves to extend and expand awareness, if just to confirm that all is well.

4   **Replication:** traditionally, the only purpose of a model was its ability to enable another to take on and replicate the desirable behaviour of the original source. 'If one can do it, others can do it' was the mantra. Then that was modified with the proviso that the acquirer had the necessary aptitudes to support it. Still full replication was the Grail.

However approximate replication can only be possible because the acquirer comes with his own physiology and neural network. If I take on a model, I will process it through my Fran-ness and create my version. The question is 'does the resultant performance meet the needs of the end user, both in terms of their personality and context?' It might be that all that is being asked of the model is to shift the end user away from perhaps a currently stuck position, into somewhere more viable.

CASE Model – Criteria for Model Design

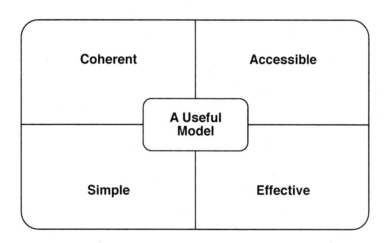

It is important that you are able to select good models to work with. If the model itself is flawed then you will perpetuate the flaws in your technique. Design criteria for models have been one of the unmapped areas in the modelling territory, so the modeller had only instinct to rely on. Often the difficulty has been framing the model in such a way that it becomes totally congruent and rock-steady.

The model needs to be robust, which means it is successful with a variety of users, in a variety of contexts, over a period of time, used a variety of techniques. Occasionally a model may be constructed just to deliver the needs of the moment, and have no further shelf life. If this disposable model does its job in that moment, then it can be deemed to be robust.

1   **Coherent:** the elements within the model need to fit together and work together. The feel of the model is all-important, or more accurately, the feel of the model's structure. When you step in and

second position it, it needs to feel balanced, with each of the elements having the same weight and this weight is evenly distributed throughout.

For those of you who find such concepts difficult to take on, I offer the metaphor of an Australian bushman's hat, with the corks around the brim. If your model were this hat, and your model's elements the corks, would the hat be resting on your head evenly, one side being dragged down, or having some corks more lightweight, with no impact at all?

- You achieve balance by making sure that all elements are the same in nature: nouns with nouns, verbs with verbs, adjectives with adjectives, behaviours with behaviours, skills with skills, beliefs with beliefs etc. If these are mixed up, you will get a lopsided feel.

- The elements also need to be at the same chunk size. If they are not, then you should look to combine some and chunk up to a higher level, or break down an element to equate with the chunk size of the others. Labelling can convey this. If one named element is at a higher or lower logical level or chunk size, it will feel lighter or heavier than the others.

- Similarly, having clearly distinct and separate logical types within the model is really important. If two named elements share similar logical types, then they will form an imbalanced cluster. If this happens then combining them into a higher logical type might be the answer.

- The arrows that indicate the dynamics and flow of the system have to be an accurate representation.

- For sequential and hierarchical models, attention needs to be given to maintaining equal spacing between the elements, so that the steps move through the time zone or space evenly, or proportionately.

Have a look at the following examples based on the well-known Disney Model – Dreamer, Realist Critic. Before you think about what is right or wrong with them, step in and *feel* the system and notice how it impacts on you somatically – by far the quicker route to discernment.

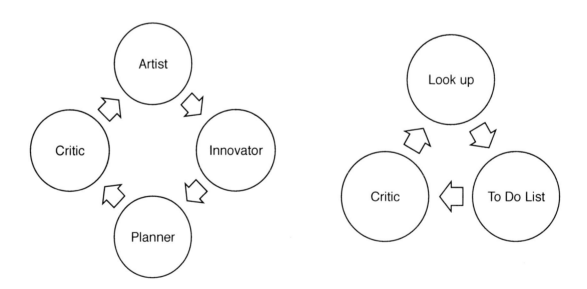

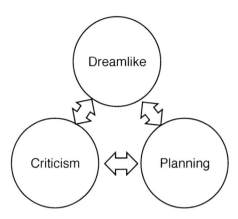

Now check your somatic findings against the criteria for coherence.

2   **Accessible:** the labelling of the elements where possible is self-explanatory, without requiring great explanations. Some modellers use words so precisely, or give their own spin on a particular word, that unless you have their definitions, the model is meaningless.   If you are also in charge of creating the acquisition process(es), your instructions and content can provide definition and direct attention appropriately.

However, language is slippery and some definitions may be required, so the model may come with a preframe.   Check this out, otherwise as the consumer, you may run the risk of making assumptions and ending up with an acquisition process that goes off in a direction not intended by the modeller. Poor understanding of the elements within the model can explain why a model gets inconsistent results. The fault is not in the model itself.

As the modeller, you determine the labels you chose.   You may go for sensory/non-sensory specific labels, metaphors or even use somatic syntax to 'name' your elements.   You may favour using Attributes or Values, as opposed to Verbs or Adjectives. Much will depend on where you want to pitch your model within the Neurological Levels.

For example, the element could be labelled at value level as Strength, or skill level as Strong, or behavioural level of Being Strong, or it could be extended into an archetype and be labelled at the identity of Warrior. Whatever is chosen, all the other elements must follow suit. Just notice how an attribute can be expressed in different ways, to convey the precise dynamic you want.

Nominalisation	Verb		Adjective	Part/Archetype
	Present	**'ing' verb**		
Appreciation	Appreciate	Appreciating	Appreciative	The Fan
Tenacity		Being Tenacious	Tenacious	The Stalwart

Labelling a Model – Burgess 2013

The end user can determine what labels you select. Pete Lindsay, Lead Sport Psychologist with the English Institute of Sport, and one of our students, finds that he gets far better results from turning the elements of a model into their respective archetypes, especially when his clients aren't that sophisticated with language. So taking the Gilligan Sponsorship Model of Tender, Fierce, Playful, this becomes The Carer, The Defender, The Joker.

3   **Simple:**   the model needs to be reduced down to its simplest form, with no repetition within it, whilst retaining its purpose and meaning. This simplicity is part of its congruence. A model with more than seven elements becomes clunky and ungainly, and suggests that the modeller has not been able to make a clear judgment about what to keep in and what to discard. This is often because the modeller feels obliged to retain much of what the exemplar has offered, not taking the bull by the horns and assertively self determining the nature of his model. As Gordon is fond of saying: 'When you are with the exemplar, your allegiance is with your exemplar. When you are with your Model, your allegiance is with your model.'

If the model has lots of elements, then it is likely that many of the elements will be subsets in service to three or four key elements. If this is the case, then what's on offer are, say, four separate and interconnected models, which are addressing more specific areas of attention.

The model ideally should be able to be represented in a simple diagram, with arrows indicating the nature of the relationship between each element: is there a two-way flow between elements, or does one element need to be activated first to inform the next one?

4   **Effective:**   the model needs to deliver its intended effect. The elements selected within the model need to combine together or sequentially to deliver the outcome promised within its name.

I suggest that there are various end points a modeller can go for. The modeller can choose to design a model and the acquisition process that goes for a very close approximation of the original behaviour. Alternatively the modeller may be happy with a loose approximation of the behaviour adapted to the personal needs of the acquirer and the situation. The behaviours are still within the same class of response as those of the exemplar. But with equal validity, it might be that the model is asked merely to act as a catalyst for shifting the acquirer in the direction of the desired behaviour.

If, however, the model produces responses totally removed from those of the original exemplars, this suggests that the modeller has gone drastically off course and overlooked vital pieces of information. In which case, it is back to data once more. Alternatively, should this 'aberrant' model consistently produce similar responses in a variety of acquirers, there is nothing stopping the modeller from quickly renaming it!

Elements of a Model

Identifying Elements

It is useful to put some distance between yourself and your data. Even the process of collating what you've gathered or typing up the transcript from a tape or video gives you some thinking space. Having a germination period, allows all the data to become absorbed into your system and make its own connections.

There may be a danger that you force yourself to 'hurry up', or you may have some tight schedule to follow, but forcing your conclusions before they are ready is not useful. The more experienced you are, the quicker you will become, since your circuitry will have become fairly hard-wired for noticing connections and patterns.

However there are some strategies I can offer to help you. Here are some ways that you can approach your data.

1   **Key words:** sort out the Key Words that your exemplars have been using – but don't necessarily assume that they are all referring to same thing. You have to check the respective contexts before you can be certain. You might also see if the same *sense* is being expressed through very different words or phrases.

2   **Emphasis:** get into the habit of circling those words that are emphasised either through volume, tone, time given, facial expression, gesture, meta comment. There are likely to be links between them.

3   **Themes:** trawl through your materials for themes. These could be beliefs or values, relationships, locations, outcomes. Then you can explore what patterns these themes have in common.

4   **Let go!:** you need to be fully predisposed to letting go of the embryonic theories you're developing and the frameworks that are forming, and starting over again. You need to pay particular attention to those elements that have held your attention the most, or which you are particularly proud of. You run the risk of including them at all cost, regardless of their dubious fit. These could always form the basis of another model later on. In creative writing parlance: 'Kill your Darlings!'

5   **Re-examine:** resist any temptation to ignore inconvenient 'bits' that don't seem to fit in. These may be the very clues to take your thinking to a higher level. Trawl through your notes, or thinking, and check out which pieces jump out and refuse to lie down.

6   **Test through your own system:** you can take the data and monitor it for your own somatic response. This will give you your sense of significance, using your own neurology or Dilts's radar to determine the common factors.

7   **Random:** this is a highly unscientific method, yet as good as any other. If you are tussling with your sheets of paper and going round in circles, ask yourself the following:

   • If someone asked me what my model is all about, what four to six words would I use to describe it?

   • If all the words you have written were thrown up in the air, what four to six words would land face up?

This process relies on the fact that your unconscious mind has already sorted the data and had a sense of the commonly held structure.

8   **Marinade it:** give yourself permission to put your data aside for a given period of time – a couple of days, weeks, or even months – and get on with something else entirely different. Pay attention to what catches your attention, on the TV, in conversation, books and articles. These items are likely to hold some key to channel your thinking. When you return to the drawing board, be aware of the thinking you are now bringing to the process.

9   **Add to it:** feel free to add in your own thinking and previous experience, or bits of models to be found elsewhere. The only final arbiter is the result you get.

And remember, if your model doesn't generate X, but consistently seems to generate Y, you've made a lucky mistake. Rename it and make out that this was what you intended all along!

Testing Elements

Once you think you have narrowed the elements down, you need to really test them, first of all against the CASE model for clear design, and then out there with willing people.

*   *Listen to your own descriptions:* how congruent are you? How fluent, or are the bits where you stumble and realise that you are uncertain?

*   *Watch their responses:* and the ease by which they could take it on. Check on their levels of politeness and encourage honesty no matter how inconvenient.

*   *Calibrate:* the end result against your expectations. Is it similar? Is it sufficient? Is it consistent?

*   *Seek feedback:* check out what wording or sequencing might be preferable. Find out ways of simplifying it if needs be. Make a note of those elements that may need extra explanation.

*   *Be honest:* you have to be squeaky clean with yourself. Are you shoehorning in or ignoring inconvenient elements? Are you putting the blame for these anomalies onto the acquirer? Are you resisting the possible truth within the feedback?

*   *Deconstruct:* be ready to dismantle the whole process and reconstruct.

*   *Self-test:* constantly be processing your various versions through your own system. You are the modeller, and therefore your neurology will be playing a vital part in the decision making process.

*   *Rehearse:* as you are introducing your model to others, notice what you find yourself regularly saying. This can form part of your preframe or the script in your instructions.

Finally

Rejoice!

There is nothing so wonderful as the moment when a model sets into its rightful resting place. The exhilaration that all the investigation has paid off. All that the churning of uncertainty has ceased. You have produced something useful, which will be in service to others. This could be the start of a new product, a new programme, and possibly a new source of income.   You have given birth to something that had not be available previously. There is little to beat the creative process.

Additional Sources of Models

It needs to be said that we are not dependent on working with models that have been generated through NLP skills, frames and modelling methodologies.

We can land upon models which many other great thinkers have come up with, and customise them if needs be to meet our CASE requirements. Once you start thinking 'Model', it is amazing just how many seem to emerge from the written or spoken word.

Personally I zone in on bullet points, since these are likely to yield a model, or succinct descriptions. I also like to go to areas that are involved with systems analysis, or technical areas where engineers have already come up with defined structures and systems.

The NLP Cookbook offers several techniques based on models created by people outside of NLP, for widely different applications. For example I delighted in discovering the work of Richard Bartle and his Gaming Stereotypes, or Thomas/Kilmann's Conflict model.

Newly Coded Model + Original Technique

The Inside Out Process

I'm putting this process into its own section because I believe that it is the most elegant way of weaving all the elements found within modelling into one streamlined process. The following account is an example of the intervention where Modelling meets Technique and vice versa. It is based on the following principles:

- Somatic Syntax allows the modeller to create a totally original description of internal processing within five to ten minutes, depending on the set up. Here the exemplar is doing most of the work, with the modeller just facilitating from a meta position if required.

- Models are digitised expressions of analogue process. Punctuation points in the analogue suggest a digital stage.

- The exemplar is the best person to test their model for congruence and full completion.

- The modeller can assist the exemplar with the labelling, operating from the CASE criteria earlier in this chapter.

- The modeller has the ability to transform a model back into an analogue experience, which is naturally and directly compatible with the exemplar's representations.

Background

I was absolutely thrilled when I devised this process, since for me it demonstrates how the whole modelling process can be refined and distilled into a 45-minute event, with next to no intervention from the modeller. It can be applied in any context and for a range of scenarios.

It came about during a training session demonstration of Gilligan's Push Pull I've mentioned in the section on Somatic Modelling. My demonstration subject was refining her combined movement of the two elements, and naturally seemed to divide the movement into four separate stages before she was satisfied that she had arrived at her integrated expression. At this stage, the Gilligan process would have stopped since the activated neurology was now 'programmed' sufficiently for new neural pathways to generate.

However what I saw was a natural digitised process within this analogue movement. I wanted to know how she might label each of these stages. A four-part model emerged which completely encapsulated the process of her desired change. We then created an acquisition process round these four labels – a spatial anchoring exercise, integrating some of her meta comments in with a mixture of linguistic frames. She experienced a profound shift within herself and need quite some time to re-emerge back into the room and to share her experiences with her fellow learners.

The Process

Fundamentally, somatic modelling can be used to represent any dynamic. You may like to check back to the section on Somatic Modelling and remind yourself of the different types of behaviour so that you know what you are looking for. Ideally the scenarios involve at least a minimum of two elements, but can incorporate three or four, but no more than seven.

1   **Identify scenario:** suitable scenarios for this application can be:
    - *Holding back/Taking forward:* this is the set up for the Gilligan Push Pull process, where you want something, or to do something, but you hold yourself back.
    - *Present situation/Desired situation:* this is a familiar pattern for NLP practitioners.
    - *Over strengths/Positive strengths/Under strengths:* this pattern can emerge from exploring 'I am too …', 'I am good at …', and 'I am not sufficiently …'
    - *Part A/Part B:* this can be The Angel and The Devil set up or any other incompatible internal relationship.
    - *Individuals or groups:* here the somatic syntax can represent the perceived relationship, and/or the desired relationship with specific individuals or bodies of people.

2   **Somatic expression:** once identified, the exemplar is required to generate a somatic expression for each element, and practise each until they are comfortable that they have encapsulated the essence of that element. When satisfied, the task is then to combine each of the elements into one flowing movement.

    It is important for the exemplar to know that it is likely that the exact nature of the original expressions will alter in the process and become integrated into one streamlined cohesive flow. To support this, the exemplar needs to be open to instinctive physical movements that emerge and to resist imposing a 'logical' description.

3   **Punctuation:** once the exemplar is completely satisfied with the composite movement, and the modeller is happy that there is full congruence, the exemplar is asked to divide the full movement into discrete blocks. When the accuracy of these blocks is tested and possibly refined, the exemplar is required to label them. The modeller needs to be aware that the punctuation doesn't conveniently fall back into the original components, and to be convinced that this new movement has an original makeup.

4   **Model construction:** now the modeller steps in and works with the exemplar and the labelling until the finished structure meets with all the conditions of well formedness (see earlier in this chapter). The labels need to be at the same logical level, yet be discrete and standalone. They

need to serve the same overarching logical type. They need to be linguistically identical – nouns with nouns, verbs with verbs.

5   **Acquisition:** the modeller pays particular attention to the comments the exemplar makes in the process regarding each of the stages and the words that are used. These can influence the type of acquisition process that is created. Use of metaphorical language can presuppose that metaphors should feature. Listening for temporal predicates could indicate a passage of time. Nominalisations may suggest introducing values and other neurological levels. Modal Operators would suggest Meta Model frames.

The modeller now takes the exemplar through an instant acquisition process, which meets all the design criteria.

By the end of this 45-minute process – provided the modeller has proficiency with model construction and acquisition design – the exemplar has now 'consumed' a second description of their desired outcome, on top of the somatic movement. Following the journey of analogue to digital and back to analogue, this powerful process provides a double description, conscious and intuitive representations, which have come solely from within the exemplar's model of the world. The level of ecology is exquisite and truly lives the presupposition that 'We have all the resources we need.'

This is putting your NLP tradecraft to the ultimate service.

Notes:

1   In the Appendix you will find a fully developed case study based on this approach, which will take you through the modelling and model construction process, and then onto the process of constructing three possible techniques right through to writing up instructions.

2   I have found that this approach works equally well working with Punctuation Modelling. Exemplars can very quickly identify the key punctuation symbols and what they represent, give them labels and frame them into a well-formed model.

Summary

The act of modelling is a powerful and efficient form of intervention as are the models and techniques that are created by it. Imagination, creativity, integrated understanding of NLP tradecraft, and a profound belief that the answers lie within the exemplar, all go towards fuelling this endeavour. Combined then with a determination and fascination to discover the structure waiting to be revealed, this amazing process comes alive for the benefit of all. If this was fully understood and adopted by the majority of NLP practitioners and specialists, I believe the influence and effectiveness of NLP would become commonly recognised and widely respected.

On the constructed model front, your model may emerge overnight, or take years to come to fruition. You may find as you explore further that just one model doesn't describe the territory, and you are compelled to reveal more. You may also discover that you have been holding your finished model just under the surface without knowing how long it's been there. And then there is the tinkering round the edges, not being satisfied until you achieve the final fit. However, you need to come out of your TOTE at some point. You have end users waiting for your discoveries. Derek Jackson came up with the comment: 'A model is an evolving approximation', which is so true. Sometimes I have wondered if this book would ever be finished!

I have only provided a tip of the iceberg in terms of modelling's potential. I know there are great numbers of inspirational and ingenious examples of good modelling practice out there, all serving to deliver desired results for the wide variety of end user. I would love to hear from you.

We are not great at promoting ourselves as a body, nor are we good at pooling our resources and refuelling our community. We are also slow in publicising our results and offering documented research. Much of this is because academia tends to legitimise quantitative research – where experimental groups are measured against the responses of norm groups – over the qualitative research approaches where individual case study evidence is gathered and conclusive patterned results are compiled. Quantitative research is naturally aligned to a constructivist way of thinking, since the 'answers' are coming only from the reality of the subjects involved.

And now

We have come to the end of the modelling story. But, for me at any rate, this book would not be complete without covering the Formal Acquisition Process as well. This is the response to the cry 'So what do I do with it now?'

The final part covers the incredibly simple process of creating wonderfully dynamic techniques that pack an exceptional punch. The modelled process I offer turns everyone of you into training developers and takes you to a level of thinking way beyond that of the average trainer.

Part 6
The Formal Acquisition Process

Introduction

I come from the position that the model forms the basis of a technique.

Having a good understanding of the different types of model available allows you to recognise a useable model wherever it is found – either self generated, created by another NLPer or found within another discipline.

At the beginning of Part 3 – The Methodologies of Modelling, *A Framework of Modelling and Formal Acquisition* is laid out, illustrating the separate activities or Modelling and Formal Acquisition. It doesn't always follow that the modeller will also be the one who designs the resulting technique. Some may say that is the domain of the professional trainer. However, I believe the modeller shouldn't be put off by such demarcation, since the process of constructing a technique is really simple – once the basic ingredients are understood.

The Formal Acquisition Process – to demarcate it from the informal acquisition of the model, by the modeller, during the modelling and model construction process – is fully independent of any modelling process. In fact, it can use models generated from any field of study and usefully turn them into a technique with recognisable NLP characteristics. All of this might suggest that there is no place for the formal acquisition process within a book whose clear purpose is to address modelling.

I've given this suggestion serious thought, and I have come to the conclusion that this process rightfully stays. If this book is to live up to its title, then formal acquisition needs to be included, because:

- Enabling acquisition by a third party is always held to be the fundamental and final part of the modelling process, by the majority of modelling authorities.

- I want to offer a fully integrated take on the field of NLP Modelling, with all aspects covered. Leaving out acquisition would require the reader to look elsewhere for this missing information.

- The process, designing a technique down to producing the final written instructions, involves the process of modelling in itself. I am providing yet another illustration of modelling and model construction at work.

- The formal acquisition process, as outlined here, answers the question modellers often have, once they have produced their model – 'Now what?'

I totally accept that many modellers may not feel the need to convert their models into a formalised technique. And some modelling methodologies, when used for therapy and coaching, don't have the requirement for digital models. Some may argue that technique design and construction is the domain of the trainer and should lie within a Training the Trainer's manual.

What you will find in this chapter is my particular take on technique construction, based on my own rationale. It comes from my thirty years as a trainer, a trainer of trainers, an NLP Master Trainer and a trainer of NLP Trainers. I totally accept that there will be other approaches that produce great results. For me, this approach brings together all the strands of NLP thinking in the most holistic way.

First of all we explore the role of techniques in the overall field of interventions, given that the application of techniques is often regarded as a primitive club by advanced practitioners. Then we delve into the detail of the technology found within a technique. You have the opportunity to explore the range of building blocks available to you, many of which are likely to be already known to you, but possibly not from this perspective. I hope you will enjoy experiencing them in a new light. And finally we go through what is involved in formalising your technique into an easy to follow set of instructions – often easier said than done.

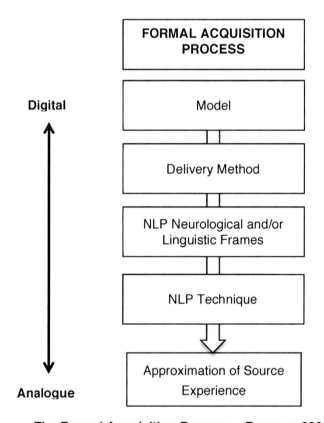

The Formal Acquisition Process – Burgess 2008

To my mind, there is no greater pleasure than to experience the fruits of your labours coming alive beneficially in another's neurology. What a gift to be able to give.

Technique Construction

When our budding modellers finally brandished their completed models, they were now ready to bring their model alive within a third party acquisition process or technique. I would casually say 'Now NLP-ise it' and be greeted with blank faces. What seemed a fairly natural process to me seemed to be double-dutch to Master Practitioners and fledgling NLP Trainers. So that set me off self-modelling once more to find out what it was that I knew and did that wasn't obvious to others. The model for technique construction emerged, after many disguises, and went on to form the basis of all the new techniques found within *The NLP Cookbook*.

Definition

A technique is a set process, constructed to deliver a predetermined outcome, whether at an individual level or with a group. It is expressed in a series of instructions, outlining predetermined stages in the process.

Model for Technique Construction

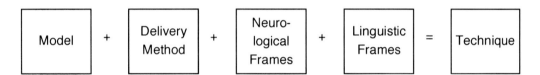

Model for Technique Construction – Burgess 2010

As I was explaining this model to others, the cooking metaphor emerged. I realised that most countries have their own recipes for chicken, and that set me thinking. How was it that this one basic component can be cooked in so many different ways – frying, grilling, baking, roasting, to accommodate availability of ingredients – vegetables, spices, herbs, sauces, and to cater for widely varying tastes? And we never seem to run out of chicken recipes!

Following the metaphor:

Chicken		The Model
Cooking Method		Delivery Method
Spices and Herbs	becomes	Neurological Frames
Vegetables		Linguistic Frames
Dish		Technique
Recipe		Written Instructions

Delivery Methods

Delivery methods are not just the domain of trainers to design training materials and exercises. The therapist and coach can really raise their game when they realise the options and distinctions they can introduce to their one-to-one work – in the moment as it is happening.

From my background as a trainer and with my NLP experience, I have identified a range of delivery methods which, when combined with neurological and linguistic frames, opens doors to a fantastic wealth of possibilities. You can never run out of new material. You will always satisfy the needs and preferences of your clients and end users, and you will be operating at the top of your game.

These delivery methods address the three major representation systems, Kinaesthetic, Visual and Auditory, plus the non-sensory Cognitive area. And then you are offered three or four different examples of each.

The Four Categories

There are the three major sensory areas of:

- *Kinaesthetic:* somatic expression, spatial anchors, hand anchors, sliding scales, and psycho-geography

- *Visual:* collages, painting/drawing, diagrams, videos

- *Auditory:* guided visualisations, sounds and rhythms, stories and anecdotes, reading and writing

And the non-sensory area of:

- *Cognitive:* questions, card sorts, and relational constructs.

This range of delivery methods is not definitive. However, they cover the territory found within NLP applications and beyond into training in general. You are offered a description of each, and a listing of the advantages and disadvantages each has to offer the designer. I wish this had been around when I first started out as a trainer!

However, before we consider these four categories in detail, it is worth taking time to consider what might be the selection criteria that will influence your choice of delivery method.

Selection Criteria

As the designer once you have your model you have the debate of how you want to 'cook' it. The treatment you choose will give the model its own distinct impact. Much of this will depend on your own mood. You may find yourself going through phases, favouring one particular approach over another. You may feel that a particular type of model is most suited to one particular treatment, to the exclusion of others. You may have blind spots, and be unaware of the effectiveness that another can offer. You may be looking for something that will particularly appeal to one person.

It can be too easy to stick with cognitive process of setting questions on a worksheet, which is known and keeps everyone within their safety zone, including perhaps yourself. Obviously cognitive processes can be exceedingly powerful – I stopped smoking in the midst of a Christina Hall series of questions for which I will be forever grateful!

Given that each model can be given multiple treatments, as the designer it is useful to be aware of the following range of criteria for selection.

1 **Safety:** if constructing a technique is a new experience for you, you may be inclined to play safe and stick with what you know, or this may be your default position. Much of NLP's methodology is offered through spatial anchors or frameworks of questions – and both methods gain great results. Handed down approaches don't necessarily imply best practice – they might suggest a lack of imagination on the part of your predecessors.

2 **Past experience:** there may be some delivery methods that you respond to more than others – possibly connected to your own preferred representation system, the person or issue you were working with, or the impact it had. The techniques that used them will possibly have more powerful memories for you than others that you encountered. This may well colour your judgment and cause you to delete the valuable engineering within others.

3 **Stuck in a rut:** most of us have continued working with the techniques as they were demonstrated. We may not have considered that there might be another way. We may feel we don't have permission. We may have wanted to but didn't know what the options were. 'Better going with what you know.'

4 **End user:** you may have a group of people who would be really resistant, say, to a somatic exercise, or be unresponsive to a guided visualisation. Or you may have an exemplar that distrusts 'mumbo jumbo' and will only respond to a cognitive process. That doesn't mean you have to ditch the model; it just means you have to select an alternative delivery method. You would need to pace those participants who are unused to personal exploration or self-reflection, and offer them something relatively safe and cognitive. Conversely, you may also opt for this approach if you wanted to rein in the more full-flowing, hyper-imaginative participant!

5 **Outcome:** what do you want to achieve? How deep an experience do you want to generate? What has gone before it? What are you planning to use to follow it, so that your overall objectives are being met? Is this a process for a trainer, coach, or therapist? Some processes may not lend themselves to one-to-one work, if disclosure by both parties is required, for example. You might just want a light sprinkling of awareness, or this exercise might be the major piece of work that is pivotal for your exemplar or group of learners. For example, a spatial anchor process is likely to generate more insightful awareness than a cognitive one.

6 **Representation systems:** personally, you may be strongly kinaesthetic and tactile and really get excited with a process involving spatial anchors. You may dismiss storytelling as a waste of time. You can't assume that your preferred delivery method is going to meet the needs of the entire group. Within any group of people there will be a spread of preferences, either for visual, auditory or kinaesthetic stimulation, and you would be wise to feed all three, if not in equal measure, certainly giving each an appearance. As a therapist, you need to pace the disposition of your exemplar. It might be a real stretch if you find him or her strongly auditory and you're not!

7 **Time:** different exercises take longer than others, both in their introduction, possible demonstration and execution. Guard against indulgence just because a particular approach is a favourite of yours. In a training context, the more complex the instructions, the longer it will take for a group of learners to start. And it may require a debriefing at the end, which has to be factored in. You may find that you are running out of time, so a pairs exercise may become a group process, a floor exercise a guided visualisation, or a card sort turns into an anecdote.

8 **Skill level:** the skill level of your acquirers, or their guides may determine your decision regarding method. If you suspect that your technique could generate a strong emotional response within the explorer, then you would want to make sure that it is in the hands of someone sufficiently skilled to handle such a situation. You may have to find a simpler route to deliver your outcomes.

9 **Own competence:** if you are also the trainer or deliverer, you want to consider your own skill level. You might find one approach too risky – group trances may scare the life out of you, or the thought of introducing a floor exercise to a group of company directors too intimidating. Or you may have insufficient experience or knowledge of one particular approach or ingredient. If you choose to pursue it, then that's great since you may surprise yourself, realise that it was much easier than you thought and that you were more skilled than you gave yourself credit for. If it doesn't work, then you will have offered yourself some tremendous learning.

To help you further in your selection process, and to deepen your understanding of what you can get from each of the delivery methods, the next section takes you through all four categories, with a short description and some useful pros and cons to help you fine tune your selection. Some of these will be fully familiar to you, some you may not have considered this way before, and who knows, you may discover some delightful and intriguing surprises. Whatever your response, you will gain a real sense of the range of possibilities presenting themselves. Never again will it be said that chicken is boring!

Kinaesthetic Delivery Methods

The majority of NLP techniques operate within kinaesthetic delivery methods, working on the principle that the body holds our neurology and has direct contact with our mind and our verbal/non verbal expression. Kinaesthetic techniques can have a strong effect on the explorer, directly accessing inner experience. Within the technique's process, the explorer can display obvious external evidence to indicate that something is going on in the inside, and this information can then be explored and developed.

Whilst the Kinaesthetic system dominates, within the experience, the explorer will be drawing vividly on internal images and sounds, creating a living metaphor in the process. This combination of senses is why the process is so effective. Care needs to be given to ensure that the emotions and memories evoked are addressed and the explorer resourced once more. It possible cases of extreme response, it might be that you suggest referring the explorer to a therapist.

1   **Somatic expression:** Judith Delozier has pioneered the use of the body as a way of conveying knowledge and revealing information directly from the unconscious mind. Information can be coded in the smallest gesture or shift in posture, as well as whole body shapes and movement. So you need to have your eyes peeled and be prepared to make significant the smallest of signs.

Internal information can be forthcoming if you work with just one single movement or a series of gestures, or if you string them all together to form their unique 'dance'.

Advantages

- It is a real energizer, and wakes people up if just because it is unusual.
- It can generate some surprising information and act as a real convincer about mind/body wisdom.
- It can be fun!

Disadvantages

- Because it is unfamiliar, explorers may be shy and self-conscious.
- If there is any incongruence in the trainer/therapist, then the process is unlikely to be successful.
- Highly cognitive explorers might find such an approach frivolous and lacking rigour.

2   **Spatial anchors:** this approach is the hallmark of NLP practices, where spaces on the floor are marked out and labelled. These labels may be an attribute, or time zone, or specific experience, or a certain person. Once that space has been set up in this way, it continues to transmit its knowledge, even from a distance. The process is quite remarkable, and I, for one, don't have a 'proper' explanation for it. How does a piece of carpet suddenly become such a rich hallucinated world, capable of evoking powerful emotions? And so quickly?

My sense is that by buying into the possibility that this might be true, the conscious mind has loosened its grip on 'reality', opening the door to the show of the unconscious mind. Whatever the reason, it is amazing stuff.

If you are going for this approach, then do include a floor plan in your instructions, so that both the guide and explorer can see as well as read your intentions. This way you can also prescribe the relationship and distance between the elements.

Advantages

- As a full body experience, it is working with the complete neurology of the explorer. This way the explorer has the greatest access to all that is going on, on the inside.
- It has the potential to evoke awareness and information not accessible through straight forward questioning.
- It is an excellent way of lubricating the explorer's access to his or her unconscious mind, opening up his or her channels of connection and increasing receptivity.

- Sustained exposure to this approach can increase access to intuition.

- This approach is truly versatile. Spatial anchors can be valuably combined both with all the neurological components and activated using many of the linguistic frames.

Disadvantages

- It can require space that you may not have. One option is to work on a tabletop and let the explorer's fingers do the walking.

- Some may be reluctant to lend themselves to such a self-conscious approach, so strong rapport and pacing would be needed. Or you may need a demonstration to provide a strong convincer.

- Some may just be unsure of the approach if this is his or her first exposure to it. It is useful to pace this uncertainty before you drag them onto their feet.

3   **Hand anchors:** I delight in this approach. It is so simple yet incredibly responsive. You are likely to have first come across it with the conflict resolution technique Visual Squash, where conflicting parts are allocated a hand each, and subsequently integrated by bringing both hands together.

This approach is widely promoted by Ernest Rossi whose change-work practices are based on the principle that the hands have by far the largest neural representation in the brain's cortex. If you want to know more, Google *Homunculus* and see what you get. Rossi's approach is also one of the quickest trance inductions that I know.

The principle is to use your hands to allocate a pair of conditions. It could be two parts, two decisions, two values, two beliefs, two states, a before and after – two of anything in fact. Allocate a function to each hand. The hands are then placed facing each other about seven to nine inches apart at about eye level, with the intention for both hands to ultimately come to rest together. The explorer puts all attention to the point between the hands. After a short while one hand or both begin to move spontaneously and this movement continues until the process is complete.

Advantages

- A certainty for any 2-element models.
- It can generate some extraordinary responses and insights.
- This approach, if successful, can provide a tremendous convincer to the explorer that he or she has a very active unconscious mind which is alert and ready to support and direct discovery.
- The first time anyone discovers the life force that comes through the spontaneous (ideomotor) movements of the unconscious mind, can be a memorable surprise!
- Since the explorer can determine how he or she is going to load their hands, the approach is a highly flexible, respectful, and places choice literally into the hands of the explorer.

Disadvantages

- You are restricted to selecting two elements at a time. If you have more, then you can pick and mix them to your advantage.
- Again some explorers might view the idea with suspicion, and force the pace consciously, not trusting that movement will flow unbidden. They may not be able to let go their conscious need to be in control, and so not give themselves up to the gentle forces directed by their

unconscious mind.

- Because it is non-verbal, some cerebral beings may distrust its efficacy.
- You don't know how long the process might take, as some people may go much deeper into a trance than others. For this reason, using this approach as a group process could mean you are left waiting for one person to complete.

4   **Sliding-scales:** I developed this approach within a therapy session with a client – one of these fertile moments of synergy. However, I'm sure that I'm not the first to have discovered it. It really works for me since the metaphors of mixing desks and dimmer switches are familiar to most people. It operates on the basis that most people are able to register the internal effects of *more of*, and *less of,* and the comparative awareness of *better* or *worse*. Increase or decrease the intensity and the outcome improves – or it doesn't. In the process, the range of flexibility can be identified. When working with three or more elements within a model, this process offers immediate information about the relationship between the respective patterns.

You can allocate sliding scales to each of the model's elements, if they are attributes or values, either as a numerical scale, or you can define their polarities. For example, you can determine the place of Vulnerability on the numerical scale. Additionally you may choose to label both ends of the scale with the defined polarities, for example Totally Exposed and Over Protected.

Sliding-scales is an excellent tool for self-modelling, combined with an immediate intervention tool. By placing, intuitively, the elements on their appropriate each of the scales, the present profile or structure is determined. And then by moving their location up or down the scale, increasing or decreasing the intensity, the explorer feels the effects and can determine independently the preferred optimum levels. This is an instantaneous process and gives great autonomy to the explorer.

What I also like about it is technical effect – it provides a somatic form of submodality change, which you don't often get within NLP processes. And it provides instant calibration.

Advantages

- It is very simple to do, highly accessible and provides immediate kinaesthetic feedback.
- Gives the explorer direct control over his or her inner experience without any outside interruption or intervention.
- You can demonstrate and expand the zone of flexibility, by extending the variables.
- It is quick and easy to explain.
- It is a great tool for self-modelling and establishing fluctuating profiles.

Disadvantages

- It only applies to simultaneous models.

5   **Psycho-geography:** psycho-geography involves the relational field that is built up in the presence of different energies, be they from people or from objects. It is similar to the repelling or attracting of like and opposite magnets. And as these energies are mostly unseen, they can go undetected unless the equivalent of iron filings is scattered into the system.

In this instance, the 'iron filings' can be literally people, fellow learners, who take on roles, or objects. Alternatively, you can have the explorer acting as each of the components, moving from one to the other. I often use bits of paper, or paper cups to represent the people or objects within the system. It is amazing just how quickly the explorer identifies with the objects and instinctively understands their relationship with each other.

By moving these around, into different configurations, knowledge can emerge out of the system, that wasn't previously available.

Advantages

*   A dynamic way to plot a system, and directly involves the explorer in a physical manner.
*   Within a physical three-dimensional system, movement is easy to effect and consequences detected.
*   It deliberately takes the explorer to different perspectives in time and space.
*   It is an unscripted process that will take on its own life, and so be totally explorer focussed.
*   It allows for flexibility in approach.
*   It works well where space is limited.
*   And they can take their cups home with them!

Disadvantages

*   A visually represented system relies more heavily on the imagination and receptivity of the explorer.

Visual Delivery Methods

We are surrounded by visual imagery, God given and man made. From cave dwellers' artwork to the great Italian painters, images have been used to describe the world around us, and offer comment through the content they contain. All TV, printed and billboard advertising talks to us through the implicit messages the images and symbols represent. Yet there is a prevailing belief amongst many that visual expression is only for the artistic few – unless you are a child that is.

Working with images draws on the intuition and innovation of our creative mind, which has a more direct contact with our unconscious mind. The principles of art therapy are based on the beliefs that there is inherent healing power within the creative process of art making, and that art is a means of symbolic communication.

Using images to evoke the message within a model can touch infrequently visited corners of our imagination. The huge benefit is that we can have a readily available and lasting representation of our exploration, so that the significance can continue to pulse its meaning.

1   **Collage:** a collage or montage is the process of gathering images and objects and presenting them collectively, either fixing them onto a surface or presenting them in a display.

It can be a highly creative approach to representing a model and its elements. Explorers are invited to gather items that for them represent the elements of the model. Traditionally, these can be images from magazines, snippets of words, photographs, postcards, or they can be textured paper or fabric, or physical sand, wool or twigs. Taken individually and together, the combination describes the essence of the model.

Alternatively, the explorer can be invited to gather physical objects – stones, clothing, books, food, instruments – which taken together also evoke the message within the model. Tracy Emin's *My Bed* (1998) and her *Tent* aka *Everyone I Have Ever Slept With 1963–1995* (1995), are perfect illustrations of this.

Advantages

- This is physical activity, involving eye and hand, which in its own way generates energy.
- It can become play, and wonderfully messy.
- It doesn't rely on any artistic merit or skill, so is free of self-imposed judgment.
- The explorer's internal interpretation becomes externally visible and possibly permanent.
- It appeals to those who delight in visual expression.
- It can be a sociable process if working in small groups.

Disadvantages

- It requires providing materials to work with. Asking participants to bring materials with them can overcome logistical problems.
- It can become messy.

2 **Painting/drawing:** inviting explorers to draw their internal experience can provide them with surprising information – not just through what they draw, but how they draw it. I am constantly fascinated to watch learners draw what they saw in a guided visualisation, and see them select particular colours, pay particular attention to specific areas, expand the details and widen the picture. After the inevitable disclaimer of 'I can't draw', it is wonderful to see them lose themselves into their creation, with the absorption worthy of any child. What is produced has profound meaning for its creator.

Present the model and invite them to provide an image for each of the elements. If it is a sequential or hierarchical model they select the elements in order. For simultaneous models they can choose the order. Then, possibly on a second sheet of paper, they now draw a representation of what all these combine to become. What is produced is a totally meaningful anchor for their experience, and one that can trigger the experience each time they see it.

Advantages

- It is an antidote to left-brain thinking and allows unconscious imagery to flow.
- It can reveal some surprising connections and meanings.
- It confounds beliefs about not being able to draw, and illustrates the power of symbolism.
- It can be fun and enjoyable.

Disadvantages

- It might be regarded as frivolous.

3 **Diagrams:** introducing a diagram into a process usually comes at the end, when all the information has emerged and is ready to be plotted. A diagram is a visual encapsulation of a system, illustrating the size and location of the elements, their inter-relationships, and strength of connection – or lack of – between each.

From a diagram you can clearly depict the centres of activity, the contributing factors and the pathway towards resolution. This two-dimensional, freeze-frame world reduces a vibrant experience into manageable summary.

Again the diagram doesn't have to be based on absolute logic. Nor does it have to be an accurate representation. It merely needs to reflect the natural logic of the explorer. Sometimes in the plotting, new awareness emerges, as the significance of some elements grow, or diminish.

The model can be offered, combined with some meta model questions: 'What could this mean?' 'What could this lead to?' 'What might others say?' 'What could be the evidence?' and a diagram can be woven between the elements and the projected beliefs surrounding the elements. An interesting map emerges of a future outcome.

Advantages

- The process provides a practical activity, which can activate both logical and creative thinking to achieve a level of integration.
- This is a means of externalising the internalised processing and summarising events. It can provide a form of tangible evidence for the explorer of his or her experience.
- It can highlight recursive patterns and strategies, as well as points of leverage and blockage.

Disadvantages

- The diagram may not contain all the systemic elements.
- It cannot easily represent a three-dimensional system.

4 **Videos:** YouTube rules! Today we have access to a seemingly endless selection of videos to illustrate our purposes. If you know the outcome you are pursuing or an angle that you want to take, you can turn an average viewing experience into something meaningful. You can select humorous extracts to emphasise your point or the elements within your model. You can choose videoed interviews with their own anecdotes.

You can of course make videos of your own. I actually sat in a lecture, where the lecturer made a video of himself lecturing and then sat with us as it played! I'm not recommending this. But again the technology is there for you to create your own visual story.

Advantages

- There is a vast selection of material to choose from.
- It activates creative inner processing.
- The process takes focus of attention to somewhere different.

Disadvantages

- The approach requires technology, which may not be your forte.

Auditory Delivery Methods

Entering our internal system through our ears can be profoundly effective. Radio plays, audiocassettes and CDs bear witness to this. Audio allows us to create our own internal worlds, placing our attention at will, without restriction or external rules. As with reading, the characters we imagine rarely show any similarities with their real counterparts.

We have permission to take ourselves wherever we choose, in whatever way we choose. We can make connections that are ours alone. We can make quantum leaps to seemingly disconnected areas effortlessly and naturally, following a seamless logic.

Using an auditory delivery method as a vehicle for conveying a model can test your creativity and challenge your language skills. It can bring you appreciation of the lyricism of words, the song of their phrases, and the dance of their rhythms.

1   **Guided Visualisations:** Guided Visualisations are common in many fields of development, and can't be claimed as belonging to NLP specifically. They have long been used in traditional hypnosis as a therapeutic intervention. However, they become the special domain of NLP when they hold a model at their heart. The model determines the script, the dynamic between the elements, and the potential outcome or processes experienced. This way, they can become an even more powerful tool to enable others to reach their awaiting insight.

Guided Visualisations take the explorer directly into a world of imagery. The words may activate a series of pictures or create dynamic three-dimensional sequences in full colour. The explorer may additionally experience sensations of temperature, fatigue or high energy, and emotions of sadness, wonder or amusement.

If the explorer stays merely listening to the words, without going inside, then this could be due to the delivery of the piece, the way it is constructed and written, or because there is insufficient rapport between the explorer and the guide, or the explorer and the piece. Going into trance requires the trust.

Whilst you, the writer, have the model as the basis of your structure and you predetermine where you want your explorers to go, you can't be certain that your explorer will go exactly where you want. Your words may set him or her off on a unique trail of discovery of even greater relevance – to them!

Advantages

- This process gives the explorer experience freely, without constraint.
- It enables the explorer to access corners of information that may have been long forgotten or unknown.
- It opens the explorer's system to the power of metaphor and symbol which carries its own language and meaning.
- It is a pleasurable experience and a great way to relax the group or individuals.
- It can act as a summary of events and forms an excellent closure to the day.
- The details can be customised to the group You can be spontaneous and create something on the spot to address particular issues that have arisen.

Disadvantages

- The process relies on the skill of the writer and the facilitator in the delivery of the words. It also relies on the skill and confidence of the facilitator to manage the process, being sensitive and responsive to visual cues.
- Some explorers may be less receptive than others and feel disadvantaged.
- Some explorers have very poor access to their visual system, and distrust their ability to visualise, especially if the person next door is having raving Steven Sondheim experiences. This seeming 'inadequacy' may lead them to believe that this sort of learning is not for them.

2 **Sounds/rhythms:** ideas and feelings can be translated into sound as any composer can tell you. Everyone can tell the difference between a sad and a happy sound, where sound is being used as a metaphor.

We can map the structure of sound over the elements of any model. The sound could be in the form of mimicry of the actual word, or if the word is an object – for example a bear, or a warrior – the sound may attempt to replicate the sound this object would make. Or the sound may represent the emotion the word evokes. Playing them together, and we can compose that model's music and perform its latent song.

We have such a wide range of variables to choose from – the nature of the sound itself, volume, tone, beat and all the other facets of a sound; and its method of delivery – voice, musical instrument, percussion objects. We can deliver the sounds standing still, or add them to the somatic syntax of movement and create an accompanying dance.

Auditory is the least preferred representation system, with only a minority feeling familiar and comfortable with the language of sound. Working with an underused channel of expression can make the explorer's experience much clearer and unedited.

Advantages

- No equipment, materials or space is required – just the voice! Instruments can be created out of any everyday objects that can produce a sound.
- This is a very primitive form of expression, and can bring the explorer with a very deep connection with his or her inner structure.
- An uplifting relational field can be created within a group, where everyone is performing their own expression of the model.

Disadvantages

- Explorers may feel inhibited, embarrassed, or unfamiliar with this form of expression.
- Explorers may not give their full, unfettered commitment to the process.

3 **Anecdotes/stories:** we are descended from an aural tradition that predates access to the written word. We have a natural desire to listen to a story, going back to our childhood days of fairy tales and mythology. Just say the magic words 'Once upon a time …' and we become transported.

Milton Erickson used stories as one of his major forms of intervention, matching the elements within the story with the problem and solution space of the explorer. He would draw on situations happening locally or nationally, descriptions of naturally occurring phenomena, or tales from his own life. Or he would make the story up completely, and present it as real, if it suited his purposes!

You can wrap your model up in a story, following its sequence or enveloping it in its co-existing elements. You can make it literal, or you can convert the elements into metaphors or archetypes (see neurological frames in the next section).

Advantages

- Stories are great for catching attention and setting the scene.
- Stories can be used to set filters, offer explanation or resolve confusion.
- You can make something up on the spot, or modify a tale, to reflect events happening in the moment.
- You can use a story to quieten energy, or to energise. The story can directly target an emotion, or activate thinking.
- You can provide the long or short version, depending on the time available.

Disadvantages

- The storyteller may not be adept, and end up being boring, or worse, embarrassing.
- There is a danger of the storyteller becoming self-indulgent, taking up time that could be better used doing something else.
- The story may not be relevant or current with the audience, even though it is one of your favourites.

4 **Readings/writings:** readings can take the form of stories and poems, in full or through selections and quotations. As with anecdotes and stories, readings can reflect the message of the model, and offer the dynamics within it through the writing.

As the designer of the experience, you may be the one to collate the material yourself to illustrate some or all of the elements within the model, or to illustrate the effects of the model's dynamics. Conversely as a task, you may require the explorer to find the stories, which will demonstrate his or her own interpretation of what the model offers.

Again you are well served if you deliberately set out to collect writings that are relevant to your message. There are increasing numbers of popular books that are compendiums of uplifting stories. You may find that, in your own reading, you have an ear or eye primed to notice if a particular section would illustrate your point perfectly.

You want to rehearse the material, reading it out loud, so that you understand the intentions of the piece, where the emphasis needs to be, where the pauses most powerfully lie. This is particularly true when reading poetry. You also want to know how much time it takes up.

You need to make sure that you acknowledge your source and don't reproduce the materials in written form without permission.

Advantages

- The authors are likely to be more skilful than you, so you can borrow from their lyricism.
- Having source materials demonstrates your thoroughness and earns you brownie points.

- Readings change the tone and energy and direct it as desired.

Disadvantages

- If you cannot 'act' the words, then the reading can descend into a meaningless monologue. You can overcome this by practising in advance, and recording it and rehearing yourself. You have to believe the words and commit to the message.

- Your attention is more likely to be on the written word, so you run the risk of losing contact with your audience.

Cognitive Delivery Methods

Cognitive learning uses the logic and reasoning of language to process information. In Western culture, where logical thinking rules, we lay great value on our ability to apply rational thought – often mistakenly being interpreted as evidence of intelligence.

For any information to have meaning, it still has to be processed through our neurology, and interpreted somatically in our internal sounds, images and feelings. We cannot make sense of a sign until we internally represent what the sign is saying – which is why visiting a foreign country, especially where the language is expressed in an unrecognisable alphabet, can be stimulating or stressful, depending on your temperament.

NLP is known for connecting this inner processing through the precise use of words. A cognitive approach can activate what we think about the subject. It can also activate *how* we think about it, which may prove to be the more useful layer of information. At both levels we are given the opportunity to discover our patterns and habitual responses.

1   **Framework of questions/statements:** asking and answering questions is so familiar and basic to all of us. It is our primary way of gathering and giving information, and it forms the dominant approach to all development activities, either in a group or individually. It relies on the questioner being able to form the question succinctly, and on the explorer having the ability to interpret the intention of the question and have a familiarity with language to express the answer.

As the designer of a cognitive exercise, knowing how to word your question is crucial to the flow, the scope and the effectiveness of the process. If in doubt, borrow from the thoroughly developed technology of the linguistic frameworks in the NLP Ingredients. You will find many questioning templates that you can take wholesale, or use selectively. You need to be aware that these questions may be part of a progressive sequence, and taken out of context may not deliver the required punch.

You also will want to consider if you want the answers to be recorded or not. Some might like to have their experience there to refer back to. Others may not want the process slowed down by the writing of it. Your decision will determine the layout you ultimately choose.

The nature of questions is covered extensively in Part 4 – The Skills of Modelling, and there are some fantastic exercises in *The Bumper Bundle Companion Workbook* to test your understanding.

Advantages

- You have control over the engineering and therefore the direction the process takes.

- You can cover a lot of ground within your framework, to meet your outcomes.

- Your explorers are familiar with the set up.

- Cognitive explorers relish this approach. It can keep them within the bounds of safety, without exposing them to too much disclosure.

- You don't require much by way of explanation or demonstration.

- Provided the participants refrain from discussing and debating merits of the answers, this can be an efficient use of time.

- You don't need additional space.

- You can use the approach easily over the phone, or by email.

- You can opt for a content free approach, where the explorer completes the internal journey without having to package his or her experience into words for the external guide. Apart from saving time, this cuts down guide 'interference'.

Disadvantages

- The effectiveness of the process is totally down to the relationship between questioner and explorer. The process could descend into an interrogation, or a robotic reading of the page.

- The questioner's attention can be held by the piece of paper and not on the effects of the question on the explorer. Often a questioner is onto the next question before the explorer has completely answered the previous one.

- An explorer may be ready for volumes of disclosure, which the questioner just can't handle.

- Familiarity with answering questions can be its downfall, since the explorer may be in danger of providing pat answers, without going into much deeper processing. Much depends on the skill of the questioner and the structure of the questions.

- If the process requires answers to be given, demands are made on the explorer to find the words, package them in a way that will be acceptable, and not invite comment, and run the risk of being judged or becoming vulnerable. Taking a content free approach here, where the explorer doesn't speak out loud, overcomes this problem.

- The process can become boring, overworked and overused.

- It relies on the delivery skills of the questioner.

2 **Card sorts:** card sorts are fundamentally a range of cards which can be grouped into predetermined piles, under provided headings or into self selecting groupings of the explorer's own choosing. The content can be anything you choose – statements, objects, states, characteristics, questions – anything that directs the explorer's attention towards your outcomes. They can be prepared, or headings written in the moment.

You may decide to use this approach deliberately to activate movement and raise energy.

Card sorts are so flexible. They activate process outcomes as well as product results. How the person sorts the cards can be significant. How the pairs or groups interact in the process can be the learning. Or how the decisions are come by might be the significant piece. The whole experience can generate rich pickings.

You will need a minimum of 12 ingredients to make it meaningful and stretch the options available. Guard against overloading the number of cards involved, since the complexity will put people off. Only the most tenacious will still be there wanting to make sense of it – with full permission from weary colleagues!

As the designer, include some blanks. These can be used to replace missing cards or for encouraging explorers to make up their own. If you are the facilitator, then you're well advised to check that each set is complete. Come with sufficient numbers of packs to accommodate groups of no more than four. Any more and you will have people opting out.

Advantages

- Card sorts involve physical movement, providing something tangible to do with the hands. Often cards are spread out on the floor that gets people out of their chairs.
- You divert attention away from the others and onto the cards.
- You can set up social sub groupings.
- You can reveal the explorer's thinking processes and highlight patterns of thinking.
- If working in pairs or threes, you can build relationship – or test it as differences are revealed.

Disadvantages

- You have to prepare them in advance. This can be time consuming unless you are buying them ready made.
- Participants may not be ready to work with differences.
- You require available flat surfaces to work on.

3   **Relational constructs:** these are delightful linguistic dances that serve to scramble the conscious mind and allow the unconscious mind full rein. Basically they involve the interplay of two, maybe three components, which are mapped against each other. This allows for subtleties of information to emerge.

As you can imagine, along with the Hand Anchors, this delivery method lends itself particularly to two-element models. However, just as usefully, you can opt to play with any two elements within a multi-patterned model and so interweave greater and greater distinctions from within the system. It certainly can expand awareness and take it to some very interesting places, as well as being fun and intriguing.

You have different types to choose from:
- *Polarities:* where you choose direct opposites – safe/unsafe, certain/uncertain
- *Cartesian Coordinates:* where two elements are combined in four different ways – Eric Bern's OK Corral is a famous example of this: I'm OK/You're OK, I'm OK/You're Not OK, I'm not OK/You're Not OK, I'm Not OK/You're OK
- *Confusion Technique:* where you take two states and mix them up – tenderly fierce and fiercely tender.

You can gain a tremendous amount of mileage out of this form of language use, since all models of two elements and above can be given this treatment. It can be fascinating to discover the distinctions that emerge which allow explorers to realise the shades of grey between their self-imposed black and white, and to discover that the space is wider than they thought it was.

Whilst this approach works excellently on paper, it can come to life when combined with a spatial anchor process. You can also successfully incorporate these language patterns in guided visualisations and trance inductions.

Advantages

- This approach is readily available and simple to construct.
- It is easy for explorers to work with.
- In some instances the combinations may start off seeming to be illogical, in which case the explorer can quickly bypass the logic of the conscious mind and get to where some useful information lies.

Disadvantages

- For the particularly picky explorer, its simplicity might offend.
- Other than that I can't think of any disadvantages. I like this one.

The Neurological Frames

We have now reached the point where we can begin to fine-tune the recipe. We know the different ways of cooking it. We now are ready to decide the particular treatment to give it.

Neurological Frames give your recipe its zing and unique experience. Selecting these well and you will create a memorable experience. The Linguistic Frames, which follow provide the textures and colour.

List of Neurological Frames

The following are the Neurological Frames found within the spread of the basic techniques appearing in a *full* NLP Practitioner programme:

- VAKOG Representation Systems
- Submodalities
- Time – Past, Present, Future
- Perspectives – First, Second, Third and Meta Position
- Space/Dissociation
- Metaphor
- Mentors
- Parts/Archetypes.

It is important that you get inside the dynamics of each of these as they activate our neurology and provoke the profound responses we get. In my mind, these are the frames that set NLP apart from any other form of intervention.

By including any of the neurological frames, you will take your explorer to a different place, perception and experience. Having an understanding of the effects of each, allows you the option of amping up the model, expanding on, deviating from, or curtailing it.

If you are operating with a client, as opposed to designing a technique, an integrated knowledge of these frames allows you to respond specifically to what is happening in front of you, as opposed to what is supposed to happen from the page. Picking up on a 'chance' comment may lead you to developing the submodality element further, or take you off somewhere in time via a dissociated route.

When a Neurological Frame is not a Model

You may remember that one of the characteristics of Natural Models is that they can lend themselves to embellishing other models. In other words, you can take the natural model of Senses as expressed in submodalities and apply its dynamics to elements of another model to enliven it. Given this fact, it is important to differentiate when the structure is being used as a model on which the technique is based, and when it is being used as a neurological frame to activate a model.

For example, Meta Mirror is based on multiple perspectives. This is its model. If you then add a step that involves dissociation, perhaps because the explorer may be unhappy about becoming fully associated into the second position, then you have operated this multiple perspectives as a neurological frame.

In the same way, parts would not be a neurological frame within Six Step Reframe, since parts form the basic model of the technique in the first place. Since nothing is added neurologically to this simple technique, it is deemed to be free of any added neurological frames.

Coming up ...

On the following pages, you are given a range of points to consider for each of neurological frame, as well as reminding you of their occurrence within the basic techniques to reactivate your own reference experiences. Then I offer you, hopefully, an inspiring creative list of ways of applying them, possibly beyond your current experience.

This breakdown, in and of itself, is a great summary of our technology and a fabulous reference resource – in my humble opinion!

VAKOG Representation Systems

Perception is all there is. Nothing exists for us, unless we can perceive it – externally or through internal remembered or constructed representations.

The representation systems are the DNA of NLP. All experience is described through our VAK representation systems.

State is described fundamentally in sensory specific language, involving VAKOG both externally and internally.

Our state is determined on which aspect of VAK we are paying attention to: externally to sounds images, or physical conditions; or internally to images, sounds, or physical sensations.

Whilst we may use the same label for a state or emotion, each of us will configure our internal experience differently and uniquely.

Our VAK configuration can be altered to produce a different state.

Techniques based on VAK are the most basic to be found. Often VAK focus is incorporated into a larger more involved process.

VAK informs the higher-level frames of eye accessing cues, submodalities and sensory predicates.

Internal and External VAK forms the basis of any inventory, and strategy, and is required to access a fully associated current or a reference experience.

The VAK profile, where internal and external attention is identified, defines and describes the state.

Actively shifting focus of attention between Internal and External VAK is a direct and effective means of resourcing an explorer.

Techniques Involving VAK:

- *Change Personal History* – working with useful and unuseful states
- *Circle of Excellence* – development of inventory
- *Neurological Level Alignment* – inventory in Environment
- *New Behaviour Generator* – use of projected screen and each eye accessing location
- *Visual Squash* – description of each part.

Applications

- A sensory specific inventory, at any stage on the timeline, or perspective, ensures full association. This level of detail is often bypassed which reduces the impact of the experience.

- Asking for a VAK inventory can provide a starting and finishing point for calibration.

- Similarly by asking for sensory specific evidence of a desired outcome will give you the EXIT point of your TOTE.

- By specifically asking 'What do you/others see, hear, feel?' you are asking the explorer to access all his or her representation systems, not just the one they favour. It could be that this produces the difference that makes the difference.

Submodalities

Submodalities are the building blocks of experience, developed by Richard Bandler. They provide the language and notation of experience.

Submodalities give the explorer the chance to crystallise how he or she is constructing inner reality, often with the option to reconfigure this structure.

Submodalities can be used to describe an internal state, a scenario, a relationship, a physical sensation, or an emotion.

Submodalities can also act as a marker to calibrate that change has taken place, by conducting an inventory before and after.

When viewing a particular scenario that took place in our past, our submodality construction of this event can alter depending at which point on our timeline we are viewing it. A bad experience when we were eight years old at school may have one configuration when we view it as if we are sixteen, which differs significantly when we look at the same event at 30 on our timeline. We then have a choice from within our own system of the configuration that serves us best.

Submodalities can be used to describe relationships, through the differences in construction between the individuals. When plotted through time, shifts in the relationship and wellbeing of the individuals can be detected.

It is important to retain an ecological use of submodalities. To make someone smaller just to make the explorer feel more powerful is perpetuating the problem. Enabling the explorer to feel comfortable when both are life size is far more useful.

Techniques incorporating Submodalities:

- *Circle of Excellence* – development of the state
- *Neurological Level Alignment* – expansion of the Spirituality resource
- *Neurological Level Alignment* – calibration tool on return to Environment
- *Phobia 'Cure'* – through the different locations, plus changing colour and movement
- *Timeline Alignment* – constructing a supportive representation of Present, Future and Past.

Applications

- Using submodalities within an exercise gives the explorer the chance to crystallise how he or she is responding internally, with the option then to reconfigure the structure. You can use them to describe an internal state, an experience, or a relationship.

- Discovering the submodality structure is a great information-gathering tool, since it can serve to explain an emotional response – something small in black and white, for example, could explain a sense of unimportance.

- You can compare one submodality profile against another, for a good and a bad experience, or actions in different contexts, or different relationships. By establishing these contrasts then you can modify one to match the more desirable other.

- Submodalities can also act as a marker to indicate that change has taken place, by conducting an inventory before and after. In most of the exercises I have used the scale method of evaluation as the means of calibrating the change. This is merely tapping in to the unseen submodality structure.

- Enabling your explorer to identify and then discover the optimum arrangement of submodalities is a great coaching aid – widening the fairway, the goal posts, the pocket will make a huge difference for the golfer, the footballer and the snooker player.

Time – Past, Present and Future

Our internal relationship with time can show up in our language: 'Always harping back to the past' 'She's ahead of herself' 'The future beckons' 'Put it all behind me' 'Stuck in the here and now'.

Everybody's timeline is a construction unique to them. Whilst there are some suggested generalisations, there is no right or wrong way to construct it. The more useful filter is how supportive it feels, and whether or not it delivers you to where you want to be.

Having said that, we have a natural instinct to arrange time mostly in a linear form, most often with our future ahead or to the right of us, and our past behind or to the left of us. Just rearranging this set-up can make a difference.

For some people the present is in front of them, which means they can view past and future readily. From this dissociated position off their line, they can view time objectively, which is really useful for planning. They are described as being 'through time'.

Others may be standing on or in their present, which enables them to be fully associated. These 'in-time' people tend to get caught up in the moment and lose track of time. This is a great place to be if you want to make the most out of an experience.

Our unconscious mind can talk through our feet. An exercise may ask the explorer to walk into the future or walk to a point in the past to gather certain information, and his or her feet know exactly where to go, or more accurately where to stop.

Hand gestures, body movements and eye locations all can indicate inner accessing of time. Spatial predicates of 'behind', or 'in front' could suggest a location in time, which could be useful to explore.

All our memories are stored chronologically within our unconscious mind, which is fundamentally concerned with keeping us safe, and will know if directly accessing a past event is useful or not.

If you are working with events in the past, you must make provision to ensure that the explorer is left in a resourceful state. Stepping off the line into dissociation is first line resourcing.

Timelines are plastic and can be stretched and shrunk, moved backwards and forwards. If you want to make time, you can stretch out the period in question. If you want to reduce the impact of a time frame then you can shrink it.

Techniques incorporating Time:

Arguably all techniques incorporate time, since future pacing to embed the resource and instruct the unconscious mind should be regarded as good practice, along with checking ecology, establishing and maintaining rapport, and calibration.

- *Change Personal History:* working with an unuseful reference experience
- *Neurological Level Alignment:* since arguably the choice of Environment is in some near future point
- *New Behaviour Generator:* projecting future scenarios
- *SCORE:* ingeniously using the pull of future Effects to over balance the hold of past Causes
- *Timeline Alignment:* discovering the internal representations for Past, Present, and Future and adjusting them to meet the demands of the outcome
- All involve future pacing.

Applications

- Stepping metaphorically by taking a physical step into the future, can help solidify goals and test their effectiveness. It can also be a source of 'wisdom with foresight', providing information regarding the effectiveness of today's decisions. Conversely stepping into the past can hand over information about the causes of a situation, and offer information that we may have forgotten.

- Combining timelines with mentors or Younger You/Older You can generate invaluable insight.

- Using our past timeline is a great way of gathering resources needed for today or a future point.

- Combining past, present, and future with submodalities can let us know, in the abstract, our response to each without having to experience the events. If it is less than favourable, then you can reconstruct the structure of submodalities into something much more acceptable.

- Understanding a relationship through time can reveal otherwise hidden dynamics. Enabling the explorer to notice when she began to become smaller or lose colour can indicate the decline in the relationship much earlier than the conscious mind might be prepared to admit.

- You can explore the parallel timelines of the people within a relationship. Going second position and experiencing someone else's journey in contrast to your own can provide essential insight.

- You can incorporate Neurological Levels with a different You at different time periods, to re-access and strengthen a resource, or to reframe the nature of that person then.

Perspectives – First, Second, Third and Meta positions

Having the skill and flexibility to view a situation from a variety of positions opens up the possibility of new learning, through widening the problem space until there is 'no news of difference'. This allows the solution space to emerge.

In first position we see the world through our own eyes and ears. For some of us this is the only place to be, and we discount any other viewpoint. Taken to the extreme this is the hallmark of bigotry.

Second position is experiencing the world through the eyes and ears of another, as opposed to projecting our map onto the other person. Some people spend most of their time in second position – to the denial of themselves and their own needs.

We can go second position with people, real or imagined, known or unknown, objects, emotions, relationships; systems expressed in diagrams or ideas; anything that has a structure, in any place in time or space.

Being able to go fully into second position is the making for deep rapport. It is also an essential skill for modelling any structure, through trying it on and feeling the inherent levels of congruence.

Whenever there is an individual and something else, there will be a relationship.

Third position looks onto the relationship between ourselves and the other person, to evaluate objectively its dynamics and notice particular contributions to outcomes. Those who spend their lives out here, run a commentary on the world without fully engaging with it.

When viewing from Third, the viewer needs to correct any bias towards one position over another, and take an equidistant stand from First and Second.

Forth position is the relational field that is the emergent property arising from the combination of the other perspectives. This is often the destination point when working with simultaneous models.

A Meta position is the dissociated first position and views self in operation.

Having the flexibility to shift perspectives at will is essential for gathering feedback and informing decision-making.

Techniques incorporating Perspectives:

- *Meta Mirror:* is based completely on first, second and extended versions of third
- *Neurological Level Alignment:* use of mentors
- *Phobia 'Cure':* if choosing to become the projectionist.

Applications

- If you want your explorer to learn more about a relationship, be it between two people, or two objects, or a person and object, then working on the system, created by first, second and third positions, will deliver the necessary information.

- Coming up with what someone else will see, hear and feel, is a way of expanding the evidence your explorer might need for a decision, or to explain past behaviours.

- Combining 2nd position with metaphor can provide profound insights. Becoming a sack of potatoes as the hurt, or stepping into the anger which is a black devil, can provoke great learning, especially if the explorer then views him or herself from that position or from 3rd.

- Submodalities can shift depending on the perspective. Your explorer can construct his or her sense of a scenario from first, then step into the shoes of another, or view it from a distance, and unsurprisingly, the whole scene can change. This creates the option of choice.

- Combining multiple perspectives with timelines can really begin to describe the wider system that is operating for the explorer, and take him or her to some new and unusual sources of insight.

- Simultaneous models generate the 4th perspective, that of Relational Field. This may be at the same level as the other perspectives, or may take on a higher overview.

Space and Association/Dissociation

We all have an unconscious concept of spatial location either for an emotion or internal structure as well as the layout of an external system. Once our attention is drawn to it, we can usually begin to construct the spatial map.

Space itself can be two-dimensional or three-dimensional, describing a systematic or a systemic system respectively.

Spatial predicates define the specific location of something, or describe the locations of various elements within a system, be they connected to or independent of each other.

Changing the position of one element within the system will cause the other elements to shift accordingly, revealing deeper connections and relationships. Homeostasis and congruence results when there is no more movement within the system.

At an individual level, the shift in location between being associated *in* the process, and being dissociated by stepping outside the process, is significant and readily marked. This is evidenced through language and gesture.

Association/Dissociation are one of the submodality categories. Association is where the experience is being sensed directly through the individual's own senses. Looking down, the feet are seen. Dissociation is where the individual is looking at or onto him or herself.

Association generates a full neurological experience. If this experience is overpowering and drowns out cognition, then stepping out into an increasingly dissociated position can reduce the emotional impact. This is an excellent means of sustaining resourcefulness.

Conversely, if individuals are too dissociated, possibly as a means of protection, then they could be usefully encouraged, and supported with the necessary resources, to move more into themself and associate fully onto their timeline.

Techniques incorporating Space:

- *Circle of Excellence:* Association and Dissociation to build up the state
- *Change Personal History:* viewing Younger Self, option not to associate into the event
- *Meta Mirror:* possible need to dissociate and avoid full association in second position
- *New Behaviour Generator:* viewing options from a dissociated position and then stepping into association to experience revised behaviour
- *SCORE:* possible dissociative position at Cause
- *Swish:* the construction of an associated and a dissociated picture
- *Timeline Alignment:* becoming dissociated as a means of resourcing, or of gaining a 'through time' perspective.

Application

- You can combine association and dissociation with parts. There may be a part that is dissociated from the others. Discovering what has to happen for that part to join up with the others could be a really significant move.

- You can create a live system either physically on the floor, or through using objects or bits of paper. Once the locations of elements within the system are defined, the explorer can move between them and explore their respective relationships, and also the shifts created by moving elements about. Vital information can be gleaned concerning the 'empty' spaces.

- Exploring timeline from a dissociated position is essential for safe working, until the timeline has become aligned and harmonised. Similarly going to a dissociated second position may be the safest way of gaining information from this perspective.

Metaphor

A metaphor is a description of what something seems like, and is the language of our unconscious mind.

Our language is full of metaphorical references, directly or indirectly offering insight of our inner constructions.

Metaphors follow their own physical laws, yet can follow the fantastic and irrational, which leaves us free to unfetter our imagination and let it really talk.

It is a great way of combining all the senses into a generalised description. We know the sack of potatoes is likely to be heavy and lumpy, and fairly static – although it is always useful to check this out.

A metaphor encapsulates all the representation systems and can be described in submodalities, without the need to do any further investigation.

Working with the metaphoric description offered by an explorer deepens rapport. It ensures that the process is unique to him or her. It also speaks of total acceptance and recognition of the worth of his or her world.

Using metaphors avoids having to bring internal experience completely to the surface and present it in fully coded language. Metaphorical descriptions allow the speaker to stay linked to deep structure.

Talking within metaphor deepens the level of association with the experience being described.

We tend to use 'metaphor' to include both simile, which is *like something*, and metaphor, which is *equal to something*.

Techniques incorporating Metaphor:

- *Neurological Level Alignment:* description at Identity level
- *SCORE:* can be delivered using metaphors for each location
- *Timeline Alignment:* can work metaphorically as opposed to pure submodalities.

Applications

- You can selectively introduce metaphor at a key part in the process. Often when touching on a sense of Identity, people may feel inhibited about talking about themselves at such an intimate level. Transforming this into a metaphor, say, of 'candle' 'wind' 'oak tree' 'eagle' allows the explorer to connect with the sense of this, without embarrassment.

- You can deliberately create the space for the spontaneous revelation of a metaphor. 'If this was an animal, which one would it be?' and then continue to run the process within the world of an animal, for example.

- You can choose to work totally in metaphor, for example, in a story. If you match the metaphor to the structure of the story, you will be able to pace and lead the explorer through the process.

- Alternatively, you can opt to create a metaphoric world with different locations on the floor, each with their own naming and relationships. Similarly you can use drawing and painting and summon up the same quality of insight.

- You can use a metaphor to describe a feeling, or range of feelings. It can be remarkable how the least likely structures reveal themselves – the sack of potatoes, the plastic spaghetti, the muscle and the blob finding ways of coexisting harmoniously.

Mentors

Mentors enable us to plug into the wisdom of others – not just a few, but anybody and everybody – to bring forth internal wisdom that usually bypasses the kneejerk editing of the conscious mind.

We can select mentors from people we currently or used to know, those who have passed on, those we have yet to meet, and those we can conjure up in our imagination.

Mentors can be all ages – often the very effective ones are children. You can invite great historical personages, characters from fiction, stars of stage and screen and cartoon. You can draw upon anyone who you feel could have something to offer.

Mentors are likely to be free of judgment; therefore their advice can be easily accepted. Mentors can lend authority or frivolity or whatever resource is in short supply.

It can be astonishing to find ourselves mouthing what this mentor is saying, when we've stepped into their shoes. 'Where did that come from?' is often the question a bewildered explorer will ask.

Mentors are a specific application of second positioning, where we are 'borrowing' the wisdom from apparently this external source. In fact the information is still coming from within our own amazing neurology.

At the same time they also work in part like a metaphor, with its symbolism. Bugs Bunny will have a different slant on life than Meryl Streep.

Techniques incorporating Mentors:

- *Neurological Level Alignment:* for the levels of Behaviour, Skills, Beliefs and Values and Identity.

Applications

- If you want to expand the problem space and provide new sources of information, introduce a mentor. It may be one of the explorer's choosing, or you may impose it as part of the design for a specific purpose.

- Selecting the cast of mentors can put a useful boundary round the experience.

- Mentors can be really useful if the explorer is feeling particularly unresourceful, lacks confidence in speaking up for him or herself, or needs external permission to state the desired truth.

- You can arrange for a cocktail of mentors to be summoned to create a designer state.

- You can organise different mentors for different time periods, and then have them hold conversations between themselves.

- Acting As If, by taking on the persona of a mentor, can be a very effective means of resourcing an Explorer, or for testing out future scenarios.

- An animal can be used as a kinaesthetic mentor, bringing its non-verbal energy and attributes.

- Mentors differ from parts or archetypes in that they bring an 'externalised' source of energy and information into the system. They can be temporary and transitory. Whereas parts are pre-existent and internal to the system.

Parts/Archetypes

Parts are aspects of our personality and together make up our whole.

Parts naturally can be evidenced through the different voices we use, our different walks, and the clothing we choose to wear.

Within NLP, we work with these aspects, as if they are separate personalities each with their own desires and purpose of how to be in service to us.

Parts wouldn't exist if they didn't have a specific positively intended purpose.

Those of the Jungian persuasion would argue that these parts are well documented archetypes, with characteristics common to most people. Such an attitude removes the uniqueness of the explorer's experience and the naming of the individuals within the system. It also predetermines what there will be to find, in a form of self-fulfilling prophecy.

Parts can hold their own unique belief system, and meta programme profile.

Congruence is achieved when all the parts are aligned and in agreement.

Parts can be any age, and not the explorer's actual age. They can be opposite gender. They may be readily available or in hiding. They form alliances and feuds with other parts, and misunderstand the intentions of each other. They may be ill equipped for the job they have to do.

Both parts and archetypes are another form of metaphor, but the source of information seems more from within, than that, say, of a mentor.

Working with parts can enable the explorer to dissociate from the direct experience and allocate emotions and responsibilities onto the relevant part.

If you are working with parts or archetypes, then you must make sure you reintegrate the whole system at the end of the process.

Parts, as a complex natural model, can be used as a modelling methodology as well as enhance the acquisition of a model.

Techniques incorporating Parts/Archetypes:

- *Disney Strategy:* working with the Dreamer, Realist and Critic

- *Meta Mirror:* some versions talk about the Director (3rd), Producer (4th), even Couch Potato (5th) and Theatrical Critic (6th).

Application

- Parts can be brought into an exercise if you want to combine certain traits, or bring a fragmented system together.

- Converting elements in a model into parts may make it easier for some explorers to access, being more responsive to the Referee and the Goalkeeper than the concepts of evaluation and defence.

- Translating emotions or resources into the appropriate archetype is great for the construction of stories.

- Working various parts together with submodalities can throw up some useful information about relationships between them.

- It is worth recognising that parts are internal expressions of dominant personality traits, having their own neurological level and meta programme profiles. This in turn can provide spontaneous departure points into an embellished spontaneous process.

- Where incongruence emerges during a process, you could invite the part (or parts) responsible to explore its sources. Similarly where there is a particularly strong meta model injunction, then finding the part it belongs to can take you straight to the heart of the matter.

Anchoring

Note: Anchoring or anchors are not, of themselves, Natural Models, since they can be composed of one element or several – a sound, or the synaesthesia of touch and image. The process of applying an anchor is a fundamental skill very closely associated with the neurology of state. However, anchors where they are applied within a technique are an essential neurological frame, and need to be included in this listing.

Anchoring, when part of a technique, is a deliberate act, as opposed to the natural anchoring that occurs spontaneously.

In the early days of NLP, when the focus was more on therapy, anchoring others through touch, gesture and voice was common. More recently, the favoured practise is to enable the explorer to self-anchor a developed resource, to encourage self-sufficiency, and reduce practitioner interference.

Some Codes of Practice make specific mention of the ecological use of tactile anchoring, lest it could be interpreted as unwanted behaviour.

Anchoring serves to embed a useful resource within the explorer, by the practitioner.

Many techniques rely on spatial anchors to activate internal processing.

The practitioner's use of hand gestures indicates location and reinforces the spatial anchors.

Anchors can be fired just through thinking about the trigger.

All change is a means of reconstructing and reframing existing anchors.

Techniques incorporating Anchoring:

- *Change Personal History:* substituting resource state
- *Circle of Excellence:* the whole point of the process
- *Disney Strategy:* chaining anchors of the three archetypes
- *Meta Mirror:* stacking of the anchors from each perceptual position.
- *Neurological Level Alignment:* Spirituality Resource, Auditory anchoring through repetition, stacking anchors on the descent
- *SCORE:* in the somatic version Dancing the SCORE, there is the chaining of the somatic anchors
- *Swish:* using one image to trigger new behaviour
- *Timeline Alignment:* anchoring time location through consistent marking of the spatial anchors by gesture and tone of voice
- *Visual Squash:* collapsing of the two anchors to create a third part

Applications

- You can deliberately introduce setting an anchor into a technique, if you know you will be creating a powerful state.

- You will be creating an anchor if you invite a somatic gesture, a symbol or a statement, to any of the elements within a model, specifically a constructed model.

- You can usefully invite a merging of these anchors to induce change, through creating a composite somatic gesture, an emergent image, and a higher level statement

The Linguistic Frames

The designer of a technique didn't pluck any old wording and slap it into the wording of an instruction. Being the engineers and technicians that we are, the language within a technique will have been selected and crafted.

The starting point for NLPers is the direct connection between language and internal processing. Words carefully selected deliberately target specific parts of the explorer's map and internal experience.

This throws up some essential points:

- As the designer, you have to be absolutely certain that the words you have written do the job you intend, taking the explorer to a particular location within internal awareness. Your words also need to be clear and unambiguous so that the guide can be confident in delivering them.

- As a practitioner you have to be careful before you start putting your own language into any set of instructions. You need to fully understand the intention behind the instruction before you deviate from the script and write your own.

Following a laid down script can be an anathema for a highly 'options' person. They will naturally want to put in their own words, and if they are 'internally sourced', they will consider their words to be better! Those who prefer 'procedures' and are 'externally referenced' will naturally fall in with the written script. Informed flexibility is key.

To understand the essential purpose of a technique, it is useful to go to the horse's mouth and work from the format that the originator proposed. It is amazing how altered a technique can become by the time it reaches the hands of a tenth generation learner. The original status quo needs to be balanced with what we know now, which may not have been available then. It can also be said that a well-formed mistake might produce even more effective results than the original.

Once you have fully understood the intentions of the developer for each step in the process, then you are at liberty to phrase the questions in your own way, provided you are certain that you are directing the explorer's attention precisely, and in the intended direction.

Listing of Linguistic Frames

All of the following Linguistic Frames resulted from modelling processes. All have the ability to access and formalise inner experience:

- Meta Model

- Milton Model

- Outcome Frame

- Reframing

- VAK Predicates

- Temporal and Spatial Predicates

- Associative/Dissociative Language.

The following additional patterns appeared after the development of the basic listing of techniques and are often introduced in NLP Master Practitioner programmes:

- Sleight of Mouth patterns

- Meta Programme language

- Clean Language.

The Profile

On the following pages, you are offered:

- A summary of considerations regarding each of the patterns, some which will be already familiar, and some which may be new to you

- A listing of those basic techniques incorporating the particular linguistic pattern, so that you can remind yourself of how they operate in action

- A useful set of suggestions regarding how you can weave these patterns into techniques, to inspire you and activate your creativity

- And finally a recap of the patterns to save you looking elsewhere.

Skills Required

Obviously there is much more that could be offered here. However, the purpose is not to develop your skills in these linguistic frames but to raise your awareness of their practical applications.

If you want to consider yourself to be a professional, then you need to develop fluency in each of these patterns. Gone are the days when you could pick and choose those you liked and discard those you didn't like or found difficult.

As a modeller, you need to know what each can do for you. And for a technician creating your own acquisition processes, you need to have a feel for which elements from what pattern you could useful incorporate into your technique. The choice is yours!

Meta Model

Meta Model questioning is an essential tool to determine the underpinning belief structure and mapping out of the problem space, especially if the practitioner doesn't have other modelling methodologies to hand.

Meta Model patterns can be expressed in language other than that commonly regarded as Meta Model statements, or questions. For example 'can or can't' may appear as 'possible/impossible' or 'limits'.

Knowing the intentions of each of the meta model patterns means that you know what missing information is being targeted for retrieval from the deeper structure.

Every statement will have several doors you could go in on. It is down to you the modeller to decide which option to follow.

If you are unaware of the Meta Model patterns being offered by your explorer, you will miss the opportunity to pick up on what is *really* happening for him or her in that moment. Happily if they are important, they will re-occur, and this time hopefully the message will get over your awareness threshold giving you a second chance to respond to them.

Whilst an explorer is going through any process, it is important to be on the lookout for throw away comments, which very often could be explored further with the appropriate questioning, and so reveal the essential deeper structure operating in the moment.

Techniques involving Meta Model:

- *Meta Mirror:* the secondary gain question 'What is keeping you behaving like this?' 'What's stopping you?'
- *Neurological Level Alignment:* during the early inventory period, seek out deletions. By Beliefs, you may offer up awareness of causal and equivalence beliefs, as well as Lost Performatives and Modal Operators
- *SCORE:* when you are working cognitively, to gain clarification
- *Timeline Alignment:* pay attention to any patterns that emerge when exploring a metaphor, which are limiting the further exploration.

Application

- Within a technique, Meta Model questions and applications can be introduced to expand the explorer's awareness. Uncovering deletions, in for example, state inventories makes the surface structure clearer. Inviting awareness of consequences or deeper meaning can take a technique that bit further.

- You can selectively use parts of the Meta Model framework of questions to include into your exercise. You need to be clear about where you want to direct your explorer's attention. You also need to predetermine the sequence and journey you want to set up.

- You can stay with one of the patterns and use it to explore further and further: 'What does that mean?', 'And what does that mean?', 'And what then does that mean?'

- You can combine a selection of Meta Model questions with questions from other frameworks.

Recap

By way of a recap, should you need it, here are the patterns. You can put your own labels to them:

- What must happen? What has to happen? What is essential here? What has to be avoided? What will it be like when you do/have?

- What stops you? What is impossible here? What is getting in the way? What would be the outcomes of this? What was removed? What did you have to overcome?

- When specifically was this difficult for you? What other events, which were successful, are you now aware of? Who has championed you?

- People who are X are like …? X types of people deserve …?

- Being X leads to/gives you … which leads to/gives you …? And also …? X & Y leads to …?

- Being X means … which means …? When X is with Y, this means …?

Milton Model

A skilled practitioner will be using trance language almost as second nature, *and hopefully serving the agreed outcome.* By pacing and leading, you will enable your explorer to enter into an altered state much more quickly.

All of NLP requires the explorer to operate in an altered state. Your effectiveness will be directly dependent on your ability to help your explorer sustain this altered state through providing trance intonation and language. Permissive trance language – *may, might, could, whichever* – gives the explorer options and self-determination, which allows for free exploration.

Using trance language, and as importantly, phrasing and intonation, will also take you, the practitioner, into a more defocused state, which will then allow you to be far more aware of *all* that is going on, in and around the actual action.

Your own trance state means you will be able to pick up in your peripheral vision much smaller movements in physiology. You will be more attentive to the explorer's language because your internal dialogue will be softened. You will also be able to listen to the communications from your unconscious mind.

Using lots of non-sensory specific language – *noticing, aware, discover, learn, seek,* etc. – will allow the explorer to explore in his or her own unique way.

Trance state allows for multi-tracking and multiple attention, since there is less mental restraint on the system.

You need to have trance phraseology and intonation at your fingertips, or you will find it difficult to lead an explorer into the required level of altered state. At the same time, you will also stay in up-time state that may not serve you.

Techniques involving Milton Model:

- *Change Personal History:* as the explorer journeys back to the reference event
- *Disney Strategy:* the trance like manner with which the Critic communicates with the Dreamer
- *Neurological Level Alignment:* from Belief level onwards
- *Phobia 'Cure':* to calm the explorer into becoming comfortable in the cinema
- *SCORE:* during Outcome and Effects and when working with metaphor or somatic syntax
- *Timeline Alignment:* to deepen the access to internal experience
- *Visual Squash:* to encourage the emergence of the parts and the subsequent assimilation

Application

- You can consciously script trance language patterns into your written instructions if you want to soften your explorer's attention and lead him or her into a deeper trance state. This way the explorer will be more receptive to what her unconscious mind has to offer.

- If your exercise requires your explorer to 'hallucinate' her own inner world, then trance language will induce this.

- You will definitely need to entwine trance language into any story you may construct, to take your listener into that far off fairy-tale world.

- You can select these patterns if you want to offer direction to your explorer without being too overt.

Recap

Should you need it, here is a recap of the patterns involved:

- And you may … You might … It's permissible …
- And you can … You could … It's possible …
- As you realise, become aware, notice, identify, recognise, sense, assume, store away, calculate, imagine, accumulate, wonder, travel, accommodate, question…
- You can … can't you? You have … haven't you? You were … weren't you? It is … isn't it?
- Imagination, satisfaction, connection, results, contribution, recognition, relationship, rewards, thoughts, questions, responses, journeys, destination, solution, implications …
- Allow yourself to … Invite part of yourself to … Ask yourself … Begin now to notice … Take a moment … whilst …
- As X happens Y will begin to … That leads to …
- When you … this now means that X has begun to …

Outcome Frame

All behaviour is outcome focussed.

All techniques should be selected on the basis of having established an ecological outcome, plus the inclusion of a sensory-based description as evidence of how this outcome will be experienced.

Your technique may seek to deliver the overall outcome, or contribute to its attainment.

All techniques should start with an ecology check. Someone says they want to change something but are they sure they're sure?

You need to establish a description of the sensory-based evidence of the outcome. Otherwise how will you know it is appropriate to exit your TOTE? Just because the session has run its time doesn't mean to say that the work is done.

Sensory acuity has to be on the look out for spotting signs of incongruence.

Within the ecology check you need to pay attention to any secondary gains which, if unattended to, will sabotage your and your explorer's chances of success.

If you are detecting incongruence, it is essential to explore what will be lost through the change.

Incongruence is directly connected to the doubt or unhappiness of a particular part. You can use this knowledge to change direction and work with that specific part – if that is ecological with the explorer.

Throughout the entire process you need to be aware of your outcome at each step – the outcome for your question, your positioning, the instruction and every other response you make.

Establishing a well-formed outcome is an intervention in its own right.

Techniques involving Outcome Frame:

- *New Behaviour Generator:* looking for different ways to achieve a desired outcome
- *Six Step Reframe:* checking out with other parts if there are any ecology issues surrounding the change.

Application

- You can select elements out of the full framework, for example the Evidence Frame, or the Ecology Frame as part of your instructions.

- You can use the framework as a story line, or a metaphor for decision-making.

- You can combine the framework with time and submodalities to gather further details about the value of the goal.

- You can use the framework to explore inner confusion caused by conflicting desires.

Recap

Here is a comprehensive listing of the questions found within a collective Well Formed Outcome framework.

- What would you rather have? What would you like to have happen?

- What is important about this? How will this be of benefit to you?

- When/Where do you want it? When/Where don't you want it?

- What has stopped you? What do you have to do differently?

- How will you know you have it? What will you/others hear, see, and feel?

- What resources do you need? How are you asking for this now?

- If you got this would you want it? If you got this, what would you gain/lose? If you didn't get this, what would you gain/lost? What do you want to make sure you keep?

- Having got this, looking back, when did you start? What was the first thing you did?

Reframing

Reframing directs the explorer to doubting a belief that is holding him or her stuck. It sets up some movement into the system.

Reframes may be written into the script, or you may find yourself using them spontaneously during the process.

Basic reframing focuses mainly on meaning and context. Here are some common examples:

- Tears are a great way of telling the explorer that something significant has happened.
- Uncertainty and reluctance is a mark of how much they want to keep themselves safe.
- Only explorers have the PhD on themselves, so whatever they say is right.
- Doing any exploring is a mark of personal commitment and such resilience can only be admired.
- Being open to the vagaries of your unconscious mind is a mark of sanity and not the opposite!
- Whenever an explorer appears stuck, this is usually an opportunity for a reframe.

Should you become stuck as well, both of you need to step into a dissociated state. From this place, you will recover and determine where to go next.

Guard against reframing heedlessly, since you may be discounting real concerns, or acting to maintain your own equilibrium.

If you are offering a reframe, either spontaneous or written within an exercise, it needs to apply *at the same level of value or above.* If you don't you will demonstrate that you don't have an understanding of your explorer's map.

Techniques involving Reframing:

- *Six Step Reframe:* the fundamental NLP presupposition that: 'All behaviour has a positive intention.'

- *Change Personal History:* to shift meaning attached to earlier decision: 'That younger You didn't have the knowledge and understanding you now have. If he/she did, then a different decision would have been made.'

- *Meta Mirror:* when looking at You and the other person, and identifying the characterlogical adjectives to each of you, this is followed up by: 'What are you doing so well to continue being like this?'

- *Phobia 'Cure':* there are two very precise reframes which are essential for the resourcing of the explorer and preframing the subsequent experience, namely: 'Phobic responses started out in an instant, which means the opposite can happen just as quickly' and 'Your unconscious mind wants to protect you from whatever threatens you.'

- *Timeline Alignment and Change Personal History:* 'We can't change what has happened in our lives. We can, however, change the meaning and response to those events.'

Applications

- Use reframing questions if you are working with beliefs in an exercise.

- You can usefully offer reframe questions when you want the explorer to come up with a range of options.

- You can artfully combine reframing questions with mentors and parts.

Recap

By way of refresher here is a listing of reframing questions:

- What else can this mean?

- When might this be useful?

- What else might the consequences might be?

- What examples do you have when this isn't the case?

- What different outcome could result?

- What might be the positive intention?

- What is this similar to?

- What is all of this part of?

- How does this reflect who you are?

- What part is not like this?

- How is this significant in the greater scheme of things?

- What is important here?

- How might someone else regard this as being acceptable?

Sensory Predicates

Whenever a technique involves submodalities, you will be working with VAK Predicates.

Similarly when you take an inventory as part of a calibration process, you will be using VAK Predicates.

You may also be particularly meticulous and select your VAK Predicates to match the preferred representation system of the Explorer, or the Explorer's internal processing representation system.

If you are having difficulty establishing rapport with your explorer, then pay particular attention to the VAK preferences of your explorer and pace them. Your explorer may, for example, be highly attuned to this dissonance.

If you have fully entered into the explorer's metaphor, and deeply second positioned, you will find yourself naturally pacing the explorer's VAK Predicates, either within the same representation system, or isomorphically in your preferred system.

Given that VAK predicates predetermine the representation system of the explorer, it is often better to use non-sensory specific words in instructions. This allows the explorer to explore in his or her own way.

If however, the technique calls for accessing a particular representation system, then the use of relevant predicates would support and assist this.

Techniques involving VAK Predicates:

- *Circle of Excellence:* development of the state
- *Neurological Level Alignment:* expansion of the Spirituality resource
- *Neurological Level Alignment:* inventory and calibration tool on return to Environment
- *Phobia 'Cure':* working with the submodalities of the film and the two rooms
- *Swish:* fundamental to establishing the unwanted and wanted images
- *Timeline Alignment:* for describing the metaphorical or submodality structure of the timeline.

Applications

- Any time you want to heighten a reference experience, create an opportunity for anchoring a state, or generate sensory specific evidence, insert a VAK inventory.

- If you are creating a story, you need to be mindful of including the full range of sensory predicates.

- You might create a process that requires the explorer to deliberately deliver her description of what is happening in representation system other than her default preference.

Recap

I have only provided a short-list of sensory predicates across the five representation systems. I strongly advise you to draw up your own listing, as this will stretch your least favoured system.

Kinaesthetic	Auditory	Visual	Gustatory	Olfactory
Warm	Booming	Shining	Tangy	Aromatic
Cool	Loud	Glittering	Bitter	Sweaty
Hot	Quiet	Sparkling	Sweet	Pongy
Cold	Tone	Dull	Salty	Smelly
Icy	Mode	Bright	Gutsy	Pungent
Smooth	Cacophony	Glowing	Tasty	Noxious
Rough	Orchestrate	Shimmering	Sour	Sickly
Hard	Tinkle	Translucent	Stomach	Perfumed
Grip	Crashing	Scenic	Swallow	Scented
Grasp	Purring	View	Guts	Malodorous
Tender	Howling	Black and white	Lump in throat	Sniff
Firm	Hooting	Any colour	Lip service	Snort
Comfort	Chatter	Shades	Digest	Turn up your
Handle	Laughter	Colourful	Thirst	nose
Dancing	Beep	Reflecting	Honeyed	Wrinkle your
Wet	Shriek	Dark	Gingery	nose
Dry	Whisper	Light	Peppery	Miasma
Damp	Click	Shadow	Spicy	Whiff
Clammy	Cluck	Contrast	Pickle	Fragrant
Sticky	Snarl	Focussed	Sugary	Fragrance
Slimy	Whimper	Hazy	Vinegary	Bouquet
Squelchy	Drumming	Fuzzy	Plummy	Rank
Furry	Whimper	Blurred	Fruity	Musty
Hairy	Crescendo	Clear	Savoury	Waft
Sharp	Silent	Monochrome	Creamy	Snuffle
Buzzing	Deafening	3-D	Stomach	Foetid

Temporal Predicates

Whenever a technique involves moving through time, you are called upon to be meticulous about using temporal predicates. This way the explorer can stay associated and gain clear direction, confident that you are in charge of the process.

Clarity and precision regarding the relative positions within the process helps to build up, and sustain, the emerging hallucination and trance created by the process. And you will achieve a deep level of rapport in the process.

Wherever the explorer finds himself, be it in the past or in the future, he has to be fully associated. So the language *always* has to be in the present. The other places in time then relate to this point. e.g. 'Away into the future up there from this point in the past ...' 'Having had this now for some time ... ' 'Looking back to today ...'

If the practitioner is fully associated and second positioning the process then this language will be automatic. It is a clear giveaway that the practitioner is somewhere else if the language is sloppy.

Part 6 – The Formal Acquisition Process

Additionally, if the practitioner is fully second position to the explorer and the hallucination that the explorer is creating, then the correct verb tenses will occur naturally. So much easier and quicker than having to consciously work out where you are!

Gestured anchors or voice intonation can also indicate positioning on the timeline.

All techniques should involve a Future Pace, to test if the desired state is achieved.

Techniques involving Temporal Predicates:

- *Timeline Alignment, SCORE, Change Personal History:* these involve particular attention to precise time based language
- *Meta Mirror:* where the relationship is based in the past, it needs to be activated as if happening now. The third and fourth positions have to be actively engaged
- *New Behaviour Generator:* this future based process operates as if happening in the present
- *Phobia 'Cure':* referring to an earlier reference experience and associated into present.

Applications

- Temporal predicates are essential if your exercise is working directly or indirectly with time.
- They are essential for providing a solid structure to a process.
- Temporal predicates can usefully be combined with Milton model language to deepen the trance effect.
- You can use a mishmash of temporal predicates in a Guided Visualisation or in a story if, for example, you are recounting a magic spell.

Recap

Here are some of the linguistic formats you can select from:

- You/They have/are … He/She has/is …
- You/They are having/are being … He/She is having/is being …
- You/They have had/were … He/She has had/was …
- You/They/He/She used to have/used to be …
- You/They/He/She will have/will be …
- You/They/He/She would have had /would have been …
- Past, then, previously, hitherto, recently, just, before, ago, yesterday, after, already
- Present, now, current, immediate, instantly, still, today, renew, continue, replace, return
- Future, soon, yet, to come, immanent, presently, later, tomorrow, next, following
- Begin, end, start, stop.

Associative/Dissociative Language and Spatial Predicates

The basic association/dissociation function is the major way we have for accessing state fully, or removing ourselves out of a state.

This is a practitioner's rescue remedy and most basic first aid tool. This allows you the confidence to bring the explorer into the exploration in the first place, knowing that the explorer can stay resourceful by stepping out at any time.

Some techniques specifically call for dissociation, some splitting the synthesis of senses or into various perceptual positions. It is really important that you coach the explorer into how to word such communications.

Where the explorer is, in relation to the various perceptual positions, will be indicated through language. You need to be alert to whether this language fits the intended position. 'I think ...' is not someone who is dissociated, but is someone who is second positioning a mentor, or another person, or else in first position. Or 'I will be doing ...' is not the language of someone associated in the future.

Spatial predicates – here/there, these/those, and now/then – all indicate the degree of association. You need to have a precision in this area, or else the explorer will be dragged back into the presenting problem, after all your hard work! 'Having had that problem when you came in ...' is a distinctly more useful construction than 'So how is your problem now?'

Location can be further emphasised by your gesture anchors.

Sometimes it is really useful to 'take 5' when both the explorer and you stand back and review how things are going, and what might be useful at this stage. Bringing yourself into the process accommodates the wider system that is operating in the relationship, and can provide an opening for working in the moment.

If you don't pay attention to creating well defined associated and dissociated positions the explorer will become confused and the state contaminated. You risk the explorer taking on responsibility for the poor outcome, when in fact it's you that should be doing the apologising.

Techniques involving Associative/Dissociative Language and Spatial Predicates:

- *Six Step Reframe:* there is a need to mark out which part is being referred to
- *Change Personal History:* if the past event is distressing and also separation from now and younger self
- *Circle of Excellence:* stepping from dissociated inventory to association
- *Disney Strategy:* when referring to the plan over there, and not the realist here
- *Meta Mirror:* again based on the triple description model
- *Neurological Level Alignment:* through the use of mentors
- *New Behaviour Generator:* associating into dissociated picture
- *Phobia 'Cure':* totally based on dissociation from one and two positions removed
- *SCORE:* as with Phobia 'Cure'
- *Swish:* mindful of the different locations of the images
- *Timeline Alignment:* being off the line while exploring the past for the first time, and connecting

with past, present and future You(s)

- *Visual Squash:* involving the different locations of the first two, then the combined third part, and the assimilation into the body.

Applications

- Spatial Predicates are great for widening the space and taking it further, higher, deeper etc. than the explorer or the guide would naturally go.

- You can combine space with multiple perspectives by inviting the explorer to stand on a chair (safely) or get onto his or her knees or sit on the floor, to create different physical levels.

Note

1   As the writer of the exercise, you need to pay particular attention to your use of this/that, these/those, here/there. If you want to bring the object close to the explorer, then you will use this, these, here. If you want to distance your explorer, then it is that, those, there. Makes a huge difference.

2   If you are working in system, for example, with multiple perspectives, what is on your left from one view may be on the right from another. Or looking down from above may make something even further below. As the writer you need to be very clear where you want to take your explorer, and your guide, spatially. This is why a diagram is really useful to illustrate the layout of the exercise.

Recap

Here's a refresher of the range of spatial predicates:

- In front of, facing, opposite, forward, beyond
- Rear, behind, at the back
- Beside, next to, adjacent, at the side of, near, nearby, close, bordering
- Inside, interior, within, far inside, internal, inner, core, central, centre, contained by, surrounded by
- Outside, outer, exterior, external, peripheral
- Below, beneath, under, underneath, bottom, underside
- Above, on top of, over, overhead, up, down
- This, that
- Here, there
- These, those

Technique Design

You have your model and you've decided upon your delivery method. You have now to decide how you're going to bring your model alive. What neurological frames are you going to select? Are you going to go for pure language or will your language complement your neurological frames?

Ecology Alert

Before you begin, you need to consider just how much exploration the end user may be prepared to undertake. Some may be up merely for a light excursion, whilst others are looking for something that really takes them to the heart of the matter. It could even be regarded as abusive if you set up a process that is demanding inappropriate levels of exposure and risk.

If you are the intended guide to the process, then you will be able to adjust as you go along. However if your technique is going to unknown hands, then design something that doesn't require too much risk on the part of the explorer. Certainly, you need to include safety warnings for the guide.

Should you anticipate that a strong emotional response is likely at a certain point, then you need to flag this up in your instructions.

Design Process

1 Clarify purpose and desired outcome

- It might be that you want to market your technique as being designed for a specific purpose, to address a specific issue – like the Fast Phobia 'Cure'. This outcome is likely to be reflected in your title for it.

- You also need to know if your technique is going to demand, for example, a specific context e.g. Working with Your Child; a particular problem e.g. Working with Bereaved Children; or certain circumstances e.g. Preparing Children for Death of Another; or can it be applied across the board e.g. Preparing for Loss.

  This is vital for how you construct your technique in terms of its complexity, and for your selection of language and neurological frames. For example, children respond really easily to metaphor and submodalities, whereas this may not be such a universal application for adults.

- You want to have a clear idea about what you want your end user to experience at the end of the process you create. Obviously everyone will have his or her own unique response, but you are identifying the class of experience you expect.

  You want to know if it is going to be a particular state, or conclusion, or are you seeking to expand awareness generally. You want to know if you are strengthening a known state or creating the opportunity for an emergent property to arise.

2 **Select ingredients:** your selection of what to put into your technique may depend on some or all of the following.

- *Selection criteria:*

  - Past experience: you may draw on techniques you know which have a proven track record. Whilst I don't advocate transferring the entire process and wrapping it round your own model, this is something you could do – provided you give full credit to the original designer. You can take bits from here and there, provided that the insertion serves the overall process. This can also apply to linguistic patterns that you may have previously experienced.

  - The downside to this pick and mix may be the potential loss of flow and cohesion since it is not you that is driving the process from beginning to end. You need to test it and test it, making adjustments until you arrive at a streamlined effect.

  - Unique combinations: conversely, you may come up with a unique taste of your own. Who would have thought chocolate and chilli would have hit the right notes! You may even consider selecting your components at random from the full listing. I have all the frames and delivery methods on individual cards. I can randomly pull frames and delivery methods out and see what I can make of the combination I've come up with. I have devised some really satisfactory and exciting techniques using this approach.

  - Constraints: you may have a space issue, not just physically, which of course is a determinant, but also the length available for your instructions – ideally on one standard size page. And, of course, the time available could also curtail your creative excesses. Your own levels of congruence as the deliverer may also be a factor. Whilst you might love to try out a new approach and produce something pretty wizzy, your common sense tells you to play it safe.

  - Personal congruence: you may have doubts about particular frames, either because you have had poor experiences with them, or you sense you don't fully understand their dynamics. If you have any incongruence this will show up in your lack of authority in your instructions, so avoid them but set yourself the task to personally revisit them.

- *Components consideration:*

  - Multiple permutations: you do know, of course, that you can make a variety of techniques out of your model, by majoring on different neurological frames.

  - Neuro technology: select the specific neurological frames that will deliver your intended outcome. Some work together better than others. Refrain from putting in more than you need. Double check if you have missed a frame that might actually do a better job more efficiently.

- Compatibility: make sure all your language is compatible with your selected neurological frames – VAK predicates with submodalities, temporal predicates with time, spatial predicates with varying locations, associated and dissociated language depending on perspective. You may have opted to major on the higher end of the neurological levels, so you need the language to match. Or you may be seeking to bring to the surface specific beliefs and so you need to select the corresponding meta model pattern.

- Milk your Information: if you also created the model, you are bound to have lots of data left over. Instead of lamenting wasting your time, go through these seemingly irrelevant bits again, since they may well bring colour and direction to your instructions. For example if there was no place for the exemplar's comment 'That was really important to me', you might find yourself writing 'What is the most important thing that you want to bring with you?'

- End user: you have to consider the skill and language levels, preferences, and previous experiences of your end users as the final consumers. I would err on the side of the acquirer who knows nothing and is an NLP virgin. This way you won't be making any assumptions.

- Questions: where you have constructed questions, as opposed to adapting ones from existing linguistic frames, make sure that they:

    o Direct the explorer's attention to the desired place within his or her map.

    o Are linguistically and technically sound involving the appropriate predicates.

    o Contain presuppositional language that avoids unethical installation.

    o Where relevant, induce trance to an ethical level.

3 **Test it:** good cooks taste their food throughout the cooking. So should you as you are designing your technique. You have to have a full sense of what your engineering is actually delivering as opposed to what is in your mind. Here the meaning of your communication is truly the response that you're getting. What excites your own imagination may not transfer that well into practice.

So at each stage of the process, step in, try it on for yourself. How does it feel to you? How much knowledge and experience are you asking for? What safety issues do you have to consider? Have you built in ways to help the explorer stay in a useful state?

Then step into the shoes of your potential explorer. Does it work for him or her as well? Who wouldn't it work for? Are there any specific conditions that you need to include to tighten it up?

But the best arbiter of your work are real live explorers and guides who are willing to take on your instructions and the dynamics of your technique and then give you feedback – no matter how irritating it may initially be.

4 **Evaluate:** the time has come to stand back now and dispassionately view what you have produced. Use the following evaluation criteria before you unleash the product of your genius on an unsuspecting world.

- *Structure:*

  - Accuracy: ensure that what you are offering is technically accurate and feasible.

  - Logic: does the combination of components create the desired conditions and generate the desired outcomes? Does it build upon the inherent logic within the system? If there isn't logic within the structure, then both your explorer and your guide will become confused and possibly lost.

  - Resilience: you don't know who will be using your original instructions. The more robust the technique's internal structure the less likely it will be badly mangled through the passage of time. Sadly misinformation and inaccuracies take root as deeply as does good practice.

- *Simplicity:*

  - Too much: This is nearly an inevitable mistake early on. Just because you know a lot, doesn't mean the kitchen sink has to be thrown in as well. Supersizing the sandwich may be interpreted as generosity. Conversely it can be taken to be a lack of discernment and discrimination. As with the finest cooking, judiciously selecting your ingredients can make the difference between an elegant masterpiece or a mishmash of tastes and textures. Restrict yourself to two – three at the most – neurological ingredients, and simple language patterns. Let the technology do the work. Trust it and everyone wins.

  - Too long: Ideally a process should be designed to take no more than 30 minutes to do. Obviously, depending on the explorer and the issues being explored, in reality the process can overrun considerably. The guide's level of experience may draw out the process as well. To maintain the levels of concentration and motivation of both the explorer and the guide, be mindful of how much time your content will demand. Obviously, stripping out unnecessary elements will help. Avoid adding on cumbersome additional stages. You can always establish a Part 1 and Part 2 if needs be. A long exercise doesn't make it any better than a shorter one.

- *Flow:*

  - Blend: your ingredients should naturally blend, and avoid clumsy bumping. This will depend on what frames you've chosen and if they 'talk' to each other.

  - Rhythm: it helps if you can build up a rhythm of movement or thought, through repeating set questions, instructions and comments. This will lead your explorer more softly into the desired semi-trance state. It can also soften your guide as well.

  - Pathway: if you have designed a spatial technique, then be clear of the layout required so that there is a natural pathway through it. Having to retrace steps leads to confusion. Of course, you may want to set up a relational field where the explorer is free to roam and gather information as it emerges for them. Your diagram will quickly throw up complexity and cluttered thinking.

5 **Await the feedback:** if you are someone who is happy to be your own judge of what works, or doesn't, then you may consider that feedback is a time consuming luxury. Yet being an NLPer, you will admit that the more you test your product, the more you will discover common quirks of preference held by your consumers – no matter how annoying that might be!

Getting good feedback is worth its weight in gold and you are really lucky that your consumers can be bothered to risk your exasperation to show you such respect. So listen to what's being said. It might just be a one-off. It might however be a serious design fault that has slipped under your radar.

6   **Congratulate yourself:** it is not every day that a unique original piece of work is born. You have made a contribution to the community and the world. Enjoy the fruits of your labours, and delight that here is something, like a newborn baby, that didn't arrive in the room through the door. Feel rightly proud.

And onto the next one! Remember, you can devise many different techniques from the one model. Don't rest on your laurels after the first one you come up with. Your model has legs and can be used in different ways, with different individuals to suit different contexts.

Key Features of a Technique

Being able to deconstruct a technique into its Key Elements, from a dispassionate perspective, is the mark of a professional practitioner. Certainly, it is essential for an NLP Trainer who is training NLP. If you are a trainer of NLPers and only have a hazy idea of how a technique is crafted, you will not only disrespect the originator, you will be giving your learners a diluted version, which they will go on to dilute further. As a coach, you will not be providing the full potential that technique can offer. As a designer, you will not be able to make clear distinctions between the effects of one component over another.

Whilst I am suggesting the *Model of Technique Construction* forms the body of the process, there are essential peripheral features to factor in as well. Within every technique, you should be able to identify the following:

- *Purpose:* why you would select it

- *Calibrated evidence:* what you're measuring at the Exit

- *Components:* what's included

- *Model:* what model forms the basis

- *Neurological Frames:* which frames are selected

- *Linguistic Frames:* which frames are selected

- *Methodology:* what delivery method is chosen

- *Skills required:* skill levels needed to perform it

- *Ecological issues:* areas of concern

- Logistics of time and space*:* effects of both/either.

1   **Purpose:** each technique is designed to produce a certain result. It may be a desired state, an altered belief, a strengthened skill, or a resourceful identity. Or else it may be engineered to create

a space to generate a higher level of awareness. As the designer, you need to state clearly the intended purpose of your technique and how it might be useful. This will help the selection process of the subsequent practitioner.

2 **Calibrated Evidence:** as you know, calibration is of fundamental importance to NLPers because its process plots the journey from Present State to Desired State – the move from the unwanted physiology, emotion and response to the desired version. And this desired version is established as part of a Well Formed Outcome.

As the designer, you need to be clear regarding the evidence that will sign off the TOTE – otherwise your practitioner will be there all day, or be satisfied prematurely.

It is useful to establish the start position at the beginning so that you can measure distance covered against the desired evidence. Often it will be an observed state that can have a sensory specific description, or an inventory that can be calibrated through submodality change, or the state can be digitally measured on a scale, most often 1 low – 10 high.

3 **Components:** we've already covered these – The Model, The Delivery Method, The Neurological Frames, and The Linguistic Frames.

4 **Methodology:** the practitioner needs to decide if the delivery method you have selected is suitable for the exemplar, or the skill level of learners. Given that you have made your preferred choice, you may opt to offer alternative approaches using different representation systems.

5 **Skills:** if your instructions are well written, and the practitioner doesn't deviate from the script, then the practitioner's level of skill may not become a consideration. What is certain is that something will happen, possibly heading in the right direction. Clumsy handling can put a prospective explorer off NLP for some time.

That said, it is always the singer and not the song. A highly skilled practitioner will be able to milk the potential of any technique, with any explorer, in any context, with any issue.

6 **Ecological issues/areas of concern:** by offering an intervention, you are inviting someone to explore unknown areas of his or her map. You cannot legislate for the hands your instructions will land in. So you need to be aware of possible ecological issues and highlight them as required – to alert even the most inexperienced user.

You also need to highlight those stages within your process that could provoke an unresourceful state. For example in Meta Mirror, the explorer should only go into 2nd position once they have become sufficiently dissociated and resourced. Similarly in SCORE, the explorer only enters Cause after experiencing the powerful resources available in Effects.

7 **Logistics of time:** you need to know how long a technique will take, roughly. This will have a direct bearing on whether or not the practitioner will either decide to select it, or find a way of adapting it to suit the time available, or the nature of the explorer.

8 **Logistics of space:** you need to be clear of the layout of your technique and provide it graphically. If there are particular requirements, for example making sure you have at least a third or a half of the space allocated to Spirituality in Neurological Level Alignment, then these need to be highlighted.

I find the following template a really useful framework to use:

Technique name			
Purpose: What is the Technique designed to deliver? This is the basis for your primary selection criteria.			**Time:** What is the average time required?
Model type	**Methodology**	**Neurological**	**Linguistic**
What is the underpinning model that governs the technique, on which the whole process rests? Don't confuse the Model with the treatments provided by the Neurological Frames.	What is the dominant delivery method? Some techniques may incorporate more than one approach so identify the main one, and the supplementary ones. Depending on the explorer's needs, time and space, you may need to either abandon or adapt this option.	What are the neurological treatments given to bring this model alive, and generate its characteristic outcomes? This is the area of creativity, where adding some, or omitting some can bring about a different emphasis, or extend the technique's impact	What are the linguistic patterns that most strongly influence the direction and the quality of the technique's delivery? The more skilled the practitioner, the more effective the process.
Skill emphasis: what skills are of particular importance in the delivery of this technique, which the practitioner needs to have to assist the explorer?		**Floor layout – if relevant:** this is applies predominately when the methodology is Kinaesthetic using Spatial Anchors	
Areas of concern and contingencies: what are the danger zones/ecology issues, and any areas that may require special attention? For your own benefit, and subsequent readers, put in suggestions for how to deal with such instances.			
Comments: here you can offer some of your thoughts either about the technique itself, or your thinking regarding the deconstruction. You can make references to other techniques, and suggest add-ons.			

Bringing It All Together

Here are some permutations for you to consider. I am offering you my model for *Happiness* – appropriate for this stage in the book!

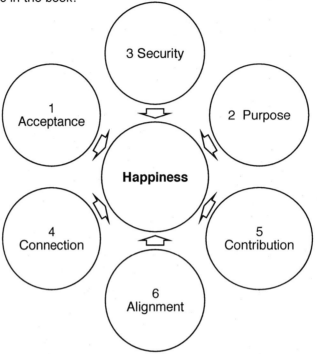

Happiness Model – Burgess 2013

Now consider the different types of techniques you could design from the following randomly selected permutations.

Delivery Method	Neurological Frame	Linguistic Frame
Spatial anchors	Submodalities	Modal Operators and Complex Equivalences
Sliding-scales	Mentors	Beliefs, Values, Identity
Drawing	Time, Metaphor	Spatial Predicates

1 **Spatial Anchors:** here you could imagine a process that has wording –

Move *Security* further away/closer: make it brighter/duller etc.

Now, stepping into this space:

- What mustn't happen?

- What can happen?

- What does this mean?

2   Sliding-scales:

As this Mentor, move **Security** to your desired position.

- What do you believe?

- What is important to you?

- What metaphor describes you in this moment?

3   Drawing:

a. Identifying a particular area for exploration – a relationship, a career path, happiness.

b. Devise a timeline and plot three time periods – a specific time in the past, the present and a specific time in the future.

c. Select five spatial predicates – in, above, below, behind, ahead.

d. Now draw metaphorically what, for example it is like to be *in the relationship, above the relationship, etc*

Already I am excited at the thought of the results we could get!

The Written Instructions

Ideally, you have already worked out the pathway of your process before you begin to write your instructions. You already know the steps involved and where you expect your explorer to be at any one time, and what sort of experience you are looking for at each stage. However, much becomes clearer once you commit to plotting your vision in the cold light of black and white. Be prepared to rewrite, rewrite, rewrite.

Writing your instructions is the last stage in your creative process. You are now ready for the final step – transferring your technique onto a personality-free, one-dimensional, disembodied sheet of paper, trusting that your words will convey and encapsulate the power of your engineering.

You might think that there's not much to say about how to write a set of instructions. You might think that all the hard work has been done. Wrong!

As learners, we have all consumed many sets of written instructions, so, initially, I just assumed that the basic rules of writing instructions were generally understood. But having handled many sets of embryonic instructions from Master Practitioners and, more particularly, from NLP Trainers, I realise that there is work to be done to shape up the ability to produce an effective set of instructions.

Understandably, when we were the consumer, our focus was on the process and not on the niceties of the sheet of paper containing the instructions. By and large, at those times, we deleted the intricacies of the mechanics involved. Only when we come to write our own do we realise there is much more to it.

Another explanation could be that when a technique is written up in an effective manner, the message is absorbed easily and doesn't bump into the critical faculties of the user. And possibly those deficient handouts, where the explorer or the guide have to struggle to make sense of what is being asked of them, might have been explained as being the 'fault' of participants, and not due to the poor craftsmanship of the designer. And the undiscerning user will make it up anyway and insert what suits his or her needs!

A handout is a model.

Think about it. Within its digital format lies the potential analogue experience. As a tabular model, you can equally apply the CASE criteria here as you can for any other model. A handout needs to be coherent, accessible, simple and effective – especially since it is unlikely that you will be around to fill in any gaps in understanding, or modify any wording.   Therefore your handout has to be:

- Logical, following a natural sequence, and laid out in a format which indicates its inherent logic

- Expressed in language that fits the experience and culture of the participants

- Stripped down to its bare components, without unnecessary additional comments and phrases

- Able to serve a range of audiences, and deliver the goods.

The participants need to be able to use your instructions to direct them clearly and accurately.   The hallmark of a well-written set of instructions is the absence of questions about the process – and a high rate of successful experiences.

The 3 C's of Written Instructions

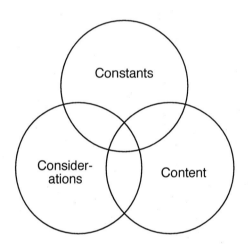

3 C's of Written Instructions – Burgess 2010

1   **Constants:**   every handout, regardless of its desired outcome, end user and content, should contain the following features.

- *Title:* the title is merely a means of distinguishing your technique from others in the field. Ideally select a name that conveys something about the topic, process or outcome. However avoid something that is too idiosyncratic since it may not last the passage of time and fashion.

- *Source acknowledgements:* all materials are required to be attributed. It is highly unethical to imply, if by omission, that the materials you are providing are original and self-generated when they are not. If you have adapted or drawn from someone else's work, then this needs to be stated. If it is self-originated, then proudly put your own name to it. If you don't know the original creator, then state your source. Avoid the liberal sprinklings of ©, ™, and ®.

- *Date:* to indicate currency, include either the origination date or revision date.

- *Model:* it is useful to include the model on which the technique is based. Where the format of the technique is kinaesthetic, then a floor plan marking out the layout of the spatial anchors is essential.

- *Length:* ideally the instructions should be no more than one side of A4. This serves to enforce the discipline of stripping out unwanted wording. Having said this, you need to be mindful of visual accessibility. Adding details about possible timings and skill level is optional.

2   **Content:** to be a bona fide NLP Technique, you need to be true to your craft and make sure you include the following stages within your instructions.

- *Outcome:* each technique is designed to deliver a specific process outcome. However the explorer will have his or her own version of this outcome and you may need to make provision for this at the beginning.

- *Health check:* you need to ensure that the outcome identified fits with the explorer's wellbeing.

- *Evidence:* you need to establish what your evidence of success is, and perform an initial inventory. This can be through a basic 1-10 scale, or it may be through calibrating shifts in submodalities, or a specific state. Whatever you choose, it must be sensory specific and measurable. This is the start of the calibration process.

- *Steps in the Process:* the steps need to be clearly outlined and ideally no more than seven.

- *Calibration:* at the end of the process, this is where your guide and explorer tests against the explorer's starting points and determines that a satisfactory difference has been achieved. When this happens they are just about finished. You need to have established a starting and finishing method of measurement.

- *Future Pace:* now you include a future pace process to ensure that the explorer has a new experience to refer to, and so offers new instructions to his or her unconscious mind.

3   **Considerations:** as the writer, you define the style and the tone of the instructions. Before you go into free flow, you need to consider the following.

- *Preframe instructions:* there may be specific directions you want to give to your guide, possibly regarding layout, possible areas of danger or difficulty, or mode of delivery e.g. content free where there is no need for the explorer to make processing known out loud, or explanations of particular terms. By preframing these you remove the temptation to insert meta comments into the piece itself.

- *The user:* who are you writing to? Personally I advocate directing your instructions to the explorer, by offering a script for the guide to follow. This way it is more intimate when the explorer reads it independently and it keeps the guide focused, whilst you keep control over the linguistic technology.

- *Layout:* number the steps clearly. As mentioned, a good exercise is unlikely to involve more than seven steps. Separate out the big chunk pieces and make these your main Steps. These should all be at the same logical level. Then indent the smaller chunk processes within that Step, as bullet points.

  Be consistent with your indentations, use numbering or bullets. Where you are using questions, then you may choose to mark these out in italics or bold. Again be consistent. This makes such a difference to the flow of understanding.

- *Language:* keep your language simple and avoid any ambiguity. Use one crafted question in place of three ones. Go for what the explorer will see, hear and feel as evidence.

You need to be firm with your instructions and very directive, leaving nothing to chance. This may be difficult for people who prefer options and are naturally inclined to let the other be self-determining. Test your instructions with guinea pigs and any whiff of confusion is an indicator that you need to tighten up on your wording.

Evaluation Template

I use the following template which summarises the *3C's of Written Instructions*.

Technical Accuracy
Are the instructions accurate? Is there a flow between each stage? Is each stage necessary? Are the instructions stripped to the essentials? Are the logical levels clearly marked and the structure of sub-steps and bullet points consistent?

Linguistic Accuracy
Does the language match the structure? Does it deliver the intended outcome? Does it target the explorer's attention precisely? Do the Presuppositions pace the explorer's reality? Is trance language free of unwarranted installation?

Constants	Content
Are the following elements included?	Are the following elements included?
Title	**Outcome**
Source acknowledgment (if relevant)	**Evidence**
Date devised	**Numbered steps**
Model name	**Calibration**
Length of time required	**Future pace**

Considerations
Are the following considerations taken into account?
End user Profile: if known does the design pace the preferences and traits of end user?
Layout: is there a floor plan If spatial anchors are involved?
Style: is the language suitable for end user?
Meta comments: have coaching comments been added to assist the guide, for example, ecology alerts?

Summary

You now have the complete package for constructing imaginative, bespoke and effective techniques targeting individuals or groups of learners. Knowing that there is a huge number of possible models out there for you to work with, and knowing that, for every model, you could come up with five, six, seven different techniques, you will always be on the curve of creativity. You will no longer have to rely on others to follow.

And in doing so, you are living NLP. Like a skilled puppet master, you are making the components of NLP dance through your imagination and dexterity. You are able to make a huge contribution to the wellbeing of others.

You are demonstrating to the world NLP's amazing depth and versatility, along with its power to create change and make a difference. And you will be a living example of someone using their talents to benefit others.

It's been quite a journey.

And Finally

Last Words

Well, here we are at the end of my endeavours. As with all models, there is stuff on the cutting room floor, either to be discarded or put aside for another book. However, the bulk of my last 25 years of exploration, discovery and learning is contained here. And as Benedict Allen insists, such learnings need to be written up for others to see.

I hope you have discovered lots of useful information, ways of thinking and practical ideas to help you on your way; and have become inspired and enthusiastic. I have sought to reproduce my thinking as simply as possible so that understanding is no effort. If I have achieved this, then I suspect you will have developed strong self-belief in your own abilities to model. As exciting, perhaps you now have clear ideas about your direction for further development.

I don't know how you've used this book: as a straightforward read; as a dipper and sampler updating your thinking as and when; or as a source of reference targeting particular aspects. If you have read it cover to cover in the process of study, then I applaud you! I hope the natural flow has been helpful.

Have you made notes, underlinings, and comments in the margins? Do you have pages turned down? I hope the book now looks really messy. Have you written up new ideas: about yourself as a modeller; about what can now be possible and available to you and your clients; and the range of approaches and applications you can take? Have I stimulated your enthusiasm to play, explore, test out, expand, discover, and learn? I so hope so.

Because, if you are able now to confidently give an explanation of NLP's potential and intentions in the face of doubt and limited knowledge, then our practice is in good hands. Your understanding and congruence regarding the authority of our modality, and your place within it, will allow others to feel more certain and reassured. We need good promotion now more than ever, when understanding and quality application can be so patchy.

I profoundly hope that what you have found here builds a belief that modelling is an everyday endeavour, without the mystique and complexity often associated with it. A model is required to simplify, aid navigation and expand awareness. This book, and all the new models it offers, hopefully, has done just that, bringing clarity about the process from the beginning to the very end. If you have gained greater confidence and congruence as a modeller, your actions will say more about NLP's efficacy and ecology than any words on a page.

I hope you realise that what you are doing naturally can be extended and formalised further, so that you can apply your talents even more extensively for an even greater contribution to the world out there. And that you also see the avenues open to you for further development, either through developing expertise in a particular methodology, or focussing on developing your modelling skills more fully to the level of expert elegance.

I sincerely wish, for all NLP practitioners, that modelling ceases to be something that has to be done for certification and then forgotten about as one-off event. It is not an optional extra. Instead I hope that you now have awareness that modelling is the heartbeat of NLP – and without it we are just going through the motions. I hope, as an NLP practitioner, you experience your identity as a modeller who has skills and methodologies to divine hidden structure and techniques to enable new acquisition and development.

Who knows what comes after this? In my fantasy I see a world where NLP is known for revealing magical truths, unobtrusively and elegantly, to the benefit and wellbeing of those involved. In this world, all for practitioners are automatic in their response that 'NLP is about revealing hidden structure', while using their honed NLP skills instinctively in this modelling pursuit. Here, there is a proliferation of new, useful and creative models with their ingenious techniques, each rippling throughout the land, serving need, expanding behaviours and generating self knowledge. Routinely, NLP is recognised for its ethical and congruent ethos, notable for having modelling at its core. And most importantly, in this make-believe, generative realm, NLP is a living metaphor for learning and for life.

In the meantime, I hope, at the very least, that every single person who considers themselves to be an NLP Trainer, and therefore an influencer of future generations to come, engages with this book: so that the message they send out is one of creativity, discovery, tenacity, logic, intuition, connection and wonder. To all practitioners I urge you: know your tradecraft; delight in its inventiveness; and love its – and your – potential.

Because Modelling is the connection with the spirit of another, and in that exchange, something magical is born.

Appendices

Appendices

A Worked Example

Moving on from the theoretical aspect of much of the content, I would like now to take you through the full process of modelling, model construction, selection of delivery method, technique design and finally encapsulating the full process in production the production of written instructions. The following worked example comes from the encounter with the Diver first mentioned in the *Inside Out Process* at the end of Part 5 – The Results of Modelling.

Constructing the Model

I wanted to come up with a model for *Handling Alien Environments Confidently*. I had in mind end users who were afraid of particular social situations, demanding business contexts, even meeting the future in-laws for the first time. I selected a Diver, since for me being 40ft underwater was the definition of an alien environment.

Somatic Modelling

I asked the Diver to give a somatic description of being a Diver. This meant I could get the exemplar to identify the punctuation points and effectively do much of the coding for me. I second positioned him and gained my own reference experiences that such gestures and verbal comments were generating within my neurology. This simplicity removes much of the noise of cognition and language, which is why I think this approach is just wonderful, and saves me much data crunching and mind churning.

Initially, the exemplar worked with right (dominant) hand only with the movement synchronised with breathing. The second hand lay passively at his side, until the awareness of Opening where both hands unconsciously became involved. This led to both hands being symmetrically involved in the movement so increasing the level of transmitted congruence, and confidence.

The exemplar came up with the following gestures:

1 Relaxation of buttocks and knees – in-breath and out-breath.

2 Opening at Belly – in-breath.

3 Hands rising up front of face.

4 Hands reach face and open.

5 Hands dropping palms up down to waist – out-breath.

6 Hands moving out to sides, palms pushing away.

Coding

The exemplar then began to break the moment into the sections each with their own label. He was not versed at working at this level of abstract awareness, so, as the modeller, I encouraged this through questions like: 'This represents what?' 'What's true in this moment?' and sought to retrieve simple deletions, cause and effects and complex equivalences.

I wrote down his meta comments and explanations since I may use them later in the process of labelling the model's elements, or for inclusion within specific questions in the instructions.

Together we came up with the following labels:

1 *Witnessing:* relaxed and resting, focus of attention outside, aware and with no judgment

2 *Opening:* readiness to receive and become involved

3 *Taking In:* gathering information, being attentive, being interested and curious

4 *Widening:* broadening perspective, reach point when have enough information, this is 'pumping up the panoramic'

5 *Deepening:* attention now inside, engagement with information, Information becomes established in body and a deepening sense of calm and certainty about being here

6 *Letting Go:* moving on from internal processing and bringing attention back out into what is happening.

During this entire process, I, the modeller, am constantly stepping into the model and testing it for authenticity and congruence. Any possible doubt I may have has to be visited and not put to bed until I am completely satisfied.

Model construction

An iterative, sequential model has emerged, with the exit of the TOTE being satisfactory levels of confidence. This is the process I took to arrive at this outcome.

Phase 1

- The Witness is a label at Identity Level, marking out its dissociated status. This is a meta position that can be returned to at any point, although the initial starting point is prior to the first element.

- The labels in the body of the sequential model started off being expressed in present continuous 'ing' words, appropriate for an on-going process, but have become nominalisations to offer more information.

- The exit state in the centre is expressed in adjectives to describe self in that moment. This is an associated expression and invites finding reference experiences to gain a neurological description of the desired outcome. Equally, it could be expressed in the nominalisation of Confident Engagement, but as you'll discover when you take it on, you place yourself in a more dissociated position – that's what frozen verbs do!

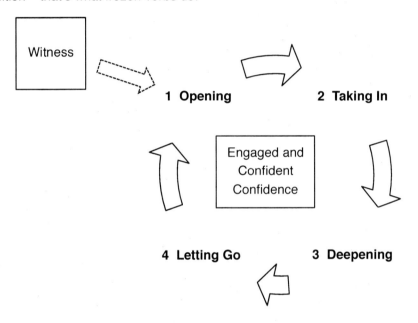

Handling Alien Environments Confidently Mk1 – Burgess 2013

Phase 2

Looking at the model, these labels didn't bring alive the process and didn't seem very meaningful to someone coming to it new. So I set about identifying what each action would achieve, i.e. nudging into the future, to find the purpose behind each action. So returning to the comments made by the exemplar and drawing from the information I was getting from second positioning, I came up with:

- I asked myself 'What does Opening lead to?' and I brought in my word, 'Commitment' – a word that the exemplar had ejected earlier, since I felt it was a moment of committing to the process. He had argued that he was already committed. I wasn't so sure.

- Following on, the 'Taking In' led me to the word 'Absorption', which felt more code congruent. (Note to self – this could be a vanity trap.) Furthermore, 'Evaluation' wasn't the end result of 'Deepening' – it was part of the process, so I was not happy with this one, although it was a word that he had used. And 'Letting Go' enabled 'Reconnection' with what was happening in the external system.

- At this stage, I wasn't fully happy with where I had got to and wanted to test it with the exemplar once more. It didn't feel meaty enough for such an important process.

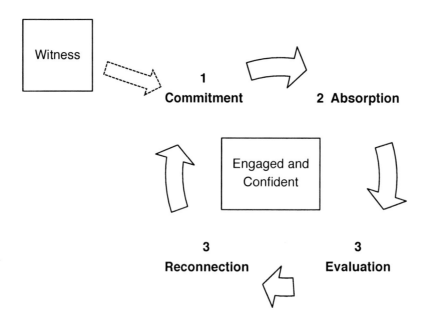

Handling Alien Environments Confidently Mk2 – Burgess 2013

Phase 3

I returned to the exemplar and together we worked on arriving at the final model. I wanted to honour his experience and at the same time form something that worked. As ever, the exemplar is unaware of what is happening at an unconscious level, so the modeller always has a job to do.

Note: It is only because this exercise is part of an overall acquisition process, that the exemplar is involved in the model construction process. Normally the modeller would be constructing the model independent of the exemplar.

- This time I looked at what Opening was a symptom of, going slightly further back in the time continuum, and suggested Acceptance – acceptance of what was going on without judgment. This allowed for permission and a desire to enter into the system.

- The exemplar immediately liked both Acceptance and Absorption. I had to control any thoughts of an 'A' alliteration!

- When it came to the third element Evaluation is what was going on. I suggested Trust and Safety, which was initially rejected. I suggested Familiarisation and he agreed that it was about sorting for sameness and difference, but it was more about an acceptable fit. To achieve what? And Trust and Safety returned. Safety I rejected because as with the other three labels Trust is something that is self-generating, whilst Safety is more dependent on the external system.

- Engagement was brought out of the outcome box as it was an end result of Reconnection.

- This began to feel right. Stepping in once more, knowing that there is an expected iteration, then there has to be an on going calibration process. So to reflect this iterative nature, the final piece was to put to the modifier – Level of Acceptance, etc.

- Throughout it became clear that the option to step out into the meta position of the Witness allowed for safety within the system and an opportunity to gather information from a dissociated perspective.

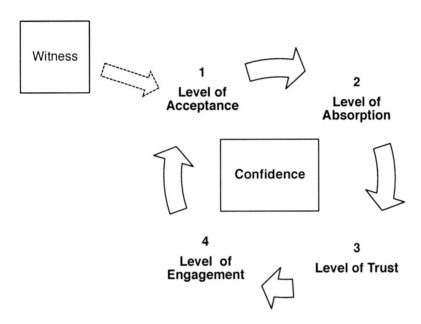

Handling Alien Environments Confidently Mk 3 – Burgess 2013

I was really excited about this model as I tested it out on myself in different contexts to see if I could raise my levels of confidence in alien situations. I was thinking of going into a room full of strangers, going to an eastern country, going into a group of people who I knew held an opposing agenda.

Selecting the Method

Now we have the model, we can go about selecting the delivery method(s) most suitable for it and for the intended Acquirers. It is useful to have at least three different treatments to play with, since (a) your model can be used in any number of formats and (b) you want to have as much flexibility as possible so that you can gain maximum mileage from it. There will always be a time when your technique won't work, and there will always be additional contexts and scenarios where your model and applications would be the most appropriate response.

Please know that there are no right answers when it comes to designing a technique. Much is down to the personality of you, the designer, and your perception of the task and the end user. So what I am offering are ideas from my map, derived from my experience as a practitioner and developer.

Possible Scenario

If you have an ill defined end user, then anything you opt for will be suitable, except when it's not. And if what you have already designed doesn't fit the purpose, then you can always come up with something else whilst retaining the model as your base point.

Should you have a specific end user in mind, or be given one, then the challenge is to come up with something that will match their profile and the conditions with the least amount of difference intruding in the process. For the purposes of this demonstration, I am opting for a known audience.

Taking the Model *Handling Alien Environments Confidently*, which has one plus four elements, and with a mandate to develop a technique(s) which would take about **twenty minutes**, for a group which is predominately '**Procedural, Internally Referenced, more Thinking than Choice'.**

I can work with all the elements, or if I feel that the group doesn't have ready access to certain elements, I may select two to work with.

Devising the Technique

I've come up with three possible techniques based on the *Handling Alien Environments Confidently* model, which I have written up as instructions – hopefully meeting the required criteria. I am also offering some comment about the design.

Technique 1 – Questions

- For this, I have taken all five elements and placed them in a cognitive series of questions as part of a written exercise. This approach appeals to cognition and can be an individual exercise with enough time to complete in 12-15 minutes and time to discuss outcomes.

- I've changed the elements into continuous verbs, to indicate a process.

- I provide a straightforward series of questions drawn from the comments and explanations gathered in the modelling process. These follow the sequence established by the model.

- You will notice that I've included particular NLP Presuppositions to build up the state of Acceptance, the use of standard reframes to open up Trust. I have invited a re-run through the questions to build a sufficient level of confidence, matching the iterative model.

Handling an Alien Environment (1)   *10 mins*

Model and Technique devised by Fran Burgess (2013)

Outcome: to gain appropriate level of confidence

Note: this is best completed working independently or content free.

1   Think of a situation that is coming up where you fear you may be out of your depth.

- How confident are you about handling this situation?   1 (low) – 10 (high)

2   Looking onto this situation, from a neutral place, breath, relax any tension in your body, and welcome the challenge ahead. Ask yourself:

- What is your outcome?
- What do you want to learn?
- What do you want to be able to do differently?

3   **Accepting**

- What has to be true for these particular individuals here?
- What might their positive intentions be?
- How are they doing the best they can?

4   **Absorbing**

- What are you paying attention to?
- Where else might you place your attention?
- What aspects do you not understand or know about?

5   **Trusting**

- What is familiar/unfamiliar to you?
- What other meaning could you be giving to the information? What else?
- When and where might people's behaviours be useful, even admirable?

6   **Engagement**

- What do you now want to know?
- What do you now appreciate and recognise?
- What personal resources do you know you can rely upon?

7   Calibration

- How confident are you now about handling this situation?   1 (low) – 10 (high)

8   Repeat stages 4-8, building upon your answers until the level of confidence has reached a 7 or above.

Treatment 2 – Spatial Anchors

- This will be a straightforward floor exercise, turning the Witness space into a Safe Place.

- This requires setting up of 1 + 4 elements on the floor and working sequentially through the four, responding to a simple pattern of questions. Since the group is predominantly Internally Referenced working individually would suit and only take twenty minutes.

- In constructing the questions, I have incorporated words from the modelling process.

- I started off using the word 'when' as in 'When I am fully accepting' but changed this to 'as' because 'when' is future referenced and 'as' is in the present and I wanted full association.

- Similarly, I altered the verb in the statement to present continuous, since I wanted the sense of on-going process.

- I opted to work with the Belief, Values and Identity from within the Neurological Levels and ! also introduced the notion of metaphor, since this leads to a powerful resource state.

- Reflecting the iterative nature of the model, I have included a walking edit once the data has been gathered which results in stacking the anchors of each of the elements and combining the physiology of Confidence into the walk.

- Given that Confidence is located in a meta position, suggesting a location for Spirituality, I have added primed this awareness and provided a metaphoric anchor which can be called upon when actually entering into the identified daunting environment.

Handling an Alien Environment (2)   *20 mins*

Model and Technique devised by Fran Burgess (2013)

Outcome: to gain appropriate level of confidence

Note: Let the guide make a note of the answers given in each of the elements.

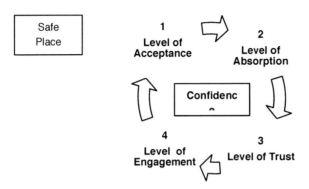

1   Think of a situation that is coming up where you fear you may be out of your depth.

•   How confident are you about handling this situation?   1 (low) – 10 (high)

2   **Safe Place:** select a safe place outside of the four elements. You can return here at any point. In front of you establish the four locations, according to the layout

3   **Accepting:** move to this place and ask yourself:

•   As I am fully accepting …

I believe …   I value …   I am like …

4   **Absorbing:** move to this place and ask yourself:

•   As I am openly gathering information …

I believe …   I value …   I am like …

5   **Trusting:** move to this place and ask yourself:

•   As I am deepening my trust for myself and others …

I believe …   I value …   I am like …

6   **Engagement:** move to this place and ask yourself:

•   As I am fully engaging with the world …

I believe …   I value …   I am like a …

7   Stand back on your neutral place, and remind yourself of your answers and your metaphors.

8   Now walk round each of the spaces, gathering up the knowledge and awareness from each. As you do, notice your level of Confidence. As it increases find yourself walking through each space in a walk that demonstrates this Confidence.

9   Calibration: Step into the centre of the space.

•   How confident are you now about handling this situation?   1 (low) – 10 (high)

•   What else or who else are you serving in this moment?

•   What metaphor represents this feeling?

Technique 3 – Relational Constructs

- I have selected pairs of elements and worked with them through Confusion Technique.

- I have framed this is as a series of questions and again made it content free to save time. This cognitive approach with step-by-step stages would appeal to the group and would take the explorer about 10 minutes – therefore twenty minutes working in pairs.

- This treatment turns the sequential model into a simultaneous model and blurs the edges between the individual elements. This results in the creation of a relational field, in this case of Confidence. As you will see from the grid, each element is represented four times, either as the nominalisation or as the verb.

- Whilst we could do this spatially, because the end users are 'Thinking' more than 'Feeling', I have made this into a straightforward paper exercise. However I fancy making it into a group exercise, so that participants can gain multiple descriptions of each of the patterns, allowing for a meta cognition to emerge. Accordingly I'm suggesting placing the formats on cards, which are then picked at random.

- I have opted to work with selections of Meta Model patterns: namely Complex Equivalence, Modal Operators of Necessity and Probability, and Lost Performatives.

Model and Technique devised by Fran Burgess (2013)

Outcome: to gain appropriate level of confidence

Note: provided – a set of 8 cards, one for each of these boxes.

It is not a problem if individuals give the same answers. Encourage participants to answer intuitively, 'off the top of their head', and leave any discussion to the end of the process.

Absorbing Acceptance means	**Absorbing Trust means**	**Engaging Trust means**	**Trusting Acceptance means**
I can … I can't … I must… I mustn't … People who do are …	I can … I can't … I must… I mustn't … People who do are …	I can … I can't … I must… I mustn't … People who do are …	I can … I can't … I must… I mustn't … People who do are …
Accepting Engagement means	**Engaging Absorption means**	**Trusting Engagement means**	**Accepting Absorption means**
I can … I can't … I must… I mustn't … People who do are …	I can … I can't … I must… I mustn't … People who do are …	I can … I can't … I must… I mustn't … People who do are …	I can … I can't … I must… I mustn't … People who do are …

1   In small groups of 3-4, take a set of cards and allocating A, B, C or D to each group member.

2   Think of a situation that is coming up where you fear you may be out of you depth. To yourself ask:

- How confident are you about handling this situation?   1 (low) – 10 (high)

3   Round One:

- A starts off by selecting one card, reading out the heading and completes the first round of statements: e.g. Absorbing Acceptance means I can … I can't … The other members follow on and give their answers

- A then carries on to the next round of statements: Absorbing Acceptance means I must … I mustn't … The other members follow on and give their answers

- A then finishes off with: People who Absorb Acceptance are … The other members follow on and give their answers

4   Rounds Two, Three and more, if time permits:

- B now picks a card and the process continues in the same way.

- Then C

- Then D

5   After three or more Rounds, the individuals check in, access the situation and calibrate their level of Confidence.

- How confident are you about handling this situation now?   1 (low) – 10 (high)

- What do you now believe about your abilities?

- What do you now believe about yourself?

Appendices

Acknowledgements

It almost goes without saying that this book would have not existed without the sources of my NLP teachers and mentors. My life and the lives of those around me owe huge gratitude to Jan Ardui, Tamara Andreas, Susan Grace Branch, Michael Colgrass, Judith Delozier, Robert Dilts, Anne Entus, Todd Epstein, Lara Ewing, Steve Gilligan, David Gordon, John Grinder, Derek Jackson, Di Kamp, Tad James, Christina Hall, James Lawley, John McWhirter, Liz Mahoney, Bill O'Hanlon, John Seymour, Penny Tompkins, Peter Wrycza.

I am also indebted to all our fabulous learners at The Northern School of NLP whose courage, inventiveness, and questioning have been huge sources of learning for me; and for the learning I've gained through working with clients whose ability and determination to take on this weird and wonderful technology, has tested and stretched my practice and taken me from the theoretical to the grounded practicalities of NLP application.

I am deeply grateful to Judith Delozier for taking the time to write the Foreword. From my earliest days she has been my consistent sponsor, valuing me and my abilities when I was unable to do so myself.

I thank wholeheartedly David Gordon who in his role as 'big chunk' editor provided me with such great direction regarding the structure of the material. He gave up precious time to help me turn my brain dump into the package you find today. And Jenny Thomas, as my 'small chunk' editor, has earned a lifetime achievement award. Her unremitting discipline and attention to detail has whipped this text into a semblance of respectability. I am also appreciative of her insightful suggestions and intelligent comments. Any lingering typos are my oversight.

I also am grateful for the support and good faith of my friends, especially Derek Jackson who has had to live with this marathon. Helen Platts and Sally Ashworth have been stalwart in their support and specific feedback.

And to Bill O'Hanlon for his insistent encouragement to put pen to paper. Look what you've done.

For the final words, here's the explorer, Benedict Allen:

> You set out with the specific objective of systematically tackling that frontier of knowledge and – here's an equally important bit – you then report back your findings. You can't claim to be an explorer unless you bring back some new insight.

Appendices

Sources and Further Reading

Unconscious Uptake

Whispering in the Wind: Carmen Bostic St Clair and John Grinder (2001) J&C Enterprises

The Real NLP Modelling Workshop: Workbook and personal notes (2008)

Personal conversation with John Grinder (2008)

Deep Trance Identification

Therapeutic Trances: Stephen Gilligan (1987) Brunner/Mazel

The Courage to Love: Stephen Gilligan (1997) W W Norton & Co

The Hero's Journey: Stephen Gilligan and Robert Dilts (2009) Crown House Publishing

Workshops, conversations and emails over the last fifteen years.

Somatic Modelling

Turtles All The Way Down: Judith Delozier, John Grinder (1987) Grinder Associates

NLP II The Next Generation: Robert Dilts, Judith Delozier with Deborah Bacon Dilts (2010) Meta Publications

NLP Encyclopedia: Robert Dilts, Judith Delozier (2000) NLP University Press

A range of workshops and conversations over the last fifteen years.

Symbolic Modelling

Metaphors in Mind: James Lawley and Penny Tompkins (2000)

www.cleanlanguage.co.uk: extensive listings of articles

Master Practitioner Workshops (2001-8) and NLP Psychotherapy Diploma (2006-8)

Punctuation Modelling

Eats Shoots and Leaves: Lynne Truss (2006)

Working with students and clients

Parts Alignment (Parts Therapy)

About 100 client sessions

Workshop deliveries

Experiential Array

The Structure of Experience: David Gordon and Graham Dawes (2005) Desert Rain

www.expandyourworld.net: in depth series of articles supporting and supplementing The Structure of Magic book and DVD

Master Practitioner Workshops (2001-11) and many many conversations

Analytical Modelling

Strategies of Genius Vol 1 – Vol 3: Robert Dilts (1994) Meta Publications

Modeling with NLP: Robert Dilts (1998) Meta Publications

NLP II The Next Generation: Robert Dilts, Judith Delozier with Deborah Bacon Dilts (2010) Meta Publications

NLP Encyclopedia: Robert Dilts, Judith Delozier (2000) NLP University Press

Workshop notes and conversations

www.nlpu.com

LAB Profile

Words That Change Minds: Shelle Rose Charvet (1995) Kendall Hunt Publishing

Email correspondence with Rodger Bailey

The Bumper Bundle's Companion Workbook

There is so much theory wrapped up in this book and the content covers so much ground, that it is not a book which helps you develop or practice your skills, other than deepen your intellectual understanding.

So for the committed learner, I have produced a Companion Workbook full of exercises to test your practical understanding and to challenge your current levels of knowledge. Hopefully not making it too easy on yourself to short change your learning, answers are supplied but not instantly accessible.

I'm told on good authority that the range of exercises are fun to do! They let you know what aspects you have already integrated and which areas you can still work with and learn more. And also make for good teaching exercises in the NLP training room.

The Bumper Bundle Companion Workbook is available through Anglo American books and Amazon.

Remember the difference between learning and assessment is a nano second!

Appendices

Index of Illustrated Models

Appendices

Index

Appendices

Lightning Source UK Ltd.
Milton Keynes UK
UKOW03f0616040615

252869UK00005B/50/P